THE SHAPE OF ENGLISH

Structure and History

THE SHAPE OF ENGLISH

Structure and History

Roger Lass

J. M. DENT & SONS LTD
London Melbourne

First published 1987
© Roger Lass 1987

This book is set in Times by
Tradespools Ltd, Frome, Somerset
Printed in Great Britain by
Mackays of Chatham Ltd for
J.M. Dent & Sons Ltd
Aldine House, 33 Welbeck Street, London W1M 8LX

British Library Cataloguing in Publication Data

Lass, Roger
  The shape of English : structure and
  history.
  1. English language — History
  I. Title
  420'.9   PE1075

  ISBN 0-460-04684-5

CONTENTS

'What a funny bag!' he said, pinching it with his fingers.
'Carpet,' said Mary Poppins, putting her key in the lock.
'To carry carpets in, you mean?'
'No. Made of.'
'Oh,' said Michael. 'I see.' But he didn't – quite.

P.L. Travers, *Mary Poppins*

The first quality, the essential quality of truth is to be simple . . . I have reduced to their simplest form the wheels within wheels that surround you, without altering the result in the slightest . . .

Truth never seems true. I don't mean only in literature or in painting. I won't remind you either of those Doric columns whose lines seem strictly perpendicular and which only give that impression because they are slightly curved. If they were straight, they'd look as if they were swelling, don't you see?

Georges Simenon, *Maigret's Memoirs*

The method of analogies is, generally speaking, a rather tormenting thing. With it, you walk in a vicious circle. It helps you to elucidate certain things, and the relations of certain things, but in substance it never gives you a direct answer to anything.

P.D. Ouspensky, *Tertium Organum*

PREFACE

A language is at least three things at once: a self-contained system, a reflection of its past history, and a prelude to its own future. If you were to ask a speaker what 'his language' consisted of (assuming he could answer such a question at all), he would probably list things that could be summed up as the forms and constructions he knows, their pronunciations and meanings, and the social and other rules for their use. So for a speaker of English, it's simply a fact that his language is partly regular and partly irregular, that some subsystems are symmetrical, and others asymmetrical. For example: the 'regular' way of forming the comparative of an adjective is by adding *-er* (*big/bigg-er*) – but there are irregular relations as well, like *good/better*, *bad/worse*. Or the marking of number on personal pronouns is asymmetrical: first and third persons distinguish singular and plural (*I* vs. *we*, *he/she/it* vs. *they*), but the second person doesn't: most standard varieties have only *you*, which serves for both numbers.

Many linguists believe in the dogma that a language is nothing more than a body of 'internalized knowledge' possessed by a speaker. If this is true, then their job is to describe this knowledge: their point of view, while analytic or 'scientific', is in the end the same as that of the speaker whose knowledge they claim to be explicating. Then think or hope they are describing some internal mental content of his.

But there's another possibility (an older and more traditional one): that it's fruitful to adopt what we might call an 'outsider's perspective', at least as a complementary position. That is, to combine the speaker's parochial viewpoint with an outsider's historical and comparative one, unbound by constraints of space or time. Thus we could look at a language from the inside (say all and only the properties of Cape Town English, A.D. 1987); or from the outside, in terms of its position in a network of related languages, its past history and its likely future evolution, its similarities to and differences from other languages . . . and so on. Or even take both points of view more or less at once, shifting from one to the other whenever it seems useful. This is what I propose to do here.

Let's return to *you*. Old English distinguished second person singular and plural pronouns: nominative singular *þū*, dative/accusative singular *þē* (later *thou, thee*) vs. nominative plural *gē*, dative/accusative *ēow* (later *ye, you*). This number/case distinction later weakened into a largely stylistic one, and eventually the nominative *ye* and the *thou/thee* system were lost, with the oblique plural *you* taking on all singular and plural functions except genitive (for which *your* from the OE genitive plural *ēower* was retained). Thus *you* as we now have it looks like the result of the asymmetrical collapse of an old number opposition (number remained stable in the other pronouns); it thus takes on a 'place' in history, which is one important dimension of its present-day status.

But the picture is more complex and interesting. If we look at certain regional and social dialects of modern English, we see that the evolution hasn't been unidirectional, but cyclic. Many dialects have now restored the old singular/plural opposition by inventing new plurals: Scots, Irish, South African and U.S. dialects with *you* vs. *yous*, southern U.S. *you* vs. *y'all*, and still others like *you* vs. *you guys*. We even see the new forms getting reabsorbed into the pronoun system and growing new genitives, as in some *y'all* dialects with genitive *y'all's*.

Without this historical background we merely have two kinds of dialects: those with a number distinction in the second person and those without one. With the history, we can see that one type continues what was once an innovation (the loss of the distinction), while the other type has reconstituted the old system that today's standard 'deviates' from. The modern distribution of forms now takes on significance as part of a larger pattern, spread out in time and space.

So scholars are not the same as speakers, and unlike them need a God's-eye view. It may not be relevant to the man on the Clapham omnibus that his language occupies a place in a patterned history, that the form he uses is either a reprise or a new direction; but it ought to be to anyone interested in language as an object of inquiry. I am, and this book is aimed at an audience that shares this interest.

The view I take here, then, is neither synchronic (the language seen in snapshot at a given moment), nor diachronic (historical): rather 'panchronic'. The subject is English of all kinds: different regional and social dialects and their structures and histories. The emphasis however is on the 'standard' varieties (see ch. 1), and on those features shared by the majority of dialects. While I don't believe that 'the only explanation for a linguistic form is an older form' (Lehmann 1952: 23), I do believe that 'genetic explanation' or historical chronicle is at least half of proper description. The Shape of English extends in three dimensions – temporal, spatial and social; and the last two have their own historical background, which is often crucial to our understanding of why things look the way they do at present.

Such a position runs counter to today's predominant orthodoxy, the view associated with Chomsky and his school that linguistics is a branch of psychology. I'm not engaged here in writing a formal grammar; but the spirit of this book is in line with that of Fred Householder's remark (1966: 100) that 'a linguist who could not devise a better grammar than is present in any speaker's brain ought to try another trade'. The English this book is about is not just a 'system of grammatical knowledge', but a complex symbolic structure emerging from and implicated in its own history.

It is in fact a structure that in some ways resembles a living organism more than a cultural artifact. Languages of course aren't really organisms, nor are they like them in any very deep sense; but because they're both historically evolved objects, they have enough in common so that certain biological modes of description can at times – as analogies anyhow – be quite appropriate. Both languages and organisms are systems, not just collections of parts. Or better, systems of systems, all collaborating in the interests of some ulterior purpose. For organisms, this is surviving and reproducing; for languages, being means of communication, badges of social identity and markers of solidarity, media for personal and artistic expression. But because they have undergone long historical evolutions, neither organisms nor languages are ever fully systematic or completely functional. Different subsystems may evolve partially independently, according to their own internal rules, and without close consultation with the wholes they're part of. Therefore both languages and organisms carry along with them much of the debris and disorder they've accumulated in the course of their history. Examples in the biological domain would be the human appendix and wisdom teeth, or the vestigial thumbs of birds; linguistic examples would be the irregular forms of the verb *to be* (*am/are/is*: cf. *walk/walk/walks*), or plurals like *mice, feet, children, sheep*.

The picture of a language I'm proposing is rather like the vision of organic structure captured by Konrad Lorenz in this extended image (1975: 25; my translation):

> The total structure of an organism is not like that of a manmade building, produced as the result of foresight and planning; it is more like the do-it-yourself house of a pioneer, who first puts up the simplest possible hut just for shelter ... and increases its size as his possessions and family increase. The original little hut is never dismantled, but becomes a junk-room; and in the course of time nearly every room in the house becomes alienated from its original purpose. But still, recognizable remains of the first hut survive; the building as a

whole cannot be torn down and rebuilt, because it is continuously and intensively being lived in and used.

Thus evolved systems are 'a collection of structural features, the remains of "yesterday's adaptations"'. For 'adaptations' read 'linguistic changes', and this isn't so far from the truth for languages as well.

ii

There is of course no such thing as 'the structure of English' or 'the history of English', independent of some particular writer's account of it. All 'facts' are mediated through theory, and through individuals' visions of their field. This book is no different: it presents, via the joint perspectives of history, dialectology, theoretical linguistics, and my own irreducibly personal way of looking at things, what might best be called 'my English'. We've had lots of others in the past (and still have, since scholarship is cohabitation, not the eclipsing of previous work), like 'Sweet's English', 'Jespersen's English', and so on. Not that I'm putting myself in that class; these are simply two familiar examples of pioneers who have left all subsequent Anglicists in their debt by defining in a highly personal and beautifully articulated way what 'the history and structure of English' are. This study is one more in a long (and I hope never-ending) line of overall views, a definition of the field filtered through a different experience and different interests. In this case, one compounded of the traditional philology I learned at Yale in the early 1960s from Helge Kökeritz and John Pope, the linguistics I learned later, and the technical linguistic-cum-philological work I've been doing ever since. Plus some special idiosyncrasy growing out of my own biography: being a native New Yorker who has spent the bulk of his professional Anglistic career outside New York (southern Indiana, Scotland, and now South Africa) has been a good cure for ethnocentrism, and the common vice of seeing the history of one's language as a steady march toward the pinnacles of one's own dialect.

I suppose what's come out of all this is a kind of hybrid: a cross between 'a book on English' and an introduction to some major aspects of English linguistics. It might have been easier to write one or the other, but this isn't possible any more. There was a time when 'English Language Studies' was more or less a discipline on its own, like the other 'philologies'; but things have changed. There are no 'language-study' disciplines any more; all of them, historical and synchronic, are now specializations within linguistics, and the language in which scholarly discourse is conducted is that of general linguistics. And this creates some problems, because the language of this subject is in many ways less familiar and accessible than the older style of discourse, and the conceptual framework is wider-ranging and more complex.

This book is neither a vulgar popularization nor a technical mono-graph, though it does have bits of both. It's aimed at an audience that has some training in modern English Language Studies or linguistics (say at first-year university level); or at the 'intelligent layman' with an interest in language who is willing to get up the necessary background. If I've done my work properly, the glossary, appendices and explanations in the text ought to introduce as much linguistic theory and terminology as are needed, and I've referred fairly generously to textbooks in the field for those who want to deepen their understanding.

But there are disparities in level. One problem (at least it was one to me in writing, and I suspect it will also be to some readers) is that certain sections, even whole chapters, are much denser and more technical than others. Those dealing with social and cultural history, the status of constructions or dialects, vocabulary, etc. are likely to be generally accessible; the two (to my mind) central chapters, those on phonology and morphosyntax, and parts of the chapter on dialects, will be much tougher going, with a lot of arcane notation and rather technical argument.

These disparities are inherent in the subject: detailed linguistic description, which I take as the major part of my brief, simply is rather hard and technical. The only way I can see of avoiding this would be to be patronizing and simplistic, which doesn't appeal to me. The material on phonology is likely to cause more trouble, if only because it is further from most people's non-professional contact with linguistic discourse than material dealing with grammar and meaning, and requires a good deal of special notation. In those parts of the Western educational world that haven't yet fallen into complete decay, there is still some grammati-cal training in the schools, most readers will be able to cope with notions like 'verb', 'subject', 'clause'. But training in phonetics and phonology has never been part of our educational tradition, and many readers may struggle a bit. This is not an apology, merely a warning.

Two more disclaimers are in order. First, since this is not intended as a 'complete' description of English (as if that were even conceivable), coverage of all areas is highly selective. A single chapter can't compete with a monograph. Each chapter is therefore a kind of 'topics in . . .', covering those things I think are most important, or likely to be most interesting. I have undoubtedly miscalculated in places.

Second, there is a distinct skewing in the coverage of the dialect spectrum, with a strong, perhaps disproportionate emphasis on England, particularly the South. This is because (a) my own expertise and experience have their limitations, and I can obviously write more (and hopefully better) about the areas I know at first hand; and (b), more importantly, because given the limitations of space I've had to make some hard decisions about overall thrust and orientation. This has led me to concentrate on England particularly, as the geographical source of all varieties of English, and on the South more than other areas, since all the extraterritorial dialects (Irish, American, Australasian, South African) derive from southern English inputs, and even the standard varieties of non-southern dialects are tilted southwards. London and the Southeast are, and will remain, at the historical and conceptual centre of English studies.

I've had to restrict myself even more when it comes to specialized subareas withing English dialect study; I have regretfully decided not to say anything about such interesting and important issues as the problems and scholarly controversies surrounding English-based pidgins and creoles, the Caribbean dialect-continua and their reflections abroad (e.g. West Indian English in Britain), and U.S. Black English. I have also left out non-native varieties (e.g. West African and Indian English) – even though in terms of both intrinsic interest and speaker numbers they're important. One has to stop somewhere, and I thought the best place would be at the edge of my own specialist competence, and more or less within the bounds of 'mainstream' English studies. There is already a fine and growing literature on 'other Englishes', and I hestitate to do an amateur job on someone else's professional pitch. The converse of this is that there will be more than might be expected on Scots and South African English, since a lot of my own research has been done on these varieties.

In spite of all this, I suspect I've covered most of the major areas. And that as an overall picture of what kind of language English is (how the machine works, as it were, and what it's made of), and as a picture of what kind of language it has been, and where it stands *vis-à-vis* its nearest relatives, this book is not likely to be dangerously misleading.

iii

A work like this doesn't get done without a lot of help, even if not all of it is intentional. Probably the first lot to be thanked ought to be my colleagues at the University of Edinburgh, from whom in the course of eleven years I learned a lot of whatever I know about how to be a linguist, and who played, for better or worse, a major part in shaping the way I now look at things: especially John Anderson, Gill and Keith Brown, Jim Miller, and Heinz Giegerich.

I am also grateful to Cape Town for being a place where I can write in winter without my toes freezing, and to its University for providing a stimulating atmosphere, helpful and critical colleagues, and an ambience in which writing books seems the proper thing to do. I owe a special debt to Menán du Plessis, Susan Wright, and Nigel Love for endless discussion, keeping me on my intellectual toes, and stepping on them when necessary. More directly, I am grateful to Malcolm Gerratt of J.M. Dent, whose idea this book was in the first place, and who has helped enormously in getting it into shape; to Nigel Love and Susan Wright for careful reading of an earlier draft; and to my wife Jaime, for her acute sense of style, her patience in listening to my attempts to formulate things, her fine ability to deflate pomposity (though I'm not sure she's entirely succeeded), and for drawing the runes in chapter 1.

Dieprivier, C.P.
July 1986

TRANSCRIPTION AND CITATION

When dealing with the actual sound structure of languages (rather than their writing systems), it is necessary, if troublesome to the non-academic reader, to use various forms of specialized transcription. A glance at the English spelling system should be enough to show why. Spelling is normally invented by native speakers for native speakers, and in a language like English, with a long history of literacy and no official spelling reform to speak of, as well as a lot of foreign vocabulary, spelling is bound to be inconsistent and uncertain in representing sound, and to incorporate devices from foreign systems in addition to the native mess. (E.g. *ph* instead of *f* in words of Greek origin like *physics* – which is itself an excrescent Hellenism in Latin orthography, where we get it from). Consider for instance the representation of the same sound in:

> *sh*ip, vi*ci*ous, na*ti*on, o*ce*an, *s*ugar, ti*ss*ue,
> *sch*maltz, *ch*arade

Or Bernard Shaw's famous spelling of fish as *ghoti* (*gh* as in *rough*, *o* as in *women*, *ti* as in *nation*).

So when particular sound qualities or sound units in a language are at issue, they will be given in a conventional transcription, here following the alphabet of the International Phonetic Association (IPA): see Appendix I for details. In addition, I will use two standard linguistic conventions: a contrastive sound unit or phoneme will be in / / (e.g. /æ/ as in English *bat*, *cat*, *mat*); a representation of a sound type in general, or a member or allophone of a particular phoneme will be in [ ] (e.g. [kʰ] as in *cat*, [k] as in *scat*, both representing members of the phoneme /k/): for unfamiliar terms see the glossary.

In citing written forms from other languages, I will generally follow the normal conventions. These are somewhat inconsistent, deriving as they do from many different traditions, and a word of what I hope is clarification is in order. In most of the older languages, Germanic as well as non-Germanic, a macron over a vowel indicates length: OE *gōd* 'good', Latin *dēns* 'tooth'. The exception is Old Icelandic, where length is represented by an acute: *góðr* 'good'. In Gothic, the acute is used to distinguish between *ai*, *au* spellings that represent diphthongs and *aí*, *aú* that stand for simple short vowels, as in *haitan* 'be called', *bauþ* 'he asked'

xix

vs. *baíran* 'carry', *baúrgs* 'city'. In Greek, Sanskrit and Lithuanian the acute marks a type of accent or tone, and length is independently marked: Sanskrit *pitár-*, Greek *patér* 'father'. The only likely source of confusion is the use of the acute also to mark stress when this is under discussion, as in *tormént* (verb) vs. *tórment* (noun). In phonetic and phonemic transcriptions, length is indicated by a colon following a symbol, as in English *boot* /buːt/.

One other potentially troublesome inconsistency, forced on us by convention, is the use of the asterisk for two quite distinct purposes. In historical discussion, a form prefixed by an asterisk is unattested or reconstructed: Proto-Indo-European */dent-s/ 'tooth'. In nonhistorical discussion, the asterisk marks ungrammatical or otherwise ill-formed or non-occurring items: e.g. *John, who and I were neighbours, *three oxes, *comed.

In grammatical discussion, I will use a hyphen to indicate boundaries between parts of words that constitute lexical or grammatical units, if the focus is on internal structure: *walk-s*, *walk-ed*, *straw-berry*.

NOTES AND REFERENCES

All bibliographical references in this book are given in the 'Harvard' format: author's name, date of publication, and page or chapter numbers if relevant (e.g. Trudgill 1983: ch. 12). This eliminates those maddening *ibids* and *op. cit.*s that make you backtrack frantically to find a first reference, and should have been outlawed from civilized scholarship a long time ago. Titles and details will be found in the bibliography at the end.

In the interests of a clean text and reasonably uncluttered exposition I have avoided footnotes; all subsidiary discussion and suggestions for further reading, and most literature citations, will be found in the endnotes to the individual chapters.

The bibliography, though probably excessively long for a book of this kind, is still highly selective; I have tried where I could to avoid citing extremely technical literature, even if reading of it lies behind my own thinking on some topic; though in many cases there was no way of doing this. I have also – again, where I could – stuck to material in English; though anybody who gets seriously interested in English, especially its history, will have to be able to read German. Where analyses or opinions of mine are particularly idiosyncratic or controversial, I have referred freely to my own more technical work and other material bearing on the controversy at issue; this is especially true in chapter 3, and §5.8.4.

The glossary at the end contains just about every technical term used in the text; the reader coming across an unfamiliar term should look it up, as the glossary often refers to an explanatory passage elsewhere in the book.

ABBREVIATIONS

Some abbreviations in this book are used in more than one sense: e.g. V = 'vowel' or 'verb'. Context should disambiguate.

A adjective
abl ablative
acc accusative
Adv adverb
Afr Afrikaans
Am(E) American (English)
Aus(E) Australian (English)

Br(E) British (English)
BV Belfast Vernacular

C consonant; complementizer
CE Canadian English
CF Citation form
CS casual style/speech
Co coda
Cons conservative
CT *Canterbury Tales*

dat dative
def definite
Du Dutch

E English; east(ern)
EML East Midland(s)
ET(E) Extraterritorial (English)
Ext extreme

F French
f feminine
Fri Frisian
FS Formal style

G German
gen genitive
Go Gothic
Gr Greek

HE Hiberno-English

IE Indo-European
imp imperative
ind indicative
inst instrumental

L Latin
Lith Lithuanian
LMC Lower Middle Class
LWC Lower Working Class

m masculine
ME Middle English
MHG Middle High German
ML Midland(s)
MMC Middle Middle Class
MWC Middle Working Class
MUE Mid Ulster English

N noun; North(ern)
n neuter
NAE North American English
neg negative
NGmc North Germanic
NML North Midland(s)
nom nominative

NP noun phrase
NW Northwest(ern)
NWGmc Northwest Germanic
NZ New Zealand

O onset; object
obj objective (case)
OE Old English
OF Old French
OFri Old Frisian
OHG Old High German
OIc Old Icelandic
OIr Old Irish
ON Old Norse
OS Old Saxon
OV Object-Verb (word order)

P peak
part participle
perf perfect
PGmc Proto-Germanic
PIE Proto-Indo-European
pl plural
Prep preposition
pres present
prog progressive

REL Relative (clause marker)
Resp Respectable
RP Received Pronunciation
RPS Reading-passage style

S strong (syllable); subject

SA(E) South African (English)
SBE Southern British English
SE Southeast(ern)
SED Survey of English dialects
SEML Southeast Midlands
Skr Sanskrit
SOV Subject-Object-Verb (word
    order)
subj subjunctive
SUE South Ulster English
SVO Subject-Verb-Object (word
    order)
SW Southwest(ern)
Sw Swedish

US Ulster Scots
U.S. United States
USE U.S. English
UWC Upper Working Class

V vowel; verb
VO verb-object (word order)
VSO Verb-Subject-Object (word
    order)

WC Working Class
WE Welsh English
WGmc West Germanic
WLS Word-list style
WML West Midland(s)

Yi Yiddish

1. ENGLISH AND ITS BACKGROUND

1.1 A Problem of Demarcation

There is a matter of definition to be settled at the beginning: what is 'English'? Or perhaps better, what, for the purposes of this book, do I take the term to mean? Within limits it's intuitively obvious to a speaker whether or not a given utterance is in 'his' language: but the limits can be hard to set. Presumably anyone who thinks of himself as an English speaker will agree that this paragraph has so far been in English; but if I now write ek het tot dusver hierdie boek in Engels geskryf, it's obvious that I've shifted to 'another language' (Afrikaans: 'I have so far written this book in English'). This is a clear case, and it would be equally clear if I did the reverse, wrote in Afrikaans with a sudden lapse into English. The boundaries would be evident to a reader who knew one – or both – of the languages. But what about this?

(1.1)

> Flooer o the gean,
> Yere aefauld white she wore yestreen.
> Wi gentle glances aye she socht me.
> Dwell her thochts whaur dwalt her een?

This is by the Scots poet George Campbell Hay (b. 1915), from a poem called 'Flooer o the Gean' (Scott 1970: 487). For a speaker of anything but a dialect related to the one this is written in, the answer may not be obvious. (See below on 'dialect' vs. 'language'.) Certainly there are some words that look English (*the*, *white*, *she*, *gentle*, *her*); but others that don't (*flooer*, *gean*, *aefauld*, *yestreen*). Some of the latter might be resolved into 'variants' of familiar English words: e.g. *socht*, *thocht* could be taken as *sought*, *thought*. But *gean*, *aefauld*, *yestreen* simply don't occur in other dialects. The writer would I imagine say he wrote in 'Lallans' (a literary variety of Lowland Scots: see §5.7.1); but would he – or a non-Scot – say it was 'a form of English'?

Leaving the question open for a moment, suppose I translate the unfamiliar words into a 'general' English that all readers will know, leaving the syntax unaltered (even if I wreck the metre a bit):

(1.2)

> Flower of the wild cherry,
> Your simple white she wore last night.
> With gentle glances ever she sought me.
> Dwell her thoughts where dwelt her eyes?

If you define English as what you *speak*, chances are that some constructions here will be ruled out: 'Dwell her thoughts where dwelt her eyes', for instance. English doesn't form questions by preposing non-auxiliary verbs, and 'where dwelt her eyes' is not allowable. 'Do her thoughts dwell where her eyes dwelt?' would be the spoken English version – and it's not certain that this use of *dwell* is really natural. But on this level the problems aren't serious, given the translation: it is recognizable as being in a 'poetic' variety or dialect of English, where the game allows certain violations of colloquial norms (archaisms like *dwell*, distortions of normal word-order, etc.).

So the limits of tolerance here extend to recognition of 'poetic English', say, as a special-purpose dialect, which at least literate speakers are familiar with, and accept as part of the complex of varieties that come under the general heading 'English'. The difficulty arises from highly localized forms like *gean*, *yestreen*; even *flooer* (if you're familiar with Scottish stereotypes like *hoose* for *house*) can be seen as a regional form of *flower*, and hence identifiable as 'English'.

The main difficulty with this passage then seems to be the presence of lexical items of restricted provenance; but with the glosses, it's easy to see that the structural framework, the basic syntax, are in fact English. Any initial hesitation seems to be based largely on unfamiliar vocabulary, which – given recognizable structure – is not a reason for excluding the passage from English. (Otherwise, any technical text in a subject you were unfamiliar with would have to be excluded, as would poems like 'The Jabberwocky' or 'The Hunting of the Snark': is 'For the Snark *was* a Boojum, you see' not English?)

But unfamiliar vocabulary and pronunciation aren't the only issue. What about the following, where all the words are undoubtedly English?

(1.3)

> i. You have to can drive a lorry to get that job.
> ii. The roof needs fixed.
> iii. Where's my book? Ah, here it's.

Sentences (i–ii) are normal in central and southern Scotland; (iii) is a West Highland type (from Trudgill 1982: 180). The dialects that use these constructions are – with a bit of phonological adjustment –

mutually comprehensible, and comprehensible to speakers of yet others. It would be virtually impossible to set up principled criteria that would for instance include *you have to be able to* (cf.(i)) and not *you have to can* within the body of 'English constructions'. Would we want to say that a Scot who says (i) has shifted into another language after *you*, and returned to English at *a lorry?* The most one could say is that in English generally the auxiliary verbs of the class *can, must, will*, etc. don't have *to*-infinitives, and don't occur in sequence with auxiliaries like *have*. This kind of construction is regionally restricted, and probably not familiar to most speakers of dialects who otherwise share the bulk of their syntax. The same would be true of double auxiliary constructions like *I might could, will you can*, which seem to be restricted to Scotland, Northern Ireland, and the southern U.S.

Sentence (ii) is again a Scots type, and also occurs in the southern midwest of the U.S. (though there it tends to be stigmatized; while the 'standard' type *the roof needs fixing* doesn't occur in Scots at all, and hence there has no social judgement except 'foreign' attached to it; all dialects on the other hand probably use or can use *needs to be fixed*).

These examples simply reinforce the problem: how do we delimit 'a language'? Any criteria we could come up with are bound to be crude and non-exhaustive; there will be loopholes in all definitions. Thus I could use 'mutual comprehensibility' (to some specified degree) as a criterion; if this could be quantified, we could set up a scale of 'comprehension distance', such that starting from a given 'base language' L, we could rank other speech forms as anything from 'closely related dialect of L' to 'other L'. So for myself as a speaker of New York City Standard English (on 'standard' see §1.2), I might set up a scale like this:

(1.4)

Base L	Close Dialect of L	Distant Dialect of L	Other L
New York Southern English Standard	Standard Scots		
		Rural Southern Scots	
		Buchan Scots	
			Dutch

The spatial arrangement suggests a continuum, not a set of clear boundaries. The comprehensibility barrier with broad Buchan (Aberdeenshire) Scots in my experience approaches that with Dutch; if

3

Buchan were in the Netherlands, I might be less tempted to take its speech as a 'distant dialect of English', and more likely to call it 'another language'.

So geopolitical factors enter into our judgements as well. It's well known that from Switzerland to Friesland there is a dialect-continuum; it's virtually impossible to say for instance where 'German' ends and 'Dutch' begins. Rural Bavarian may be close to incomprehensible to a monodialectal speaker of standard North German; conversely, the 'Low German' spoken just east of the Dutch/German border and the 'Dutch' spoken just west of it are more alike in many respects than the two varieties of 'German' just mentioned. The fact that two historically related speech communities coexist within a geographical boundary and are given the same name by their speakers doesn't make them 'the same language' in practical (communicative) terms; nor does the fact that two such speech forms exist in different countries make them 'different languages'.

In any case, it's worth remembering that terms like 'language' and 'dialect' do not represent 'natural kinds', features of the external world independently verifiable by some kind of general and agreed-on criteria. The objects that (may) fit what these terms are taken to mean – assuming agreement even on that – are not just 'out there' to be discovered. These classifications are imposed on continua of speech for various reasons: political, social, and linguistic. And we can't even necessarily take a speaker's word for the best (linguistic) designation of what he speaks. Many Scots, for instance, who (aside from some lexical and phonological differences) are fully comprehensible to non-Scots English speakers, might for historical, nationalist and political reasons deny that they spoke 'English'. An utterance like *I'm no speakin' English, I'm speakin' Scots* would not be contradictory or odd to the speaker.

Part of this of course is due to the feelings that many Scots have about England and the English; as well as to a common lay misunderstanding (helped along, as usual, by education) of locutions like 'Scots is a dialect of English'. The non-linguist takes this to mean (and uses it in the sense of) 'Scots is a debased/uncouth/provincial deviation from some standard', with all its associations of historical priority for 'English', etc.

My usage here will be the usual technical one, which does not make invidious comparisons. To say that 'Scots is a dialect of English' does not imply the (real) existence of an 'English' of which it's a dialect. Rather that 'English' is the name given to a cluster of (relatively) mutually comprehensible speech forms (the dialects) that share more features with each other than they do with any other conventionally named dialect clusters ('Dutch', 'German', etc.). In this sense to be a 'dialect of L' is to be a member of the cluster called L: 'Scots' is parallel to

'Northumbrian', 'Capetonian', 'Southern English Standard', 'Somerset Rural', and so on.

I've skirted the demarcation issue rather than grappling with it; but even if there's not much principle in the preceding reflections, it should be clear what I mean by 'English'. 'Custom and repute' will serve as a rough delimitation; except for some problems concerned with 'Scots', users of all the varieties I deal with here generally take themselves to be 'speakers of English'. This self-assessment is historically justified (§§1.3-4, ch. 2). All the speech forms under consideration are descendants, in one way or another, of a group of continental West Germanic dialects with certain common features, which were transplanted from northern Europe to the British Isles in the 5th century A.D.

1.2 'Standard' vs. 'Dialect' and Related Problems

If 'English' is a cluster of related but different dialects, I have a problem. Should I try to describe all of them? Or certain 'representative' types only? Or perhaps rather set up a semi-fictitious idealized 'core English', say, consisting of the features that seem to be most widespread across the dialects? The first is impossible; this book is too short, and anyhow nobody knows how many distinct varieties there are. Are Middle Class Bradford and Middle Class Leeds similar enough to count as 'one variety'? And what about Working Class Bradford and Leeds? Or would we be better off idealizing 'West Yorkshire' as a type, or 'West Yorkshire Middle Class' and 'Working Class'? Most sociolinguists would consider this far too crude: Trudgill (1974), in his account of Norwich speech, has a well-justified stratification involving Middle and Lower Middle Class and Upper, Lower and Middle Working Class. It's obvious we can't get into that kind of detail here, since this is a survey, not a monograph. (See further §5.1.)

Extracting widespread features and producing a kind of 'core' English is also problematical, because we might end up with a useless fiction, a pseudo-dialect that can't be identified as anyone's. On the other hand, everything I have been saying so far suggests that there is at least a core of syntax, morphology and lexis that can be taken as 'generally' English (on phonology see below). In purely practical terms, this is whatever it is that allows an American to visit London for the first time, give directions to a cab driver, and hand him the right amount of money when he tells him what the fare is.

To revert to an earlier example, *you have to can drive* is 'local'; but *you have to be able to drive* probably belongs to all dialects, including those that also say *you have to can*. From this point of view it makes sense to say that (overall) English modal auxiliaries do not have *to*-infinitives; and we add a rider 'except in Scots ...'. Obviously nobody has investigated enough of English to be able to say things like this with full confidence; there may be dialects that have no paraphrases of the *have to be able* type. But I don't know of any; so in a way the limits of reliability of this book are defined by the boundaries of my own ignorance. Every statement about 'English as a whole' is corrigible.

Actually the strategies of extracting a core, and taking one dialect as representative, tend to fall together, and for most of this book (except ch. 5 on dialects) I will adopt a slightly uneasy compromise between them. I will mean by 'English' (with no further qualifications) the set of features that seem to hold for the main so-called 'standard' varieties. These are in fact, for various historical reasons, a much more homogeneous group than say 'all rural dialects', and a much more representative group than 'all Northern English dialects' or something of the sort.

'Standard' is difficult; it is not properly an evaluative term (though laymen often use it that way), but describes a set of functions and a social status. The notion is important, as standards have arisen a number of times in the history of English, and the development of a standard has played its part in the efflorescence of English as a 'World Language'.

In a multi-dialectal situation, such as we find in virtually any nation of reasonable size, one dialect, or a set of similar ones, is usually the medium in which government and public affairs are conducted, the dialect of the universities and the church, the media, etc. In short, the mark of the educated speaker, the 'passport' to the non-local world of affairs. The standard is generally the most 'developed' dialect, in that it is used for all possible purposes, and there are (normally) no situations in which its use is inappropriate; it can be used in the most colloquial and intimate as well as the most formal and public settings, and it alone both has the vocabulary, and is judged appropriate, for technical uses. It would be distinctly odd, for example, if a paper appearing in an agricultural journal, even in Scotland, began: 'It is weel kent that tattie-bogles is no always effective like in preventing agricultural depradations by members of the *corvidae*'. (A *tattie-bogle* is a scare-crow.)

It is also the dialect that – in nations where a standard in this sense exists – is normally meant by the simple national term: *A grammar of English*, *German syntax*, etc. would be taken as referring to the national standard; a title not so referring would specify the dialect intended (*A grammar of the dialect of Dentdale*, etc.).

But 'standard' is not always a monolithic notion, particularly in a language with the kind of territorial extension English has. We could however characterize the current English standards as follows:

(i) For written English there is a supranational standard, most of

6

whose features are shared by all writers who write standard English. I suspect for instance that nothing I've written so far is marked as particularly 'American'.

(ii) On the other hand, 'the standard' in fact consists of a large set of regional standards, i.e. varieties which contain usages and vocabulary that are regional but not 'nonstandard': e.g. Scottish *outwith* 'outside', *furth of* 'beyond', South African *timeously* 'in good time', the U.S. English two past participles for *get* (*I've got* 'I have' vs. *I've gotten* 'I've obtained'). But for this dialect, by and large, there is little grammatical variation from region to region.

(iii) Many writers distinguish between spoken standard English with 'different accents' and 'different dialects'. The assumption behind this view (especially widespread among British linguists) is that there exist language varieties whose phonologies are (often quite) different, but which are the same in all other respects. Thus I would be said to 'speak standard English with a New York accent'. But in fact my standard has quite a number of regional grammatical features as well (e.g. *dove* as the past of *dive*, the *got/gotten* distinction, frequent use of simple past with perfect meaning, as in *did you read the book?* = British *have you read the book?*, etc.) For this reason I will not differentiate accent and dialect, but will assume that everyone has a dialect, which may (and probably will) differ from others elsewhere than in the phonology.

(iv) So the written standard is (relatively) homogeneous, the spoken one considerably less so; and the homogeneity is greatest in syntax and morphology, least in phonology and lexis. The 'core' I spoke about will then be essentially the grammatical base common to the (admittedly somewhat heterogeneous) set of standard dialects – more or less. As the discussion above suggests, this will be easiest to define for morphology and syntax: despite *got/gotten*, *dove*, *this roof needs fixed*, etc., it's still true that verbs in the present tense agree with their subjects in number, passives are formed the same way in all standard dialects, and so on.

(v) The worst problems will arise in phonology, since both phonological systems (the number and character of distinctive units) and phonetic realizations, as well as, to some extent, which units occur in which words, vary enormously (cf. chs. 3, 5). To take one example, Scottish English (§5.7.1) makes no distinction between the vowels of the (non-Scots) *pull* and *pool* classes: it has /ʉ/ in both, whereas other dialects normally have /ʊ/ vs. /uː/. Thus with respect to southern English or U.S. dialects the Scottish ones are 'one vowel short', and *pull/pool*, *boot/foot*, *good/food* are rhymes. On the other hand, many Scottish speakers distinguish three vowel qualities in *bird*, *heard*, *word* (usually /ɪ/ vs. /ɛ/ vs. /ʌ/), so that none of the three rhyme. The two lines from the popular American song 'Home on the Range'

> Where never is heard
> A discouraging word

simply do not work for Scots: I recall hearing a group of Glasgow schoolchildren singing 'Where never is [hɛrd] a discouraging [wʌrd]'. But both types rank as standards. Phonologically and phonetically there is no 'universal' standard in English, only a set of regional standards; though one particular 'supraregional' variety, RP or 'Received Pronunciation' (a bit anachronistically 'BBC' or 'Oxford' English) has to some extent that function. At least (if decreasingly) in the British Isles, and to some extent still in South Africa (§5.8.4).

(vi) Whatever its supraregional status, RP is a southern English dialect; and the larger number of standard dialects (mainly for historical reasons – see §§2.8-9, 5.8.1) belong to the same general type. That is, they have (roughly) the same number of consonants, the same number and type of rhyme classes, and rather similar phonetics. E.g. they all have different vowels in *bat* and *father*; though some will have the same vowel in *bat* and *fast*, and others in *fast* and *father*; they will all have different vowels in *look* and *Luke*, *put* and *putt*, *house* and *loose*, the same vowels in *grown* and *bone*, etc. (Scottish and northern English will have the same vowel in *look* and *Luke* – though the North of England will distinguish *pull* and *pool*; non-standard Northern will have the same vowel in *put* and *putt*, non-standard Scots in *house* and *loose*, non-standard Northern will have different vowels in *grown* and *bone*, etc.)

So to begin with, on historical and geographical grounds, I will connect (if not fully legitimately) the standard grammatical core with a southern English type of phonology, and assign symbols to phonological categories on that basis. Unless I am referring to specific regional or social varieties, then, I will use the following symbolization for 'the segments of English':

(1.5)

		Short Vowels				*Long Vowels*			
BIT	ɪ	FOOT	ʊ	BEET	iː	BOOT	uː
BET	ɛ	BUT	ʌ	HURT	3ː	BOUGHT	ɔː
BAT	æ	POT	ɒ			FATHER	ɑː

Diphthongs

MATE	eɪ	OAT	əʊ	IDEA	ɪə
BITE	aɪ	OUT	aʊ	FAIR	ɛə
BOY	ɔɪ				

Consonants

PIT	p	FEW	f	MEW	m
BIT	b	VIEW	v	NEW	n
TIP	t	MOTH	θ	SING	ŋ
DIP	d	THE	ð	RUE	r
KILL	k	SUE	s	LOO	l
GILL	g	ZOO	z	WOO	w
CHEW	tʃ	SHOE	ʃ	YOU	j
JEW	dʒ	ROUGE	ʒ		
		LOCH	x		
		WHO	h		

(For details and articulatory descriptions, see Appendix I.) I will use the general symbol [ə] for unstressed, reduced vowels as in *America*, ph*o*tography, *e*ffect, unless finer distinctions are at issue.

So if I say something like 'Middle English /oː/ > Modern English /uː/', I mean: Middle English /oː/ became the vowel in the *boot* class, whatever it happens to be in a given dialect of the southern English type. Thus RP /uː/ in this sense is systematically and historically equivalent to South African standard /ʉː/, Midwestern U.S. /ʊu/, etc.

Indirect as this notation may be, it should enable speakers of virtually any variety of English to identify the category in question, and relate their own dialect to the somewhat idealized one used as an example.

1.3 Origins, 1: Indo-European and Germanic

Genetically, English is a member of the Germanic subfamily of Indo-European (IE); more narrowly, of the Anglo-Frisian subgroup of West Germanic (WGmc) – see §1.4. That is, it is a descendant, by a process of unbroken transmission (involving of course massive internal change and important contacts with other languages) of an exceedingly distant parent language. This parent, called Proto-Indo-European (PIE) no longer survives; it is however 'available' to us through the results of a long tradition of historical scholarship, in the form of reconstructions. The same is true of closer ancestors such as Proto-Germanic (PGmc) – see below. I assume that the traditional techniques of reconstruction give us fairly reliable results; for the purposes of this book we can take reconstructed forms more or less as 'facts' (see the further discussion in §1.6). So if I say that the first consonant in *father* goes back to PIE */p/, what I mean is this: all our knowledge, plus a complex network of inference and argument, suggests that if we had a time-machine and

9

could go back and find a PIE speaker, we'd be very surprised indeed if his word for 'father' did not begin with [p].

The Indo-European family contains most of the languages spoken in Europe today, except for Basque, Hungarian, Finnish and its close relatives Karelian, Estonian and Lapp. (All these except Basque are members of another major family, Uralic.) It also contains a number of Near- and Middle-Eastern languages (e.g. Persian and Armenian), and most of the languages of Afghanistan and Northern India (e.g. Pashto, Hindi, Gujerati); as well as a number of now extinct languages of Asia (Tocharian), Asia Minor (Hittite, Luwian) and Europe (Illyrian, Mycenean). Thus – using modern languages only – we could say for example that English is very closely related to Frisian, slightly less so to Dutch, still less so but closely to German and Swedish, and distantly to French, Irish, Russian, Persian and Hindi. 'Closeness' here reflects roughly the time elapsed from a point when the parent language or subfamily had not yet undergone a major dialect split.

A word about linguistic 'speciation' (to borrow a term from biology) as we now understand it. New languages seem to originate basically by 'fission' – though there are other mechanisms involved. That is, if a single linguistic community splits up for any reason (migration, development of social or cultural barriers within the community), each resulting new community will continue to develop independently, and their speech will become increasingly different. All languages are in a constant state of change; and independent languages, even if related, will change more or less independently (though there may be similarities in closely related ones: see ch. 6). This is a simple observational fact, for which we have no equally simple explanation.

If the process of change goes on long enough – and especially if there is no extensive contact between the two groups – the end result will be that they 'speak different languages' (in the practical sense defined in §1.1).

Thus the early stages of a split lead to 'dialects', and the later ones to 'different languages'. We can visualize this in a simple 'family tree' model of speciation:

(1.6)

$$L_1 \quad\quad\quad\quad\quad (i)$$
$$L_1' \quad\quad L_1'' \quad\quad (ii)$$
$$L_2 \quad\quad\quad\quad L_3 \quad\quad (iii)$$

(where L_1', L_1'' are still recognizably 'dialects of L_1'.)

But there are other mechanisms as well. First of all, a primary split

10

like that at level (ii) does not have to be complete; L_1' and L_1'' can still be in contact, and speakers of one may borrow forms, sounds and structures from the other, thus leading to overlapping of features and discontinuities in the otherwise clear pattern of split. (E.g. Scots speakers whose normal form for *do* is /de/ may also use English /du:/.) This sort of interchange may continue at level (iii), where we might have bilingualism in the usual sense. This was the case with English and Scandinavian (remotely descendants of the same parent language) in the 9th–12th centuries (cf.§2.6). Hence Modern English has numerous forms of Scandinavian, not Old English, origin: e.g. the pronouns *they/ their/them*, and words like *egg, window, skirt*. Thus the model can be complicated, as in (1.7(a)) below:

(1.7)

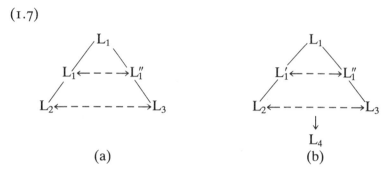

(a)   (b)

(where the broken arrows represent contact between speakers.)

In extreme cases (1.7(b)), the result may amount to a 'fusion language'; there is so much mutual borrowing that the speakers in contact develop a new speech form; and if the earlier contributors vanish, or the new one develops extensively on its own, we get a language that appears to have no direct ancestors, but rather to combine features of the dialect groups around it. (Dutch seems to be the result of this kind of development; there are clearly Saxon, Franconian and Frisian elements, but what we now call Dutch emerges quite suddenly in the 13th century.)

The fusion model does not seem to be applicable to the development of English, but the complex one in (1.7(a)) does; we will return in ch. 2 to the contacts between English and other (related and unrelated) languages.

Because of its antiquity, the IE family is a very complex network of relationships, and it is impossible to draw up an uncontroversial family tree. But it is possible to give a brief inventory of its members, to help set English in its larger context. Here are the major IE subfamilies, with some representative members († marks an extinct language):

Indo-Iranian: $\begin{cases} Indic: \text{†Sanskrit, Hindi, Bengali, Romani} \\ Iranian: \text{†Avestan, Persian, Pashto, Kurdish} \end{cases}$

Armenian:	†Classical Armenian, Modern Armenian
Illyrian:	†Illyrian, †Messapic
Albanian:	Albanian
Tocharian:	†Tocharian A, †Tocharian B
Anatolian:	†Hittite, †Luwian
Hellenic:	†Mycenean (Linear B), †Classical Greek, Modern Greek

Italic:
  { *Osco-Umbrian*: †Oscan, †Umbrian
  { *Latin-Faliscan*: †Faliscan, †Latin, French, Spanish, Italian, Rumanian

Celtic:
  { *Brythonic*: †Cornish, Welsh, Breton
  { *Goidelic*: †?Manx, †Old Irish, Irish, Scottish Gaelic

Germanic:
  East Germanic: †Gothic, †Crimean Gothic
  North Germanic: †Old Icelandic, Norwegian, Swedish, Danish, Icelandic, Faroese
  West Germanic: †Old English ('Anglo-Saxon'), English, Frisian, Dutch, Afrikaans, German, Yiddish

Baltic:	†Old Prussian, Lithuanian, Latvian

Slavonic:
  { *East Slavonic*: Russian, Ukrainian
  { *West Slavonic*: Polish, Czech, Slovak
  { *South Slavonic*: †Old Church Slavonic, Bulgarian, Macedonian, Slovene, Serbo-Croat

I have put Germanic among the groups it shows the closest affinities to; current scholarship suggests that Germanic is part of an ancient (perhaps Bronze Age) north-western IE group, including the ancestors of Italic and Celtic, and has some close relations to Baltic and Slavonic, probably due to contact: see below and §2.2.

The IE languages have been thought at different times to have originated in a number of different places; at present the best candidate seems to be somewhere in northern Europe, with later radiations to the east (as far as India) and to the west (Britain in the first instance, then America), and finally to the south (Africa and Australasia in the 16th to 19th centuries).

IE as a whole is traditionally divided into two groups, called *centum* and *satem*, from the words for 'hundred': e.g. Latin *centum* with initial /k/, and Avestan *satəm* with /s/. Germanic is on the *centum* side (/h/ in *hundred* is from earlier */k/: see below). This split seems – very roughly – to reflect an early east/west division: thus Celtic, Italic, Germanic and Greek are *centum*, while Armenian and Indo-Iranian are *satem*. (The terms of course do not refer merely to the word for 'hundred', but to the regular development of PIE */k/ in certain environments. Thus to English *heart* correspond Latin *cord-* (*c* = /k/), Greek *kardía*, Old Irish *cride* for the *centum* languages, Armenian *sirt*, Old Church Slavonic *srĭdĭce*, Lithuanian *širdìs* for the *satem*.)

The east/west split is not exceptionless: European Baltic and Slavonic are largely *satem*, as is Albanian, which suggests they might be relatively late arrivals from the east; while Tocharian (Chinese Turkestan) and Anatolian (Asiatic Turkey) are *centum*, but east of some *satem* groups. On comparative and other evidence the *centum* type is older; so it looks as if Tocharian and Hittite may have split off from the early IE community before the /k/ > /s/ change. This is largely conjectural; what is important is that being *centum* is by and large equivalent to being European; even though Germanic has close associations with *satem* Baltic and Slavonic, it clearly arose in northwest Europe.

The affinities with other IE groups can be illustrated as follows. For the oldest relations, we find a number of IE roots that appear uniquely in Italic, Celtic and Germanic; an example is IE */waːt-/ 'divine inspiration', which appears in Latin *vātes* 'soothsayer', Old Irish *fáith* 'priest', Old Icelandic *óðr* 'mad', the noun *óðr* 'mind, poetry', and the god-name *Óðinn* (Old High German *Wōtan*). There is also a unique perfect formation in /eː/ that occurs only in Italic and Germanic: Latin *vēnimus* 'we have come', Gothic *qēmum*.

The later affinities between Germanic and Baltic and Slavonic are of the same type; there are unique lexical roots, such as the one in 'gold': Go *gulþs*, OIc *gull*, OE *gold*, Lith *želtas*, Latvian *zèlts*, Old Church Slavonic *zloto*. The root here is IE */ghel-/ or */ghl̥-/, with a suffix */-to-/; the same root appears in *yellow*, G *gelb*. (Other IE groups show completely different roots in this word, e.g. L *aurum*, Gr *khrúsos*.) In addition, there are interesting grammatical parallels, especially in the formation of numerals, and certain case-endings. Thus Germanic and Baltic are unique in IE in forming the numerals 'eleven' and 'twelve' with (respectively) the numerals 'one' and 'two' and a suffix meaning 'left-over': Gothic *ain-lif*, *twa-lif*, OHG *ein-lif*, *zwe-lif*, Lith *vienúo-lika*, *dvý-lika*. (The remnants of this of course can be seen in *eleven*, *twelve*.) In the noun cases, Germanic, Baltic and Slavonic uniquely have an /-m-/ in the dative and instrumental plural endings, vs. /-b(h)-/ elsewhere: for dative plural we have Lith *-ms*, Old Church Slavonic *-mu*, Go *-am/-ōm/ -im/-um*, OE *-um*, vs. Sanskrit *-bhyah*, L *-bus*, Gaulish *-bo*. These shared innovations in morphology suggest a period of extensive and intimate contact.

It is not easy to put either a date or a place to the origins of Germanic as a recognizable subfamily; but by late Classical Antiquity the Germanic tribes are recognized (and named) as a distinct ethnic group, and clearly Germanic words and place-names appear in the writings of Roman historians at least as early as Caesar. (E.g. Caesar mentions a place called *Sylva Bāconis*, which seems to show the Germanic version of the root meaning 'beech', L *fāgus*, OE *bōc*.) As for the place of origin, the best candidate is an area east of the River Elbe, west of the Oder, and north of the Harz mountains, extending into southern Scandinavia. We can take this as the original homeland of the Germanic-speaking peoples, the place where a speech-community showing distinct features of its own, different from those of the surrounding IE languages, first developed.

The identity of Germanic – in an IE perspective – is defined by a group of innovations, both phonological and morphological. The most important of these involve (i) the vowel system, (ii) the consonants, (iii) the position of the accent, and (iv) the marking of past tense on the verb.

Without going into excessive detail, we can define the major phonological and grammatical innovations in Proto-Germanic (PGmc) as follows:

(i) Merger of PIE */a/ and */o/ in PGmc */a/, and PIE */a:/ and */o:/ in */o:/. To illustrate from early dialects that show this clearly: the distinction in L *ager* 'field', *octō* 'eight' is merged in Gothic *akkrs, ahtau*; that in Gr *phrátēr* 'brother', *plōtós* 'swimming' is merged in Go *brōþar, flōdus* 'flood, tide'. (The letter *þ* 'thorn' in older Germanic scripts represents [θ] or [ð], just like modern *th*.)

This does not mean of course that Greek or Latin are ancestors of Gothic; merely that they represent an older IE state of affairs, in which two categories were distinct that collapsed in the ancestor of Gothic.

(ii) 'Grimm's Law' or the 'First Consonant Shift'. The PIE consonant system was transformed by a massive shift, in which voiceless stops became fricatives, voiced stops devoiced, and 'voiced aspirated' or as we would now say breathy-voiced stops became first voiced fricatives and then voiced stops. The shift can be illustrated by these typical correspondences:

(1.8)

IE	Example	Germanic	Example
*p	L *p*iscis 'fish'	f	OE *f*isc
*t	L *t*rēs 'three'	θ	OE *þ*rēo
*k	L *c*ord- 'Heart'	x (h)	OE *h*eorte
*b	Gr kánna*b*is 'hemp'	p	OE hæne*p*
*d	L *d*ent- 'tooth'	t	OE tō*þ*
*g	L *g*enus 'race'	k	OE *c*ynn 'kin'
*bh	Skr *bh*ára-mi 'I carry'	b	OE *b*eran 'bear'

| *dh | Skr bán*dh*anam 'binding' | d | OE bin*d*an 'bind' |
| *gh | Skr *gh*ánti 'he strikes' | g | OE *g*ūþ 'battle' |

This highly simplified version omits some original consonants, but the import of the changes is obvious enough. Among other things, the correspondences make it clear that when two versions of the same root exist in English, with different consonants in the crucial places, the one with the expected Germanic consonant is native, and the other(s) borrowed, usually from Latin or Greek. Thus we have native/borrowed sets like *father/pater(nal), patri(ot)*; *three/trio, triad*; *heart/cord(ial)/ cardiac*; *hemp/cannabis*; *tooth/dent(al), (ortho)dont(ic)*; *kin/gen(us)/ gener(ic)*, etc. (If this kind of thing appeals, it's worth following up the etymologies of some apparently more far-fetched sets, like *bear/(de)fer/ (spermato)phore/(Christo)pher*; *bind/(of)fend*; *whale/baleen*; *quick/ vivid/biology*. A good etymological dictionary will show that these more distant-seeming relations are the same in principle as the more transparent ones above.)

(iii) Fixation of Accent. In PIE, as in the older dialects, word-accent (§3.4) wasn't fixed in a particular place. Within a paradigm, for instance, accent could shift in response to various morphosyntactic categories, some prefixes carried accent and others didn't, and so on. Thus the moveable accent in the Greek verb: taking 'loose', root *lū-*, we have root-accented forms like pres 1 sg *lū́-ō*, future 1 sg *lū́-s-ō*; suffix-accented ones like imperative 3 sg *lū-é-tō*; and prefix-accented ones like aorist 1 sg *é-lū-sa*.

In late PGmc the accent was shifted to root-initial syllables; affixes (except for certain prefixes: §3.6) could no longer be accented. Curiously, this accent-shift actually has historical reflexes in Germanic in the consonants of certain forms. At some point after Grimm's Law, the voiceless fricatives from IE */p t k/ became voiced if they were followed by an accented syllable; these voiced fricatives later became stops in the dialects. This led to apparent 'violations' of Grimm's Law, in which a given root could appear in two forms, one of which had the predicted consonant, and one of which didn't. Thus OE *weorþan* 'become', past sg *wearþ* with expected /θ/ < */t/ (cf. Skr *várta-mi* 'I turn'), but past plural *wurdon*, past participle *ge-word-en* with /d/, which is unexpected if the IE root ended in */t/. This problem was solved in 1875 in a brilliant paper by Karl Verner, who showed that the unexpected consonants turn up in just those places where the original IE form did not have an immediately preceding accent: thus to *weorþe* 'I become' corresponds Skr *várta-mi* as above; and to *wurdon* corresponds Skr *va-vr̥t-imá*. This set of correspondences is now known as Verner's Law. Other reflexes in English are *was* vs. *were* (where *were* is from the old past plural root: the original consonant in *were* is *[z], and the /r/ arises by a process called rhotacism: see §1.4). Verner's Law also shows up in *seethe* vs. *sodden*.

(iv) The Weak Verb. The oldest IE way of marking tense and related distinctions on verbs is by means of stem-internal vowel change or Ablaut (along with prefixes, suffixes, and other devices). Thus Greek *léip-ō* 'I leave' (pres), *lé-loi-pa* 'I have left' (perfect), *é-lip-on* 'I left' (aorist). The root of the verb could be represented as *l...ip*, with different vowel 'grades' for the present, perfect and aorist. We could thus define the alternation or 'filling in' of the vowel slot as: *e* for present, *o* for perfect, zero for aorist. I.e. *é-lip-on* shows 'no vowel' strictly speaking in *-lip-*, since the *-i-* is part of the root.

Germanic kept this system, with modifications, for a large number of verbs. We can see its relics clearly in the tense forms of a Gothic verb like *ur-reisan* 'to arise', root *r...is* (the prefix means something like 'up'):

(1.9)

	Present	Past Sg	Past Pl
	reis-an	rais	ris-um

Here the spelling *-ei-* = [iː] (i.e. [i] + [i]: IE /e/ becomes /i/ in Gothic), and is thus equivalent to Greek *-ei-* in *léip-ō*; the *a* to Greek *o* in *lé-loipa* (remember that earlier PIE */o/ becomes Germanic */a/); and the 'zero' in *risum* is like that in *é-lip-on*. Verbs of this type, forming their tenses essentially by modification of vowels within the root, are called strong verbs. But Germanic developed another type, in which tense-related information was carried by a suffix containing a dental or alveolar consonant. An example would be Gothic *lag-jan* 'to lay', past 1 sg *lag-i-da*. This type, with suffixation, is a Proto-Germanic invention, and is called the weak verb. Both of course survive in English: using the relatives of the two Gothic forms mentioned, we have *rise/rose/ris-en*, and *lay/lai-d*. As time progressed the weak type became more and more common, strong verbs became weak, and now the weak conjugation is the only productive one; English today has only about 60 of the original 300-odd Old English strong verbs (see further §4.5.5).

So, very briefly, the ancestor of all the Germanic languages, called Proto-Germanic (by us: we don't know what its speakers called it) was a dialect of Indo-European, and developed in north-west Europe in pre-Christian times. It was characterized (among other things) by marked phonological and grammatical innovativeness. This ancestral dialect has of course left no direct records; but there are early inscriptions in Germanic dialects, from about the middle of the 2nd century A.D.

onwards, that are much closer to the original than the later textual traditions, and give us the best direct idea we can get of what very early Germanic looked like. As a point of departure for what follows it's perhaps worth looking at one of these ancient inscriptions.

One of the most syntactically complete early Germanic texts is the famous inscription on the Golden Horn of Gallehus from South Jutland, written in North-West Germanic (see §1.4) of about 400 A.D. I give it below in the original runes, with a transliteration indicating grammatical divisions:

(1.10)

ᛖᚲ ᚺᛚᛖᚹᚨᚷᚨᛊᛏᛁᛉ ᚺᛟᛚᛏᛁᛃᚨᛉ ᚺᛟᚱᚾᚨ ᛏᚨᚹᛁᛞᛟ

ek   hlewa-gast-i-z   holt-ija-z   horn-a   taw-i-d-o

This transliteration can be glossed as follows: *I, Hlewa-Gast*-noun class marker-nominative singular *Holt*-patronymic-nominative singular *horn*-accusative singular *make*-pre-tense marker-past-first singular. Or, to put it in English, 'I, Hlewa-Gast, Holt's son, made (this) horn'. A comparison of the grammatical analysis with the modern translation gives some idea of how Germanic dialects have changed in the past millennium and a half; and we will see later that the earliest attested forms of English are in many ways rather closer to this than to the modern language. Indeed, the earliest English is only about three centuries later.

1.4 Origins, 2: The Ancestry of English

It used to be assumed that PGmc split early into three groups: North, East and West Germanic, as in the previous section. Scholarly opinion has now swung to the view that this trichotomy is relatively late, and follows an earlier two-way split into North-West and East Germanic. Many inscriptions that used to be assigned to 'Proto-Nordic', like the Gallehus text above, are now taken to be in North-West Germanic. The revised family tree looks like this:

(1.11)

```
                        PGmc
            NWGmc                    EGmc
        NGmc  WGmc
```

NWGmc is thus the ancestor of both the Scandinavian dialects and of

English and its relatives; EGmc is the ancestor of Gothic and its descendant Crimean Gothic.

Within WGmc itself there are a number of later splits, ultimately giving rise to the modern groupings: English and its close relative Frisian, the Netherlandic dialects (Dutch and Afrikaans), the North German dialect complex usually called Low German, and High German (now usually called simply German). (The terms 'High' and 'Low', by the way, are not evaluative: they refer to origins respectively in the mountainous interior and the coastal plain.)

What follows is necessarily rather detailed and technical; but it is of genealogical interest, and gives some insight into the criteria linguists use for the subgrouping of dialects within a family. Each subfamily is defined by shared innovations, here mainly phonological. This is not a complete account, but a sketch of the most salient features. For the sake of an overall picture, I will begin with the features that separate NWGmc and EGmc, and then look at NGmc vs. WGmc, and finally at the subdivisions within WGmc itself, ending up with English.

North-West Germanic vs. East Germanic. Phonologically, NWGmc shows a change of PGmc */e:/ to /a:/, as in OIc *láta* 'let', OHG *lāzzan* vs. Go *lētan*, and a change of PGmc */z/ to /r/, called 'rhotacism', e.g. Go *huzd* vs. OE *hord* 'hoard'. Morphologically, it develops a new past-tense in *ē* for certain verbs which replaces the old IE type formed by reduplication of the first syllable (as in Greek perfect *lé-loipa*): OIc *heita* 'to be called', past sg *hét*, OE *hātan, hēt* vs. Go *haitan, haí-hait*.

North Germanic vs. West Germanic. North Germanic is distinguished by some phonological losses, e.g. deletion of initial /j/ and /w/ under certain conditions: OIc *ár* 'year', *úlfr* 'wolf' vs. OE *gēar* (*g* = [j]), *wulf*. Also loss of the velar fricative /x/: OIc *nótt* 'night', *þó* 'though' vs. OE *neaht, þēah* (*h* = [x]). But the most striking innovation is a new definite article that follows its noun: OIc *úlfr-inn* 'the wolf' vs. OE *se wulf*. In addition, nearly all prefixes were lost, incuding the marker of the past participle: OIc *orðinn* 'become' vs. OE *ge-worden*. (English of course lost this particular prefix at a later stage: *has come* vs. Afrikaans *het ge-kom*, G *ist ge-kommen*, etc.)

West Germanic is partly defined negatively – in its earlier stages it is more conservative than NGmc; but two innovations do stand out. One is the West Germanic Gemination: a lengthening (in effect 'doubling') of all consonants except /r/ in certain contexts – generally after a short vowel and before one of the consonants /r l j w m n/. Thus OE *settan*, OS *settian* 'set' with medial *-tt-* vs. Go *satjan*, OIc *satja*. The single/double consonant distinction isn't just a matter of spelling: historically vowels behave differently before single and double consonants (cf. *over* vs. *offer* < OE *ofer, offrian*); and the singles and doubles themselves may develop differently, as the above example suggests (cf. §3.8). In WGmc, PGmc */z/ was also lost in unstressed syllables, leading to a loss of many noun endings: thus Go *dag-s*, OIc *dag-r* 'day' (nom sg: OIc *-r* from earlier *[z]) vs. OE *dæg*, OFri *deg*, OHG *tac*.

Within WGmc, there is an important split into two groups: Ingvaeonic or North-Sea Germanic (see §2.2) vs. High German. Ingvaeonic includes such early dialects as Old Low Franconian, Old Saxon, Old English and Old Frisian; High German contains the dialects collectively known in their early stages as Old High German.

High German is characterized mainly by a medieval innovation, the so-called second consonant shift (Grimm's Law was the first). The effects can be seen by comparing a modern Ingvaeonic dialect, English, with modern High German. The English consonants here represent the original types:

(1.12)

English	German
pound	*Pfund*
tongue	*Zunge* (*z* = [ts])
make	*machen*
water	*Wasser*
that	*das*
three	*drei*

Ingvaeonic is characterized by three main phonological innovations. First, monophthongization of the PGmc diphthong */ai/ to /aː/ or /eː/: OHG *bein* 'bone' vs. OE *bān*, OFri *bēn*. Second, loss of final /r/ in monosyllabic pronouns: OHG *mir* 'me' vs. OE/OFri *mē*. And third, loss of nasals and lengthening of the preceding vowel before voiceless fricatives: OHG *finf* 'five', *gans* 'goose', *tand* 'tooth' vs. OE *fīf*, *gōs*, *tōþ*.

And within the Ingvaeonic group, to narrow it down still further, we distinguish an Anglo-Frisian subgroup, characterized mainly by the development of the earlier low back vowel */ɑ/ to a front vowel spelled *æ* in Old English and *e* in Old Frisian: OHG *tac* 'day' vs. OE *dæg*, OFri *dei*.

This mass of philological detail can be summarized in an extended family tree, showing both early and late relationships within West Germanic:

(1.13)

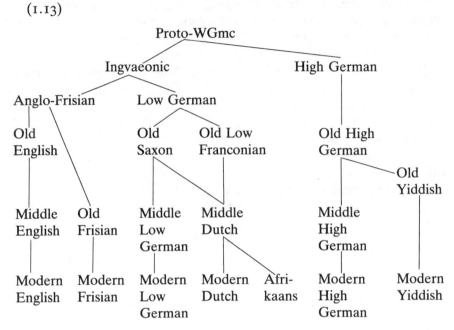

So in a fairly complicated way we have established something of a genealogy; the following chapters will consider both what the earlier stages looked like, and their relation to the structure of Modern English.

1.5 Structure and History

This book is about the 'structure and history' of English. Throughout this chapter I've talked about both: about structure in saying that a dialect has a particular set of vowel contrasts, a certain syntactic rule, and so on; about history in referring to linguistic changes. To the non-linguist (and sometimes the linguist) it is not always clear how these two categories are related; this is a short introduction to some complex issues which are crucial to an understanding of how languages work in time, and of two different modes of discourse I will be switching between.

Structure and history are intimately connected. If a language didn't have a relatively fixed structure it would be unlearnable, and useless for communication; language-understanding is partly a matter of prediction and anticipation on the part of the hearer. E.g. if you hear *the* you know that a noun or adjective plus noun is coming, if you hear a word beginning with /st/ you know that only a vowel or /r/ can follow. And conversely, such structural principles serve as constraints on what speakers can produce.

On the other hand, today's English is not the same as Pope's or Shakespeare's or Chaucer's or King Alfred's. The structural changes that have taken place over the last millennium are so massive that the English of 900 A.D. is a foreign language to us. As a concrete example, consider these three versions of the same biblical passage (Luke 2:8-9): the first in Old English, the second in Middle English, and the third in Early Modern English, the Authorized Version ('King James Bible') of 1611:

(1.14)

> (i) And hyrdas wæron on þam ylcan rice waciende, and nihtwæccan healdende ofer heora heorda. Þa stod Drihtnes engel wiþ hig, and Godes beorhtnes him ymbe scean; and hi him mycelum ege adredon.

> (ii) And scheeperdis weren in the same cuntre, wakynge and kepynge the watchis of the nyȝt on her flok. And lo! the aungel of the Lord stood bisidis hem, and the cleernesse of God schinede aboute hem, and thei dredden with greet drede.

> (iii) And there were in the same countrey shepheards abiding in yᵉ field, keeping watch ouer their flocke by nyght. And loe, the Angel of the Lord came vpon them, and the glory of the Lord shone round about them, and they were sore afraid.

The continuity between (ii) and (iii) is clear, as is that between (iii) and any modern version you might care to imagine. Aside from matters of spelling (y^e, v for initial u, u for medial v) and style, this English text of the early 17th century is more or less in 'our language'. But (ii), about 300 years earlier, shows striking systematic differences: e.g. third person plural pronouns *thei* for nominative, but genitive *her*, dative/accusative *hem*; and the verb is marked for number: sg *stood*, *schinede* vs. pl *weren*, *dredden*.

And the OE text, perhaps 400 years earlier still, is in 'a different language': word order (the second sentence reads 'Then stood God's angel before them, and God's brightness them about shone; and they them with great fear dreaded'), inflection, vocabulary (*ylcan* 'the same' (acc sg), *Drihtnes* 'God's', *ymbe* 'about') are very different. Yet we can see continuities between (i) and (ii): *wæron* = *weren*, *stod* = *stood*, *adredon* = *dredden*. And with a bit more thought, between (i) and (iii) via (ii): *were*, *stood*. (The spellings conceal some other differences: e.g. OE *stod* and ME *stood* were both /stoːd/, whereas Early Modern *stood* was /stuːd/, with the vowel later shortened to /ʊ/: cf. §3.10.) But it is important to remember that in principle the sequence (i–iii) represents an unbroken transmission of English from generation to generation.

As a summary, the following statements describe number-agreement on the verb, and the 3 pl pronoun system in the three temporal dialects represented above:

(i) In OE, there was a sg/pl distinction in the past, where pl was marked with *-on*. The 3 pl pronouns were nom *hi(g)*, gen *heora*, dat/acc *hem*.

(ii) In ME, there was a sg/pl distinction in the past, where pl was marked with *-en*. The pronouns were nom *thei*, gen *her*, dat/acc *hem*.

(iii) In Early Modern English, there was no number distinction in the past. The 3 pl pronouns were nom *they*, gen *their*, dat/acc *them*.

We have three distinct language-states, and each pair is related (in this data-sample) by among other things two changes:

(1.15)

> (i) > (ii): *-on* > *-en*; *hi(g)* > *they*.
> (ii) > (iii): *-en* > $\emptyset$ (i.e. '*-en* becomes zero');
>   *her*, *hem* > *their*, *them*.

(The two changes are of different types: *-on* > *-en* is a transformation of native material, while *they*, *their*, *them* are borrowings; but this is not relevant here.) Note that despite the changes, the continuous transmission and intergeneration communication are never broken. How is this possible, given the radical differences?

The answer is of course that linguistic change is rarely if ever 'catastrophic', as the above account would imply. Englishmen didn't suddenly wake up one morning saying *thei* instead of *hi*. The actual mechanism of change is something quite different, even if the end result is very like (1.15).

To clarify this, we will have to look briefly at some basic properties of languages spoken in normal speech communities (see further §5.5). As long as a language is spoken, it's never fully stable or 'fixed'; like all other cultural institutions languages are constantly changing. If you have speakers, you have a certain amount of variation; and if you have variation, you have the precondition (and enabling mechanism) for change.

There is in fact a certain similarity between linguistic and biological change: the establishment of a new form is rather like the origin of a new species. We begin with a pool of variants in the community, and some have a greater survival value than others. In a biological population this means greater reproductive success; individuals with the 'better' features leave more descendants, and eventually their descendants may replace the original population. With linguistic innovation there is no question of 'fitness' in a functional sense – one linguistic form is as good as another for purposes of communication. But there are still selective pressures of a social kind that will favour (for reasons we don't understand) particular variants: and these are selected cumulatively, with the result that over time the older forms gradually disappear (or nearly disappear) and are substituted for by newer ones. It is this cumulative, directional survival that we call 'language change'.

On the basis of textual evidence, and much recent observation of change in progress in contemporary speech communities, we could visualize for instance the substitution of *they* for *hi* this way:

(1.16)

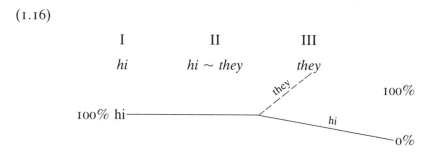

(The positive slope of the broken line for *they* indicates an increasing proportion of *they* to *hi* occurrences, leading to takeover by *they*; the negative slope of the solid *hi*-line indicates decrease leading to loss.)

At any given time a language will show instances of this general type of variation (whether in syntax, morphology, phonology or vocabulary). Some will be of the *they* ~ *hi* type, i.e. directional over time – a gradual increase of one variant at the expense of another. Some on the other hand will be what might be called 'stable variation': sets of options that appear to be going nowhere. An example is the alternation of what are called the *wh-*, *th-* and zero markers of relative clauses (cf. §4.6.3), what we get in respectively *the man **who**(**m**) I saw* vs. *the man **that** I saw* vs. *the man I saw*. This pattern, with the *wh*-forms tending to be more formal, and the *th*/zero more casual, seems to have been stable in English since at least the 16th century; in its own way as much a part of the solid core of English structure as the forms themselves. (But it could of course be taken up at any time as the basis for a change: variation generally is a necessary condition for change, but not a sufficient condition.)

But if languages typically show this kind of variation, and if changes proceed by small increments over long periods of time, how can we sensibly talk about either 'structure' or 'change' the way we do, as if they were discrete phenomena? The answers differ slightly in the two cases, but they both hinge on the need to idealize and abstract in order to describe intelligently. The principle involved can be put (perhaps a bit cryptically) like this: the existence of totally bald and one-legged men does not falsify the claim that human beings are bipeds with hair. The rest of the discussion may clarify this.

We generally describe the structure of a language at a given time in terms of a set of fixed categories and rules; and this level of description does not have to take account of the fact that languages exist in time, and are always changing. In a sense we can't even describe processes of change without prior description in terms of fixed categories. And this idealization is harmless in the end because of one simple fact: by and large most of the structure of a language will not be changing at a particular moment.

Take modern English: very few of the major grammatical rules seem to be undergoing any significant change at the moment in most dialects. Word-order is stable, as are the forms of nouns, verbs, pronouns, the structure of relative clauses, and the like. But there are some areas of variation leading to change in some dialects: e.g. in my own, the old perfect/past distinction appears to be eroding; I now have *did you eat yet?* and *I ate already* alongside of *have you eaten yet?* and *I've eaten already*. This might well be the beginning of the loss of the perfect, and a generalizing of the old past form to all uses (see §6.4 for further discussion).

A 'complete' description of a language (if such a thing were possible) would take into account both its time-bound and stable properties. There will always be a 'core' of fixed, categorical structure, surrounded by a 'periphery' of exceptions, variation, and anomalies of various kinds. And the periphery will include both fairly stable relics of the past (what I have elsewhere called 'undigested history': Lass 1981), and instances of variation either directed toward getting rid of the undigested anomalies, or suggesting future developments. The case of the past and perfect in my dialect is an example of the latter.

To illustrate undigested history of various kinds, and the core vs. periphery distinction, consider English noun plurals. The basic rule is that plurals are formed with -(*e*)*s*: but we also have the types represented by *mice, sheep, children, cherubim,* and *strata,* among others. The first three are older native types that were once much more common; the others are foreign borrowings (Hebrew and Latin respectively). There seems to be no evidence that the 'umlaut plural' class (§3.8) – or what's left of it – is anything but stable: *mice, feet,* etc. don't have alternatives like **mouses, *foots*. The same is true of the tiny *n*-class (*children, oxen*). But some of the foreign types are getting Anglicized: *cherubs* is heard as well as *cherubim* (for some speakers, with a difference in meaning: *cherubim* are biblical, while *cherubs* occur in Watteau paintings). And *strata* is also occurring increasingly often (normally, so far, in the speech of the semi-educated) as a singular, with a new plural *stratas*. (The same thing happened with *agenda*, historically the plural of L *agendum* 'that which is to be acted on' – but this was long enough ago for it not to be stigmatized any more.)

Again, consider the nouns that form their plurals by changing the final consonant from voiceless to voiced before the suffix: *house, wolf, knife, life, sheaf, leaf, mouth*. These members of the class seem stable enough: *wolves, knives, sheaves*, etc. But other items in this group seem to be changing: thus *roof* and *hoof* are losing for many speakers their historical plurals *rooves* and *hooves*; I have for instance *roofs, hoofs*, and the latter has the same vowel /ʊ/ in both singular and plural. It looks very much as if there is a kind of clean-up operation in progress on this particular bit of undigested history (for its origins, §3.8); it's not unlikely that in a generation or so *knife* will behave like *fife*, with final /f/ in both singular and plural.

There are further complications, in that certain classes of nouns have two plurals: e.g. *fish* vs. *fishes*, as in *the pond is full of fish* vs. *the fishes of the South Atlantic* vs. **there are lots of fishes on the fishmonger's slab*. Or the use of a zero-plural in predatory contexts: *I bagged six eland, I caught a lot of flounder*. This may be an instance of a countable noun turning into a mass noun like *sugar*: there is a clear difference between countable *sugars* (glucose, sucrose, lactose) and mass *sugar* (a bag/cup full).

But none of this affects the general validity of the rule that 'English plurals are formed with -(e)s'; and in fact any other statement, despite the exceptions, would be misleading, and in an important sense 'untrue'. The -(e)s plural is core, and the others periphery. Most important, perhaps, core statements are predictive: to say that -(e)s is the core of the plural system is to predict that new words in English will take it, and that a speaker presented with nonsense-words (*skrulf, blotz*) will use it and not vowel-change, -en, or zero.

We can now see why it's legitimate to talk of structure in a static and categorical way even if variation exists; the other side of the coin is showing that it's permissible to talk of change in 'catastrophic' terms even though it usually proceeds by variation. Despite the scenario in (1.16) for the triumph of *they* (and similar ones we could construct for -*on* > -*en* > -∅, and so on), it's still true that 'there was a change' from *hi* to *they*, from -*on* to -*en*, from -*en* to zero. How you describe a change depends on your focus; if you're interested in the overall development of the language, in 'landmarks' or what we might call 'macrohistory', then there was a simple change from one state to another. If you're interested in the mechanism and intimate details of a change, i.e. 'microhistory', then there was a long period of cumulatively weighted variation. Both accounts, given the differing perspectives, are 'true'; but because of this difference in perspective they're complementary. This kind of macrohistorical perspective is common in many fields: e.g. we know that 'the romantic period succeeded the classical' in western music, even though Beethoven was writing his violin concerto during Haydn's lifetime, and Schubert was writing his late chamber works during Beethoven's.

To use a more mundane but perhaps clearer illustration: say I drive south from Newcastle to London, but at one point I cut east and spend a day in Norwich. My journey ('the change') can still be adequately and truly described as 'Newcastle > London'; if you ask me how I got there, I could tell you about Norwich.

1.6 How Do We Know Anything About Early English?

Since much of this book is concerned with pre-modern English, it's worth saying a bit about how we know what we think we know. The reader unfamiliar with the technicalities of linguistic reconstruction and historical argument may wonder about my apparent confidence in discussing what – from a common-sense viewpoint – I can't really know anything about at first hand. What may be particularly problematical is claims about the phonology of say Old or Middle English, or to a lesser degree, about word-meaning and grammar.

A complete explication and evaluation of the sources of historical knowledge even for one language would be the subject-matter for a whole book (or indeed for the lifelong education of a historian); I will look at a couple of test-cases here, to rough out the kind of networks of inference that support our reconstructions.

Let's begin with morphology, syntax and vocabulary, and with the earliest attested stages of English. As an exercise, imagine that we have all the presently known manuscript sources for Old English, but that none of the scholarship has been done; we're starting from scratch, more or less like Champollion with the Rosetta Stone. How might we begin to work out the meanings of words and endings, and the basic syntactic rules of the language? Old English, in this situation, is a problem: the language has died out, even if its descendant survives. And modern speakers can't understand it at all – even though it looks in bits as if it's 'English'.

We may not have precisely a Rosetta Stone, but we do have some similar aids – texts involving Old English and another language: Latin. Now Latin has never died out; from late Roman times to the present there has been a continuous tradition of Latin teaching, and good grammars are available; we 'know' (or can know) Latin in a way close to the way we might learn any modern foreign language. So let's look at some of the Latin-connected sources for knowledge of OE, and see what they can tell us.

First, the early glossaries: these are lists of Latin words with OE equivalents, normally fairly recondite or at least unusual vocabulary, presumably for use once the reader has mastered the classroom vocabulary and is reading sophisticated texts. The 8th-century *Corpus Glossary*, for instance, has among others the following entries:

(1.17)

> *abortus*: misbyrd
> *alnus*: aler
> *albipedum*: huitfoot
> *anethum*: dili
> *ablata*: binumine

Our knowledge of Latin enables us to gloss the Latin words on the left: 'abortion, miscarriage', 'alder', 'white-foot(ed)', 'dill' (whose botanical name is still *Anethum graveolens*), 'deprived' (the past participle of *auferō* 'deprive'). Even this tiny bit of data, combined with other knowledge, tells us more than we might suspect: e.g. the connection between *mis-* in *misbyrd* and modern *mis-*, *-byrd* and *birth* seems clear, and *huitfoot* looks a lot like *whitefoot* (good working hypotheses anyway, which are supported by other evidence). From these two glosses, in addition, we can already suspect that OE had derivational prefixes (§4.8.5), and formed Adj + N compounds of a particular type (§4.8.2). Looking a little further afield, a comparison of *binumine* 'deprived' with German *benumen* (past participle of *benehmen* 'deprive') suggests a segmentation *be-num-ine*, i.e. *bi-* is a prefix, and *-ine* represents an earlier version of the participial suffix (which in fact we find in later OE as *-en*). And so on.

Slightly more detailed information comes from the many surviving interlinear glosses (word-for-word translations) of Latin texts; these give a lot of morphological information, but virtually nothing on syntax, since they generally follow the Latin. But in some cases where the structures of the two languages diverge, we can learn a great deal – especially from information which OE is forced to supply, but is not explicitly stated in Latin. Here is an instructive example from the gloss to Psalm 29 in the *Vespasian Psalter* (9th century):

(1.18)

EXALTABO	TE	DOMINE	QUONIAM	SUSCEPISTI	ME
ic uphebbu	ðec	dryhten	forðon	ðu onfenge	me

NEC	DILECTASTI	INIMICOS	MEOS	SUPER	ME
ne ðu	gelustfullades	feond	mine	ofer	mec

(Authorized Version 'I will extol thee, O Lord; for thou hast lifted me up, and hast not made my foes to rejoice over me'. In the AV this is Ps. 30, since the numbering in the Latin Vulgate is one out.)

Latin normally does not express the pronominal subject of a verb: *exaltabo* '(I) shall exalt', *dilectasti* '(thou) hast delighted'. The OE gloss puts in the subjects (*ic uphebbu, ðu gelustfullades*); thus telling us that OE is a subject-expressing language, that it shows person agreement on the verb in both present and past (*ic . . . -u, ðu . . . -es*), and also giving us some useful pronoun forms in different cases for first and second person (*ic/me/mine, ðu, ðec*: see §4.3.3). This brief example gives some idea of the utility of glosses as sources of both morphological and lexical information.

With this kind of background, we can turn to free (or freer) translations of known texts into idiomatic OE: in particular parts of the Bible, which were normally translated from the Vulgate. In some cases, where OE and Latin syntax coincide, the translation seems to be word-for-word, indistinguishable from interlinear glosses; thus Genesis 1:1:

(1.19)

In principio	creauit	Deus	coelum	et	terram
On angynne	gesceop	God	heofonan	&	eorðan
In beginning-dat	made	God	heaven-acc	and	earth-acc

But in other cases the rendering is much freer, and hence more indicative of OE structure (and translator's style, which we assume to be within the bounds dictated by the basic grammatical rules); so Genesis 18:1:

(1.20)

Apparuit	autem	ei	Dominus	in	conaulle	Mambre
Appeared	then	he-dat	God	in	valley-dat	Mamre

sedenti in	ostio	tabernaculi	sui	in	ipso
sitting in	mouth-dat	tent-gen	he-gen	in	same-dat

feruore	diei
heat-abl	day-gen

vs.

God	þa	æteowde	eft	Abrahame	on	þam	dene
God	then	appeared	again	Abraham-dat	in	the-dat	valley-dat

28

Mambre,	þær	þær	he	sæt	on	hys	geteldes	ingange
Mamre	there	where	he	sat	in	his	tent-gen	ingoing-dat

on	þære	hætan	þæs	dæges
in	the-dat	heat-dat	the-gen	day-gen

(AV: 'And the Lord appeared unto him in the plains of Mamre: and he sat in his tent door in the heat of the day'.)

It's reasonably easy to project from this kind of material to untranslated texts; thus over about 400 years of scholarship we have built up a detailed knowledge of OE morphology, syntax and vocabulary – enough to write confident pedagogical grammars, scholarly monographs, etc. And of course as English develops, and becomes more like its present form, the task becomes easier; and the knowledge we obtain from later stages also feeds back into our understanding of the older ones.

The procedures we use are in fact similar in kind – if different in detail – to what we would use in extracting information about any language: the first requirement for effective 'decipherment' of an unknown language (whether dead or still spoken) is an informant who is at least reasonably bilingual in that language and one you already know. A parallel to the development of our preliminary knowledge of OE might be an English-speaking linguist with a good command of French learning German from a native speaker with good French but no English. The shared language (which is native to neither linguist nor informant) serves as the medium until the learner is good enough to start using German as a source of further knowledge.

Of course there are differences: e.g. one can ask a living informant direct questions ('How do you say X?' or 'Is Y grammatical?'); with a language surviving only in dumb texts the questioning must be indirect. Another, and more serious problem is the representativeness of the texts that happen to have survived. A speaker of a language has a vast repertoire of styles and usages, and a vocabulary bigger than might be imagined from any given collection of his utterances; a dead language may be attested in a limited number of texts, and a quite limited variety of styles. For instance, we have no 'colloquial' Old English: the whole surviving corpus is pretty much elevated (poetry or serious prose; even the large number of riddles, which are often extremely witty, are in highly formal verse).

So there are enormous and often unfillable gaps in our knowledge even of the history of our own language; much of what does survive seems to have done so accidentally. For instance the word *thimble* (OE *þȳmel*) occurs only twice in the surviving OE materials, and is unattested between then and the 15th century. It wouldn't have taken much in the way of accidental loss of manuscripts (say two small monastery fires) to leave the word 'sourceless', appearing out of thin air in the 15th century. Yet with what we have it's clear that it didn't die out and suddenly get reinvented; either nobody happened to write it down between the attested occurrences (possible, but only just); or none of the cases where it was written down have survived (much more likely, considering the destruction of MS materials during episodes of vandalism like Henry VIII's expropriation of the monasteries, and the years of thuggery under Cromwell).

In written texts the forms themselves appear on the page, and using procedures like those sketched above we can reconstruct morphology, syntax and meaning reasonably well. But phonology is a different matter: how can we tell what kinds of sounds the letters in early texts stood for? As far as English goes, there are no reliable descriptions of pronunciation until the 16th century (and even these can be hard to interpret); yet we're pretty confident about many of the claims we make.

This topic is enormously complex; I'll look in (perhaps tedious) detail at one example, to show just what kinds of evidence we can bring to bear, and the sort of arguments linguistic historians use. The example is actually quite simple, but typical, and shows something of the infrastructure that linguistic history is built on. Similar arguments (even if virtually never unpacked and laid out in the literature in precisely this form) underpin most of our historical beliefs.

It's pretty much an article of faith among Anglicists that the *-gh-* spellings in modern (standard) words like *night, bought* represent an old velar fricative /x/ (as in G *Nacht*), which was pronounced at least as late as the 15th century, and probably well into the 16th. And that therefore ME spellings like *niʒt, nicht, nyght*, etc. (ʒ 'yogh' was often used where we use *-gh-*) represent something like /nixt/. We can reconstruct the sources of this belief in more or less this way, using *night* as an example:

(i) The *-h-* in the ancestor of the ME forms (OE *niht, nieht*) is assumed to have represented /x/, and there is no reason to think that there was any change in ME. The OE claim is justified as follows:

(ii) Other related dialects show /x/ or something similar (i.e. a fricative in the velar-to-uvular range): G *Nacht* /naxt/, Du *nacht* /nɑχt/, etc. This represents an older state of affairs than modern English /naɪt/, with nothing intervening between the vowel and consonant, because:

(a) Our knowledge of typical sound changes says that by and large arbitrary consonants don't get inserted in the middle of words, and loss of segments is commoner than gain;

(b) The only Germanic languages that don't have /x/ here are those that have lost it in all positions (English *night*, Swedish *natt* /nat:/, etc.);

(c) There is a regular correspondence between this /x/ in German, etc. and /k/ in other IE languages: thus L *nox* /noks/, stem /nokt-/ (cf.

gen sg *noct-is*), Lith *naktìs*, Skr *nakt-*. And Germanic /x/ is regularly related to /k/ in other IE groups (Grimm's Law, §1.3): L *octō* 'eight', Gr *oktō*, Tocharian B *okt* vs. G *acht*, OE *eahta*, etc. Therefore Germanic /x/ looks like a weakened survival of an earlier /x/: i.e. a fricative, with a passage for turbulent airflow, is weaker than a stop, which at some point completely closes off the airstream.

(iii) Now to later survivals. Phonetic accounts of standard English from the 16th century (e.g. John Hart's *Orthographie*, 1569) describe a consonant in this position that they identify with orthographic *h*, which is clearly [h]. Similar pronunciations are attested at least up to the early 17th century. Now if [x] is the natural weakening of [k], [h] is the natural weakening of [x]: the typical sources of [h] in many languages involve the loss of oral articulation of some other consonant, usually a fricative (e.g. Classical Greek /h/ < IE */s/: Gr *hépta* 'seven' vs. L *septem*, and the English prefixes *hyper-* from Greek and *super-* from its Latin equivalent). Thus the sequence IE /-Vkt/ > OE /-Vxt/ > 16th c./-Vht/ > modern /-Vt/ is entirely what we would expect.

(iv) Further, many forms ending in OE *-h* /x/ have come down with /f/: e.g. *tough*, *rough*, *enough* (OE *tūh*, *rūh*, *genōh*). Since *f*-spellings are attested as early as 1300 (*thurf* 'through' < OE *þurh*, cf. G *durch*), it is unlikely that /x/ had lost its articulation and become /h/ any earlier. It is typical of /h/ that it either remains or gets lost; it does not seem to become anything else. And if OE *h* was in fact a velar, the change to a labial consonant is also a well-known type: thus Latin velars often become labials in Rumanian, as in *opt* 'eight' < L *octō*.

(v) In addition, some modern English dialects as late as the 19th century show developments of our hypothetical /x/ such as /k/ or /g/ – which are reasonable from /x/, but not from /h/ (and much less from nothing): Wright's *English dialect grammar* gives /ɛkθ/ 'height' (OE *hēahþu*) in Oxfordshire, Buckinghamshire and Essex, /ɛkfə/ 'heifer' (OE *hēahfore*) in East Anglia, and /flɪəg/ 'flea' (OE *flēah*) in Yorkshire at that period. And of course in the more conservative varieties of modern Scots, a velar fricative occurs just where we'd expect it: e.g. /nɛxt/ 'night', /bɔxt/ 'bought' (OE *bōhte*, northern ME *boȝt(e)*). So at least some dialects in both England and Scotland must have gone through the whole period without even reaching the stage /h/.

(vi) Throughout the ME period, forms in *-gh-*, etc., where we posit /x/, generally rhyme only with members of the same class, not with words with the same vowel but no hypothetical /x/. Thus Chaucer rhymes *wight*: *knight* (OE *wiht*, *cniht*), but does not rhyme either with *delit* (OF *deliter*), nor does he rhyme this with any other member of the OE *-ht* class. Even though modern *delight* is spelled with (unhistorical) *-gh-*, and *delight*: *wight*: *knight* are perfectly good /-aɪt/ rhymes now.

31

This apparent piece of scholarly overkill is in fact a simple (!) illustration of what a historical argument looks like; but it demonstrates the inextricable connections of general linguistic theory, modern dialectology, comparative historical linguistics and direct historical testimony. All are part of the converging network of sources in historical linguistics, and underpin and lend reliability to the historian's productions.

CHAPTER 1: NOTES AND REFERENCES

1.1 For discussion of some of the constructions mentioned here, and the general problem of dialect-differences and mutual comprehensibility, see Trudgill (1982). On the 'dialect'/'language' question, Haugen (1966), Hudson (1980: ch. 2), Chambers & Trudgill (1980: ch. 1).

1.2 On standard languages, Haugen (1966) is a classic; see also Hudson (1980: §2.2.2), and on English in particular Trudgill (1983: chs. 11–12), and Strevens (1985). For the accent/dialect pseudodistinction, Wells (1982), Strevens (1985).

1.3–4 For a general outline and introduction to the IE family, Lockwood (1966). This is a bit dated and unsophisticated, but contains useful examples and a lot of information, and some analyzed texts. A more technical and up-to-date introduction is Baldi (1983). Beyond this, one has to get into the technical literature – though the textbook summary in Bloomfield (1933: chs. 18ff) is also useful (if also dated). The question of the IE homeland is still debated; suggestions range from Central Asia through the Caucasus and Anatolia, the Balkans, Central Europe, to an area stretching from the North Sea to the Ukraine. For recent discussions see the critical survey in Szemerényi (1985) – a technical and difficult but important state-of-the-art report on IE studies.

On historical linguistics, including reconstruction, the best textbook (though not all that elementary) is probably Bynon (1977). On reconstruction see also Lass (1984b: §13.4), Bloomfield as cited above, especially ch. 18, and Hockett (1958: chs. 42–61). There is a very readable general introduction to some important aspects of the historical study of language (or the study of language history) in Sapir (1921: chs. VII–VIII).

On the Germanic languages and their ancestry, there's little of a non-technical nature that's worth reading. The classic handbook in English is still probably Prokosch (1938). The early stages are excellently if very technically treated in van Coetsem & Kufner (1972), which has copious references. Of particular interest in this collection are the papers by Polomé (on the relations between Germanic and other IE groups), and Kufner (on the internal dialectology of Germanic). On runes and runic inscriptions, Elliot (1959) and Antonsen (1975); the latter contains transliterations and analyses of all the interpretable early inscriptions, and a valuable linguistic commentary. Verner's 1875 paper on the IE consonants in Germanic is one of the most important landmarks in historical linguistics, and set standards for historical argumentation and use of evidence that are still in force. For readers whose German is good, the original is well worth reading; there is also a quite good translation in Lehmann (1967).

For the more direct affinities of English, the commentary and texts in Markey (1976) are useful; the introduction gives a detailed treatment of the dialectology of Ingvaeonic, and its wider relations. For references on the early history of English itself, see the notes to chs. 2–4 below.

1.5   On the interrelationships of structure and history, see Lass (1984b: ch. 13) and Lass (1981). On variation as a prime mechanism in linguistic change, Lass (1984b: chs. 12–13). For a difficult but rewarding discussion of this area, see the classic paper by Weinreich *et al.* (1968); this is one of the monuments of recent historical linguistic theory, and one of the most important papers in the field in recent times. On linguistic and biological change, and the problem of 'function', Lass (1980); the view I take in that book is not a popular one, and anyone who reads it should also read at least one hostile review – I'd recommend Itkonen (1981). Texts cited in this section are from Görlach (1974).

1.6   The material from OE glosses is from Sweet (1885); the biblical translations from Crawford (1922). The comment that interlinear glosses don't tell us about syntax is not necessarily true: some OE glosses have an elaborate system of numerical or alphabetic coding that tells the reader what order the words ought to go in to make good OE sentences, not just literally translated Latin ones (see Robinson 1973). For *thimble* and similar cases, see Hoad (1984).

2. THE EXTERNAL HISTORY OF ENGLISH: A SKETCH

2.1 External vs. Internal History

It is customary to talk of languages having 'external' and 'internal' histories. The internal history is that of the language itself – its sound system, grammar, etc. But languages are spoken by communities which themselves have histories; and these interact with the purely internal evolution of their languages. This is external history. To take a simple example, the lexicon of a language may reflect the contacts its speakers have had with other speech communities. In the previous sentence, which contains twenty different words, twelve are native English (*to*, *a*, *the*, *of*, *given*, *may*, *speakers*, *have*, *had*, *with*, *other*, *speech*), one is Scandinavian (*take*), six are either directly from Latin or from Latin via French (*simple*, *example*, *language*, *reflect*, *contacts*, *communities*), and one is Greek (*lexicon*). This kind of 'hybrid' vocabulary is the result of past contacts: either through actual interaction of speakers in mixed communities, or through the medium of the written word. So it's clear that at one level at least – that of vocabulary – the history of the speech community itself contributes to our understanding of the present situation.

But contact isn't the only aspect of external history that concerns us. There is the interaction of language and society in general: the uses that a language is put to (e.g. whether or not it is the 'official' language of religion, government, education), which particular dialects have greater or lesser prestige, the geographical sources of standard dialects that may develop, and the like. These things are often intimately connected with shifts of power or of prestige from one area to another, the influence of particular social classes, etc. So some aspects of the evolution of a language will be related to the extralinguistic environment of its speakers; in this sense language history is part of cultural and political history. This chapter is a broad overview of this complex relationship as it has affected the development of English, setting the language in context as part of the broader history of its speakers.

But it's important to note that except for lexical borrowing, there is little if anything in the external history of a language that can be said to 'cause' internal events in any direct way. The socio-political setting of a speech community can affect vocabulary; and the selection of particular dialect bases for a standard (cf. §§2.8–9) is obviously socially motivated, by virtue of the association of dialects with places and social groups. But these factors do not affect linguistic structure *per se*. In the 17th century the old question-type *where live you*? was gradually replaced by the modern *where do you live* structure; and in England the originally distinct vowels in *bird, fern, hurt* merged into one (§3.8). But there was surely nothing in the 17th-century political or social climate that could be sensibly implicated in these changes: at the structural level there is no connection between language and society.

The internal life of a language is close to autonomous, and periods of (relative) stability or instability, for instance, do not match neatly with periods of stability or instability in other aspects of cultural life – except again for vocabulary. But the lexicon is the least structured and in a formal sense the least important part of a language. Certainly as far as major classes like nouns, verbs, etc. are concerned, it's the easiest thing in the world to make up new words; but it's quite a different matter with a new case-ending, pronoun, or syntactic construction. The social valuations attached to particular linguistic structures will obviously prompt their adoption or rejection; but these are imposed valuations, and no change can be said to be 'socially caused'. With all this out of the way, it's still the case that the history of its speakers is part – and an important part – of the total picture of the history of a language.

2.2 The *Völkerwanderungen*

Nobody knows who the first human inhabitants of Britain were, or what language(s) they spoke; but we do know when Germanic speakers in any numbers first arrived, and what they found when they got there. The arrival of these settlers (or invaders) was not however an independent event: it was part of a long series of demographic shifts, among peoples of many different linguistic stocks, that occupied much of the first half-millennium or so of the Christian era in Europe. These tribal movements are generally known by their German name, *Völkerwanderungen*; in this section we will be concerned with the wanderings of the Germanic speakers.

The best place to begin, perhaps, is the 1st century A.D. when the first reliable documentation appears. We can then move in two directions: back to the origins, and forward to the setting for the invasion of Britain. Judging from accounts like Tacitus' *Germania* (A.D. 98), there seem by the first century to have been a large number of culturally and linguistically related tribes (Tacitus lists 40) identified conventionally as 'Germani'. They were spread out over northern and north-central Europe, with pockets to the South: from Scandinavia and Lithuania in the North to Hungary in the Southeast and Switzerland in the South-west, and along the North Sea from Friesland to the mouth of the Elbe, and thence along the Baltic to the Gulf of Finland. Many of these tribes have names we can recognize easily from later history: Frisii, Anglii, Gotones; but others are more obscure (Manimi, Lemorii, Aestii). Tacitus, like other Romans of his time, tended to assume that just about any hairy non-Romans were 'Germans' (he was wrong about the Aestii, who were Balts); but in general his account is backed up by later literary and archaeological evidence, and presents a substantially accurate picture of the early Germanic world.

Of particular interest for us is Tacitus' mention of a western tribal alliance, consisting of three groups he calls Ingvaeones, Istvaeones and Erminones. The Ingvaeones lived along the North Sea, the Istvaeones along the Upper Rhine, and the Erminones to the South and East, in what would now be Germany. This seems to correspond reasonably to the later WGmc dialect divisions: Old English, Old Saxon, Old Frisian (Ingvaeonic: cf. §1.4), Franconian (Istvaeonic) and Upper German (Erminonic) – though only the first term is now used.

Given the original homeland of the German peoples in north-central Europe (cf. §1.4), it's clear that by Tacitus' time there had been a lot of movement to get them as far east as Lithuania and as far south as Hungary. And much more was to take place in the next few centuries, bringing Germanic speakers to their early southeast limit in the Crimea, and their western one in Britain.

In the last two centuries B.C. we can assume a fairly unified Germanic community in northwest and central Europe: dialectally diversified, but still probably speakers of 'one language'. Perhaps a situation rather like that of English itself today. During this period the Goths moved from their Scandinavian home (probably Sweden: cf. names like *Västergot-land*, *Gotland*, *Göteborg*) to the southern shores of the Baltic, where they remained for a couple of centuries at least. Here they came into contact with Baltic and Finnic peoples; from this period we can date early Germanic loans in Finnish, which often show more archaic forms than are attested in any Germanic language. E.g. Finnish *kuningas* 'king' (cf. OIc *konungr*, OHG *kuning*, OE *cyning*): on comparative grounds we would reconstruct PGmc */kuniny-a-z/, where /-a-/ is a declension marker like the -*u*- in L *domin-u-s*, and /-z/ is the nominative singular ending (like Latin -*s*). This ending is gone in OHG and OE, and is represented in OIc by the relic -*r*. Other archaic loans in Finnish are *ruhtinas* 'prince' (cf. OE *dryhten* 'lord'), *rengas* 'ring' (cf. OIc *hrengr*) – all reconstructed with PGmc nom sg */-a-z/. There are also some loans in Baltic languages, e.g. Old Prussian *asilis*, Lith *āsilua* 'ass' (cf. Go *asilus*), Old Prussian *catils*, Lith *katilas* 'kettle' (OIc *ketill* < */katil-/), and many more. We also owe to this period of contact the oldest form of the name of the Goths that has survived: Lith *Gudaī*, showing pre-Grimm's Law PIE */d/ (§1.3: cf. Tacitus' later form *Gotones*, OIc *Gautar* with shift to /t/).

In the 2nd–3rd centuries A.D., the Goths migrated to the Southeast, and settled on the northern shores of the Black Sea. These tribes separated into two groups, Ostrogoths and Visigoths, respectively east and west of the Dniepr. The Visigoths, christianized by Bishop Wulfila (d. 383), are the source of our only substantial remains of an East Germanic dialect, and indeed the earliest sizeable sample of written Germanic that we have. Some of their descendants – or at any rate some East Germanic speaking community – were still there as late as the 16th century, the source of the fragmentary corpus called 'Crimean Gothic'.

The West Germanic group seems to have been geopolitically coherent by the end of the first century, according to Tacitus; we can assume it was beginning to develop a linguistic identity as well. By Tacitus' time, indeed, we must have a dialect-picture rather like that presented by the earliest texts: though we know very little about the ancestors of the Scandinavians in this period.

During the early Christian centuries there was also considerable movement in the rest of Germania; a group of North Sea tribes (known collectively as 'Saxons') began to move south into Germany, towards the Weser and Rhine, thus bringing Ingvaeonic speakers back into contact with other West Germanic groups; another wave of migration to the West led to the settlement of Britain (cf. §2.3). This pattern of split and re-establishment of contact is pervasive in the early history of Germanic, and continues (if less intensively) until about the 11th century; the Scandinavian settlement in Britain in Alfredian times, and the later invasions, are part of the same ceaseless movement (cf. §2.6). This constant re-establishment of contact between related languages is one of the most problematic aspects of this period for linguistic historians: it makes it nearly impossible to unravel the ancestry of some of the Germanic languages with any precision.

At the same time, there was activity in the South: in the first century Erminonic tribes moved from the Elbe into southern Germany. Some of these appear later as the *Baiuvarii* (hence G *Bayern* 'Bavaria'), and the *Alemanni*, whose name is given by linguists to a dialect-complex including Swiss German (Alemannic). And various Istvaeonic tribes had emerged as an alliance under the name 'Franks' or 'Franconians'; these were to form the basis for the central German dialects, as well as contributing to the complex interaction between Low Franconian, Saxon, and to some extent Frisian, which eventuated in modern Dutch. Thus by about the fourth century we can see the outlines of the dialect-clusters that were to develop into the modern 'national' languages (Dutch, German), as well as others with no particular modern states attached to them (Frisian, Low German). The beginnings of High German as distinct from the rest of non-Ingvaeonic West Germanic dates from the end of this early period: this is signalled by the 'second' or High German consonant shift (cf. §1.4) which probably began in the South in the 5th or 6th centuries and spread northwards.

At the end of the 5th century, the Franco-Istvaeonic tribes moved west into northern Gaul (then Latin-speaking) and a bilingual state was formed under the Merovingian kings (whose name may survive in the Dutch/Afrikaans surname *van der Merwe*: cf. OE *Merewīoingas*). These and their successors, the Carolingians, brought about a political unification of most of the continental West Germanic peoples, which was the nucleus for the emerging German identity.

The picture in Scandinavia is less clear; the northern tribes did not come into contact with Rome as the Goths and the West Germanic tribes did, and at this early stage didn't write their own histories. But we can assume separation of Scandinavian from West Germanic by the 5th century, and from the 7th century on, a split into eastern (later Danish and Swedish) and western (later Norwegian, Icelandic and Faroese) groups. Jutland, earlier the home of the West Germanic Cimbri (whose name may survive in *Himmerland*: another example of the shift of IE */k/ in Grimm's Law), was colonized by the Danes (5th–6th century); and later (9th century) the Norwegians colonized Iceland and the Faroes. But it is only in this later period (the 'Viking Age') that the North Germanic peoples really appear as a historical presence: we will look at their effect on English when we consider their contacts with the Ingvaeonic settlers of Britain (§2.6).

So the main dialect-divisions within Germanic are fixed by, say, the 6th century at the latest; but we have very little textual evidence for most of the dialects until much later. The early runic inscriptions (3rd–6th centuries) are mostly very short, and not always unambiguously de-cipherable; many of them appear to have no very certain dialect provenance, but are written in a kind of 'classical' and rather archaic Northwest Germanic *koiné* or literary *lingua franca*. By the time the earliest substantial bodies of written material appear (6th–8th centuries), the individual dialects have evolved considerably; yet in the early texts their common Germanicness is a good deal clearer than it would be in a similar sample taken today.

To close this section on the Germanic heritage of English, it might be interesting to look at Old English as compared with the other early dialects; this will give an idea of the state of Germanic in general in the early days. Below are the first three sentences of the Lord's Prayer in Old English and a series of early dialects increasingly distant from it:

1. OE   Fæder ūre þū þe eart in heofonum, sī þīn nama gehalgod.

    OS   Fader ūsa, thū bist an them himila rīkea. Geuuīhid sī thīn namo.

    OHG   Fater unsēr, thū in himilon bist, geuuīhit sī namo thīn.

    OIc   Faþer várr sa þú ert i hifne, helgesk nafn þitt.

    Go   Atta unsar þu in himinam, weihnai namo þein.

2. OE   Tōbecume þin rīce.

    OS   Cuma thīn rīki.

    OHG   Quaeme rīchi thīn.

    OIc   Til kome þitt ríke.

    Go   Qimai þiudinassus þeins.

3. OE   Geweorþe þīn willa on eorþan swā swā on heofonum.

    OS   Uuertha thīn uuilleo, sō sama an ertho, sō an them himilo rīkea.

    OHG   Uuerdhe uuilleo thīn, sama sō in himile endi in erdhu.

    OIc   Verþe þinn vile, suá a iorþ sem a hifne.

    Go   Waírþai wilja þeins, swē in himina jah ana aírþai.

Even long after the establishment of distinct literary languages, the common vocabulary and structure are clear. There are of course differences in syntax and lexical choices: e.g. the OE/OIc use of a verb whose root means 'holy' (*gehalgod*, *helgesk*) vs. the other dialects' 'consecrated' (*weihnai*, *geuuīhit*); Gothic *þiudinassus* 'kingdom' (whose root means 'people, nation': cf. its survival in *Teuton(ic)*, G *Deutsch*) vs. *rīki*, *rīce* (with an original sense like 'power': G *Reich*); the forms of the verb 'to be' (OE *þū eart* vs. OS *thū bist*). But on the whole the similarities are greater than the differences, and they make it unsurprising that contact and borrowing were common, and persisted even well into the Middle Ages.

2.3 The Germanic Settlement of Britain

The first Germanic invaders (the 'Anglo-Saxons': see below) did not arrive in linguistically virgin territory. They came to an island with a long settlement history, which was at the time a Celtic-speaking Romanized former Imperial province. Britain had been continuously if sparsely settled since the late Stone Age; earlier settlements existed, but had been wiped out by the last glaciations. From late palaeolithic times (say c. 9000 B.C.), however, there was a stable population. What language(s) they spoke is unknown, and even beyond conjecture; given the limitations of our reconstructive techniques, it is not clear whether we could speak of language families and relationships in the usual sense at this time-depth even if we had any linguistic remains – which we don't. Indeed, we know nothing about the linguistic provenance of any British population until the first documented Celtic invasion, that of the Belgae who according to Caesar came from northern Gaul in the first century B.C. Though some authorities consider the Bronze Age people called 'Beaker Folk' (after their characteristic pottery) to have been Celts (fl. c. 2000 B.C.), and others suggest that the Celts first came over in a series of migrations in the 6th–1st centuries B.C. But our story really begins later: by the beginning of the Christian Era Britain was Celtic-speaking, if with a fair amount of Celtic-Latin bilingualism. The history of English as a geographic and cultural phenomenon in the British Isles is in essence the history of the displacement of the Celtic languages – a process that is still continuing, and may now, unfortunately, be nearing completion.

There are two major Celtic dialect groups, Brythonic (Welsh, Breton, extinct Cornish) and Goidelic (Irish, Scottish Gaelic, extinct Manx); they are also (a bit confusingly) called respectively P-Celtic and Q-Celtic. These names derive from the developments of IE *$/k^w/$: P-Celtic $/p/$ vs. Q-Celtic $/k/$, often spelled *q* in early sources. This can be seen in the words for 'head' and 'four' in modern Welsh and Irish: *pen*, *pedwar* vs. *ceann*, *ceathair*. P- vs. Q- is a distinction relevant mainly for the history of Celtic: but it leaves its traces in British place-names, which thus reflect early settlement history. In Scotland, where there were settlements of both groups, we get *Kenmore* < *ceann mòr* 'big hill', *Kennet* < *ceann ath* 'chief ford' vs. *Penicuik* 'cuckoo's hill' (cf. Welsh *pen y cog*) and *Pencaitland* < *pen chet* 'head of the wood' + *llan* 'enclosure'.

The earliest Celtic settlements were probably Goidelic; there may have been Celts in Ireland as early as 700 B.C., and until well into the Christian Era the Gaels (as we will call them) inhabited – as they still do – Ireland and the western fringe of northern Britain (Goidelic dialects are now spoken in Ireland and on the western edge of Scotland, mainly the Western Isles).

The early history of the Brythonic peoples (henceforth Britons) is unclear; it is not even certain whether the Brythonic/Goidelic split is continental or British. But the bulk of the early Celtic settlement was Brythonic, and by the time the Romans occupied the island in A.D. 43, most of mainland Britain was Brythonic speaking. The Britons have left traces, especially in the form of place-names, from Wales (their last stronghold today outside of Brittany) to East Anglia, and from Orkney to Cornwall.

Roman historians have left us the names of many of the Brythonic tribes and their leaders: some of the most famous are the Ordovices in North Wales and the Silures in South Wales (who gave their names, ultimately, via rock formations in their former territories, to the Ordovician and Silurian periods of the Cambrian era: L *Cambria* 'Wales'); the Iceni in East Anglia, known mainly for the exploits of their leader Boudicca (Boadicea); and the Cantii, who gave their name to Kent (cf. OE *Cantwarabyrig* 'town of the Cant-inhabitants', now *Canterbury*).

In the Christian era, Gaels from the West raided the coasts of Wales and Scotland; the Irish raided South Wales c. 270–275, and established small Irish-speaking kingdoms; and there were Irish colonies in Cornwall and Devon in the 5th and 6th centuries. In about 450 the Gaels of Dálriada (Co. Antrim) crossed to Argyll, and established a new kingdom of Dálriada; there were settlements about the same time in the Isle of Man and the Western Isles.

So the Romans invaded, and largely Romanized, a predominantly Brythonic island in A.D. 43, and held it until about 410, when for both military and political reasons it became more of a liability than an asset. After their withdrawal, the defences of the former province were left to the Britons; and their tendency to use, without sufficient power-base, Roman techniques of defence led to the eventual takeover of Britain by Germanic peoples.

The Romans had for a long time been in the habit of either hiring foreign mercenaries, or employing non-Roman allies to assist them in both defence and conquest; a reading of Caesar will show how cleverly the Romans managed to pit 'friendly' against hostile Celtic tribes during the campaigns in Gaul. After the Roman withdrawal, the Britons apparently tried to use the more militaristic and competent Germanic peoples of northern Europe in their own intertribal struggles; and one such attempt precipitated the resettlement of Britain.

North Sea tribes had been raiding the British coast for a good part of the Roman occupation; the coastline from the Wash to the Isle of Wight was in fact called the *Litus Saxonicum* 'Saxon Shore', and there was a specific Roman official (the *Comes Litoris Saxonici* 'Count of the Saxon Shore') entrusted with its defence. So the Ingvaeonic peoples were apparently well known: the name 'Saxon' may actually mean nothing more than 'North Sea German'.

According to the Venerable Bede (*Historia Ecclesiastica gentis Anglorum*, c. 731), the British leader Vortigern, beset by Picts (Britons) and Scots (Gaels) from the North, invited a Germanic army to assist him, in return for land. The traditional date for this invitation and acceptance is 449, but this is not actually clear from Bede's account: 449 is the year of the accession of the Emperor Martian, who ruled until 456. All Bede says is that it was 'in his time' that the invasion occurred. Bede's account of the invasion and its consequences is worth quoting; even though he was writing nearly three centuries after the event, he was a careful scholar, and availed himself of the best archival materials available, both in Britain and on the Continent. However problematic some of his statements may be, he is still a unique authority.

Bede says (ch. 15) that in the time of Martian,

> the Angles or Saxons came to Britain at the invitation of King Vortigern in three longships, and were granted lands in the eastern part of the island on condition that they protected the country; nevertheless their real intention was to attack it. At first they engaged the enemy advancing from the north, and having defeated them, sent back news of their success to their homeland, adding that the country was fertile and the Britons cowardly. Whereupon a large fleet quickly came over with a great body of warriors, which, when joined to the original forces, constituted an invincible army. These also received grants of land and money from the Britons, on condition that they maintained the peace and security of the island against all enemies.

(Which they eventually did, more or less; especially as it was now theirs.)

According to Bede, the invaders came from 'the three most formidable races of Germany, the Saxons, Angles, and Jutes'. The Jutes were the ancestors of the peoples of Kent and the Isle of Wight, the Saxons (from 'the country now known as Old Saxony') were the ancestors of the East, South and West Saxons (whose names survive in *Essex*, *Sussex*, and the now archaic *Wessex*), and the Angles (from 'Angulus', i.e. roughly Schleswig-Holstein) are the ancestors of the 'East and Middle Angles, the Mercians, all the Northumbrian peoples ... and other English peoples'. Indeed, Bede's three divisions tally reasonably well with the three major Old English dialect groups; but whether these divisions arose on the Continent or in Britain is debated (see notes to this section). There is another problem, in that other authorities give different versions of the ethnic make-up of the invaders: the 6th century Byzantine historian Procopius (who may have got his information from members of a Frankish embassy to Constantinople) lists Angles and Frisians; and the Welsh historian Gildas (c. 550) mentions only Saxons. There is also the possibility that other Germanic tribes as well were involved: *Swaffham* (Norfolk) may contain the name of the *Suebi* (Swabians: OE *Swæfe*), and there is archaeological and linguistic evidence for Frankish involvement as well. All we can say certainly is that the bulk of the invaders (judging from their later attested language) were Ingvaeonic speakers, and that there was some Franconian element as well, either initially or not too long after.

The invaders, in a not unfamiliar fashion, set themselves to driving the natives out of the main centres, and establishing total political hegemony. By about the 6th century, the Celtic population had been driven to the margins of the island, split by incessant battles with the invaders (which they normally lost) into three relic populations: one in Devon and Cornwall (where Cornish remained a spoken language until the 18th century), one in Wales, and one in southwest Scotland and northwest England. Their legacy remains in the name *Cumberland*, and the now artificially revived *Cumbria* for the administrative convenience created out of Cumberland and Westmorland: the origin of the name is L *Cumbri* 'Brythonic Celts' < Celtic *cymry* 'fellow countrymen'.

Celtic left a remarkably small impression on the language of the invaders. Aside from place-names, which tend to remain stable under conquest, about the only certified Brythonic loans into Old English are *bratt* 'cloak', *binn* 'manger', *brocc* 'badger', *carr* 'rock', *torr* 'peak', and *cumb* 'coomb(e)'. Other possibles are *bannoc* 'bannock, small cake', *dunn* 'dun-coloured', and *assa* 'ass'. There are also a few Goidelic loans, notably *drȳ* 'magician' < Old Irish *drūi* (the same root occurs in *Druid*). All in all, not much of the vocabulary of a conquered people in the language of the conquerors: but then the conquerors had less contact than normal. Compare the situation in South African English: a glance through just the entries under the letter *I* in Branford (1980) reveals more than 25 loans from southern Bantu languages alone, of which at least ten are in common use. There are of course more Celtic loans in modern English, but these are later (see §2.11).

From the 6th century on, then, the Celts as such cease to play any role to speak of in the linguistic history of the dominant group (except marginally through the Irish Church: §2.5); for our purposes, chauvinistic as it may sound, the history of English is the history of Germanic speakers, with one important though traditionally overrated interlude following the Norman Conquest (§2.7).

2.4 The Old English Kingdoms and Dialects

Within about a century and a half after their arrival, the 'Anglo-Saxons' had a monopoly of what organized political power there was in the larger part of Britain. (In all sections of this book dealing with pre-modern times, 'Britain' is a geographical term: the main island, including what are now England, Scotland and Wales. Ulster does not become 'British' until the 16th century, and it may be questionable whether Orkney, Shetland and the Hebrides are yet.)

But Britain in the early days is a geographical notion, not a politically unified kingdom or nation-state of the modern type. Certainly until the end of the 9th century we have a rather fluid collection of independent kingdoms, often at war with each other, and a shifting balance of power.

In the 7th–8th centuries, Britain was divided up into a number of independent kingdoms, the most important of which are shown in the map below:

Map 1. The Main Anglo-Saxon Kingdoms
[Modified after Bourcier 1981: 52]

These kingdoms were partly linguistic as well as political entities; well into Middle English times, and even to some extent now, we can see the remains of the old boundaries in the rough apportionment of certain linguistic features (cf. §§5.2–4).

In the later part of this period, we can really speak of three main kingdoms: Northumbria, Mercia, and Wessex, with the smaller kingdom of Kent largely under Wessex control. Political and cultural supremacy passed from one major kingdom to another: in the 7th century to Northumbria, in the 8th to Mercia, and in the 9th, largely due to King Alfred, to Wessex. This latter change of fortunes is linguistically important in the 9th–11th centuries, since for a time the southwestern (West Saxon) dialect of Old English became as close as anything ever got in the early Middle Ages to being a standard form of English.

Until at least the end of the 9th century, then, we have a relatively non-unified England, with no one of its major dialects of greater (overall) importance than another; literary and non-literary texts appeared in all of them, and they had fairly clear identities. We can get a slight idea of the state of dialect differences even in quite early times by comparing two 10th-century glosses to the same Biblical passage. Below are a Northumbrian (Lindisfarne Gospel) and a Mercian (Rushworth Gospel) version of Matthew 7:15, with the Latin text. In the Authorized Version the passage reads: 'Beware of false prophets, which come to you in sheep's clothing, but inwardly they are ravening wolves'. (L = Lindisfarne, R = Rushworth, V = Vulgate):

L	behaldas	gē		from	leasum	wītgum	ðā	ðe	cymes	to	īuh	in
R	behaldeþ	ēow	wið		lease	wītgu	þā	þe	cumaþ	to	ēow	in
V	attendite		a			falsis	prophetis	qui		veniunt	ad	vos	in

L	wēdum	scīpa	innaueard	uutedlīce	sint		uulfes	fērende
R	gewēdum	scēpa	ininnan	þanne		sindan	wulfas	rīsænde
V	vestimentis	ovium;	intrinsecus	autem	sunt		lupi	rapaces

Aside from different lexical choices, which are probably a matter of the individual glossator's style (e.g. *uutedlīce* 'truly' vs. *þanne* 'then' for *autem*), and spelling conventions (L prefers ð, R prefers þ), there are important structural differences. The two most notable are the different vowels in 'sheep' (L *ī* vs. R *ē*, a distinction parallel to that between modern *sheep* and *shape*); and the verb-inflections. Northumbrian has replaced the older -*þ* endings for imperative plural and present 3 plural with -*s* (*behaldas*: *behaldeþ*; *cymes*: *cumaþ*). The Northumbrian -*s*, which also occurs in other persons, is an important innovation: it is ultimately the source of modern standard third-person singular -*s*. (See §2.9 on Northern influence on London speech in the 14th century.)

45

There happen to be no contemporary West Saxon or Kentish versions of this passage; but to illustrate further, if there *were* a West Saxon one, it would probably look like this:

> *behealdaþ gē from lēasum wītegum þā þe cumað to ēow in gewēdum scēapa; beinnan sindon wulfas fǣrende.

Despite the lack of either political unity or 'nationalism' in the modern sense, there was certainly a consciousness – both inside and outside Britain – of an ethnic and linguistic identity. The early use of *Saxones* for all the invaders by Latin writers was largely superseded by *Angli*; in 601 Pope Gregory refers to Ethelbert of Kent as *rex Anglorum* (for some possible reasons for this counterfactual title see the next section); and a century or so later Bede called his book an ecclesiastical history *gentis Anglorum*, where the name applies to everyone from Lothian to Sussex. From earliest records, however, the vernacular name for the language is never anything but *Englisc* (from *Engle* 'Angles'); the people and sometimes the nation are normally called *Angel-cynn* 'Angle-kin'. The name *Englaland* 'land of the Angles' seems to appear first in the 11th century, thus considerably postdating the name of the language. (In Celtic references, they were still 'Saxons'; even now the old name is retained in Scots Gaelic *Sassunach* 'Englishman', lit. 'Saxon'.)

2.5 Christianity and Latin

The English (as we will now call them) were, in the familiar sense of the word, 'Pagan'; non-Christian, adherents of traditional Germanic religion. (Roughly the sort of thing we would call 'Norse Mythology'.) Indeed, relics of the old religion with a clearly northern flavour remain in as basic a field as our day-names: e.g. *Wednesday* 'Woden's day', *Thursday* 'Thor's', *Friday* 'Freya's'.

But in those days (as now) the old religions rarely managed to hold their own in the face of determined missionary onslaught; within about two centuries the Germanic population of Britain was at least superficially Christianized. The conversion was achieved by a kind of pincer movement, the Irish-based Celtic church coming in from the Northwest, and the Roman from the Southeast. (Not by concerted action, but historical accident; the two churches were not on the best of terms.)

The Celts (except for the northern Picts) were already largely Christian by the time of the *adventus Saxonum*; the first northern mission of importance was that of St Columba, who came from Ulster in 563 and set up a community in the island of Iona, off the west coast of Scotland, which served as his missionary base. From this centre churches were established in much of what is now Lowland Scotland; and it was probably in the area of Edinburgh that the Irish missionaries first came into contact with English speakers: Edwin of Northumbria set up a fortification on the Castle Rock in 632, which is supposed to have given the city its name: *Eadwinesburh* 'Edwin's fort' (though the first element of the name might as easily be the less romantic Scandinavian *eiðinn* 'gorse'). At this stage, it is worth remembering, the Irish were Irish-speaking. Thus the first contacts with Christianity the Northern English had were via the medium of Irish, a point we will return to.

Less than half a century after the start of St Columba's mission, the Roman church sent its first evangelists. In 596 Pope Gegory dispatched Augustine (later St Augustine of Canterbury, not the more famous Bishop of Hippo) and a party of about forty monks to preach the Gospel to the English. In 597, according to Bede, they landed on the Isle of Thanet, which was part of the Kingdom of Kent. King Ethelbert was not unfamiliar with Christianity; though he was unconverted, his wife was a Christian Frank, who came with her own bishop. Augustine had provided himself with Frankish interpreters, which suggests either that Ethelbert had learned Frankish from his wife, or that 6th-century Frankish was close enough to English for some kind of mutual communication to be possible.

Bede tells us that Ethelbert received Augustine cordially, and was impressed with his preaching (which he must have listened to via one of the interpreters; presumably Augustine preached in Latin). But he refused to accept the new religion. He did, however, in a spirit of tolerance it's doubtful Augustine would have shown, give the missionaries *carte blanche* to proselytise, and left it to his subjects to convert or not as they chose.

Over the next half-century missionary activity proceeded in two ways: *ad hoc* conversion of individuals, and 'official' conversion of kingdoms, through acceptance of the new faith by royalty. In 604 the East Saxons converted; in 625 Paulinus of Nola was made Bishop of Northumbria, and set about the conversion of King Edwin, which took place in 627; the West Saxons yielded in 635, and the Mercians in 655. At this point we could say that despite the frequent backsliding recorded by Bede, Britain was essentially Christian.

From a cultural and ultimately political point of view, the conversion of the English is of paramount importance. Just as in the case of Charles Martel (if he'd lost the battle of Poitiers in 732 we'd all be Muslims), the result of non-conversion would be an unimaginably different history. But closer to our concerns here, Christianity had an effect on the language of the invaders (or by now 'natives'): it marked the beginning of a long and intimate contact between English and Latin. Germanic

47

speakers had of course been exposed to Latin quite early on, when they first made contact with Rome in pre-Christian times. From this 'continental' period we have in Old English a number of more or less pan-Germanic loans that reflect (as loans usually do) the nature of the cultural contacts between the two linguistic groups. Coming as they did from north of the olive- and grape-lines, for instance (though grapes were grown later in Britain by the Romans, and viticulture was revived in the Middle Ages), the Germanic peoples obviously learned about both oil and wine from the Romans: OE *oele* 'oil' (L *oleum*) and *wīn* 'wine' (L *vīnum*) date from this period. Among the other early borrowings are *mynet* 'coin' (L *moneta*), *teped* 'curtain' (L *tapētum*), as well as perhaps *pise* 'peas' (L *pisum*) and *sæturnesdæg* 'Saturday' (L *Saturnī dies*; OE simply substitutes its genitive singular in *-es* for the Latin *-ī*).

The loans from this period are 'everyday' vocabulary, and undoubtedly derived from face-to-face spoken contact; though the extent of Germanic-Latin or Latin-Germanic bilingualism is unknown. (Not that mutual bilingualism is a precondition for borrowing, of course; very few English-speaking South Africans ever spoke a Bantu language, but words like *sangoma* 'witch-doctor' < Zulu *iSangoma* 'diviner', *indaba* 'conference, parley' < Zulu *indaba* are common currency; and cf. §§2.7, 2.11–12.)

The advent of Christianity however led to a much more extensive contact with Latin; in the early days mainly via the Bible and Latin-speaking clergy, in later periods through bilingual literacy, and exposure to a wider range of Latin literature. The Latin influx came at first through two sources, one minor and one major. The first and minor one is borrowing through Irish; there is relatively little of this, since the contacts between Irish and English were restricted mainly to the northern outposts of Northumbria. To this group of words belong *ancor* 'hermit', *cross*, *cursian* 'to curse', and a handful of others.

The early material directly from Latin is much more extensive. A large part consists of items conceptually or ritually central to the new faith: *abbod* 'abbot', *ælmesse* 'alms', *scrīn* 'shrine', *tempel* 'temple', *mynster* 'minster'. There are also some important non-religious loans from the early period, some Biblical, others from what must have been a growing bilingualism among imported Roman clergy, and English speakers' experience of other Latin literature: *purpl* 'purple', *pīn* 'pine', *plante* 'plant', *līlie* 'lily', *fefor* 'fever', *gīgant* 'giant'.

During the Scandinavian invasions (8th–10th centuries) there was a decline in the fortunes of the church. Monasteries and churches were sacked regularly (one of the first to go was the great Northumbrian centre of Lindisfarne in 793, followed by Bede's monastery at Jarrow the next year), and as might be expected there was something of a cultural eclipse (or that's how it looks by hindsight) during this time of siege and turmoil. It is certainly the case that there was a falling-off of clerical quality; in the 9th century King Alfred remarks, in the preface of his (?) translation of Gregory the Great's *Cura Pastoralis*, that knowledge of Latin had

> so totally fallen away among the English that there were very few [priests] on this side [i.e. south] of the Humber that could understand what the liturgy meant in English, or even translate an Epistle from Latin to English; and I do not think there were many beyond the Humber. There were so few that I cannot think of one south of the Thames when I succeeded to the crown.

Alfred goes on to say that even before the Viking destructions, although the churches were full of both books and clergy, the latter made little use of the former 'because they could not understand them at all, since they were not written in their own language'.

Alfred's answer to this was not – as one might have thought – an immediate reform of the teaching of Latin; rather, since as he says the Law was first written in Hebrew and then translated by the Greeks, etc. into their own vernaculars, that translation should be encouraged. The thing to do is to put into English 'those books it is most needful for all men to know'. And the procedure he suggests is that 'all the young freemen of England' who can should be taught first to read English; 'then let those who want to learn more, and aspire to higher things, be taught Latin'.

One result of the Alfredian reforms was a wealth of translation of Patristic and other religious writings, as well as secular and philosophical works: Alfred translated, assisted in translating, or gave his name to translations of – it is not always clear which – Boethius' *De consolatione philosophiae*, Orosius' *Historia adversum Paganos*, and other works. This vernacular revival, which included original material as well as translation, was accompanied – if later – by a revival of Latinity, which meant in effect a reestablishment of contact with European culture, and especially with the Mediterranean world.

In the late 10th century, continental monastic reforms reached England, in the form of adoption of the Benedictine Rule; this was accompanied by a general revival of religious life, and of education – since this was the province of the church. The newly reformed monasteries became major literary centres, both in Latin and English; and it must have been the growth in numbers of bilingual monastics that led to a vast increase in Latin borrowings.

49

Many loans of this later period have a distinctly bookish flavour; apart from new religious terms like *cell, clūstor* 'cloister', there were grammatical terms like *accent* and *declīnian* 'to decline', medical terms like *cancer, scrofel* 'scrofula', and a host of exotic plant and animal names, like *coliandre* 'coriander', *gingiber* 'ginger', *cēder* 'cedar', *camell* and *tīger*.

The lists given so far – especially the religious terms – suggest that English was a kind of impoverished tongue, with no resources other than importation for handling new concepts. This is misleading: the larger number of religious terms were actually not borrowed, but developed out of indigenous material. Some were literally translated (a process known as calquing or loan-translation): e.g. *patriarchus* as *hēah-fæder* 'high father'. Others were substituted for by semantically shifted native terms: e.g. *baptizāre* was rendered by *fullian* 'to consecrate' (older **fulwīhan* 'make wholly consecrated'), which led to new formations like *fulluht* (< *full-wīh-t*) 'baptism', *fulluht-bæþ* 'baptismal font', and so on. Other Germanic dialects did similar things: Old High German usually renders *baptizāre* as *touffan* 'immerse'.

Despite the loans, in fact, Old English (compared say to Middle or Modern English) was quite resistant to borrowing. In this respect it was rather more like modern German, which frequently avoids classical learned terms, and remakes vocabulary out of native resources. Thus while English unselfconsciously uses Greek terms like *larynx* and *oesophagus*, German has *Kehlkopf* 'throat-head' and *Speiseröhre* 'food-pipe', even in technical contexts.

2.6 The Scandinavian Invasions

In the 8th century the North Germanic peoples embarked on a great territorial expansion, which ended up with Swedes in Russia and Turkey, Norwegians in Iceland and the Faroes, and Danes in Normandy (whose name contains 'North-man') and England. We will be concerned here solely with the incursions into Britain, which cover a period from the end of the 8th to the late 11th centuries.

These, beginning in 787 according to the Anglo-Saxon Chronicle, were at first mainly small-group raids, restricted to targets near the coast – typical hit-and-run Viking sorties, undisciplined but no less effective episodes of pillage, murder and rape. This lasted until about 850. In that year, a Danish fleet of 350 ships invaded the Southeast of England, and the Danes eventually captured London and Canterbury; by 867 they had taken York. So at this point most of eastern England was in Scandinavian hands ('Dane' in Old English meant any Scandinavian, but most of the invaders probably were from Denmark). The pattern had shifted from raiding to conquest – as we have already seen with the Saxons, who began as maritime raiders. (Though apparently nobody invited the Danes.) After consolidating their hold on the East, the Danish hosts turned their attention to Wessex in the late 860s or early 870s; and would probably have taken that too, if Alfred had not finally defeated a large Danish army at Ethandun (Wiltshire) in 878. This defeat was massive enough to force the Danes to recognize Alfred's sovereignty over Wessex, and under the terms of the Treaty of Wedmore in that year the Danes withdrew from Wessex – but not from England. In effect Alfred saved Wessex and most of the West of England by ceding to the Danes roughly all of England east of a line from Chester to London – what is called the 'Danelaw' (i.e. that place where the Danes were legal authorities). A codicil to the treaty insisted that the Danes also become Christian, which they apparently did.

The position of the Danelaw can be seen clearly in map 2, which uses Scandinavian parish names as indices of Danish settlement.

But things did not stay quiet. The Danes were inclined from time to time to want more territory, and there were also new invasions. After a series of Danish attacks and English reprisals, King Athelstan defeated an army of Danes and Scots at Brunanburh (somewhere in Northumbria) in 937; and by the end of the century much of eastern England was back in English (i.e. Wessex) hands.

The last phase of the Danish Conquest (not the usual term, but as appropriate as the Norman Conquest) began with an invasion by a fleet under Olaf Tryggvason (later king of Norway) in 991. This culminated in the battle of Maldon on the Essex coast in which Olaf defeated the East Saxons under earl Byrhtnoth – a defeat memorialized in the best of the OE Battle poems, *The Battle of Maldon*. After this, the process of large-scale invasion began, in Baugh's felicitous phrase (1957: 110) 'to assume an official character'. In 994 Olaf was joined by King Sveinn of Denmark in an attack on London, and Denmark became established as the major political power in Britain; Sveinn's son Cnut (often anglicized as Canute) was crowned king in 1014. For the next quarter-century England was in effect a Danish province, ruled by Danish kings. (Much of Scotland at this time was in Norwegian hands, particularly the Western and Northern Isles.)

The Danish-English relationship was very different from the Saxon-Celtic; for one thing the Danes, however rude the manner of their arrival, did not drive out the local population, but settled in the midst of it. Even though places like York, Stamford, Lincoln, Derby were 'Danish towns', they were populated by Englishmen as well, most likely

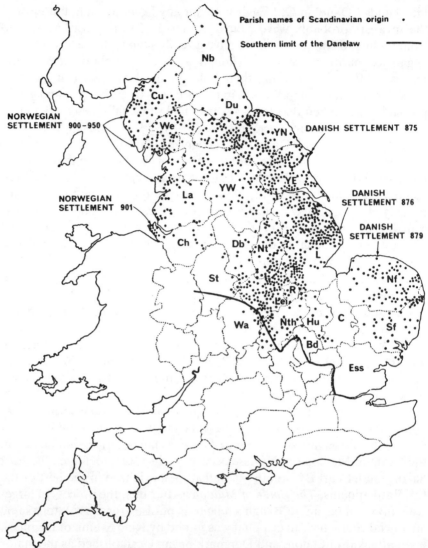

Map 2. Scandinavian Settlements (on the basis of Parish Names) and the Boundary of the Danelaw. [From Wakelin 1972: 20]

in the majority. 'Conquerors' or not, the Danes formed part of a mixed population.

In addition, they spoke a language closely related and in many ways structurally similar to English; though whether the two were mutually comprehensible, as some historians claim, is dubious. But whether they were or not, the overall similarities undoubtedly made bilingualism easier: in the same way as (say) it's easier for a German to learn Dutch

than English. At any rate there's no doubt that at least the later stages of
the Danish presence – before they were absorbed, as the Normans were
later to be – were characterized by fairly extensive bilingualism.

Unfortunately we have no direct evidence for what the contact
situation was like; most of our knowledge is built on inference from
borrowing (see below). But there is one tantalizing piece of hard data:
an 11th-century runic inscription in a church at Aldburgh (Yorkshire),
which reads:

(2.1)   Ulf let aræran cyrice for hanum and for
        Gunware saula

i.e. 'Ulf caused (this) church to be erected for him(self) and for
Gunwaru's soul'. The entire inscription is in English except for the sixth
word, *hanum*, which is North Germanic; OE would have *him*. This kind
of intimate mixture suggests a speaker so used to operating in both
languages and switching between them that he has, in a moment of
inattention, let the boundaries blur. To see the effect in more familiar
terms, imagine a German-English bilingual writing 'Wolf erected this
church for *sich* and ...'. (Incidentally, the fact that the name is *Ulf*
rather than *Wulf* is interesting: was the inscription the work of a Dane
writing in English and letting his Danish slip through, or of a bilingual
from a Danish/English family given the Danish form of the name, or
what?)

Whatever the bilingualism was really like, it's clear that the 'Anglo-
Norse' dialects (i.e. the varieties of Danish and Norwegian spoken in
England) retained their identities and continued in use as late as the 12th
century – though the remains are pitifully thin, consisting of only about
four legible inscriptions, the latest (in Norwegian) about 1150.

The extent of bilingualism is suggested mainly by the amount of
borrowing; Baugh gives a figure of 900 North Germanic items in English
from this period. And most of them, significantly, are not learned or
technical, but the sort of everyday lexis that we might expect to pass
from language to language under the unspecialized conditions of
everyday conversation. One can see similar effects with Afrikaans loans
in South African English, where the scope and nature of the contact are
better documented. An utterance like '*Ag*, man, why didn't you put the
boerewors on the *braai*?' (Oh, why didn't you put the sausage on the
grill?) is in principle the sort of thing we might suspect to have been
fairly normal in the Danelaw.

The borrowing is well-treated in the standard histories: a few
examples will suggest the kind of items that make up the bulk of the
Norse legacy: *egg, dirt, fellow, leg, sky, skull, take, window, ill, bask,
skill*. Sometimes Norse forms simply ousted the English: *take* supplanted

OE *niman, window* (ON *vind-auga* 'wind-eye') replaced OE *ēag-þyrel* 'eye-hole'. In other cases, both Norse and English forms remain, with a split in meaning: *die* replaced OE *steorfan* for the general sense, but the latter still remains as *starve*, i.e. to die of cold/hunger in the North of England, or merely of hunger elsewhere. Other Scandinavian: English pairs like this are *skirt : shirt, dike : ditch* (except in the North, where only *dike* is used), *kirk : church*. (The latter pair only in Scotland, where *kirk* normally refers to the Church of Scotland or the dissenting 'free' churches and their buildings, and *church* to the Church of England and other foreign bodies and theirs.)

The intimacy of contact between the two languages is also suggested by the borrowing of rather unlikely items. In general, the most borrowable are members of the major 'open' lexical classes, like nouns, verbs, adjectives; primarily structural forms, like pronouns and prepositions, are normally resistant. Yet in English the Scandinavian pronouns *they, their, them* (ON *þeirr, þeirra, þeim*) have replaced OE *hīe, hiera, hem*; and we have at least the preposition *till* and (archaic) *fro* – the latter in the mixed *to and fro*, which ought of course to be **till and fro*. In some regional dialects, especially in the North, much more Scandinavian material has survived; modern Scots for instance has among other forms *gar* 'make, cause', *big* 'build', *waur* 'worse' (cf. OIc *gøra, byggva, verre*).

The Danes also left a legacy of place-name elements: *-by, -thorpe, -thwaite, -toft* are uniquely North Germanic, and occur most frequently in the Danelaw. There is even one possible syntactic Scandinavianism in English: the ability to 'strand' prepositions at the end of relative clauses, as in *the car he was in*: cf. The Swedish equivalent, *bilen som hann var i* 'car-the relative-marker he was in'. This construction occurs commonly only in English and North Germanic. (The other Germanic languages have things like the English alternative *the car wherein he was*, or less often *in which he was*.)

The intensive contact seems to have lasted until the 11th or 12th centuries (except in the Northern Isles of Scotland, where Scandinavian dialects were spoken until the late 17th century). By the end of this period the Danes had simply been absorbed into the English-speaking community, memorialized by loans, place-names, and the surname element *-son*.

2.7 The Norman Conquest

The Danish hegemony lasted until 1042, when the royal line apparently expired. The throne passed back to the English, and Edward (later known as 'the Confessor' because of his extreme piety) became king. He died without issue in January 1066, and a problem of succession rose. In those days kings did not automatically succeed by primogeniture; there was a still rather obscure process called 'election', which among other things involved the possibility of a king naming his successor regardless of family ties. The English finally decided on Harold Godwinsson, whose father was the powerful Earl Godwin of Essex.

But William Duke of Normandy (among others) contested Harold's election. William, the illegitimate son of a Duke of Normandy and a tanner's daughter, and Edward's second cousin, claimed that both Edward and Harold had promised him the throne: the former apparently freely, the latter under duress, while a captive in Normandy.

The English disagreed; and in September 1066 William sailed from Normandy with a large fleet to enforce his claim. At the time of his landing in Sussex Harold was unfortunately in Lincolnshire, fighting a Norwegian army under Harald Harðráði (also a claimant to the throne). After dispatching the Norwegians, Harold marched to Sussex in an incredibly short time, collecting more troops on the way, and met William at Hastings. Harold's death in battle, and the superior Norman strategy, demoralized the English, and William won. He then embarked on a campaign of pillage and destruction until the English capitulated, and he was crowned king at Westminster on Christmas Day 1066.

Being more sophisticated, politically, than the Danish kings, William entrenched himself in power with superior efficiency. Among other things, he brought with him his own nobility and higher clergy, and replaced the indigenous ones, thus setting up a new loyal French-speaking bureaucracy in both state and church.

The Conquest was certainly a major event in English political (and to some extent social and cultural) history; but its linguistic importance is a matter of controversy. The received view is that it was cataclysmic: it 'changed the whole course of the English language' (Baugh 1957: 127). French under this interpretation is supposed to have 'ousted' English, and to have been the 'dominant' language until the late 13th–early 14th centuries, when it began to decline, and English, after having been 'subjected', was 're-established' (see Baugh 1957, titles of chs. 5–6); during much of this period all social groups except the peasantry were bilingual.

Against this is a 'revisionist' view: that even though the Conquest had superficially striking effects (notably a huge influx of French loanwords), (a) there was never any dominance of French outside the specialized spheres of government, the court, and the aristocracy; (b) there was no widespread practical or everyday bilingualism; and (c) the loan-influx can be explained without the sociolinguistic assumptions of the received view. Evidence for (a) and (b) comes from a combination of careful demographic and historical scholarship, plus a certain amount of common sense; and evidence for (c) from a consideration of similar loan-effects in the documented absence of bilingualism, plus – again – common sense and some knowledge of the typical behaviour of languages in contact.

To begin with demographics: the mere population figures, as far as we can reconstruct them, make any sort of cataclysm unlikely. Far from swamping the English, the Normans never made up more than (generously) 10% of a population of 1.5 million (some estimates are as low as 2%). Modern research gives the following picture of French-English relations in the immediate post-Conquest period:

(i) The native peasantry constituted upwards of 80% of the population, and everyone admits they never learned French. This leaves us with 20% in which bilingualism was even feasible.

(ii) Perhaps 1% of the small farmers at the time of the *Domesday* survey (1086) were French; and they employed English labourers, with whom they had to communicate.

(iii) The French urban presence was small, consisting mainly of enclaves in otherwise English towns, e.g. 160 in Norwich, 145 in York in the late 11th century.

(iv) Of the lower clergy, perhaps 2% were French; and since the bulk of their parishioners (see (i) above) must have been monolingual English, preaching in the ordinary churches would have been in English. (The liturgy – i.e. the mass, etc. – would have been in Latin; but sermons obviously would not have much effect in a language the audience didn't know.) In any case there is a long tradition of pre-Conquest vernacular preaching, preserved in the sermons of Ælfric and Wulfstan, among others, and there is no evidence that this deteriorated or died out.

By the late 12th century, the situation is:

(v) Royalty, the feudal aristocracy (c. 1200 about 197 lay and 39 ecclesiastical barons) and the upper secular (non-monastic) clergy, e.g. the major bishops and the archbishops of Canterbury and York, were French by birth and language, as were a good proportion of the monastics, especially the abbots of French foundations.

(vi) Only the court and the feudal barons were likely to be monolingual or virtually so; they were a closed social circle, with primary ethnic and cultural ties with France. Further, they had no need to learn English, since lower-level communication could be handled by a bureaucracy, at least some of whose members had to speak English. These circles remained French-speaking until well into the 13th century. Even Henry II (1154–89), the first post-Conquest king supposed to have known any English, only understood it, but needed an interpreter to talk to English-speaking subjects.

(vii) The lower nobility (i.e. knights holding land in fee from the barons) was mixed, a considerable number being English. And many of the Norman knights ended up marrying English women. In this group we can assume gradually increasing everyday bilingualism, leading to English monolingualism among the French as they gradually assimilated.

(viii) The urban middle-class French (mainly merchants) lived among the English, and transacted most of their business with them; it's more likely that they would have to learn English to function adequately than that the English would bother to learn French: especially since there's no evidence that the sub-aristocratic social fabric of England was much affected by the Conquest.

(ix) The French speakers who had to learn English were those who needed it for everyday life: government functionaries, clergymen, etc. The bilingualism that arose in these circumstances was precisely the kind that would militate against the survival and spread of French as a vernacular. The more competent the functionaries became, the less motivation there would be for the English to manage in French; it was the invaders who had to accommodate, by sheer force of practical circumstances – not the invaded.

Points (i–ix) do not however imply that at least the educated English never learned French, or that French didn't have a very special and prestigious position. But its relation to English was not that of a competing vernacular. French did have, all through the early post-Conquest years and well into the 14th century, enormous prestige, but its position was in principle no different from what it was in Germany or Iceland. That is, it was the fashionable language of European culture, and some competence in it was a mark of non-insularity. Certainly all educated Englishmen in the 12th and 13th centuries could read French, and probably spoke it after a fashion; perhaps a situation not unlike what prevailed among the upper classes in 19th-century Russia. The real difference between English-French contact and contact with French in other countries, and one of the factors that accounts for the great number of loans, is the presence of a resident body of native speakers, perhaps the bulk of whom were at least in the early stages themselves engaged in learning English; loans do not come into a language only through the activities of its own speakers.

And there was as well some use of French in special contexts, like the universities, the law-courts, and parliament: though this of course affected only a minority of Englishmen. And even here French was in decline as early as the 13th century; the Visitor of Merton College

57

Oxford (an ecclesiastical official whose function is to see that the statutes are being held to, etc.) was distressed to find in 1284 that even the Fellows were speaking English instead of Latin or French.

The situation overall does not show practical bilingualism or a linguistic takeover, any more than the use of Latin for diplomatic and scientific discourse in the 17th century implied a Romanization of England. There has been a long-standing confusion between French as a cultural *lingua franca*, gentleman's accomplishment, and special-purpose language and French as a competing vernacular and supplanter of English.

It is in this light that we should take the frequent rather self-conscious remarks in English vernacular literature of the 12th–13th centuries on the position of English and the snob-value of French, like this famous one from Robert of Gloucester (c. 1300):

> þus com, lo, Engelond in-to Normandies hond:
> And þe Normans ne couþe speke þo bote hor owe speche,
> And speke French as hii dude atom, and hor children dude
>   also teche,
> So þat heiemen of þis lond, þat of hor blod come,
> Holdeþ alle þulke speche þat hii of hom nome;
> Vor bote a man conne Frenss me telþ of him lute.
> Ac lowe men holdeþ to Engliss, and to hor owe speche ȝute.
> Ich wene þer ne beþ in al þe world contreyes none
> þat ne holdeþ to hor owe speche, bote Engelond one.

['Thus came, lo, England into Normandy's hand: and the Normans could speak only their own language, and spoke French at home, and taught it to their children, so that nobles of this land that come of their blood retain the speech that they got from them; for unless a man knows French he is held of little worth. But low men still keep to English, and to their own speech. I expect that there are no countries in the world that do not keep to their own speech, except England alone.']

Even native English writers used French – as they used Latin – as one of their literary languages. As late as the 14th century major figures like John Gower wrote large-scale works in French and Latin as well as English. The higher literary culture was essentially trilingual; two 13th-century examples will give some idea of the contexts in which we would expect languages other than English to figure. These are 'macaronic' poems, one in English and French, the other in English and Latin:

(a) MS Harley 2253	(b) MS Trinity Coll. Camb. 323
Mayden moder milde,	Leuedi, best of alle þing,
oiez cel oreysoun;	*rosa sine spina*,

from shome þou me shilde,	þou bere ihesu, heuene king
e de ly malfeloun.	*gratia diuina.*
for loue of þine childe	of alle þou berest þat pris,
me menez de tresoun;	heie quen in parais,
Ich wes wod & wilde,	*electa,*
ore su en prisoun.	moder milde and maidan ec
	efecta.

I will attempt only prose translations:

[(a) Virgin mother mild, *hear this prayer*; shield me from harm, *and from the wrongdoer*. For love of thy child, *lead me from wicked deeds*; I was mad and wild, *therefore I am in prison.*

(b) Lady, best of all things, *rose without thorns*, (may) thou bear Jesus, king of heaven, *by divine grace*. Thou bearest the prize above all, *chosen* high queen in paradise, *made* both mild mother and virgin.]

The immense number of French loans into English over the whole Middle English period (as many as 10,000) has inclined scholars to assume that only active bilingualism is a reasonable source. But significantly, about 90% are attested only after 1250, when even the strongest proponents of the eclipse-of-English scenario admit that French was on the decline as a spoken language. If this indicates late borrowing rather than merely late attestation, then it also suggests the probable mechanism behind the bulk of the loans: borrowing via passive knowledge.

It is possible to have extensive borrowing without anything approaching 'bilingualism' in the normal sense, or even active command of the source language – as long as there is an extensive literary acquaintance. We can see less striking but relevant examples in borrowings from Latin in the 16th–19th centuries, which amount to about 200, and from Italian in the same period, which amount to about 400. Latin-English bilingualism in the usual sense is ruled out because there were no native speakers of Latin, but only texts as sources; and there was certainly no large-scale intimate Italian-English contact.

Words encountered only in written texts can percolate easily into spoken language – even the everyday speech of people with no knowledge of the source. The following for instance are all post-medieval Latin loans which are now surely part of the core vocabulary of all speakers of English: *genius, extra, area, exit, pus, veto, album, lens, bonus*. All that is needed for words from any written source to get into a language is for someone to adopt them and use them; if he is a prestigious enough source, or if others for one reason or another accept his importations, the process of borrowing is completed. And lexical material does drift quite easily from technical and learned sources into popular speech, as the above examples show.

The French loans cover all the usual categories: many represent cultural items brought in by the French (e.g. terms of chivalry), or things they were particularly famous for; others are simply miscellaneous. In the category of things the French were known for we have the old chestnut, famous from a passage in *Ivanhoe*, ch. I, that after the Conquest the names for animals on the hoof were still English, but their processed forms were French: *cow*, *calf*, *sheep*, *pig* vs. French *beef*, *veal*, *mutton*, *pork* – a testimony to the *cordon bleu* image of the French chef even in the 11th century. Similarly, borrowed terms include items connected with the feudal aristocracy (*baron*, *minstrel*, *juggler*), government (*government*, *crown*, *empire*, *scepter*), the church (*religion*, *theology*, *abbey*, *convent*), and with the general superiority in the finer things connected with Frenchness (*fashion*, *adorn*, *dress*, *robe*, *luxury*, *satin*, *diamond*).

The influx of loans did have one structural effect on English of some importance – though it did not change 'the whole course' of the language. This is due to a difference between French and English phonology of the period. In Old English, the voiced fricatives [v z] occurred only in word-medial positions, after a stressed vowel and before either another vowel, or a nasal or liquid plus vowel: thus *f* was pronounced [v] in *ofer* 'over', *wulfas* 'wolves', but [f] in *faran* 'to go', *æfter* 'after', *wulf* 'wolf'. And [s] and [z] were similarly distributed (see §§3.9–10). There was thus no possibility of a contrast between the voiceless and voiced fricatives in the same position, as in modern *few*: *view*, *seal*: *zeal*, etc.

Old French, on the other hand, had distinctive /f v s z/, all of which occurred freely in initial position. Thus when French loans like *virgin*, *vice*, *victory*, *zeal*, *zodiac* came in, their acceptance set up a new structural pattern, which is now thoroughly integrated into English phonology. (This is one kind of borrowing that does presuppose a spoken source – if not necessarily a command of the source language on the part of the recipient; in Old English, when words with initial [v] in Latin were borrowed from written sources, they appeared with [f]: e.g. *fann* 'fan', *fers* 'verse', L *vannus*, *versus*.)

This change in segment distribution is probably the only structural effect of the long English-French contact. The Conquest was – linguistically – not a cataclysm: its effects, outside of the lexicon, are barely noticeable. If English had not had this long contact with French, the chances are that the more systematic aspects of its structure would be the same as they are now; though we might of course say *sheep-meat* instead of *mutton*, *lift* (OE *lyft*) instead of *air*, *doom* (OE *dōm*) instead of *judgement*. Lexis changes easily, but the structural frames it fits into are more resistant, and tend to remain, changing only under language-internal conditions.

And in fact the resistance of structural categories to borrowing provides an interesting contrast between the French and Norse contacts. As I mentioned above, it is usually only the major lexical categories (noun, verb, adjective, adverb) that are prone to borrowing under normal contact conditions, i.e. the so-called 'open classes' (classes whose membership can be easily increased); members of 'closed classes' (pronouns, prepositions, conjunctions, inflectional endings) are not borrowed except in intimate bilingualism. Thus the borrowing of *they*, *their*, *them*, *till* from Scandinavian suggests a much more intimate functional bilingualism than ever was the case with French.

Languages tend to retain their overall structural integrity and identity, even in close contact; after more than 300 years in South Africa, and contact with English for more than 200 of them, Afrikaans is still recognizably a Dutch dialect; after perhaps a millennium of contact with Slavic, Yiddish is still German – even if both Afrikaans and Yiddish have changed radically. By the same token English is still an Anglo-Frisian dialect of West Germanic – if a rather deviant one. (On 'deviance' in this connection see §6.2.)

2.8 Dialect and Standard in Middle English

Standard languages in the modern sense – particular high-prestige dialects in which the nation's business is conducted, in which serious (or any) literature is normally written, in which children regardless of their home dialects are to some extent or another educated – are not typical of the Middle Ages. Even highly educated people, if they wrote their language, normally wrote in their own regional dialect. Even in Old English times, when dialect differences were in some respects less clear-cut than they were later, every text we have is by and large identifiable as having a regional provenance. There was, it seems, a kind of 'poetic dialect' or *koiné*, largely West Saxon but with a considerable admixture of archaisms and non-WS forms; but normal prose writing was generally local. As it happens, the bulk of OE prose is West Saxon: largely because most of it dates from post-Alfredian times, i.e. during the supremacy of Wessex, and was written in Wessex or adjacent territories. And texts from other areas often show WS influence; since obviously the language of the ruling coterie is going to be highly prestigious, and 'provincial' writers will attempt to capture some of its features. (We still see this for instance in the orotund public speech of the semi-literate, e.g. shop-stewards who will say things like 'Me and the lads is engaged in an ongoin' conflict situation', in a broad local accent.)

The attribution of particular prestige to a local dialect of a language depends on having a ruling class or other focus of prestige that produces extensive material in that dialect. In the first two and a half centuries after the Conquest, this situation did not really exist in England. The literature produced by and for the highest classes was mainly in French, and even royal proclamations were issued in Latin and French; the first post-Conquest proclamation in English was promulgated by Henry III in 1285. The natural effect of this lack of a single prestige model is a proliferation of local standards; and the whole Middle English period is characterized by the development of rich vernacular literatures in the various regional dialects. Until the ascendancy of an English-speaking, London-based court in the 14th century, there was no dialect that had much more overall prestige than any other; to 'write in English' meant to write one's own dialect, using local forms and spellings. And it was not uncommon for texts to be translated from one dialect to another in the course of copying.

Here is a striking instance; two versions of an early 13th-century poem usually called 'Three Sorrowful Things'. The first (probably from the SW Midlands) is clearly the original; note that the rhymes work. The second (E. Midland?) has two false rhymes, due to the fact that in the dialect of its scribe, the infinitive had not lost its -(e)n ending, whereas the dialect of the original had. Thus the first version rhymes þre 'three': be 'be'; the second has ðre: ben:

(a)   Wanne ich þenche þinges þre
        ne mai neure bliþe be:
        þat on is ich sal awe,
        þat oþer is ich ne wot wilk day.
        þat þridde is mi meste kare,
        i ne woth nevre wuder i sal fare.

(b)   Wanne i ðenke ðinges ðre
        ne mai hi neure bliðe ben:
        ðe ton is dat i sal awei,
        ðe toþer is i ne wot wilk dei.
        ðe ðridde is mi moste kare,
        i ne wot wider i sal faren.

['When I think on three things, I can never be happy: one is that I must go away, the second is that I know not what day. The third is my greatest care, I know not whither I shall fare.']

Not also *meste* vs. *moste*, *wuder* vs. *wider*, where the spelling reflects major pronunciation differences; and the contrasting forms of the first person pronoun, *ich* vs. *i*. (The use of *þ*, *ð* is a matter of local spelling traditions, and has no linguistic implications.)

These kinds of differences are still apparent a century later. Here are brief extracts from two versions of *Cursor Mundi*, an extremely popular poem probably composed in the North of England in the late 13th century. Version (a) is from Lancashire and (b) from Bedfordshire:

(a) Bifil þan in a litel quile
     Iacob yode walcand be þe nile
     He sagh apon þe watur reme
     Caf flettand dunward þe strem
     O þ^t sight wex he ful blith
     And til his suns he tald it suith

(b) Sone afftyr in a litell whyle
     Iacob ʒede be þe watyr of nyle
     he se opon the watyr gleme
     Chaf come fletyng w^t þe streme
     Of þe Syght was he bliþe
     And to his sones he tolde it Suiþe

[(a): *qu* = *wh*; *yode* 'went', *caf* 'chaff', *flettand* 'floating', *suith* 'quickly'; (b) *ʒede* 'went'.]

Aside from textual discrepancies due to 'scribal editing', the dialect features of both areas show clearly: northern present participles in *-and* vs. Midland in *-yng*, N *tald* vs. Midland *tolde*, and the characteristic northern *qu*-spellings where other areas show *wh-*.

But even if people spoke and wrote their own dialects, with no sense of a 'superordinate' or 'supraregional' standard, there was awareness of dialect differences, and a certain amount of stereotyping. In the South, particularly, people were sensitive enough to these differences to be able to use them – accurately – for comic literary effect. Chaucer for instance, in the *Reeve's Tale*, has two northern characters among his Southerners, and clearly differentiates their speech. His northern clerks, John and Alleyn, born 'Fer in the north, I can nat telle where' (*CT* A 4015), use well-attested northern forms: thus (A 4035–8):

     'By God, right by the hopur wil I stande,'
     Quod John, 'and see *howgates* the corn *gas* in.
     Yet saugh I nevere, by my fader kyn
     How that the hopur wag*ges til* and *fra*.'

Here we have a northern vowel in 'go' (/aː/ rather than S /ɔː/: cf. §3.8), the local expression *howgates*, the *-(e)s* 3 sg present ending on the verb (cf. §§2.4, 2.9), and northern (ultimately Scandinavian) *til and fra* (cf. §2.6). Whereas the narrator and the southern characters use southern forms, e.g. the Miller's wife who says (A 4080–1):

> Allas! youre hors *goth* to the fen
> With wilde mares, as faste as he may *go*

(cf. the Northerner John's *gas* above).

In the late ME period the dialect of the SE Midlands, particularly London and environs, began to assume – at least for written English – something of a standard function. Except for the far North, which then as to some degree still was culturally as well as geographically separated from the Midlands and South, an essentially SE, ultimately London English began to function throughout the country as 'English', and dialectal differentia become rarer in written texts as we move into the 15th and 16th centuries. There are a number of factors – demographic, socioeconomic, political and cultural – that led to the eventual 'triumph' of London English.

On purely linguistic grounds, first of all, there is some evidence that in general Midland dialect types, by virtue of their 'transitional' status between the more extremely local northern and southern dialects, constituted some kind of 'mean'. Ranulph Higden in his *Polychronicon* (c. 1327) remarks that Midland speakers have special comprehension advantages. In John of Trevisa's translation of 1385:

> ... men of þe est wiþ men of þe west, as hyt were undur þe
> same party of hevene, acordeþ more in sounyng of speche þan
> men of þe norþ wiþ men of þe souþ; þerfore hyt ys that
> Mercii, þat buþ men of myddel Engelond, as hyt were
> parteners of þe endes, understondeþ betre þe syde longages,
> Norþeron and Souþeron, þan Norþeron and Souþeron
> understondeþ eyþer oþer.

The social, cultural, economic and political reasons for the eventual dominance of the SEML dialect are also suggested by Higden in an acute comment (again in Trevisa's translation – which is in a south-*west* Midland dialect!): Northerners especially are incomprehensible to Southerners because they live 'nyȝ to strange men and aliens þat spekeþ strangelych', and also because

> þe kynges of Engelond woneþ alwey fer fram þat contray:
> For a buþ more y-turnd up the souþ ... and ȝef a goþ to þe
> norþ contray, a goþ wiþ gret help and strengthe. þe cause why
> a buþ more in the souþ contray þan in þe norþ may be
> betre cornlond, more people, more noble cytes, and more
> profytable havenes.

(*woneþ* 'dwell', *a buþ* 'they are', *ȝef* 'if'.)

He is clearly right. The conditions for the development of a regional dialect into a supraregional standard are all here: the region is the seat of government, is agriculturally rich, has good ports, and is a focus of urban culture with London as both the political and cultural capital, the seat of the court and the judiciary, not far from the major universities and the chief archiepiscopal see, it's no wonder that when a standard did emerge it was London-based (see the next section for more comment).

The fact that southern English was becoming prestigious during the 14th century, and developing 'Establishment' associations, is negatively reflected, unsurprisingly, in northern writings. In the *Second Shepherds' Play* from the Towneley Cycle (Yorkshire, late 14th century), Mak the sheep-rustler puts on airs and claims to be a 'yeoman of the king': in doing so he uses southern forms like *ich* for *I*, *mo* for *ma* 'more', *goyth* for *ga* 'go!'; and the shepherds he's talking to respond by saying: 'Now take outt that sothren tothe/And sett in a torde' (2.5–16), i.e. 'Now take out that southern tooth and go sit in a turd'. (In northern perceptions, southern and southern Midland are conflated.)

2.9 Development of the Southern Standard

A successful standard must be widely comprehensible, socially highly valued, and 'codified' to some extent; that is, if as is usual, control of the standard is a key to social advancement, a mark of having arrived (or being there already), there must be some authoritative consensus, preferably in written form, on what it consists of. The genuinely standard – especially in a class-conscious society – must be distinct from what is 'ignorant', 'provincial', 'lower-class', etc. This is not to say that such a consensus, in any form that would pass muster among professional linguists, is normally achieved – or even fully achievable; but one of the uses of a standard in the lay sense is as an exclusion-device, and a means for identifying and pigeonholing other people in an efficient and comfortable way. All dialects of course are 'markers' in this sense, catering to natural human xenophobia: but with standards the question of 'authority' arises, whereas nonstandard (and non-aspiring) speakers are normally confident enough in their intuitions about what counts as a legitimate sample of their native speech to distinguish ingroup from outgroup without assistance.

The authority problem becomes particularly acute when large numbers of speakers have to use the standard, but as a 'second language': e.g. learning different phonology or lexis or syntax, or in many cases learning to write (and perhaps speak for special purposes) a non-local form of their language, or at least a form based on a variety not their own. Or becoming fully bidialectal, using the standard for 'public' purposes and their local variety at home. This began to surface explicitly in the 16th century, largely in terms of pronunciation; but the fact that lack of standardization could be a problem for language users was apparent earlier.

The first clear treatment of this difficulty comes in the early days of printing in England: how do you assure wide comprehensibility and acceptance, and what kind of language do you use for it? For Caxton, as the pioneer English printer, this was a matter not merely of principle, but detail: what forms ought to be used in printed books? In the prologue to his *Eneydos* (1490), he tells the famous story of a sailor coming ashore in England and asking for *egges*; and being told by a shopkeeper that she doesn't understand French. Whereupon he is instructed by a companion to ask for *eyren*, which is successful. Both forms existed, that is, but were unevenly distributed among speakers; and Caxton uses the story as a microcosmic illustration of his problem. There is so much diversity, he says, and 'in these dayes euery man that is in ony reputacyon in his countre. wyll vtter his commynycacion ... in suche maners & terms/ that fewe shal vnderstonde theym'.

He defines his solution in an interesting way, that comes close to an explicit definition of what a standard – at least a literary one – should be:

> And for as moche as this present booke is not for a rude vplondysch man to laboure therein/ ne rede it/ but onely for a clerke & a noble gentylman. . . . Therefor in a meane bytwene bothe I haue reduced & translated this sayd booke in to our englysshe not ouer rude ne curious [i.e. recondite, refined] but in suche termes as shall be vnderstonden by goddys grace accordynge to my copye.

Until about the 17th century the basic concern seems to have been what phonological type would be taken as the standard (or as people tended to say 'best') one: concern with grammatical features comes later, and is in general more a matter of codifying particular points of syntactic and morphological usage than actually choosing a base. It seems that once a local dialect type (identified by its phonology) was selected, the grammatical structures more or less agreed on by educated speakers, which were less in flux than phonological properties, went along with it.

The early debate on the standard was cast largely in terms of what was not 'provincial' or 'affected'. The details of what constituted standard or acceptable pronunciation were much debated among phoneticians from the 16th through the 19th centuries: but the various disagreements (early ones like whether *weight* and *mate* should rhyme, late ones like which words should have /ɑː/) are less important, from a sociolinguistic point of view, than the agreement on matters of principle.

The consensus from quite early on is that educated London is 'that speach which euery reasonable English man, will the nearest he can, frame his tongue therevnto' (John Hart in his *Orthographie*, 1569). Though Hart does admit that no one 'could justly blame' a native of Newcastle or Bodmin for writing in his own vernacular 'to serue hys neyghbors' – adding significantly 'yea, thogh he wrate to London (i.e. 'odd as it might seem for someone to use provincial speech forms in such a setting'). Twenty years later Samuel Puttenham, in a famous passage from his *Arte of poesie*, says that the best English is 'the vsual speech of the court, and that of London and the shires lying about London within lx. miles'. Puttenham, like Hart, allows that Northerners and Westerners might properly use their own speech in their own surroundings; but acceptance as non-provincial in educated circles (i.e. in London and environs) seems to depend on lack of recognizably local forms. Later writers make the same point: Christopher Cooper in 1685 says that in the south 'purissima & emendata loquendi consuetudo est' ('the most pure and correct speech is the norm'). The result is the development of a non-local standard pronunciation with a London base: ultimately what is now generally known as Received Pronunciation.

Without going into detail, it's clear that from the 14th to the 17th centuries the notion of 'standard' English became increasingly London-centred: with a cultural circumference including the ancient universities and the church. It's no coincidence that Puttenham's sixty-mile radius touches – as near as makes no difference – Oxford, Cambridge, and Canterbury. Until the autonomous development of American English in the early 19th century, and of South African, Australian and New Zealand standards later on, it's safe to say that by and large southern English defines standard English – even to a large extent in Scotland, where the native standard began to recede from public use after the death of Elizabeth I in 1601, when James VI of Scotland became James I of England, and removed his court from Edinburgh to London (see §5.7.1).

But however 'southern' people thought the standard was, it was not from a historical point of view dialectally all of a piece. Though its phonological basis is SE Midland, at least one aspect of its morphology – though not stabilized till late – is distinctly northern: the third person singular verb ending in -s. In ME generally, there were four major types of present-tense paradigms:

(2.2)

		Northern	E Midland	W Midland	Southern
	1	-e	-e	-e	-e
Sg	2	-(e)s	-(e)st	-es(t)	-est
	3	-(e)s	-eþ	-eþ/-es	-eþ
Pl		-(e)s	-en/-es	-es/-en	-eþ

That is, in the North -s forms were generalized everywhere except 1 sg (a feature that goes back to Northumbrian OE); in the EML they occur occasionally in plurals, and in the WML (in the more northern parts) in 3 sg as well. These -s forms do not begin to gain much currency in London until the 15th century, and in the 16th they start to become common in informal and personal writing. But the old -eth remains in more formal usage: even as late as 1611 the Authorized Version of the Bible has no instances of -s. It's hard to work out exactly how (much less why) this change occurred; while there was certainly a large and increasing influx of Northerners into London and East Anglia during the period, it seems rather odd that only one form out of the paradigm should have been borrowed.

The position of London at a kind of crossroads between the Southeast and Southwest has left a certain amount of non-EML material in the modern standard. For instance, the voicing of initial fricatives characteristic of the South in ME times (see §5.2) has left van, vane, vat, vixen, vent, vial (cf. phial), all of which began with /f/ in non-southern Middle English. And while the EML should have ME /i/, modern /ɪ/ for OE /y/ words, many southeastern forms with /e/ (OE /y(:)/ became /e(:)/ in the southeast in pre-ME times) have remained: dent (but cf. dint, both < OE dynt), fledge, hemlock, kelp, knell, left, pebble, shed, merry.

Still on OE /y/, this remained as /y/ in the SW, and became /u/ in ME: thus from SW dialects we have blush, clutch, crutch, cudgel, much, rush (n), shut, shuttle, thrush, thrust. There are also some forms of this type where because of later developments, only the spelling survives: burden, church, furze, hurdle (ME /i/ or /u/ or /e/ before /-rC/ would give the same pronunciation: cf. §3.10). Similarly there is a SE spelling in kernel (WS cyrnel). Then we have bury with a SW spelling but a Kentish pronunciation, and busy with a SW spelling but an EML pronunciation.

Some of these developments have been claimed to be due to 'functional' considerations. Thus M.L. Samuels argues that the SW shut was borrowed into London English because of the fact that the normal EML development would be homophonous with shit; but in fact shit for shut persists from ME times through the 16th century; why should this homophony become a 'problem' after centuries of coexistence? I think the general motivation for interdialect borrowing will turn out to be purely random.

To round out the picture of non-EML elements in the standard, we can instance some northern forms: (a) with undiphthongized ME /uː/ (except in the North, ME /uː/ comes down as modern /aʊ/: §3.10): *uncouth*, *gruesome*, *croup*, *dour*; and (b) with the modern reflex of northern ME /aː/ < OE /ɑː/ instead of the non-northern ME /ɔː/ (§3.9): *hale* (cf. S *whole*), *kale* (cf. *cole*(-*slaw*)), *race*, *raid*, *scale*.

2.10 Grammarians and English: 'Authority' and 'Correctness'

A major source of insecurity for many English speakers is the existence of supposed 'authorities': dictionaries, grammars, the works of Fowler and other self-appointed linguistic guardians. There is a widespread assumption that these ought to take priority over native-speaker judgements. It's a commonplace, for instance (especially if you play scrabble or listen to radio quizzes), that you go to a dictionary to find out if a word 'exists' – no matter that you happen to use it. Or that to find out if a usage is 'correct' or (in the amateur sense) 'grammatical', you look it up in some grammar book. This rather odd notion of the authoritativeness of external (especially written) sources has a long pedigree, and has had its effects on the use of English – or at least on speakers' attitudes towards it.

Except for details, the codification of a standard phonology came relatively early, as we saw; and in any case, since phonetic discussion is likely to be more technical and less intimately tied in to everyday experience of language than grammatical discussion, the focus of public (rather than learned) debate, when it arose, was primarily on syntax and lexical usage.

In the late 17th and early 18th centuries more general views of culture and human society were imported into attitudes toward language; and this led to the development of a 'prescriptivist' and 'authoritarian' attitude toward language use that still plays an important role in what survives of traditional education in the English-speaking world. But whatever its effects, the rise of the power of 'the grammarian' is an interesting chapter in the intellectual history of Enlightenment England.

In late Roman days, the question of 'correct' usage was not an emotive one, as it is now. The grammarian Quintilian, for instance (*Institutio oratoria* I.vi.45), defines what is proper in speech as simply stemming from agreement in practice: 'consuetudinem sermonis vocabo consensum eruditorum' ('The norm of speech I take to be the agreement of educated men'). There is no need for external authority; the judgement of cultivated speakers is sufficient.

But this kind of relaxed confidence was not sufficient for the late 17th century. For one thing, the very Latin about whose norms Quintilian could be so certain was now for all practical purposes a dead language (even if a written and spoken one). That is, it was immune to change because its structure, and the range of allowable constructions, were institutionalized in grammars, which – in the absence of native speakers – were fixed 'courts of appeal'.

Such an institutionalization seemed highly desirable to what we might loosely call the 'Enlightenment temper'; the Italians and French had already set up academies to produce authoritative grammars and dictionaries (1582 and 1635 respectively), and at least the dictionaries had appeared by the 1690s. The Royal Society attempted, from the 1660s on, to do the same thing; due perhaps to a fortunate streak of anarchism in the British temper the attempts never really got off the ground. But the attitudes that provoked the formation of academies are clear in the attitudes toward their own language even of gifted writers like Dryden; in his dedication to *The Rival Ladies* (1664), for instance, he remarks that 'I am Sorry, that (Speaking so noble a Language as we do) we have not a more certain Measure of it, as they have in France, where they have an Academy erected for the Purpose'. And in the dedication to *Troilus and Cressida* (1679) he says poignantly: 'how barbarously we yet write and speak, your Lordship knows, and I am sufficiently sensible in my own English. For I am often put to a stand, in considering whether what I write be the idiom of the tongue, or false grammar.' A modern linguist might be tempted to ask: if Dryden couldn't tell, who could? But this would be insensitive to the point of anachronism, because there was a powerful ideology behind the attitude.

Perhaps the most important component of this ideological complex was the desire to 'ascertain', to use the 18th-century term, the language: to determine on some principled basis what was 'real' or 'correct' English, and to fix it immutably in print, so that the question of 'false grammar' could be settled. Change in language – except for the necessary importation or creation of new lexis for particular purposes – was felt to be a danger; change if left unchecked could lead to loss of comprehensibility (as had happened to Chaucer to some extent, and even more of course for earlier English): a language with a newly established 'classical' status should ideally be as fixed as Latin.

Some of the flavour of this state of mind can be sensed in the remarks of one of the more sophisticated writers on language in the period: Dr Johnson. In the Preface to his *Dictionary* (1765), he remarks that when he began his work, he

found our speech copious without order, and energetick
without rules: wherever I turned my view, there was perplexi-
ty to be disentangled, and confusion to be regulated; choice
was to be made out of boundless variety, without any
established principle of selection; adulterations were to be
detected, without a settled test of purity, and modes of
expression to be rejected or received, without the suffrages of
any writers of classical reputation or acknowledged authority.

Unlike many other writers (down to this day) Johnson realized his
own limitations and the size of the job – to some extent. On the one
hand, he was clear that 'there is in constancy and stability a general and
lasting advantage, which will always overbalance the slow improvements
of gradual correction', and insistent that 'our written language' should
not 'comply with the corruption of oral utterance, or copy that which
every variation of time or place makes different from itself'; on the other
hand, he says:

I am not yet so lost in lexicography, as to forget *that words are
the daughters of the earth, and that things are the sons of
heaven*. Language is only the instrument of science, and words
are but the signs of ideas: I wish, however, that the instrument
might be less apt to decay, and that signs might be permanent,
like the things which they denote.

But this does not mean that one ought to give up: indeed, Johnson
attempts a retarding action by deliberately not using examples from
living writers ('that I might not be misled by partiality') – except in
special cases, such as 'when some performance of uncommon excellence
excited my veneration'. This is in keeping with his desire for a fixed, non-
contemporary (or pan-temporal) standard. In the end, he suggests a
programme of action: the dramatic language is not merely a reflection of
Johnsonian melancholy, but of an attitude that is probably as common
now as it was then:

If the changes that we fear be thus irresistible, what remains
but to acquiesce with silence, as in the other insurmountable
distresses of humanity? It remains that we retard what we
cannot repel, that we palliate what we cannot cure ...
tongues, like governments, have a natural tendency to de-
generation; we have long preserved our constitution, let us
make some struggles for our language.

The linguist's comment would be: if this is what you can do with a
'decaying' language, why worry? The point that seems to evade Johnson,

and is still far from obvious to most people, is that 'language' itself is neutral: there are only good and bad users.

These quotations encapsulate a number of persistent themes, many of which have had a significant effect on educational practice, and hence on speaker attitudes – largely through the dictionaries that followed Johnson's, and the grammars of English that began to proliferate during the second half of the 18th century. One important factor to note is the element of personal taste or preference: Johnson takes as worthy of citation things that *he* perceives to be of 'uncommon excellence', and this kind of personal predilection or antagonism to words, usages, and constructions often ended up being elevated to 'authoritative' status.

The history of this frame of mind is long and complex; it's notable that children are still being exposed in the schools to ideas about language that originated in 18th-century linguistic ideology, and – even then – had only the most tenuous foundation (if any at all) in the actual practice of educated speakers. E.g. avoidance of split infinitives (attested in writers of the first class since at least the 14th century), not ending sentences with prepositions (which Churchill once remarked was 'something up with which I will not put'), making a rigid distinction between *shall* and *will*, avoiding double negation on the pseudo-logical grounds that 'two negatives make a positive'. (It's interesting that this objection is refuted by its own data: if a double negative is in fact a positive, how were the grammarians able to interpret it as an ill-formed negative?) This is not to say that standard speakers should use double negatives: in my speech *I don't have none* is ungrammatical not because it's (universally) 'wrong', but because it's not a construction in my dialect; and I wouldn't recommend a foreign learner to use it, because it belongs characteristically to lower-prestige dialects.

Perhaps the most lasting effect of the 'authoritarian' or prescriptive tradition however is an attitude: that the language is 'under threat' or 'decaying', that there are rearguard actions to be fought against all kinds of novel diseases affecting our speech. And one of the most interesting properties of this constellation of attitudes is the general lack of historical perspective, and the invincibility of opinion in the face of contrary data.

Since in the tradition (cf. Johnson above) the new is generally suspect, the tendency remains to consider anything you don't like as a pernicious novelty, usually attributed to whoever your private xenophobia selects as the most likely target: 'the Americans', 'the young', the ill-educated, or anyone else who fits the bill (closet liberals at the BBC, etc.).

In a recent study of prescriptive attitudes, Crystal (1985) takes a sample of comments on terrible 'new' usages sent into the BBC in the 1980s, and shows that a large number of them were condemned in Henry

Alford's *The Queen's English* (1863); one has to say little more. Crystal sums up the attitudes of 'usage-conscious' people this way: in talking about readers' reactions to a book based on his BBC programmes on usage, he says

> I am gaining the distinct impression that knowing the facts . . . *makes very little difference.* The main reaction so far can be summarized thus: 'I was very interested to read about X (where X is any of the usage topics covered), and I agree that I am silly to worry about it so much and should be tolerant when I observe it – but I still *hate* it and wish you would condemn it!'

I suspect that what we are dealing with in the end is a matter of social psychology, only incidentally concerned with language: one of the best ways for the unconfident members of an orthodox faith to define their status is to have a good eye for heresy. After this brief socio-historico-psychological excursus, I return to English.

2.11 Later European Contacts

The early Scandinavian and French contacts produced a great influx of loanwords: but this was not the end of it. There were no other contacts of precisely the same kind – the English never again were conquered, and didn't (on their own territory) ever live in the same kind of intimacy with foreign populations (on the special case of the Celts, see below). But Britain is an island nation; it has been for a long time a maritime and commercial one; and – despite its periodic claims to the contrary – it is culturally and geographically part of Europe. So seafaring and commercial contacts with other European nations, and perhaps even more importantly participation in a 'common European culture', have had a significant effect.

The history of foreign lexis in English has been well covered; all I can do in this and the following section is look at a small sample of the major post-medieval borrowings. But before we turn to the rest of Europe, we ought to consider the strange relation between English and the one language group that was continuously (if increasingly precariously) spoken on its own home territory: Celtic. As we saw earlier (§2.3), English-Celtic contacts in the OE period resulted in very little borrowing; and the continuing negative prestige of the Celtic languages and their speakers make the paucity of loans less surprising. Indeed, the standard reactions of the English – who were generally in the position of an occupying power *vis-à-vis* the Celts – to Celtic languages was either to

73

ignore them in the hope that they'd go away (as was the case in Wales from the Act of Union in 1536 until the 19th century), or to mount official efforts to supplant them. In Scotland, for instance, the Statutes of Iona (1609) made it mandatory for the eldest child of every Highland family to be educated at Lowland (i.e. English-medium) schools; and even missionary societies like the SPCK did their best to Anglicize the Gaels in Scotland, proposing as one of their aims 'rooting out their Irish language' ('Irish' was often used as the name for Scots Gaelic, which is historically reasonable since the original Goidelic settlement was Irish: cf. §2.3).

Under these conditions, the bulk of the loans are, expectably, distinctly 'local': items specific to the Celtic cultures, topographical or natural terms. In the 14th century we have *loch*, *mull* from Scots Gaelic, and *crag* from Welsh; in the 15th, *clan* from Scots Gaelic and *lough*, *shamrock*, *brogue* from Irish; in the 16th, *coracle* from Welsh, *bog*, *plaid*, *ingle*, *caber*, *slogan*, *cairn*, *ptarmigan* from Scots Gaelic; in the 17th, *leprechaun*, *ogham*, *galore* from Irish and *strathspey*, *quaich* 'drinking cup', *dulse* 'a kind of seaweed' from Scots Gaelic. (The fact that the two last have to be glossed for most readers, I suspect, makes one wonder if they are really 'loans into English' in the same sense as *clan* or *plaid*.) In the 18th century Irish gives *banshee*, *shillelagh*, and Scots Gaelic *whisky* (from the first element of *uisge beatha* 'water of life'), *claymore*, *cairngorm*, *sporran*. In the 19th century we have *blarney*, *colleen*, *keen* 'lament' from Irish, and *eisteddfodd* from Welsh. If we add to this (only slightly reduced) list the handful of loans into Old English, we have an extraordinarily poor showing for something like 1300 years of contact: a fine example of the importance of prestige in borrowing.

The major sources of post-medieval loans – at least of non-exotic items (I take *kangaroo*, *gorilla*, *hookah*, *mikado* and the like to be exotics, and will deal with them in the next section) are other Germanic and Romance languages: especially Dutch, French and Italian. We will look first at Germanic loans (including the rather minor influence of German and Scandinavian). The types of loans here and below reflect a fairly general principle: when a nation is famous for something, the period of its dominance in the field is the period when its lexis is borrowed. As we will see below, particularly in the case of Italian, borrowings into English (the same would be true, say, of Dutch or German) give a kind of capsule history of the role of a nation in European cultural life.

For Dutch, perhaps the largest amount of material is in the field of seafaring: 15th-century *buoy*, *deck*, *hoist*; 16th-century *dock*, *splice*, *yacht*; 17th-century *smack*, *keelhaul*, *cruiser*, *jib*, *yawl*; 18th-century *schooner, scow*. Many others are in the visual arts, e.g. 16th-century *landscape*, 17th-century *easel, sketch, stipple*. There are also miscellaneous items, like *hops, boor* 'peasant' (15th c.); *isinglass, muff, split, burgher* (16th c.); *brandy, smuggle* (17th c.); and *geneva* 'gin' (Du *jenever* < OF *genevre* < L *juniperus*) in the 18th century; the shortening *gin* was first attested in 1714.

German provides a number of mineralogical and chemical terms: *zinc* (17th c.), *cobalt, shale, quartz, nickel* (18th c.), and *protein, paraffin* (19th c.); as well as local edibles (19th-c. *lager, kohl-rabi*), educational terms (19th-c. *kindergarten, seminar*), dog-breeds (19th-c. *poodle, dachshund*, 20th-c. *weimaraner*), and miscellaneous terms like *hinterland, zeitgeist, yodel, zither* (all 19th c.). War with Germany in this century has provided among other words *blitzkrieg, strafe, panzer*; and other cultural contacts have yielded beer varieties (*bock*) and foods (*strudel, (wiener)-schnitzel, (sacher)-torte*, etc.).

Among the other Germanic languages, there is a handful of later Scandinavian loans: *link, silt* (15th c.), *rowan, slag, scuffle, snug* (16th c.), *troll, squall, keg, skittles* (17th c.), *cosy, muggy, tungsten* (18th c.), *vole, floe, ski* (19th c.), *ombudsman* (20th c.).

One other Germanic language which has furnished a fair amount of lexis is Yiddish: but it's not always clear whether this component should be treated under the heading of European or extraterritorial contact. Some Yiddish loans like *goniff/gonoph* 'thief' (ultimately Hebrew) are traceable to as early as the 1830s; but in the main these are not items that have become naturalized English (certainly this one isn't, even if Dickens used it). Perhaps the greatest amount of Yiddish lexis came in via contacts in the U.S.: this is certainly the case with *schmuck, bagel*, and a number of others. But whatever the sources (and the history isn't always clear), the majority of these forms are late (19th–20th century), and many are of somewhat restricted use (cf. the comments on 'Judaeo-English' in §3.2.1). But we can list the following as being widespread enough to count as 'English' – even if they tend to be used more in areas with large Jewish populations than elsewhere. If forms that are familiar in London, New York and Cape Town count as nativized, then we can probably include (with glosses for people in whose areas they are not current) *goy* 'gentile', *chutzpah* 'gall, nerve', *shlep* 'drag', *drek* 'shit', *shlock* 'cheap merchandise', *latke* 'pancake', *matzo* 'unleavened bread', *nosh* 'food, snack', *schlemiel* 'fool, clumsy person, drip', *shiksa* 'gentile girl'. At least I've seen all of these in the feature pages of South African newspapers, unglossed: so here they're 'native' words now.

Among the Romance languages, the most influential have been French and Italian. For French, the chief imports are military and gastronomic terms, and items connected with what could broadly be

75

called 'fashion' and the arts. Military: *trophy, pioneer, pilot, colonel* (16th c.), *stockade, dragoon, brigade, carbine* (17th c.), *caisson, terrain, espionage* (18th c.), *barrage* (19th c.). In the gastronomic field we have *soup, champagne* (17th c.), *aubergine,* (usually replaced in the U.S. with the later formation *egg-plant,* and in South Africa competing with *brinjal* < Portuguese *bringella*), *picnic* (18th c.), *gourmet, restaurant, menu, mousse* (19th c.). Under the loose heading of 'fashion' (for want of a better cover-term) we have *indigo, gauze, vogue, genteel* (16th c.), and *moiré, crochet, blouse, beige* (19th c.). In the arts we have *scene, grotesque* (16th c.), *rôle, ballet, crayon* (17th c.), *vignette, nuance* (18th c.), *format, renaissance, nocturne, baton* (19th c.). Other loans include *moustache* (16th c.), *emigré, guillotine, débris, glacier, plateau, migraine* (18th c.), and *acrobat, croquet, ravine, crevasse* (19th c.).

The Italian contribution is in many ways quite similar: both Italian and French were the languages of prestigious cultures from the Middle Ages onwards. And most important, of fashionable cultures: in music, to take one example, we find German composers like Schütz going to Venice to study in the 17th century and bringing back new styles, the 'French overture' becoming the stock in trade of German baroque composers, and so on. The Italian influence focusses on a number of fields similar to French, but with a preponderance of loans in music and the visual arts. Some examples: Military: *cavalier, squadron, bandolier, duel, salvo, frigate* (16th c.), *attack, rocket, barrack* (17th c.). In the visual arts (including architecture) we find *cupola, cornice, frieze, stucco* (16th c.), *portico, villa, balcony, corridor, filigree, cartoon* (17th c.), *mezzanine, arcade, picturesque, portfolio, terra-cotta, torso* (18th c.), *studio, replica, tempera* (19th c.). In music, however, the influence is greatest; a small sample includes *madrigal, fugue* (16th c.), *opera, recitative, sonata, solo, allegro, largo, piano, presto, vivace* (17th c.), *soprano, mandolin, trombone, viola, cantata, duet, oratorio, concerto, aria, quartet, forte, staccato, tempo* (18th c.), and *piccolo, sonatina, cadenza, legato* (19th c.).

Among other loans are *nuncio, artisan, mountebank, carnival* (16th c.), *intrigue, charlatan, gala, gazette, manifesto* (17th c.), *bronze, lava* (18th c.). And in the 19th century, in addition to names for cultural specialities like *Mafia, vendetta,* we have foods: *risotto, canteloupe, spaghetti* – as well as what you can get from them (*ptomaine*), and what you can get if you don't eat the right ones (*pellagra*).

The Spanish and Portuguese contributions are smaller, but important; they are also complex, in that historically they consist of two layers, items borrowed direct, and those which came into Spanish and Portuguese from other languages, and were borrowed during English contacts with Spanish in America and Portuguese in Africa and Asia, or in other ways. Without discriminating these in detail, we can list the major loans as follows.

From Spanish: *cask, rusk, sherry, renegade, galleon, grenade, tornado, cannibal, iguana, banana* (16th c.), *cargo, desperado, matador, granadilla* 'passion-fruit', *embargo, junta, parade, guitar, plaza, peon, llama, chinchilla, cockroach, vanilla, avocado* (17th c.), *albino, stevedore, quadrille, flotilla, cigar, cinchona* (18th c.), and *cigarette, guerilla, picaresque, lasso, mustang, rodeo, stampede, lariat, bronco, nutria, bonanza, patio, adobe, canyon* (19th c.). Obviously the bulk of these latter items come from English-Spanish contacts in the Americas, and could as well be treated in the next section; their currency in non-U.S. English is probably a function of inter-variety contact in English rather than borrowing *per se*, but it seemed convenient to group them together here.

The Portuguese element is much smaller, and largely exotic; aside from *port* (wine) in the 17th century, the main borrowings are *flamingo, molasses, sargasso, madeira, yam, buffalo, mandarin* (16th c.), *pagoda, peccary, macaw, macaque, assegai, dodo* (17th c.), and *palaver, verandah* (18th. c).

Other European languages have provided very little. Direct contact with Russia through the Muscovy Company in Elizabeth I's reign opened the way to a few early loans like *ruble, czar, beluga* (16th c.); others include *mammoth, knout, astrakhan* (18th c.), *vodka, droshky, tundra, troika* (19th c.), and *pogrom, soviet, bolshevik, intelligentsia, sputnik* (20th c.). From other Slavic languages there is very little: *polka, mazurka*, (Polish), and *robot* (Czech, in a way: from a play by Carel Čapek, translated into English in 1923, and based on the root *robot-* 'work').

The non-Indo-European languages of Europe have given very little: from Hungarian we have *hussar, coach* in the 16th century (via French), *Magyar* in the 18th, and *shako* in the 19th. More recent Hungarian loans include *czardas, goulash, paprika*. From Finnish as far as I know we have only one, the recent *sauna*.

2.12 The Spread of English

In 1655, Flecknoe (*Relation of ten years Travell*) remarked that Dutch was an extremely useful language for travellers, since it was used 'everywhere by sea, which is as properly the Hollander's Country as any land they inhabit or possess'. As for Latin and English, 'they only served me to stop holes with, the English Language out of our Dominions being like our English money current without much ado in neighbouring countries who traffick with us; but further off you must go to Banquiers of your own Nation, or none will take if off your hands'. Three hundred years later there is probably no single language likely to be understood in more places than English (among other things it's the international medium for air-traffic control).

In the reign of Elizabeth I, English had according to our best estimates somewhere in the order of 5–7 million mother-tongue speakers. We don't have even approximate figures for second-language speakers, but it's unlikely that these were more than negligible outside the British Isles (at this point many speakers of Welsh, Cornish, Manx, Irish and Scots Gaelic would have spoken English as a second language). And certainly there was no place except the 'Celtic fringe' where English had any kind of official (non-native) status.

As of 1985, if we count only first-language speakers, the numbers are probably something over 316 million. If we also count countries where English has some official status as a language of education, government, etc., we can add something upwards of another 1,400,000,000. A slightly finer (if not exhaustive) breakdown of the figures may be interesting. The following countries have more than one million native speakers: Australia (14m), Canada (17m), U.K. (56m), Irish Republic (3.3m), New Zealand (3m), South Africa (2m), and the U.S.A. (215m). If we want to add the complex creole-to-standard 'continua' of the Caribbean, we could also cite Jamaica (2.3m) and Trinidad and Tobago (1.2m).

But Canada, the U.S., and Australia also have large numbers of second-language speakers; and even in countries where English is really nobody's first language, there are about 1m speakers in Botswana, 12m in Ghana, 700m in India, 2m in Liberia, and 50m in the Philippines. Of course in many of these cases the figures are probably inflated: there is a difference between 'speakers' and 'users', and the extent to which these figures really represent what we'd want to call 'speakers' is debatable. Still, over 300m mother-tongue speakers, and nearly a billion and a half people who use it to some degree or other, on every continent – quite a move from what Flecknoe describes, in a little over three centuries.

What accounts for this? It's important to note, as a matter of general principle and because of a tendency toward inflated ethnic pride among English-speakers, that the development of 'world-language' status is not a linguistic phenomenon: it's a cultural, and perhaps more basically a political and economic one. It's not the inherent 'superiority' of a language that increases its speaker-numbers and geographical spread, but at least three other things: (a) the extent to which it is imposed as a colonial language on non-speakers; (b) the extent to which it is of economic utility for non-speakers to learn it; and (c) the extent to which access to the language means access to a culture felt to be in some way a necessary, useful or prestigious possession.

The last is probably largely a function of the others: the prestige of the culture carried by a language is matter of the 'public relations' salience of its speakers, or of the image of their nation. The fact that many non-speakers of English want to learn it to read Shakespeare or Dickens in the original, or that non-speakers of German might learn it for access to Goethe or Thomas Mann, does not in itself say anything about the greatness of Shakespeare of Goethe. Any more than the relative paucity of people learning Greek to read Cavafy or Afrikaans to read van Wyk Louw says anything about *their* greatness. When a national literature comes – however it does – to play a certain part in the perceived image of a 'common culture', the importance of its language comes to mirror the importance of this perceived role. But behind all this is political and economic muscle: it's probably true that no nation that fails to conquer others ever has its language spread much beyond its own borders. (Prestige of course can persist long after physical power is gone: England lost much of its world-power status when it lost its empire, but this hasn't affected the prestige of English – the investment is already too great.)

Until about the end of the 15th century England's political and economic focus was pretty much its own doorstep; trade and war were conducted with nearby countries like Holland and France. This was the norm for medieval Europe: except for great trading powers like Venice, which maintained the bulk of Europe's links with the East, life was fairly parochial.

But in the late 15th century, the beginning of the 'Age of Discovery' as schoolbooks like to call it, there was a gradual opening up of the non-European world – Asia, Africa, America, later Australasia – which led in time to colonization, and the establishment of European populations in distinctly exotic places. Along with other gifts to the Heathen like missionaries and measles, the expanding colonial powers brought their languages; and along with receipts like syphilis and potatoes, they brought back, or had incorporated into the extraterritorial varieties of their languages, a host of new loanwords. And, of course, each new foreign community formed the nucleus for the development of new dialects as well.

As early as 1497 an English expedition under John Cabot visited Canada, and the first English colony under Sir Humphrey Gilbert was established in 1583; from the 1480s on there was an English presence in West Africa, with English ships reaching Benin in 1553, and establishing a flourishing trade in ivory and pepper by 1555.

By the 17th century, an English presence was established in the Caribbean and in North America (Jamestown 1607, Plymouth 1620); by the late 18th century India was under English rule (1765: but the presence goes back to the exclusive Indian and South Asian trading rights granted to the East India Company in 1600); and the first English-speaking settlement in Australasia, the penal colony at Sydney, was set up in 1788. In the next century, the British were in the Western Cape in 1806, in the Eastern Cape in 1820, and in Natal in the 1840s; and New Zealand was established as a colony in 1840.

English was at this time also busy spreading through the originally Celtic-speaking parts of the British Isles. By the Acts of Union of 1536 and 1542 English was established as the official language of Wales; and in a complex series of waves of colonization culminating in the 16th and 17th centuries, it began to take over Ireland as well. (The influence of Celtic was however minor: see the previous section.)

We will have more to say about the details of the spread of English in these various areas when we come to consider the individual dialects (ch. 5); for now what's important is the general picture, and a brief idea of the contribution of the various languages English made contact with during this expansion.

As is usually the case, the influence of exotic experience on the language was virtually confined to lexis: even extensive bilingualism rarely if ever left traces on English structure (except perhaps in Ireland (§5.7.2) and South Africa (§5.8.4)). The fact that transported languages tend to change radically and rather quickly is often attributed to the contacts they make; but in most cases this is impossible to demonstrate, and is the result of a simple logical fallacy in argument – *post hoc, ergo propter hoc* ('after it, therefore because of it'). All languages of course change, as long as they're spoken; and the freer a transplanted language is from the prestige norms of its source (or the more, as in the U.S., it desires to free itself from them and establish its own identity), the quicker change is likely to be.

We will look here, for illustration, at the lexical effects of six major contacts, resulting from trade or actual settlement: the Middle East, India, the Far East, the South Pacific, Africa and the Americas.

There had been an indirect influence of Arabic and Persian (largely via French) all through the Middle Ages; but direct loans began to multiply in the 16th and 17th centuries. From Arabic we have *sultan, sheik(h), muezzin, magazine, hashish* (16th c.), *fakir, imam, emir, sherbet, sofa, harem, minaret, henna* (17th c.), *Allah, tarboosh, genie, hookah, ghoul, kohl* (18th c.), and *wadi, yashmak, alfalfa, loofah* (19th c.). There are not many direct loans from Persian: but among those we have are *shah, divan, caravan, bazaar* (16th c.), *shawl* (17th c.) and *carboy, bulbul, attar* (18th c.). From various Turkic languages (mainly Turkish) we get *horde, turban, coffee, caftan* (16th c.), *odalisque, kiosk*

80

(17th c.), *caracal* (18th c.), and *fez, kismet* and *macramé* (19th c.).

Indian loans come from two sources: Sanskrit, which furnishes a group of mainly 18th- and 19th-century items like *avatar, suttee, yoga, nirvana, karma, swastika*; and various Indian vernaculars, both Indo-European (mainly Hindi, Marathi and Bengali) and Dravidian (Malayalam and Tamil). The earliest vernacular loans are Dravidian: *calico, coir, copra* (Malayalam) and *curry, coolee* (Tamil), in the 16th century. The 17th century yields *nabob, guru, sahib, pundit, maharajah, chintz, dungaree, punch, ghee, cot, bungalow, cowrie* (Hindi), *mongoose* (Marathi), *pariah* (Tamil), and *atoll* (Malayalam). In the 18th century, Hindi gives *bandana, sari, mynah, cheetah, bangle, jungle, shampoo*, and Bengali *jute*; Dravidian loans include *bandicoot* and *mulligatawny* (Tamil). In the 19th century Hindi gives *dacoit, thug, puttee, topi, pyjama, chutney, dinghy, loot, gymkhana, polo*; and from Tamil we have *patchouli*.

From the Far East the Sino-Tibetan languages give *lama, yak* (Tibetan, 17th c.), *ketchup, pekoe, kaolin* (Chinese, 18th c.), *kow-tow, loquat, oolong, tong* 'secret society' (Chinese, 19th c.). From Japanese we have *shogun, kimono, sake, soy* (17th c.), *mikado* (18th c.), *gingko, hara-kiri, tycoon, samurai, geisha* (19th c.), and *kamikaze, karate, bushido, sukiyaki, tempura* (20th c.).

The English experience in the Pacific has produced a number of loans, mainly from Malayo-Polynesian and Australian languages. In the 16th century we have *sago* (Malay), and in the 17th from the same source *cassowary, rattan, amok, lory, orang-outan*. In the 18th, Malay gives *bantam, kapok, gecko, pangolin*; and Australian languages *kangaroo, wombat, dingo*. In the 19th we get *dugong, sarong* from Malay, *raffia* from Malagasy, *kiwi, moa*, from Maori, and Australian *koala, boomerang*. Later loans from Australian languages (perhaps doubtfully integrated in non-Australian English) are *kookaburra, didgery-doo*.

The African experience has produced a surprisingly small number of loans from indigenous languages; and many of those we have are difficult to trace, as their sources are uncertain. In the early days we get *potto* and *chimpanzee* from unknown West African languages (18th c.), and little else (though some words of ultimately West African origin like *okra, gumbo, voodoo* come in through contact with African slaves in the West Indies).

Bantu languages give us *zebra* (from a language of the Congo) in 1600, followed by *baobab* and *kudu*. Other Bantu loans begin to appear in the 19th century, e.g. *tsetse* (Tswana). More come into English through contact with the Zulu during the Zulu Wars – though most of these now have little currency outside South Africa (exceptions are *donga* and *impi*). South African contacts also yield a few loans from 'Hottentot' (Khoi) languages: e.g. *quagga* – probably via Afrikaans, judging from the -gg- spelling for /x/: the normal South African pronunciation is /kwäxä/. From 'Bushman' (San) we get *gnu* (1777), normally not used in South Africa (where the local term is *wildebees*(*t*) from Afrikaans).

Many other 'African' loans are in fact from Dutch or Afrikaans (depending on what you want to call the language at the time): from the 18th century we have *steenbok, springbok, eland, hartebeest*; and from the 19th *meerkat, aardvark, wildebeest, veld*(*t*), *trek, laager* (originally from German), and *spoor*.

The English settlement in the Americas was a rich source of material; we will be concerned here only with those items that found their way into English generally (even if they refer to specifically American things), as distinct from words that remain strictly regional. Thus *raccoon, skunk, tomahawk, wigwam* are English in a non-regional sense; even for people who may not be at all sure what any of them look like. (Most non-Americans tend to use *wigwam* for the classic conical Amerindian tent, which is in fact a *teepee*; a *wigwam* is a hemispherical hut with a hide framework over bent poles.) Whereas other words from indigenous languages like *quahog* (a kind of hard-shell clam) or *muskellunge* (a large fish of the pike family) are clearly regional.

Tracing the etymologies of loans from Amerindian languages is difficult; none of the languages had written forms before the Europeans arrived, and in many cases identification of a source depends on our (often doubtful) knowledge of what people were living in a given place at a given time, and what dialect-group their language(s) belonged to. The settlers naturally attempted to represent borrowed words in English spelling, which is also a problem in deciding on the shape of the original (and not a uniquely American one of course): thus *raccoon* first appears in a narrative of Captain John Smith (1608) as *rahaughcum* and *raughoughcum*; in later sources we have *aracoune* (1612) and *rarowcum* (1624); the modern form first appears in 1672.

But many loans can at least be traced to distinct language families; and the largest group of these is from Algongquian (the family including Fox, Cree, Ojibwa and a number of extinct languages). About the earliest Algongquian loan of general currency is *skunk* (1588); the bulk of the others came in during the 17th century, e.g. *hickory, moccasin, moose, raccoon, oppossum, squash* 'marrow', *powwow*. There are also indirect early loans (via French) from native languages, e.g. *caribou, bayou, toboggan*.

In the 19th century we get loans from native languages of the southwestern U.S. and Mexico, usually via Spanish: e.g. from Nahuatl or other Uto-Aztecan dialects *tomato* (17th c.), *avocado* (18th c.), *coyote* (19th c.).

Indigenous languages or perhaps (it's not always easy to tell) imaginative reconstructions of them have also led to a number of real or spurious loan-translations: e.g. *warpath*, *paleface*, *war-dance*, *war-paint*, *bury the hatchet*, which found their way into non-American English via the spread of the mythology of 'the Pioneers' and 'The Old West' through popular fiction and the cinema.

The American settlements also led to renewed contact with Dutch (in New York especially), and a number of general terms have come in this way: e.g. *boss* (Du *baas*) as early as 1650, *coleslaw* < *kool slaa* 'cabbage salad' (now often folk-etymologized to *cold slaw*, hence the possibility of *hot slaw*, a kind of sauerkraut), and a host of others like *spook*, *cookie*, *sleigh*, *Santa Claus* and *waffle*.

The continued use of normal word-formation processes like compounding (cf. §4.8) also led to the creation of new lexis, much of which has found its way into non-regional English. To give an example of the richness of this source, the 18th century alone is responsible for *bullfrog*, *tree frog*, *butternut*, *beef cattle*, *backwoods*, *shotgun*, *buckshot*, *snowplow*, *grizzly bear*, and *slippery elm*.

CHAPTER 2: NOTES AND REFERENCES

2.2 On the early history of the Germanic peoples, see the brief account in Prokosch (1938: 21–34), and Kufner's chapter in van Coetsem & Kufner (1972). Most of the major work in this area is in German (see Kufner for references); if this is accessible, Karsten (1928) is useful, if dated, as is the conservative Krahe (1963: 10–42). Texts in this section from Prokosch (294ff).

2.3 On the prehistory of Britain, Price (1984: ch. 1) and his references. On early Celtic Britain Price (chs. 2–11, passim), and for technical detail Jackson (1953). For an overview of the history of the Celtic languages in Britain, Thomson (1984).

The Germanic invasions are covered in the standard histories, e.g. Baugh (1957: ch. 3), Robertson & Cassidy (1954: ch. 3). There is a revised version of Baugh (rev. Cable, 1978), but the chapter contents are largely the same, and the numbering holds for both. On the general subject of this chapter a critical reading of Leith (1983: chs. 1–2, 6–7) may be useful; there is a lot of interesting material, marred somewhat by a vulgar egalitarian-cum-Marxist bias.

For the Germanic settlements and christianization, Bede himself is still a prime source, and fascinating reading; there is an excellent Penguin translation (Sherley-Price 1955). The Angles-Saxons-Jutes scenario, for all its traditional charisma, is problematical; for an idea of some of the difficulties, and the complexity of the early settlement, see De Camp (1958) and Bennett (1955). De Camp in fact proposes that the basic OE dialect divisions arose in England, not on the continent.

2.4 On Anglo-Saxon England in general, Stenton (1955). For a readable and authoritative account of OE society and culture, Whitelock (1952). In a more technical linguistic vein, see the fascinating and important synthesis of political history, modern techniques of variation analysis, and traditional OE linguistics in Toon (1983). Texts cited are from Sweet (1967: 216ff).

2.5   For Latin loans see Campbell (§§493–564), and Jespersen (1948: ch. III).

2.6   On the Scandinavian invasions, Baugh (ch. 4), Price (ch. 15); on 'Anglo-Norse' Ekwall (1930), Gordon (1957: 326ff). On Scandinavian loans and other possible influences Jespersen (1948: ch. IV). Some recent scholarship has claimed that the Scandinavian influence was much more far-reaching, and that Middle English was actually an Anglo-Norse creole. For a determined espousal of this view see Poussa (1982); for counter-arguments Görlach (1986).

2.7   For standard accounts of the Norman Conquest and its effects, Baugh (ch. 5), Jespersen (ch. V), and Legge (1941). A major revisionist paper, which I follow here, is Berndt (1965); for a modern synthesis and useful references. Price (ch. 17). On post-Conquest England see Stenton (1952), and the references in Bourcier (1981: 124f). On the French element in English, Baugh (ch. 5), Serjeantson (1935: ch. V). The Robert of Gloucester extract is from Dickins & Wilson (1956: 14); the two macaronics are from Brown (1932: 24f, 155).

2.8   On the rise of a southern standard in ME, Schlauch (1959: ch. I), Strang (1970: ch. III) for the general picture, and for the detailed dialectology of the London area and the rise of the 'Chancery Standard' or 'Type IV' dialect see Samuels (1963), Fisher (1977). 'Three Sorrowful Things' from Brown (1932: 19); *Cursor Mundi* from Jones (1972: 195ff), Chaucer from Robinson (1957), Trevisa from Mossé (1950: 285ff), Townely Play from Cawley (1958: 48).

2.9   On the development of the post-ME standard see Schlauch (chs. II–IV), Baugh (chs. 7–8), and Dobson (1955). Dobson is concerned solely with phonology and its social implications; on the same topic, with extension to the present, see the discussion of the rise of RP in Holmberg (1964). Caxton citations from Crotch (1928); Hart from the Scolar Press facsimile (1969), Cooper and Puttenham cited after Dobson. On the development of the verb inflections, Wyld (1936: ch. IX). For non-EML forms in the southern standard, see Jacobson (1962); for supposed functional motivation for dialect borrowing Samuels (1972) and the counter-arguments in Lass (1980: ch. 3).

2.10   The 'authority' and 'correctness' problems are treated in detail in Baugh (ch. 8), Schlauch (chs. IV–V). For historical background, Dykema (1961). On the problem of lay attitudes toward language generally, see Bloomfield's classic paper on 'secondary and tertiary responses to language' (1944), and Crystal (1985b); the most recent treatment of the whole issue is Milroy & Milroy (1985). Dryden quotations from Baugh (ch. 9); Johnson from unnumbered pages of the preface to the 1785 edition.

2.11   The standard history of foreign lexis in English is still Serjeantson (1935); much of this chapter (except for American English) draws on her work. For Celtic loans, Serjeantson (ch. IX); for English-Celtic contacts generally Price (ch. II). Dutch and other European loans mostly after Serjeantson; Yiddish material is not from written sources, but my own observations.

2.12   Flecknoe citation from Craigie (1946: 119); figures on English speakers from Crystal (1985(b)). On the spread of English generally, Baugh (chs. 10–11), Schlauch (chs. VII–VIII), Bailey & Görlach (1982: Introduction). The various papers in Bailey & Görlach contain good historical introductions to the extraterritorial dialects; I will mention some of these in more detail in the notes to ch. 5. Data on exotic loans generally from Serjeantson; U.S. material from Marckwardt (1958) and Mencken & McDavid (1963).

3. PHONOLOGY

3.1 Preliminaries

By the phonology of a language we mean those aspects of its structure connected with its 'sounds', both in terms of their organization and systematic properties (phonology proper), and their physical properties (phonetics). The two, as we will see, intersect in a very intimate way, and it is not really possible to talk of one without invoking the other. This section is intended as a brief introduction to the kinds of phenomena that generally come under the heading of phonology, for the reader who may not be acquainted with basic phonological terminology and theoretical concepts.

There are at least six major areas that concern us in describing the phonology of a language:

(i) *Phoneme Inventories* (Phonological Systems). Every language has a set of contrastive segmental units or phonemes, whose primary function is distinguishing items in the language. E.g. *cap, cab, cat, cad, catch, cadge, cam, can* are clearly 'three-unit sequences', where the first two units are identical, and whatever it is that distinguishes them resides solely in the final segments. (Don't be misled by the spelling: *-tch* and *-dge* represent functionally single units just as much as *-p* or *-b*.)

In terms of phoneme composition, we might represent these words as linear strings of three elements, /kæp/, /kæb/, /kæt/, /kæd/, /kætʃ/, /kædʒ/, /kæm/, /kæn/. And *scab, scat, scam, scan* are four-unit sequences, distinct from *cab, cat* etc. only by virtue of the initial /s/ (/skæt/ ≠ /kæt/), and from each other by virtue of their final consonants. Similarly *kip, kit, kin* are distinguished from *cap, cat, can* by their second units, and from *tip, tit, tin* by their first.

So a language has an inventory or system of vowel and consonant phonemes, such that the substitution of one for the other will – under normal conditions – produce either a change of meaning, or a word that for some reason or other isn't in the language. Thus if we substitute the vowel /ɪ/ (as in *sit*) for the /æ/ in the first set, we get *kip, *kib, kit, kid, Kitsch, *kidge, Kim, kin*. The forms **kib, *kidge* happen not to exist – but they clearly could: they are potentially well-formed. (See (iii) below for a different kind of nonexistent form.)

86

(ii) *Allophonic Rules.* Consider *cat, cad, scat.* It is clear that phonemically they are /kæt, kæd, skæt/. But if we look at the actual pronunciations, we find that there are differences not apparent in the phonemic representations. First, the /k/ in *cat* and *cad* is aspirated [kʰ], while that in *scat* is unaspirated [k]. Further (for my dialect, which I'm using as an example, but for many others as well), the vowel in *cad* is a long [æː], while that in *cat, scat* is a short [æ].

Thus each of these items must be described in terms of at least a pair of representations:

(3.1)

		cat	cad	scat	
PHONETIC	[	kʰæt	kʰæːd	skæt	]
PHONEMIC	/	kæt	kæd	skæt	/

The phonemic representation contains information relating to distinctiveness or 'identity' of form: it answers the question: 'Which of the possible vowels and consonants of English does this item contain?' The phonetic representation is an idealized version of something closer to the actual speech-event: it answers the question: 'How are the particular units of English identified in the phonemic representation physically realized?' The phonetic information is to a large degree redundant, or rule-governed: that is, given a phoneme of a particular kind in a particular position, many aspects of its physical realization can be predicted.

Thus we have rules like: (a) 'voiceless stops /p t k/ are aspirated syllable-initially unless /s/ precedes'; (b) 'short vowels lengthen before voiced consonants (like /b d g/)'. In standard terminology, we would say that English 'has a phoneme /k/', and that this 'has the allophones [kʰ], [k]' in certain positions. A phoneme is thus an 'ideal' or 'abstract' but essentially phonetic unit in a language's code-system, which has particular physical characteristics in certain contexts.

The most important point is that phonemes are contrastive (informative, meaning-distinguishing) units, but allophones are not; characteristically, the allophones of a given phoneme occur in complementary distribution, i.e. one can never appear in place of another. Thus one could say *cat* as [kæt] and *scat* as [skʰæt]; but the result would not be of the type you'd get if instead of [kʰæt] you said [sæt], etc.

When we refer to 'the sound system' of a language we normally mean its phoneme system, not the set of its allophones. To take an often-used example, both English and Hindi 'have' the sounds [p pʰ]; but the two are contrastive in Hindi ([pʰəl] 'fruit' vs. [pəl] 'moment'), whereas no English words can be distinguished solely by aspirated vs. unaspirated voiceless stops. Aspiration 'occurs' as a phonetic phenomenon in both languages, but it has an informative function only in Hindi. (By 'informative' I mean lexically informative; if you were to substitute say [p] for [pʰ] in *pat*, the result would – for most standard English speakers – be an effect of 'foreignness' or 'oddity' – but not a different word. (This is not the case in final position: both [ætʰ] and [æt] are perfectly acceptable versions of *at* for most English speakers.)

(iii) *Phonotactics*. This term refers to the set of constraints on the arrangement of phonemes, and the nature of the higher-order structures built out of them, especially syllables. (In linguistic terminology, '-tactics' refers to arrangement: cf. the same root in 'syn*tax*'.) Two languages may have virtually the same set of segments, but have different rules for their deployment: both English and German, for instance, have /s z ʃ/ (as in *sip, zip, ship*), but treat them quite differently. As the examples show, all three can occur initially in English; in standard German, only /z ʃ/ can: *Sohn* 'son' /zoːn/, *Schiff* 'ship' /ʃɪf/. In English all three can occur finally as well (*ass, as, ash*); in German only /s ʃ/ (*Spies* 'spear' /ʃpiːs/, *Fisch* 'fish' /fɪʃ/). The exclusion of /z/ from final position is part of a larger pattern in German, which again makes an interesting contrast with English: both languages have the stops /p t k b d g/ and the fricatives /f v s z/; but in German only the voiceless /p t k f s/ can appear in syllable- or word-final position, whereas in English they all can.

Given larger sequences, such as consonant clusters, we can see similar constraints: e.g. in English /bl/ can appear only syllable-initially (*blue*), and its inverse /lb/ only finally (*bulb*); any three-member initial cluster must begin with /s/, its second member must be one of /p t k/, and its third one of /r l j w/ (with further restrictions: see §3.3).

The phonotactic restrictions of a language enable us (cf. (i) above) to distinguish between two classes of non-existent forms: those which are 'accidental gaps' in the lexicon but are phonotactically well-formed (**kib, *kidge*) and those which are 'principled gaps' (**stling, *lbub*).

(iv) *Casual Speech ('Allegro') Rules*. The three components mentioned so far are concerned with word-structure 'in the abstract', as it were: with careful pronunciations of individual words. And indeed this is the basic – and necessary – level of phonological description. We don't however typically speak in words, but in utterances consisting of strings of words, put together in real time. And we don't always (or even typically) speak slowly, with maximum attentiveness and self-monitoring. In connected colloquial speech, where words 'meet at the edges', and where the segments that make them up come in more rapid sequence than they would in isolated one-word utterances, all sorts of things happen. Long vowels shorten, final consonants drop, segments become more like each other, etc. To take two instances: (a) In my speech the word *in* /ɪn/ is typically pronounced [ɪn], with a final alveolar nasal; but in connected speech, the final /n/ assimilates to a following consonant. Before a velar it becomes velar, as in *in Cape Town* [ɪŋ kʰéɪp tʰàʊn], before the labial it becomes labial, as in *in Paris* [ɪm pʰǽrɪs]. (b) Still with my own speech: words like *camp, can't, bent* are pronounced in isolation as [kʰæːmp, kʰæːnt, bɛnt]; in slightly more casual speech, the vowels anticipate the nasality of the following consonants, and become nasalized: [kʰæ̃ːmp, kʰæ̃ːnt, bɛ̃nt); but in rapid colloquial speech, the following nasal drops completely, leaving [kʰæ̃ːp, kʰæ̃ːt, bɛ̃t]. In this kind of speech, the difference between say *bet* and *bent* is carried entirely by the nasality of the vowel: [bɛt] vs. [bɛ̃t].

Let's look at the implications of this last process: every English speaker who has learned (or tried to learn) French knows that 'French has nasalized vowels; English doesn't'. But in fact this is true only at the level of very careful, maximally monitored speech. In normal running speech, every variety of English I've heard has nasalized vowels. But as speakers we're not conscious of them: (a) because they don't contrast with non-nasalized vowels in careful speech; (b) because they only occur in those speech styles where we pay minimal attention; and (c) because as long as there's nasality, it doesn't much matter where it is; *bet* and *bent* will still be distinct.

For this reason English speakers will often have enormous difficulty in learning to pronounce (phonemic) nasalized vowels in careful speech in a foreign language – even if they have them all over the place in their own everyday speech. (Hence the cross-linguistic vulgarisms represented by Thackeray in *The Yellowplush Papers* as *O mong Jew* 'O mon Dieu', *bong jour* 'bon jour'.)

(v) *Stress-Rules.* Languages tend to have rules by which certain syllables are made more 'prominent' than others, i.e. are stressed or accented. Thus all speakers of English would agree that the following stress assignments (and no others) are correct: *cáttle, belíeve, álgebra, detérgent*; while most British and American speakers would disagree on *salívary* vs. *sálivary, contróversy* vs. *cóntroversy*. In English, stress is not arbitrary; it is largely controlled by rules sensitive to syllable-structure and syllable-number. Any account of the phonology of a language with an accentual system (it is not certain whether all have them, but most do) will have to say something about it; for some languages the rules will be very simple (in Finnish, stress falls on the first syllable of the word, and a weaker stress on every odd-numbered syllable except the last; in Polish stress falls on the penultimate syllable of the word), or quite complex, as in English (see §§3.4–6). We will also be connected with stress-patterns beyond the simple word, e.g. with the difference between compound stress (*bláckbird*) and phrasal stress (*black bírd*).

(vi) *Morphophonology*. Since words and smaller grammatical elements (suffixes, etc.) are made up of strings of phonemes, it is in principle possible for sound-structure to be implicated in grammatical structure as well. Thus there is a large class of items in which root-final consonants vary before particular suffixes: *electric/electricity/electrician, physics/physicist/physician* (/k/~/s/~/ʃ/: ~ = 'alternates with'). Related alternations occur in *educate/education, critic/criticize, divide/divisible/ division*, etc. Vowels alternate as well: /aɪ/~/ɪ/ in *divine/divinity, crime/ criminal, sign/signify*, /eɪ/~/æ/ in *sane/sanity, humane/humanity, grain/ granary*, and so on. Such alternations are called morphophonemic or morphophonological – i.e. they involve the implication of phonology (in terms of phoneme-alternations) in morphological (= word) structure.

For some linguists, these alternations are a fundamental aspect of the phonology of a language – *the* fundamental one, in fact; for others, they're not genuinely phonological at all, but are part of the morphology. The debate on these issues is complex, unresolved (like nearly all interesting debates in linguistics), and in the context of this book pretty much irrelevant; I will take a rather conservative point of view, and consider most of the alternations cited above and many similar ones as primarily relics of historical change, remnants of what were once living processes in the language. They will come up mainly in the historical section of this chapter (§3.8), and in the discussion of modern English word formation (§4.8). (See the notes for some references to the literature on this topic.)

In the following sections, we will look first at the consonant and vowel systems of English, and some of the most important and widespread allophonic rules; after this we will turn to phonotactics, stress and allegro rules, since both vowels and consonants are involved. Later sections will examine the historical origins of the present-day states of affairs.

3.2 The Segmental Phonology of a Standard Dialect

3.2.1 INTRODUCTION

In this chapter the problems posed by the dialectal diversity of English will be most acute. Dialects differ more in phonology than at other levels; yet it would be virtually impossible to treat these differences adequately while at the same time trying to draw a coherent general picture. As a compromise, I will devote this chapter for the most part to as 'representative' a dialect type as possible, with notes on major divergences where appropriate; more details will appear in ch. 5.

The dialect type I'll concentrate on here is a standard variety of Southern British English (SBE). Its 'representativeness' can be defined as follows:

(i) The consonant and vowel inventories of most standard dialects are quite similar to SBE, for two historical reasons:

(a) The post-medieval British standard was largely based on London and Home Counties English, which is the geographical core of SBE (cf. §§2.8–9).

(b) When English was exported as a colonial language, the main input to the extraterritorial dialects, and in large part the basis of their emerging standards, was SBE.

(ii) These historical factors have assured that in outline at least U.S., South African, Australian and New Zealand English are structurally SBE types (cf. §§5.6, 5.8).

(iii) The similarities involve not only (rough) phonetic likenesses, but overall system-shapes as well. That is, for all these dialects it would be reasonable to say for instance that *bit, pit* are members of a rhyme class distinct from *beet, peat*; that the *beet*-class will have a closer and longer and probably fronter vowel than the *bit*-class; that *good, flood, food* are distinct; that *good* and *flood* will have distinct short vowels (respectively those of *put* and *putt*) and *food* a long vowel, etc. (This description will not hold in detail for Scots, even the standard: see §5.7.1).

There are of course differences between the extraterritorial dialects, as well as differences separating most American ones from the others: e.g. SBE and non-U.S. extraterritorials show a distinction of the type /æ/ vs. /ɑː/ in the *bat* and *bath* classes, while most U.S. and Canadian dialects don't; but such details will require only minor adjustments for non-SBE speaking readers.

3.2.2 CONSONANTS

We will look first at the consonant system, which is less complex and problematic than the vowel system. English is one of the large group of languages (like the rest of Indo-European) that divides its obstruents (stops, fricatives, affricates) into two broad classes – traditionally 'voiced' and 'voiceless'. These terms are crude, but will serve. For the voiced set, the vocal folds are vibrating at some point during the consonantal closure; for the voiceless set, voicing on a following vowel begins either simultaneously with the release of the closure, or some time after release. If voicing is delayed after release, there is a period of [h]-like friction, known as aspiration (cf. §3.2.4). Thus /p t k tʃ f θ s ʃ h/

are voiceless, and /b d g dʒ v ð z ʒ/ are voiced. The other consonants (the sonorants: nasals and liquids) are normally voiced: i.e. there are not usually voiced: voiceless pairs like /t/:/d/, etc., but simply a voiced series /m n ŋ r l w j/ (see below for one exception).

The basic inventory of English looks like this (for unfamiliar terminology see Appendix I and the Glossary):

(3.2)

		Labio-Dental	Labial	Dental	Alveolar	Palato-Alveolar	Palatal	Velar	Glottal
STOP	vl		p		t			k	
	vd		b		d			g	
FRICA-TIVE	vl	f		θ	s	ʃ			
	vd	v		ð	z	ʒ		(x)[1]	h
AFFRI-CATE	vl					tʃ			
	vd					dʒ			
NASAL	vd	⌐	m		n			ŋ	
LIQUID	vd		w[2]		r, l		j		
	vl		(w̥)[1]						

1. Only certain dialects have /x/ or /w̥/: see below.
2. /w/ normally has both labial and velar articulation, but phonologically tends to behave like a labial.

As a reminder, here are key-words for the items in (3.2):

(3.3)

{pit		tip			kill	
{bit		dip			gill	
{few	thigh	sue	vicious		SA ag	hill
{view	thy	zoo	vision		Scots loch	
			{chew			
			{Jew			
	moo		new		ring	
{ wail		rue, loo		you		
{US whale						

The classifications are non-controversial, except for the grouping of /r l j w/ together as liquids. Many linguists reserve this term for /r l/ only, and call /j w/ 'glides' or 'semivowels'. I see no need for this distinction, since all four behave as a group in English: they are the only segments that can follow an initial sequence of /s/+stop: *spring, sclerosis, skew, squeal* /sprɪŋ/, /sklərəʊsɪs/, /skjuː/, /skwiːl/; they all devoice after initial voiceless stops (listen to the difference between the /r j/ in *brew, beauty* vs. those in *pray, pure*), etc.

The system in (3.2) minus the bracketed /w̥x/ is a minimal 'core'; the only dialects with smaller inventories are regional ones with no /θ ð/, e.g. some Irish varieties (see §5.7.2). But there are standard dialects with the expanded inventory. Scots, some northern English dialects, and many North American ones have two labial liquids, voiced /w/ in *Wales, witch* vs. voiceless /w̥/ in *whales, which*. This is an ancient contrast: cf. OE *Wealh* 'Welshman', *hwæl* 'whale', *wicca* 'witch', *hwilc* 'which'. It now seems to be receding except in Scotland, where it is fully stable. Many (non-Scots) dialects that have it show variability tending to loss – though speakers who have been influenced by spelling, or by teachers in love with the written word, will tend to try and retain it – usually with indifferent success.

At least two national standards, however, have a stable and fully integrated velar or uvular fricative, which we will represent as /x/ (as in G *Bach*). In all Scottish varieties except the most Anglified this occurs in words and place-names of Celtic origin like *loch* /lɔx/, *clachan* /kláxʌn/, *Auchtermuchty* /ɔ́xtərmʌ̀xte/, and other items like *pech* /pex/ 'pant', *driech* /drix/ 'dreary'.

In South African English /x/ occurs much more widely, because of the immense number of fully integrated loans from Afrikaans (especially) and indigenous languages that have /x/. These words, probably because of long-standing Afrikaans/English bilingualism (see §4.8.4 for details), are generally not (much) altered to conform to English patterns – certainly not to the extent that foreign words are in most other dialects. Items like *ag* /äx/ 'oh', *dagga* /dáxä/ 'cannabis' are simply as English as any others. The same is true of Afrikaans place-names and place-name elements, e.g. *-sig* /sïx/ 'view', *-gracht* /xräxt/', *groot* 'great' /xrʊət/, as in the Cape Town local names *Bothasig, Buitengracht, Groot Constantia*.

One might also suggest that other varieties have at least a marginal /x/: e.g. those of Jewish speakers (whether Yiddish-speaking or not) who normally use words like *chutzpah* /xʊ́tspə/ 'gall, nerve', *toches* /tʊ́xəs~ tʌ́xəs/ 'ass', *chupah* /xʊ́pə/ 'bridal canopy'. It is questionable in some cases how integrated these are: if a Jew doesn't normally use them with non-Jews, they might belong to a specialized supranational ethnic register ('Judaeo-English'?).

As far as dialectal norms go, there is remarkably little overall variation except in the alveolar series /t d n l/, and /r/. Most dialects have alveolars (except before dentals: e.g. in *tenth*, which is [tʰɛn̪θ] with a dental [n̪] even for speakers with alveolar [n] elsewhere); though some dialects do have dental norms. Dental /l/ is widespread even in dialects with alveolar /t d n/; and dental /t d n/ occur in the West of Scotland and are common in U.S. urban speech (e.g. in New York and Chicago).

The distribution of types of /r/ is more complicated. Perhaps the majority of speakers regardless of origin have some kind of approximant – i.e. a vowel-like segment with no actual contact between the tongue and anything else. These may be postalveolar (as in most British dialects), retroflex (with the tongue-tip curled back, as in some U.S. varieties, southwestern British English and western Scots); or a very complex articulation with the main constriction opposite the velum and secondary constriction of the pharynx, as in much U.S. English. Other kinds do however occur: an alveolar tap [ɾ], rather like a very short [d], produced by a single quick contact of the tongue-tip against the alveolar ridge is common in less prestigious Scots and South African dialects, and occurs in many high-prestige British varieties as a variant of [ɹ] between vowels (as in *very*), or after /θ/ (as in *three*). Some old-fashioned Scots varieties have a trilled [r] (like Italian *r*) – but this is recessive. Finally there is a uvular fricative [ʁ] (like French r): this is pretty much confined to older, largely rural speakers in Northumberland and Durham, though there are pockets in Aberdeen (among standard speakers), and the West of Scotland. Because of this variety, I will use the general symbol [r] in all transcriptions, except when the particular quality is at issue.

There is a major division between English dialect types with respect to the phonology of /r/. This could be discussed under any one of a number of headings, but I will deal with it here, while we're focussing on the consonant inventory. The treatment of /r/ is – in this precise form – unique as far as I know to English.

The distinction is between those dialects that allow /r/ to appear in all positions, and those where its occurrence is systematically restricted. These are called respectively rhotic and non-rhotic (terms coined by John Wells – though the less elegant '*r*-ful' and '*r*-less' are often used by American linguists). The distributions of /r/ work out this way:

(i) Rhotic. /r/ occurs in all positions: initially (*red*), between vowels (*very*), before consonants (*part*) and finally (*four*). There may be allophonic differences in some positions, but the /r/ is always pronounced.

(ii) Non-Rhotic. /r/ occurs initially and between vowels (*red, very*); it does not occur before consonants (*part*). In final position it occurs only if there is a following word beginning with a vowel, i.e. when it is effectively between vowels; before pause or a word beginning with a consonant it does not occur. Thus *four* will have final /r/ in a sequence like *four and five*, but never in *four men, only four*. RP for instance will have invariable [pʰɑːt] *part*, but [fɔːr ænd faɪv] *four and five* vs. [fɔː mɛn] *four men*.

Such dialects exhibit what is known, for obvious reasons, as 'linking *r*'. The more conservative non-rhotic types have linking *r* only when there is a historical or orthographic *r* at the end of the word: thus *law and order* will be [lɔː ænd ɔːdə], with no /r/ at the end of *law*, while *four and five* will have /r/ at the end of *four*, as above. Many varieties of SBE, however, have extended the linking principle so that /r/ occurs not after certain words but after certain vowels – regardless of history or spelling. Dialect of this type will have [lɔːr ænd ɔːdə] as well as [fɔːr ænd faɪv]. This is known (again for obvious reasons) as 'intrusive *r*'. It occurs most commonly after /ɔː/ (*law and order*), /ɑː/ (*bra and knickers*), /ɪə/ (*the idea of it*), and unstressed /ə/ (*China and Japan*). This usage is sometimes stigmatized, or at least treated humorously; I recall reading somewhere of a child who had a Siamese cat named *Annaran* (after *Anna-r-and the King of Siam*).

Some non-rhotic dialects display much less linking than others; South African English for instance tends to have a glottal stop [ʔ] initially in words that would seem to be vowel-initial, which acts like a consonant and blocks linking: thus [fo: ʔænd fäːv] *four and five*. Intrusive *r* seems virtually never to occur.

The rhotic/non-rhotic distinction has its origin in the loss of post-vocalic /r/ that began in the South of England in the 17th century and was completed during the 19th. The loss seems to have begun before consonants, and was only extended to stressed final position much later. But the change did not extend to all parts of Britain, and extraterritorial dialects that either developed earlier than the loss or had large inputs from parts of Britain where it didn't occur are still rhotic.

At present, rhoticity is distributed more or less as follows: (a) non-rhotic: all of England except the Southwest and portions of the Northwest Midlands; Wales; east coast and southern coastal U.S.; Australia, New Zealand, South Africa. (b) rhotic: Southwest England; West Lancashire; Ireland (north and south); Scotland; the rest of the U.S.

The other segment prone to loss is /h/ – which has a very restricted distribution to begin with, occurring only in syllable-initial position in most dialects. All dialects appear to drop /h/ under low stress, e.g. in *give him one, who's he think he is*. It would be unnatural for most speakers to have /h/ anywhere in these examples except in stressed *who's* in normal casual speech. But in England, at least, perhaps the largest number of (non-standard) dialects have lost /h/ completely, and only retain it unsystematically under the normative influence of the schools and the standard varieties. This leads to the familiar literary device of indicating semi-education or (partly undeserved) upward mobility or lower-class pretension in English characters by having them produce a nearly random distribution of /h/: *I just 'ave to get to the hoffice*, etc. The only parts of England where /h/ seems to be retained in popular speech are Tyneside and East Anglia; but it is fully stable in all varieties in Ireland, Scotland, and the U.S. (The letter *h* is in fact normally called /heːtʃ/ in Ireland.) /h/-dropping does occur in Australian and New Zealand English of the less cultivated types, and to a certain extent in South Africa as well – though in the latter case the phonetic quality of /h/ is such (often only a slight breathiness) that an outsider could miss it and think he was hearing a 'dropped *h*', whereas the native would know that it was there.

It used to be thought that /h/-dropping was relatively recent; but it now seems clear that it began at least as early as the 11th century, and that the current *h*-fullness of the English standard varieties is the result of a school-imposed reintroduction, under the influence of spelling.

3.2.3 VOWELS

The description of vowel systems is complex and controversial, and this is particularly true for English. A few words on the model I use in this book are in order. Phonetically, virtually all English dialects have three vowel types: short vowels (*sit, sat*); long vowels (*boot, bought*); and diphthongs (*bite, boy*). In most dialects, however, there are no pairs distinguished solely by length: there are quality differences as well (e.g. SBE will have [ɪ] in *bit* and [iː] in *beet*). This has led to many widely-used transcription systems for English indicating only quality at the phonological level, since the length differences can generally be predicted on the basis of quality: thus *beet* /bit/ vs. /bɪt/ *bit*. This is phonetically misleading; and what's worse, makes the incorrect claim that the vowels in *bit* and *beet*, for example, are phonologically 'the same kind of animal'. Such an approach misses major insights into the organization of the English sound system, and makes it impossible to relate contemporary structure and history in a coherent way.

There are important phonological reasons why vowels of the *bit* and *beet* types ought to be distinguished by something more than quality. The long vowels behave differently from the short ones in ways that have nothing to do with their quality; and further, long vowels and diphthongs group together as a class, as against short vowels. The arguments for this classification are somewhat complex, but important; the whole character of most English (and other Germanic) vowel systems is based on this two-way split. We will look at some of the main evidence and its significance here.

First, distribution. Both long vowels and diphthongs can appear in final stressed open syllables; short vowels can't. Thus *tea* /tiː/, *tie* /taɪ/, *paw* /pɔː/, *how* /haʊ/; but no words of the types */pæ/, */hʊ/.

Second, cross-dialect equivalences. Given a particular lexical set (say the *bat* set or the *mate* set – i.e. those words that 'have the same vowel as . . .'), we can predict:

(i) If one dialect has a short vowel in a given set, the others will – even if the qualities differ vastly;

(ii) If one dialect has a long vowel, the others will have either long vowels or diphthongs.

We can illustrate this with some selected lexical sets from four dialect types: SBE, South African standard (SAE), East Yorkshire urban (EY), and rural Northumberland (RN):

(3.4)

		SBE	SAE	EY	RN
Short	bit	ɪ	ï	ɪ	ɪ
	bat	æ	ɛ	a	a
	bet	ɛ	e	ɛ	ɛ
	but	ʌ	ä	ʊ	ʊ
Long/ Diphth.	beet	iː	iː	iː	iː
	mate	eɪ	eɪ	eː	ɪə
	boat	əʊ	ɞ̈ʊ	oː	ø̞ː
	out	aʊ	ɑʊ	aʊ	uː
	boot	uː	ʉː	uː	ɪə
	bite	aɪ	äː	aː	ɛɪ

Thus across dialects shorts are short, longs and diphthongs are interchangeable. (We will see the structural reasons for this below, and the historical background in §§3.8–10). Of course the actual members of some of the sets will vary from dialect to dialect: e.g. while in SBE and related dialects *head* and *deaf* are in the (short) *bet* class, and *look* and *hook* in the (short) *foot* class, in much northern English these items have long vowels: the first two in the *beet* class and the second in *boot*. (This is due to shortening of the vowels in these words in the South, but not in the North.)

These equivalences are of course also reflected in the morphophonology. Given alternations of the *divine/divinity, insane/insanity* types, all dialects will have either a long vowel or diphthong in the first alternant and a short vowel in the second – regardless of quality. So SBE will have *div*[aɪ]*n/div*[ɪ]*nity, ins*[eɪ]*n/ins*[æ]*nity*, and the Yorkshire dialect in (3.3) will have *div*[aː]*n/div*[ɪ]*nity, ins*[eː]*n/ins*[a]*nity*, etc. (see further §4.8.4).

Thus English – except for Scots (§5.7.1) – has a 'split' or dichotomous vowel system: two distinct vowel sets with different phonological behaviour. For convenience we can call the sets 'short' and 'long'. The short set contains (generally) simple short (steady-state, monophthongal) vowels; the long set contains either long steady-state vowels or diphthongs.

But why should these groups of vowels pattern this way? It is in fact quite expectable, and a very widespread pattern across languages. If say [e] is a short vowel, what is [eː]? Simply an [e] followed without a break by another [e], or a continuation of the [e]-articulation over a longer time than is normally given to a short vowel. Thus an alternative notation for [eː] would be [ee]. And a diphthong of course is a vowel cluster: thus [ee] is parallel to [eɪ]. It's only a matter of convention that we write [eː] but [eɪ]. We might say then that a long vowel is simply a diphthong whose two elements or morae (singular mora) are the same; or that a diphthong is a long vowel whose two morae are different. The closeness of the two types will become more apparent in the historical sections, when we will see that long vowels frequently diphthongize, and diphthongs monophthongize to long vowels: thus the source of modern /aɪ/ is ME /iː/, and that of modern /ɔː/ is among other things ME /au/.

Many languages in fact recognize this parallelism in their spelling systems: e.g. Dutch and Afrikaans distinguish long from short vowels in certain environments by writing the former double. So *Cape Town* in Afrikaans is *Kaapstad*, with long /ɑː/ in the first syllable and short /ɑ/ in the second; and diphthongs are also written with two vowel symbols: *hou* /höu/ 'to hold'. (Like nearly all orthographies, this is inconsistent: the diphthong /ɛi/ is written either *y* or *ei*.) There are even relics of this technique in English spelling: *beet, beat, boot, boat, house,* etc.

Given these facts, it would be more precise to refer not to 'long' and 'short' vowels, but to 'complex' and 'simple' ones – as is often done in the technical literature. But this would add yet another terminological distinction to a chapter already overfull of them, and I will stick to the traditional terms.

A typical SBE system:

(3.5)

SHORT		LONG				
		Monophthong		Diphthong		
ɪ	ʊ	iː	uː	eɪ	aɪ	ɒɪ
ɛ	ʌ	ɜː	ɔː	əʊ	aʊ	
æ	ɒ		ɑː	ɪə	ɛə	ʊə

Observe that characteristically for English, there are three series of diphthongs: in /-ɪ/, in /-ʊ/, and in /-ə/. For ease of identification, the symbols represent the following lexical classes:

(3.6)

SHORT		LONG					
		Monophthong		Diphthong			
bit	foot	feet	boot	mate	bite	boy	
bet	but	hurt	bought	oat	out		
bat	pot	part/		idea	fair	poor	
		fast					

(The vowels in *hurt, fair, poor* are characteristic of non-rhotic dialects: §3.2.2.) These displays and others of a similar type to follow show monophthongal vowels roughly in their location in the 'vowel-space': conventionally the front of the mouth is to the left, and the roof of the mouth at the top, so the front/back axis runs left-to-right.

From a comparative and historical point of view, it is of interest to compare a system of this type with that of standard German:

(3.7)

SHORT			LONG				
			Monophthong			Diphthong	
ɪ	Y	ʊ	iː	yː	uː	ae	
ɛ	œ	ɔ	eː	øː	oː	ao	
a			ɛː			ɔY	
				ɑː			

Again, for identification:

(3.8)

SHORT			LONG				
			Monophthong			Diphthong	
mit	Stück	Schutt	Lied	grün	Gut	Zeit	
Bett	höchst	Gott	Beet	schön	tod	aus	
Stadt			spät		Staat	heute	

Overall – except for the front rounded vowels /Y œ yː øː/ – the two systems are quite similar. We will see later that modern SBE (along with all other dialects) descends ultimately from a system rather like this, with two front rounded vowels, short and long.

3.2.4 MAJOR ALLOPHONIC PROCESSES

While the phonetic realizations of the various phonemes, and the effects of phonetic context, vary widely from dialect to dialect, there are a few processes that are so widespread as to be highly typical of English in general. Among the most important are:

(a) *Aspiration*. Voiceless stops (and often the affricate /tʃ/) are aspirated in syllable-initial position: e.g. [tʰ] in *town, today,* [kʰ] in *cow, collect,* etc. Most dialects do not aspirate intervocalically after a stressed vowel (*bitter, backer*), or after /s/ (*spot, stop, scat*). In syllable-final position (as in *tap, cat*) /p t k/ may be aspirated, unreleased, or ejective (produced with an airstream initiated by an upward movement of the closed glottis).

Aspiration is widespread; perhaps more dialects have it than not. It is however notably lacking in much of Scotland, in parts of the North Midlands (Yorkshire and Lancashire), and in working-class South African English.

(b) *Palatalization*. The velar stops /k g/ have strikingly different allophones before back and front vowels. In general, the fronter (and closer) the vowel, the more palatal the realization. E.g. if you compare the initials of *coo, key* and *goose, geese,* you will find that in the first of each set the back of the tongue contacts the velum (soft palate), and in the second the contact is between a more forward part of the tongue and the hard palate. Phonetically, we could write the two pairs as [kʰuː], [cʰiː] and [guːs], [ɟiːs] ([c ɟ] are voiceless and voiced palatal stops). Phonemically, of course, since degree of frontness is predictable, the pairs are /kuː/, /kiː/ and /guːs/, /giːs/.

(c) '*Clear*' vs. '*Dark*' /l/. In many dialects (virtually all SBE, South African, and southern U.S.), /l/ has two major allophones, depending on syllable position. One is a 'clear' (neutral or slightly palatalized) [l] syllable-initially, and the other a 'dark' (with a secondary stricture between the back of the tongue and velum or uvula) [ɫ] syllable-finally. Thus *lull* in such a dialect would be [lʌɫ]. Intervocalic /l/ in this kind of set-up is usually treated as syllable-initial: thus *feel* [fiːɫ] vs. *feeling* [fiːlɪŋ].

Other dialects however lack this alternation: eastern and central Scots, most non-Southern U.S. dialects, and Australian and New Zealand English have dark /l/ in all positions (except sometimes before /j/, as in *million* [mɪljən]); Tyneside, most forms of Hiberno-English (Irish English) and some western Scots dialects have clear /l/ in all positions. So /l/ can be clear everywhere, dark everywhere, or clear initially and dark finally; as far as I know an alternation dark initially vs. clear finally doesn't occur.

In some dialects, the secondary back articulation of syllable-final /l/ is so prominent that the alveolar stricture is dropped, leaving behind a diphthong instead of a vowel + /l/ sequence; this is typical of working-class London and Home Counties speech, where *fill, milk* are often [fɪʊ], [mɪʊk].

In addition to these widespread rules, there are two others sufficiently common to be worth mentioning:

(d) *Glottalization and Glottal Stop Substitution.* In perhaps the bulk of British dialects and many U.S. ones, syllable final voiceless stops /p t k/ often have a preceding or simultaneous glottal stop [ʔ] with them. This has the phonetic effect of shortening the preceding vowel; in much Scots, for instance, where the voiced stops /b d g/ are voiceless finally, a pair like *cat*: *cad* might be distinguished only the presence of [ʔ] and a very short vowel in *cat*, and no [ʔ] and a longer vowel in *cad*. In dialects of this kind the stop following [ʔ] often deletes in casual speech, leaving behind only the glottal stop: thus *cat* as [kaʔ]. In such dialects /t/ is usually the most often replaced by [ʔ]; less often /k/ and /p/, in that order. Replacement also occurs intervocalically, as in [bʌʔər] *butter*, [pʰaʔɪŋ] *packing*.

Glottal stop substitution is common in non-standard speech throughout most of the U.K. In standard varieties that have accompanying [ʔ] with voiceless stops, substitution tends to occur only when another consonant follows, e.g. [fʊʔbɔːɫ] *football*.

(e) *Voicing and Tapping of Intervocalic* /t/. One well-known marker of much U.S. speech is the apparent merger of /t/ and /d/ in an alveolar tap [ɾ] after a stressed vowel and before an unstressed one, so that e.g. *latter* and *ladder* sound the same. This effect is due to two factors: a shortening of the stop articulation in this environment, and a voicing of /t/ in voiced surroundings. In U.S. English generally this process occurs both within the word and across word boundaries; [bɪɾər] *bitter/bidder*, [hɪɾ əm] *hit him/hid 'em*. In RP and many British dialects, tapping occurs only across word boundaries, i.e. in the *hit him* types; between vowels there are either ordinary stops [t d] or a voiceless tap [ɾ̥] for /t/. Something like the U.S. situation appears to be the case in informal speech in many Australian and South African varieties as well.

3.3 Syllable Structure

Just as words group into phrases and other syntactic constituents (cf. §4.3.1), so phonemes enter into higher-order structures as well. The most important of these is the syllable – perhaps the key item in phonological structure. As we will see, many of the most important phonological generalizations (including some made earlier in terms of segments) are most naturally cast in terms of the syllable and its parts.

Syllables are not just strings of segments, but independent units with an internal structure. A syllable (σ) has two main constituents; an onset and a rhyme. The rhyme is the syllabic element (normally a vowel) plus any following material; cf. the everyday use of the term in '*cat* rhymes with *fat* and *sprat*'. The onset is any material preceding the rhyme. Thus the basic division in a monosyllable like *cat* would be:

(3.9)

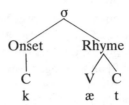

But the rhyme itself has two constituents (see below for evidence): the peak (syllabic) and the coda (any following material). So the complete syllabic structure of *cat* is:

(3.10)

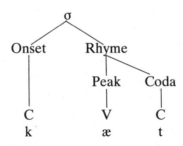

This is the model we will use for talking about syllables: the constituents defined as above, plus fairly obvious derivative notions like 'CVC syllable', '-VC rhyme', etc.

Of these constituents, the onset or coda or both may be empty (here indicated by 0):

(3.11)

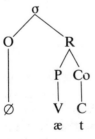 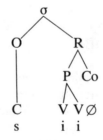 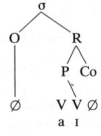

Empty Onset: Empty Coda: Empty O, Co:
    at   *see*   *eye*

But peaks may never be empty; they are the defining category of the syllable. (The syllable is thus a 'phrase' – i.e. it has an obligatory and characteristic constituent that can function in itself as the whole. Compare the 'head noun' of a noun phrase: e.g. *boys* is the head of *the big spotty idiotic boys*, and can fulfil any syntactic function of the larger construction: §4.3.1.)

Each syllable constituent has its own particular properties and distributional limitations; we will first consider the structure of English onsets and codas, and then the rhyme as a whole. To illustrate the independence of onsets and codas, we can look at what consonants and clusters can appear in them. There are some very simple restrictions: e.g. /h/ can only occur in an onset, and /ŋ/ only in a coda: *hang* /hæŋ/, but not */ŋæh/. But now consider a selected group of CC clusters, in terms of their possible appearance in onsets and codas: in the table below, + = is allowed, − = is not allowed:

(3.12)

	(a)				(b)		
	sp	st	sk		ps	ts	ks
Onset	+	+	+		−	−	−
Coda	+	+	+		+	+	+

	(c)				(d)					
	pl	lp	pr	rp	mp	nt	ŋk	mb	nd	ŋg
Onset	+	−	+	−	−	−	−	−	−	−
Coda	−	+	−	+	+	+	+	−	+	−

Summarizing these results:

(a) /sC/ clusters are legal in both onsets and codas (*spat/asp*);

(b) /Cs/ clusters occur only in codas (*apse, cats, axe*); initial /ts/ occurs for some speakers in foreign words (*Tsar, tsetse*) – but these are often nativized, e.g. /zɑː(r)/, /sɛtsiː/~/tɛtsiː/.

(c) Stop + liquid and liquid + stop clusters have 'mirror-image' restrictions, being confined respectively to onsets and codas (*play* vs. *help, pray* vs. *carp* – the latter for rhotic dialects only, of course).

(d) Nasal + stop is restricted to codas (*hand, hank*); further, no dialects seem to allow /mb/ in codas, though some do allow /ŋg/, e.g. those in the Northwest of England that have /sɪŋg/ for *sing*. Nasal clusters in onsets are tightly constrained as well, normally to /s/ + nasal (*smooth, snow*), though some speakers have /ʃ/ + nasal as well (*schmuck*: see below).

Let's consider onsets in more detail. To get some idea of how restricted they really are, it's worth comparing the number of mathematically possible onset clusters with what actually occurs. If English has 22 consonant phonemes (cf. §3.2.2), this should allow, for two member (CC-) clusters, a total of 22 × 22, or 484. If we disallow clustering of any consonant with itself, since English does not have long or double consonants within the word, this removes 22, leaving 462. The actual number (generously – see (3.13) below) is in fact 48, a little over 10% of the possibles. And of this maximal set, many dialects may lack up to half a dozen or so. We can represent the maximal set this way:

(3.13)

	r	l	j	w	m	n	f	v	s
p	pray	play	pure	—	—	—	—	—	—
t	try	—	tune[1]	twin	—	—	—	—	tsetse
k	cry	clay	cure	queen	—	—	—	—	—
b	bray	blue	beauty	bwana[2]	—	—	—	—	—
d	dray	—	duty[1]	dwell	—	—	—	Dvořák	—
g	gray	glue	gules[3]	Gwen	—	—	—	—	—
f	free	flea	few	—	—	—	—	—	—
θ	three	—	thew[1]	thwack	—	—	—	—	—
s	—	slay	suit[1]	sweet	smoke	snow	sphere	—	—
ʃ	shrimp	shlock	—	Schwartz	schmuck	shnook	—	shvartse[4]	—
v	—	—	view	—	—	—	—	—	—
h	—	—	hue[5]	which[5]	—	—	—	—	—
m	—	—	muse	—	—	—	—	—	—
n	—	—	new[1]	—	—	—	—	—	—
l	—	—	lute[1]	—	—	—	—	—	—

Notes

1. For some dialects: British ones typically have /tjuːn/, etc.; most U.S. /tuːn/. The alveolar + /j/ seem to be rarest with /l/: very few speakers now distinguish *loot* and *lute*.
2. In a scatter of foreign words only. Labial + /w/ is not an English pattern.
3. As far as I know, the only word with /gj-/.
4. /ʃC-/ clusters define a special Yiddish/German subset for some speakers; only a few items like *schmaltz* (musical or artistic) are of general currency.
5. Many speakers (especially British) do not have phonetic [hj-], but a palatal fricative [ç] (as in German *ich*); such dialects could be said to have a separate phoneme /ç/, parallel to the /w̥/ in dialects that contrast *witch* : *which*. Conversely, if [ç] can be /hj/, then [w̥] could be /hw/.

Note that quite a number of these are highly restricted, e.g. to foreign items only, like /dv bw/. And /sf/ occurs only in Greek loans, e.g. *sphere* and its derivatives, and a few others like *sphinx, sphincter, sphagnum*. If we make the assumption that proper names aren't really 'words' in the normal sense, then /dv ʃw/ drop out.

The constraints on CCC- clusters are even tighter. C_1 is always /s/, C_2 a voiceless stop, and C_3 one of /r l j/:

(3.14)

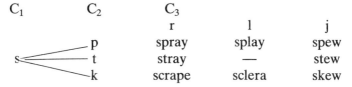

C_1	C_2	C_3		
		r	l	j
	p	spray	splay	spew
s	t	stray	—	stew
	k	scrape	sclera	skew

/stl/ is excluded on the same principle as /tl dl/ in (3.13); speakers with /tj-/ in *tune* will have /stj-/ in *stew*, otherwise /st-/. Only a few Greek words have /skl-/ (all as far as I can tell derivatives of *sklēros* 'hard').

The exclusions in (3.12–14) are clearly not necessary. Even if clusters like (say) /ml-/ seem outlandish or 'unpronounceable' to an English speaker, they are not to speakers of Polish (*mleko* 'milk'). And even other Germanic languages are happy with clusters impossible for English, e.g. Afrikaans /kn-/ in *knie* 'knee'. Indeed, a number of now 'un-English' combinations were normal in earlier times: OE had /wl-/ (*wlite* 'face'), /wr-/ (*wrītan* 'to write': the /w/ here did not disappear until well into the 17th century), /kn-/ (*cnēo* 'knee'), /fn-/ (*fnæst* 'breath'). In cases like *write* and *knee*, spelling, as is often the case, lags centuries behind pronunciation. (Some modern dialects incidentally have /tl- dl-/ in *clean, glove,* etc. – mainly in rural Cumbria; these exclude /kl- gl-/. And /sr/ occurs for /ʃr/ in some southern coastal U.S. dialects.)

Turning our attention to codas, it looks as if many more cluster types are legal: stop + fricative (*apse, adze*), nasal + stop (*limp, lint, link*), nasal + fricative (*bronze, ponce, hams*), nasal +fricative + stop (*rinsed* /rɪnst/), nasal + stop + fricative (*pants*) – even nasal + stop + fricative + stop (*glimpsed* /glɪmpst/). But most of the more complex clusters are of a special type: they are morphologically complex as well. The final consonants in *rinsed, pants, glimpsed* are all grammatical endings. *Apse* and *adze*, for instance, seem to be the only common English monosyllables with stop + fricative codas that do not have a grammatical boundary between the two consonants: much more typical would be *cap-s, add-s*. Similarly, most stop + stop codas (except for *act, apt, inept* and a few others) are also morphologically complex; the characteristic type would be *crack-ed, crapp-ed,* etc., where the /t/ is a verbal past marker.

Even given the differences between onsets and codas, though, certain general constraints apply to both. For instance, clusters of obstruents always agree in voicing: they are either all voiceless like /sp st pst/ or all voiced like /bz dz gd/. Further, no two members of the sibilant class /s z ʃ ʒ tʃ dʒ/ may cluster. In addition, no two stops at the same place of articulation may cluster; it would seem that this follows from the voicing rule (e.g. */td/, */dt/ would be ruled out by that); but there is a further complication, in that while according to the voicing rule */tt/, */dd/ would be legal, there is also a constraint against self-clustering (mentioned above in relation to onsets). We'll see one implication of this below. (A very marginal exception to the voicing rule appears to occur in those dialects that have /-dθ/ rather than /-tθ/ in *width, breadth*.)

These restrictions have repercussions on the phonological shape of certain grammatical endings – an illustration of the overall coherence and interrelatedness of the components of a linguistic system. Consider the plurals of regular nouns, the present 3 sg of verbs, and the past tense of weak verbs:

(3.15)

Noun Pl	Coda Cluster	Verb 3 sg	Coda Cl	Verb Past	Coda Cl
cat-s	/t-s/	hit-s	/t-s/	walk-ed	/k-t/
dog-s	/d-z/	dig-s	/g-z/	nabb-ed	/b-d/
fish-es	/ʃ-ɪz/	bash-es	/ʃ-ɪz/	wound-ed	/d-ɪd/

That is, the 'sibilant suffix' (noun plural, verb 3 sg) agrees in voicing with a preceding obstruent (except a sibilant); if there is a sibilant, a vowel is inserted between the two, so an illegal cluster will not arise. The same principle applies to the verbal past: as long as the two final stops disagree in place of articulation, the only constraint is agreement in voicing; if they are both alveolars, the past suffix takes a vowel, just like the plural after a sibilant. (With sonorants, of course, there is more freedom, since the possibilities of legal clustering are greater; thus while voicing is normal for the past after nasals and liquids as in *climbed, filled*, there are alternants like *dreamed ~ dreamt, smelled ~ smelt*, etc.)

The identity of the rhyme is again defined by cooccurrence restrictions between segments; though here some more complex issues arise, bearing both on the long/short split in the vowel system and the distribution of stress (§3.4 below). First, it is notable that a stressed syllable with an empty coda may not have a short vowel: the minimal short-vowel rhyme is -VC (*cat*). A stressed syllable may however contain a long vowel or diphthong alone (*see, how*). I.e., given the model of syllable-structure we have been using, the rhyme-types (a), (b) below are allowed, but not (c):

(3.16)

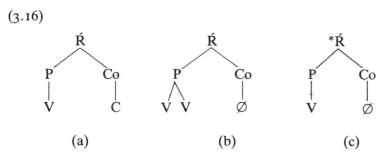

(a)   (b)   (c)

This applies only to stressed syllables; we will return to the reason for this in the next section, as well as to the influence of rhyme shape on stress.

Within the rhyme itself there are certain cooccurrence restrictions; e.g. in most dialects long vowels may not occur before /ŋ/ (though some U.S. ones have /ɔ:/ in *song*, etc.); and for non-northern dialects the diphthong /aʊ/ may not occur before labials (/p b f v m/) or velars (/k g/). Otherwise there are few restrictions within the rhyme itself: there are no general constraints controlling vowel length and coda complexity as in some languages; both long and short vowels occur before complex clusters (*mists, beasts*).

It is the rhyme as a whole that plays a major role in phonological organization; and at this point we must introduce a new terminological distinction that will enable us to characterize this. This is the distinction between light and heavy rhymes (and by extension, light and heavy syllables). Consider the rhyme of *cat* vs. those of *cast, key*:

(3.17)

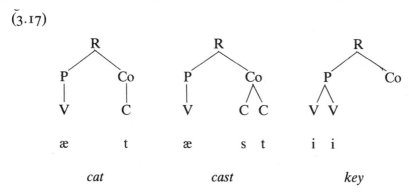

cat   cast   key

A rhyme like that of *cat*, which branches only at the topmost level, is light; one that branches at the next level – i.e. has either a complex peak or a complex coda (or both) – is heavy. As we will see in the next section, there is a tendency in English for stress to be attracted to heavy rhymes.

This distinction played a more important part in the earlier history of English than it does now: for instance certain classes of nouns in Old English took nominative plural endings only if their first syllables were light; otherwise they were endingless. Thus light *hof-u* 'dwellings' vs. heavy *wīf* 'women', *word* 'words'. That is, -VCC and -VVC form a class opposed to -VC. (It is important to distinguish between length – a durational property of segments – and quantity or weight – a structural property of syllables. Segments may be short or long; syllables are light or heavy. I raise this terminological point because many older works tend to use 'long' and 'short' for both length and quantity, and this can be confusing: you get 'long syllables with short vowels', etc.)

We might add that a rhyme that does not branch at all at any level – as in the first syllable of *alone* – is also light. This type is excluded from stressed position in English, as we have seen; the reasons may become clearer in the next section.

3.4 Rhythmic Organization: Stress

Every English word in isolation has a particular stress-pattern: one syllable is more 'prominent' than the other(s). Let us mark stressed syllables S (strong) and unstressed syllables W (weak). Then *carriage, hurry* are SW; *believe, prefer* are WS; *character, delicate* are SWW; *Johannesburg, perennial* are WSWW, etc. The prominence of a stressed syllable may be achieved in a number of ways: in relation to an unstressed syllable, a stressed one may be longer, louder, higher or lower in pitch, show greater pitch-movement – or any combination of these. In most SBE, Ss tend to be louder, longer and higher than Ws; in Northern Irish English and Danish they are louder, longer and lower. The only 'universal' requirement is that Ss be different from Ws, and that this difference be perceived as a difference in prominence. Thus stress is a relational category: a stressed syllable is S not by virtue of any particular absolute property, but in comparison to a W. Stress in this sense might be said to be a kind of 'foregrounding' of particular syllables: an S is defined as such by its difference from an adjacent W.

Ss in spoken English tend to occur at roughly equal intervals in time; there is a degree of isochrony. E.g. in a pair like *wood/wooden, wood* as a whole is approximately the same length as *wooden* (the vowels in the latter are shorter). English then is a so-called 'stress-timed' language (like most of the rest of Germanic) – as opposed to 'syllable-timed' languages like French, where what could be called the rhythmic 'beat' is defined by the recurrences of syllables, not stresses. The rhythmic organization of a language then is that set of principles that defines the occurrence in time of some basic unit; in English, rhythm is primarily a matter of the succession and juxtaposition of Ss and Ws. And the basic unit of organization is the foot. We will define a foot as a unit made of a stressed syllable plus anything to its right before the next stress. Thus *wood* is a monosyllabic foot, *wooden* a disyllabic, *character* a trisyllabic, and so on. And above word-level, a sequence like *Johnny ate a poisoned mushroom* is a sequence of four feet: *Johnny, ate a, poisoned, mushroom* – each as it happens SW. We could represent it as:

(3.18)

Thus the foot does not necessarily coincide with the word – or even the syntactic constituent, as *ate a* makes clear: this latter is a 'unit' on the rhythmic level only. (In a natural reading of (3.18), you will notice that some SW feet are as wholes more prominent than others: probably the last is the most prominent. We will take up this problem below.)

But if stress is defined as essentially a relation, how do we represent a monosyllabic foot, like e.g. *ate*, in isolation? If it were simply marked S, there would be nothing for the S to contrast with. This appears to be merely a notational problem; but one proposed solution to it enables us to capture some interesting relations among items that might not seem related. This is the rather abstract notion of the 'zero syllable'. If we take it that the minimal 'normal' foot is a sequence S̄W, where both S and W contain phonological material, then a zero-syllable is an 'empty W' after a monosyllabic S, which is normally filled by an extension in time of the S. I.e. S and W together constitute a 'norm' for a disyllabic foot. Thus the rough temporal equality of *wood* and *wooden* mentioned above would be characterized as:

(3.19)

This gives us a motivation for the frequent attachment of reduced low-stress items to preceeding monosyllables, as in *would not → wouldn't, have to* → *hafta* (cf. *wooden, rafter*). That is:

(3.20)

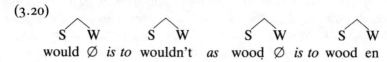

Feet may however have a more complex structure, with 'layers' of prominences. Take a form like *character*, where even though the overall pattern is S W W, there is a sense in which the ŜW unit *charac-* is as a whole more prominent than *-ter*. We could represent it naturally this way:

(3.21)

I introduce this notion of 'layering' because of a complication that needs some discussion. The presentation so far claims merely that any syllable in English is either S or W; but in fact there are 'degrees' of stress, which are often of linguistic importance. To take a simple example, both *black* and *bird* in isolation are monosyllabic ŜW feet, with zero W. But in the compound *blackbird* and the noun phrase *black bird*, the overall stress patterns are respectively ŜW and ŴS: yet it's not the case that either *bird* in *blackbird* or *black* in *black bird* is 'unstressed'. This can be seen easily by comparing them to unambiguous ŜW and ŴS feet like *blacker* and *believe*.

A representation of these four items will make clear what the differences really are:

(3.22)

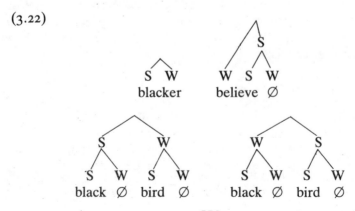

That is: *blacker* is only $\widehat{SW}$; but in *blackbird*, the full stress on *bird* is subordinated to that of a *black* at a higher structural level: in traditional terms, *black* has 'primary stress' and *bird* has 'secondary stress'. These terms are in fact rather unrevealing, since what's involved is not separate categories, but the same mechanism and the same two elements, S and W. And the same analysis applies in reverse to *believe* and *black bird*.

These examples illustrate two major facts about English stress: (a) that prominences can be greater or lesser depending on higher-level structure; and (b) that stress is not a purely phonological category, but interacts with syntax and morphology as well. Both points are worth some comment.

(a) Even within the word – even within the disyllabic word – there can be distinctions of primary vs. secondary vs. lack of stress. Compare the contours of *rabbit* and *rabbi*. Both are '$\widehat{SW}$'; but in *rabbit*, the W is weaker in relation to the S than it is in *rabbi*; *rabbit* has a reduced, centralized vowel in its W, *rabbi* has a full diphthong. We could represent them as:

(3.23)

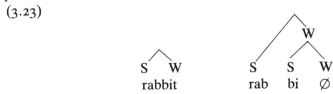

That is, *rabbi* has a 'complex W' which contains an S (exactly the same structure, in fact, as *blackbird*); only this S is weakened by a superposed W.

The purely segmental structure of *rabbi* should in fact have predicted something of the sort, since the final syllable with its unreduced diphthong [aɪ] is heavy, as opposed to the light [ɪt] of *rabbit*, and it is a general property of English that you don't get fully unstressed heavy syllables. The shape [ræbaɪ] should suggest that the second syllable couldn't be merely a W.

This way of looking at things suggests that we can now reformulate the prohibition against short vowels in stressed final open syllables (§3.2.3). The constraint can be expressed in rhythmic terms: no foot-initial syllable can terminate in a short vowel. And this also predicts that in disyllabic forms where the first syllable ends in a vowel and the second begins with one, and the two syllables constitute a foot, the first vowel will be long: *neon, briar, faïence, bowie* (knife), *Louis*. What appear to be purely phonotactic constraints on sequences of phoneme types can be referred to higher-level rhythmic structures.

(b) In *blackbird* vs. *black bird*, the stress contour is determined by fairly general rules, often called respectively the Compound Stress Rule

(CSR) and the Nuclear Stress Rule (NSR). These go roughly as follows:

> (i) CSR. Any structure A B where A, B are separate words has
> the contour SW if it is – as a whole – a lexical category (i.e. a
> noun, verb or adjective). Thus *blackbird, skin-dive, dog-like*
> are S͡W.
>
> (ii) NSR. Any structure A B where A, B are separate words
> has the contour W S if it is – as a whole – a phrasal category (i.e.
> a construction like Noun Phrase, Verb Phrase, Sentence). Thus
> *black bird* (NP), *loves Mary* (VP), *Sam died* (S) are W͡S.

There are many complications, problems, and exceptions; but the
overall point holds, and is important. That is, prominence in English at
levels above the single word is sensitive to syntax. (Even at word level it
can be: compare S W nouns like *suspect, torment* with the corresponding
verbs.)

So at these higher levels anyhow, stress is to a considerable extent
predictable: there are general rules that assign contours to words in
combination. Thus in a sentence like *the blackbird was sitting on the
fence*, while each word has its own stress pattern, the phrases themselves
have their own higher patterns. To take one example, *blackbird* is S W,
but *the blackbird*, being a phrase, is W S:

(3.24)

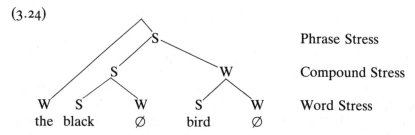

	Phrase Stress
	Compound Stress
	Word Stress

And similarly, *fence* will probably have the highest stress in the whole
sequence, because it in turn is the right-hand member of a higher phrasal
category – the sentence. And so on.

This discussion applies of course only to 'neutral' utterances, i.e. those
with no particular emphasis. Contours like those in **John** *died* (*not Sam*),
the *blackbird* (*not a blackbird*), etc. are possible. But these have special
motivations within the discourse, and in fact are only interpretable (or
noticeable) because of the fact that they violate the 'normal' patterns.

The stress contours of word sequences are, then, apparently controlled by the syntax. We ought now to see what the situation is at word-
level, i.e. whether word stress is controlled by any general principles like
the NSR or CSR, or whether it's completely unpredictable, or 'free'. At
first glance the patterns are so diverse that they seem random: *phýsic* vs.

physique, cháracter vs. *coróna*, etc. But there are a number of major generalizations – enough so that it makes sense to talk of a basic stress rule for English words, usually called the Main Stress Rule (MSR). It's a matter of technical controversy just how far-reaching the MSR is (i.e. whether all stresses are rule-governed); the topic is extremely complex, and not suitable for a treatment like this. (See notes to this section.) All I can do here is sketch some of the central regularities in the English stress system; exceptions will no doubt come to mind, but this does not destroy the validity of the regularities that constitute a kind of core.

A stress rule, given the model we've been using here, is in essence a procedure for constructing feet; obviously if a syllable gets marked S, anything to its right will be W. For readers unfamiliar with the technical sense of 'rule' in linguistics, a rule can be regarded as a set of instructions which takes a string of elements as input, and does something to these elements which produces an altered output, in a predictable way. We will operate here on the assumption that for the most part English words do not have to be marked for stress; the stress rule will accept as input a string of phonemes organized into syllables, and will produce a stress contour.

English stress is sensitive to two main properties of syllables: (a) their distance from the end of the word, and (b) their weight (whether they are light or heavy: cf. §3.3). That is, the MSR scans a word from the right, and also looks at the weight of the syllables it encounters. With monosyllables there is obviously no problem: the stress rule simply assigns an S to the syllable, and a zero W to its right, creating an SW foot. Since the zero W isn't stressable, all monosyllables get the one possible pattern.

But with disyllables we get both SW (*physic*) and WS (*physique*). To take a representative list:

(3.25)

(a) SW: (i) cattle, baggage, slalom, finish, bosom
        (ii) carcass, carton, basic, consul, China

(b) WS: (i) physique, careen, cartoon, delay, carouse
        (ii) collect, prevent, disturb, usurp, arrest

Consider group (b) first. These all have heavy final syllables, -VV(C) in (i), and -VCC in (ii). And all are WS. So the first part of the MSR seems to be:

(3.26)

MSR, 1: Stress the final syllable if it's heavy

(A special set of exceptions involves certain consonant clusters mainly in nouns: *locust, mollusc, ballast* are SW instead of expected WS, as are inflected forms where a suffix produces a cluster, as in *cover-s, suffer-ed*; here the MSR apparently takes the final consonant as 'extrametrical', and disregards it. On 'skipping', see below.)

Group (a) has light finals (-V or -VC); subgroup (i) has light first syllables, (ii) heavy. But both take stress on the penult. So to (3.26) we add:

(3.27)

MSR, 2: If the final syllable is light, go back one to the penult and stress it, regardless of weight.

Obviously (3.27) is a kind of 'default' clause: there's no other syllable to stress. But it's actually part of a larger pattern, as we can see if we look at polysyllables. Here – pretty much regardless of actual syllable count – the options are -WSW (*arena, Catalina*) and -SWW (*catheter, anthropology*). Consider:

(3.28)

(a) -WSW: angina, arena, collector, dispenser, Catalina
(b) -SWW: (i) catheter, buggery, drosophila, anthropology
            (ii) harmony, ultimate, lexicon, philanthropy

This looks very like the disyllable case: if the final is light, go back to the penult; if this is heavy, stress it (*arena, Catalina*). Thus *arena* is in principle stressed the same way as *China* – the first heavy syllable from the end receives S. If however the penult is light, as in (3.28(b)), the procedure is repeated: we move one to the left again, and stress whatever is there, either heavy (as in b.ii) or light (as in b.i). Thus *anthropology* is stressed in the same way as *catheter* or *ultimate*. All this is controlled by an overriding principle: stress, where possible, should not come more than three syllables from the end. I.e. the largest well-formed foot within the word generally has no more than two Ws in it. All of this can be summed up informally in the following two principles:

(3.29)

(a) Stress falls on the rightmost heavy syllable in the word.
(b) The search for a heavy syllable is restricted to the last three syllables.

Perhaps a comparison of a number of types will make this clearer:

(3.30)

W	W	S	W	W
		scene	Ø	
	ca	reen	Ø	
A	ber	deen	Ø	
		Chin	a	
	an	gin	a	
Cat	a	lin	a	
		fun	er	al
anth	ro	pol	o	gy

(Only the last shows an S on a light syllable.) Stress also interacts with prefixation and suffixation in complex words: see §4.8.4.

3.5 Excursus: Stress and Syllable Division

We have said nothing so far about a rather difficult problem: there are heavy and light syllables, but how do we tell, given a consonant cluster between two vowels within a word, which of the syllables it belongs to? Or even a single consonant, for that matter. E.g. where do we divide in say *butter*, *aster*, *athlete*, to take three examples to start with? *Athlete*, for instance: in principle we could syllabify *a-thlete*, *ath-lete*, or *athl-ete*. (In this section we are not talking about purely written conventions for dividing words at line-ends; these may have nothing to do with phonological syllable structure, which is our topic here.)

If we take it that any syllable in a polysyllabic word ought to be well formed by the general principles that govern monosyllables (since a monosyllabic word is by definition a well-formed syllable), then to begin with *a-thlete* is out: we recall the general rule that a foot-initial syllable may not end in a short vowel. Therefore either *ath-lete* or *athl-ete* must be right. If we look at the rules for English onsets and codas (§3.3), we find that /θl/ is not a possible onset or coda: so we have two reasons for barring *a-thlete* and one for barring *athl-ete*. The syllabification must be *ath-lete* $[_1æθ]_1$ $[_2li:t]_2$. (We will use brackets with subscript numerals to indicate syllables.)

The same strategy will serve for *butter*: /bʌ/ is out because of the restriction on foot-initials, and this apparently leaves us with $[_1bʌt]_1$ $[_2ər]_2$. But does it? Consider the apparently analogous case of *beater*. If we divide $[_1bi:]_1$ $[_2tər]_2$ we get two well-formed syllables; and if we divide $[_1bi:t]_1$ $[_2ər]_2$ we do as well. The answer in such a case is to take the medial consonant as ambisyllabic, i.e. as belonging to both syllables: hence *beater* will be syllabified $[_1bi[_2t]_1ər]_2$. That is, the /t/ belongs both to the coda of the first syllable and the onset of the second. Perhaps a tree representation will clarify:

(3.31)

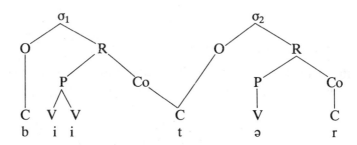

The same would hold for *butter*. Clusters can be ambisyllabic as well. A good case is the type /sp st sk/, which make legal onsets and codas. A word like *aster* would have the whole /st/ cluster belonging to both the first and second syllables: $[_1æ[_2st]_1ər]_2$.

This way of dividing syllables, according to whether the onsets and codas formed at the junction of two syllables are allowed or not, can straighten out some apparent anomalies in stress assignment, by clarifying the weight of given syllables.

Take for instance *álgebra* and *comménsal*: why should these be stressed differently? If stress is assigned on the basis of syllable weight as I suggested in the last section, then *commensal* must have a heavy penult and *algebra* a light one. Looked at in purely linear terms, this appears not to be the case: the last two syllables in both forms contain the sequence -VCCV-. But if we look at the syllable division, it's clear that -CC- in *commensal* can form the coda of a syllable: /ns/ as in *bounce*, *ponce*. Therefore the orthographic sequence -*ens*- represents the rhyme of a heavy syllable. But in *algebra*, the sequence -*ebr*- can't; the division must be between /b/ and /r/, so that the /b/ belongs to the coda of one syllable and the /r/ to the onset of the next. Hence the penult is -VC-, i.e. light. The syllabifications of the two forms are thus: $[_1æl[_2dʒ]_1ə[_3b]_2rə]_3$ and $[_1kə[_2m]_1ɛn[_3s]_2əl]_3$. (If the complicated ambisyllabicity is disturbing, look at the previous section again; all the divisions correspond to the principles introduced there.)

3.6 Latin and Germanic Stress

The reader who has studied Latin in any detail will by this point probably recognize the MSR: it is virtually the rule for Latin accent-placement (see the pronunciation section of any good Latin grammar). And the reader with any etymological knowledge will note that most of the examples I've used in the last two sections are loans – Latin, Greek or Latin and Greek via French. The MSR in its present form is of course a relatively late development in English: it came in along with borrowed vocabulary.

The pervasiveness of the essentially Latinate MSR seems to contradict the rather emphatic case I made in §2.7 for the Norman Conquest (and by implication loans in general) having a very minor structural effect on English. The central stress rule now appears to be borrowed, and in fact to govern native vocabulary as well (*cattle*, *bosom*, *butter*, *believe*, *Easter*). But this is more apparent than real: the Germanic vocabulary is governed by the Latin rule only by default – because virtually all of it falls under an older Germanic stress rule which while quite different in principle happens to coincide with a section of the MSR applicable to disyllables.

To see how this works, let's look at the way stress functioned in the quite purely Germanic Old English system. Old English stress was assigned by what we can call the Germanic Stress Rule (GSR) – one of the defining features of the IE-Proto-Gmc transition (§1.3). To recapitulate and expand: the GSR was essentially a rule of initial stress, which managed to produce final stress as well, as follows:

(3.32)

(i) Stress the first syllable of any lexical root, whether in isolation or in a compound; stress those prefixes specified as stressable; all other syllables are W, including all other prefixes.

(ii) Assign the contour S W to any sequence S S produced by (i).

To make this more concrete: disyllables like *fæder* 'father', *hūsas* 'houses' are SW; trisyllables like *loppestre* 'lobster', *wunian* 'to dwell' are SWW; prefixed forms with unstressable prefixes like *be-foran* 'before', *ge-feoht* 'fight' are WS – all by clause (i):

(3.33)

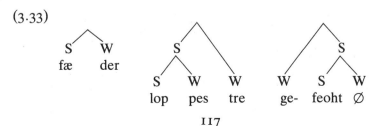

(Note that the simple exclusion of certain prefixes from the foot formed by the GSR in effect produces the same contour as the modern MSR applied to a word with a heavy final syllable: *ge-feoht* is like *arrest*.)

On the other hand, forms with stressed prefixes and compounds have their rightmost S weakened by the overall S W contour that is imposed on any sequence of two equal stresses: thus for *and-saca* 'apostate', *or-þanc* 'mind' with prefixes, and *hron-rād* 'whale-riding' (= sea), *gamol-feax* 'old-haired': (= gray-haired):

(3.34)

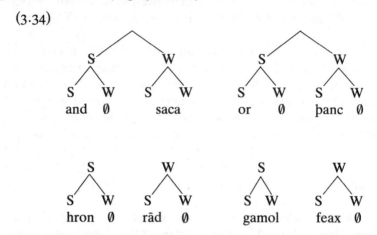

The GSR pays no attention to syllable weight; and most importantly, from the historical point of view, it starts at the other end of the word from the MSR – it works left-to-right, not right-to-left. Accentually, English has changed its 'handedness' over time. The reason the MSR and GSR tend to coincide for native vocabulary is simple: (a) very few native non-compound words are longer than one or two syllables; (b) there are very few heavy non-initial syllables in OE. Thus the penulti-mate stress-assigning parts of the MSR cover nearly all cases. In fact nearly the only modern forms of Germanic origin with final stress are from OE forms with unstressed prefixes: *before, behind, above, with-stand* (OE *be-foran, be-hindan, on-būfan, wiþ-standan*). And the modern compound stress rule is of course the same as the OE one.

3.7 Allegro Speech

Fast speech processes seem to vary less across dialects than phoneme inventories, and to some extent allophonic rules – partly because they are to a large degree controlled by the physical properties of the vocal tract, and their interaction with tempo. In this section we'll look briefly at some major allegro modifications in an SBE-related dialect, which seem to me to be highly characteristic.

In rapid casual speech (which might untraditionally but more accurately be called simply 'normal speech') a number of things happen: final segments of words come into contact with the initials of following words, creating new combinations; boundaries are blurred, so that separate words tend to cohere into rhythmic groups (e.g. a sequence like *in Cape Town*, rather than being preposition + NP, will be simply a WSW prosodic unit like *believer*: see below). In addition, the inherent stresses of less important items will weaken, leading to vowel reduction (vowels becoming [ə] or something similar); the 'fine tuning' of carefully monitored speech is relaxed, since attention is focussed on the message and the social setting, not on speech itself; what counts in normal discourse is communication with maximal ease in the least time possible. This all results in a tendency to what might be called 'efficiency': less informative items are pronounced less carefully, or even dropped; single articulatory gestures are substituted for sequences of different ones.

These phenomena surface under three main headings (examples below):

(i) *Assimilations*. Single articulatory configurations are maintained as long as possible, and complex ones are simplified. Thus we get apparent 'replacement' of one segment by another, adjacent ones tending to become more similar or even identical. Any feature can be affected: in English most commonly place of articulation, glottal state (voicing or lack of it), and nasality.

(ii) *Weakening (Lenition)*. This is a cover-term for a number of different but related processes, including voicing of voiceless segments, opening of stricture (stops become fricatives, fricatives lose their friction), reduction of vowels, and loss of oral articulation (e.g. stops become glottal stops, fricatives become [h]).

(iii) *Deletion*. What it looks like: loss of segments. In English allegro speech this happens most commonly at the end of a word, especially with consonants; though as we will see below, vowels can get lost as well.

As an example, let's look at a short passage, read by a native speaker (myself, as it happens) in two styles: once very carefully with all words separated ('Lento'), and once in the most casual possible conversational style ('Allegro'), to illustrate both ends of the continuum. (The vowel-transcription is somewhat simplified and normalized here, to avoid the reader having to focus on irrelevant details; for a better transcription for this dialect see §4.8.2.)

(3.35)

(1) TEXT: The next time you're in Cape Town,why don't you
    LENTO: ðə nɛkst tʰaɪmjuːr ɪn kʰɛɪp tʰæʊn ʍaɪ dəʊnt juː
    ALLEGRO: nːɛkstaɪm   juɪŋkʰɛɪptæʊn   ʍaɪ dəʊntʃuː

(2) TEXT: go to   Woolie's and see if you can get me a
    LENTO: gəʊ tʰuː wʊliːz ænd siː ɪf juː kʰæn gɛt miː ə
    ALLEGRO: gəʊʃə wʊliːz n̩ siəf juxŋgɛpmiə

(3) TEXT: nice pair of shoes. And just have a look at their clothes
    LENTO: naɪs pʰɛər əv ʃuːz ænd dʒʌst hæv ə lʊk æt ðɛər kl̥əʊðz
    ALLEGRO: naɪs pʰɛər ə ʃuːz n̩ dʒʌs hæv ə lʊk ət̪n̪ðɛər kl̥əʊz

Assimilations are frequent: nasals assimilate to following stops (*in Cape* (1), *can get* (2)); stops do the same thing (*at their* (3), *get me* (2)); and in reverse, the final [n] of *can* (2) assimilates to a preceding velar (see below). There are also complex assimilations, as in *don't you* (1), where alveolar + palatal 'fuse' into a 'compromise' segment, a palato-alveolar. (Historically, this kind of assimilation is responsible for the /tʃ/ in *Christian*, the /dʒ/ in *soldier*, and the /ʒ/ in *vision*: originally /tj dj zj/ (§3.10)). This is an instance of the very common process whereby allegro rules gradually 'move up' over time into lento styles, and become general, not tied to the speech situation.)

Weakenings show up as well: vowel reductions (*you're* (1), *to* (2), *if* (2), *at* (3)); we also get voicing of [t] (*go to* (2)) and change of stop to fricative (*can* (2)).

Deletions are also common: *next time* (1), *and* (2), *can* (2), *of* (3), *just* (3), *clothes* (3). It seems that overall alveolars delete most frequently in English.

There are also complex cases where a number of processes interact even in the realization of a single word. Consider [xŋ] for *can* (2): here the original [kʰ] has weakened to a fricative, the vowel has been deleted, its syllabicity has been transferred to the nasal, and the nasal has assimilated to the initial consonant. Another complex case occurs in *the next* (1), where [ðə] has lost its vowel and assimilated to the [n] of *next*, giving a long [nː] – a segment type that we know 'doesn't occur in English'. This points up one of the most interesting effects of casual speech: the creation of sequences that in lento speech – according to what we would normally take to be 'the rules of English' – can't occur. Other typical examples I have come across elsewhere are [tsiːmz] 'it seems', [pstə] 'Mr', [pxɔːz] 'because', [fnɛtɪks] 'phonetics': all of these violate restrictions on English onset-clusters (cf. §3.3), and all are quite common.

Looked at in cold blood, the modifications are so radical that it's hard to imagine a text containing a lot of them would be comprehensible; yet casual speech is characteristically modified in this way. The reason it can be processed without difficulty is that speakers 'know the rules' for converting lento representations into allegro ones; they can 're-synthesize' them, given an allegro input. It is in fact typical for an untrained speaker hearing a modified allegro sequence to be quite convinced that he heard the lento form. And for a speaker pronouncing an allegro form to insist that he's produced a lento form.

3.8 Origins, 1: The Old English Period

This and the following two sections are a somewhat breathless romp through the history of English phonology, with a special eye on systems and their shapes. The focus will be on the major changes: this is not even a potted history, really, but a selection of milestones, a look over our shoulder at the chief transformations that have led from Old English to the present-day situation detailed in the previous sections.

Old English in the 9th century had the following phonological inventory:

(3.36)

(a) VOWELS:

	SHORT	LONG	DIPHTHONGAL
	i y u	iː yː uː	æɑ æɑː
	e ø o	eː øː oː	eo eoː
	æ ɑ	æː ɑː	

(b) CONSONANTS:

	Labial	Dental	Alveolar	Palato-Alveolar	Palatal	Velar
STOP	p(ː)		t(ː)			k(ː)
	b(ː)		d(ː)			g(ː)
FRICATIVE	f(ː)	θ(ː)	s(ː)	ʃ		x(ː)
AFFRICATE				tʃ(ː)		
				dʒ(ː)		
NASAL	m(ː)		n(ː)			
LIQUID	w		r(ː), l(ː)		j	

A number of details are worth noting: (a) the vowel systems, both short and long, are much more symmetrical than in modern English; further, the two inventories are identical; (b) there are contrasting long and short diphthongs (the latter patterning with – and eventually merging with – the short vowels: see below); (c) both consonants and vowels can be either short or long; (d) the diphthongs are not of the modern 'closing' type in /-i, -u/, but both elements agree in height; (e) there is no phonemic /h/ ([h] as we will see is an allophone of /x/);

(f) while the stops are paired for voice, there is only one set of fricative phonemes, and these are voiceless; (g) there is no phonemic velar nasal: [ŋ] is an allophone of /n/ before /k, g/.

Some long consonants are original (of PIE or PGmc date), e.g. the /l:/ in *full* 'full' < */fuln-a-z/, where /ln/ assimilates to /l:/ (cf. L *plēn-u-s* for the two consonants); but may arise from a prehistoric change called West Germanic Gemination (§1.4). In this change, a consonant (except /r/) ending a light syllable and preceding /j/ (or occasionally other liquids or nasals) lengthened: thus Go *sat-jan* 'to set' without WGG vs. OS *sett-ian*, OE *sett-an* (OS still shows the /j/, spelled *i*). All of these are from PGmc */sɑt-jan-ɑm/ (on the PGmc infinitive see §4.5.5). This led to a type of alternation now impossible in any WGmc dialect: long vs. short of the same consonant. E.g. in certain weak verbs, those members of the paradigm with historical /j/ following the stem end up with long stem-final consonants, while those without it have short ones: *sett-an*, pres part *sett-ende*, pres 1 sg *sett-e* vs. past 1 sg *set-e-de*, past part *ge-set-ed*.

The difference in vowels between Go *satjan* with /ɑ/ and OE, OS with /e/ is due to a later and very important change, in which non-initial /i, j/ altered certain preceding vowels. This is usually called *i*-umlaut. 'Umlaut' does not mean the two dots on top of a letter as in G *schön*; these are called 'umlauts' (inaccurately), but are merely diacritic symbols indicating specific vowel qualities due to the historical change of that name. Umlaut, technically, is 'regressive vowel harmony': assimilation of a vowel to a vowel or vowel-like segment in a following syllable. *I*-umlaut is a post-PGmc change, affecting all dialects except Gothic, with the following effects: back vowels become front, and low front vowels raise before /i, j/.

The motivation for this can be seen in the diagram below:

(3.37)

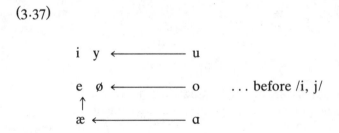

That is, the quality [i] (or [j]) acts as a 'goal' or 'point of attraction' for other vowels, which move toward it on one dimension or another. *I*-umlaut affects both long and short vowels, but the quality changes are more or less the same.

Since there were many environments where /i, j/ followed a stem – especially inflectional and derivational suffixes – umlaut had a widespread effect on OE morphology, traces of which still remain. For instance, certain noun-classes had suffixes of the appropriate type in nom/acc pl, dat sg in WGmc and prehistoric OE: hence paradigms like *mūs* 'mouse' (nom/acc sg), *mȳs* (dat sg, nom/acc pl), likewise *fōt/fēt* ('foot/feet'), where *ē* /eː/ is from earlier /øː/ (see below). Thus modern *mouse/mice, foot/feet*. The nominalizing suffix */-iθu/, which converted adjectives to nouns, also caused umlaut: hence OE *strang* 'strong', *strengþu* 'strength', likewise *lang* 'long' and *lengþu*, and – with some other changes intervening – modern *foul/filth* < *fūl/fȳlþe*. The suffix */-jan/ was also used to form derived verbs from nouns, adjectives, and other verbs: hence *trum* 'strong'/*trymman* 'to strengthen' < */trum-, trum-jɑn/, *talu* 'tale'/*tellan* 'to tell', *sagu* 'saying'/*secgan* 'to say', etc.

But for our concerns here the phonological effects of umlaut are more important. The pre-umlaut vowel system was like that in (3.36), minus /y(ː), ø(ː)/; so that part of the process that created new [e(ː), æ(ː)] merely increased the incidence of these vowels. But the umlauting of /u(ː) o(ː)/ created a new vowel type – front rounded – that had not occurred in Germanic before – though it has now become very characteristic.

At first the new vowels were simply allophones of /u(ː) o(ː)/: e.g. */muːs-iz/ 'mice' was phonetically *[myːsiz], */foːt-iz/ 'feet' was *[føːtiz]. The new qualities were predictable, given the following [i]. But at a later period /i j/ that were not in the strong syllable of a foot either dropped or became /e/, and many endings disappeared altogether. This made the new vowel types contrastive, i.e. we have new phonemes. If you drop the endings on the forms cited above, you get minimal pairs like [muːs]/ [myːs], [foːt]/[føːt], which must now be analyzed as /muːs/ vs. /myːs/, etc. At this point the characteristic OE vowel system appears. (The diphthongs had been created earlier by changes of the old Germanic ones, and special OE developments of short vowels in certain contexts that led to the formation of short diphthongs.) But the system was not to remain stable into the ME period.

Neither PGmc nor early OE had any palato-alveolar consonants, and the only palatal was /j/. That is, the stop series had only labials, alveolars and velars; there were no affricates, and the fricatives were only /f θ s x/. But at some point before *i*-umlaut, there was a palatalization, which affected /k g/ (short and long), and probably the cluster /sk/ as well, producing a pair of palatal stops [c ɟ] and the fricative [ʃ]. After umlaut and deletion of /i, j/ there was a process of 'palatal softening', whereby [c] became [tʃ] and [ɟ] became [j], whereupon the latter merged with original /j/.

This sounds complicated (and it is); but it might be cleared up by a look at the histories of some exemplary OE forms, which will show the interaction of the various processes discussed here. The words are *cinn* /tʃin:/ 'chin', *cynn* /kyn:/ 'kin', *fisc* /fiʃ/ 'fish', *gieldan* /jeldɑn/ 'to yield', *gyldan* /gyldɑn/ 'to gild', and *geong* /jung/ 'young':

(3.38)

Pre-OE:	kin:i	kunj-	fisk	geldɑn	guldjɑn	jung
WGG	–	kun:j-	–	–	–	–
Palatalization	cin:i	–	fiʃ	ɟeldɑn[1]	–	–
i-umlaut	–	kyn:j-	–	–	gyldjɑn	–
i/j-deletion	cin:i	kyn:[2]	–	–	gyldɑn	–
Palatal softening	tʃin:	–	–	jeldɑn[3]	–	–
OE sp.	*cinn*	*cynn*	*fisc*	*gieldan*	*gyldan*	*geong*

Notes

1. At this stage [c ɟ] are allophones of /k g/: they are predictable before a front vowel.
2. At this stage /k c g ɟ/ are in contrast, because the triggering environments have vanished, and both velars and palatals can occur before front vowels. Also /y/ is now a separate phoneme, not an allophone of /u/.
3. At this stage /ɟ/ merges with Germanic /j/. This does not hold for long /ɟ:/ which becomes /dʒ:/ by palatal softening, as in *secgan* /sedʒ:ɑn/ 'to say' < /seɟ:ɑn/ < */sɑgjɑn/.

At the end of this series of interacting changes, the consonant system is that in (3.36).

On the consonants in general, there are a few other items of importance. First, note that the system contained only the voiceless fricative phonemes /f θ s ʃ x/; [v ð z] did appear, but only as allophones of /f θ s/ in foot-medial position, if short and not followed by a voiceless consonant. Thus /f/ is [f] in *faran* 'to go', *offrian* 'to offer', *wulf* 'wolf', but [v] in *ofer* 'over', *wulfas* 'wolves'; /θ/ is [θ] in *þā* 'then', *moþþe* 'moth', *oþ* 'until', but [ð] in *ōðer* 'other'; /s/ is [s] in *sellan* 'to sell', *cyssan* 'to kiss', *hūs* 'house', but [z] in *hūsas* 'houses'. (The voiced fricatives became phonemic in Middle English: see §3.9.)

Short /x/ did not occur intervocalically, but only /x:/ as in *hlæhhan* 'to laugh', /xlæx:ɑn/; [h] was the foot-initial allophone of /x/, and became an independent phoneme only in Early Modern English times, when /x/ was lost in other positions.

Toward the end of the OE period, the vowel system was radically transformed, resulting in very different-looking descendant dialects. The changes are exceedingly complex, and vary from dialect to dialect; I will give only the briefest sketch here, concentrating for the most part on the developments in the eastern and southeastern dialects, which formed the basis for London Middle English.

(i) *Changes of Vowel Length.* In PGmc length was pretty much free; in PWGmc short vowels were barred from terminating foot-initial syllables, and this constraint has remained in force ever since (§3.4). But in Old English a number of alterations had begun to occur which gradually restricted the environments where long and short vowels could contrast freely.

(a) In the 9th century short vowels lengthened before a cluster of nasal or liquid plus voiced obstruent (usually a stop) at the same place of articulation. Thus *cild* 'child' > *cīld*, *climban* 'to climb' > *clīmban*, *grund* 'ground' > *grūnd*. (In historical discussions where only length is at issue, I will use the conventional device of marking length in orthographic forms.)

(b) In the 6th–7th centuries, long vowels shortened before -CCC-clusters, and before -CC- in antepenultimate syllables: *gōdspel* 'gospel' > *gŏdspel*, *brǣmblas* 'brambles' > *brǎmblas*; *sāmcucu* 'half-alive' > *sămcucu*, **ǣndleofan* 'eleven' > *ĕndleofan*.

Rule (b) was picked up and generalized in late OE (11th century): shortening now occurred before all -CC- clusters (except those that were by nature ambisyllabic, like /-st-/, which sometimes caused shortening and sometimes didn't), and before a single -C- in antepenults: *cēpte* 'kept' > *cĕpte*, *mētte* 'met' > *mĕtte*; *sūþerne* 'southern' > *sŭþerne*, *hāligdǣg* 'holiday' > *hăligdǣg*. This set of changes is responsible for the dissociation between certain simple and complex forms in modern English: e.g. *keep* with /iː/ from OE /eː/ vs. *kept* with /ɛ/ from OE /e/, *south* with /aʊ/ from OE /uː/ vs. *southern* with /ʌ/ from OE /u/ (on the split of long and short vowel qualities see §3.10).

(ii) *Changes in Vowel Quality.* The shape of the OE system was transformed by, among others, the following:

(a) Monophthongization. The long and short diphthongs monophthongized, the former merging with the long vowels identical to their first elements, the latter with the equivalent short vowels: thus *bēam* /bæaːm/ 'tree', *glǣm* /glæːm/ 'gleam' ended up with /æː/, *eall* /æalː/ 'all', *sæt* /sæt/ 'sat' with /æ/; *hrēod* /xreoːd/ 'reed', *grēne* /greːnə/ 'green' with /eː/; *heorte* /xeortə/ 'heart', *bedd* /bedː/ with /e/, etc. These changes added nothing new to the system, but left it without diphthongs, and increased the statistical incidence of the vowels /æ(ː) e(ː)/.

This picture applies primarily to the northern and eastern (Anglian) dialects; in the West Midlands and Southwest /eo(ː)/ became /ø(ː)/. We will not be concerned with this rather short-lived development, which has no significance for the modern dialects.

(b) Within historical OE times /ø(:)/ had merged with /e(:)/: hence *fēt* 'feet' < /fø:t/. In late OE, /y(:)/ unrounded and merged with /i(:)/ in the relevant areas: hence *bīdan* 'bide', *hȳdan* 'hide' came down into ME with /i:/.

(c) Short /ɑ/ fronted to /a/; then short /æ/ merged with it. Thus OE *bæt* 'bat', *catte* 'cat' come down into ME with /a/.

(d) Long /æ:/ became /ɛ:/ everywhere.

This leaves us at the end of the OE period with a diphthong-free system of this shape:

(3.39)

i:	u:		i	u
e:	o:		e	o
ɛ:				
	ɑ:		a	

3.9 Origins, 2: The Middle English Period

The 12th–14th centuries saw a radical reorganization of the vowel system, producing a new type closer to (though still with major differences from) the modern ones. 'Gaps' in the old system were filled, and a new set of diphthongs developed.

Early on (beginning in the 12th century) OE /ɑ:/ underwent a twofold development: in the non-northern dialects it raised and rounded to /ɔ:/, and in the North it fronted to /a:/. Thus OE *bān* 'bone' was represented in northern ME by /ba:n/, and in the South by /bɔ:n/. Hence – by developments we'll consider in §3.10 – SBE /bəʊn/, Scots /ben/ and Northumbrian /bɪən/. The change of /ɑ:/ created two different long vowel systems; I give them below along with the short vowels, to clarify the relation between the two sets, and set the stage for the next change:

(3.40)

i:	i	u	u:		i:	i	u	u:
e:	e	o	o:		e:	e	o	o:
ɛ:					ɛ:			ɔ:
a:	a						a	
	Northern					Non-Northern		

The final gaps in the long monophthong system were filled by a complex change generally called 'Open Syllable Lengthening' (OSL). In any disyllabic word with an SW stress pattern and a -VC first syllable, the vowel in that syllable lengthened; and if it was not already low, it lowered one height. It is clear from (3.40) that if northern /o/ were to lengthen and lower, it would produce /ɔː/, which the system lacked; and if southern /a/ were to lengthen, it would produce the missing /aː/. The outputs of the change for the rest of the vowels would fall in with segments already there. The effects of OSL are (new vowels circled):

(3.41)

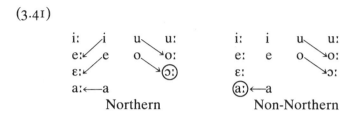

Examples: OE *wicu* /wiku/ 'week' > [weːkə], *mete* /mete/ 'meat' > [mɛːtə], *sama* /sɑmɑ/ 'same' > [saːmə], *duru* /duru/ 'door' > [doːrə], *nosu* /nosu/ 'nose' > [nɔːzə]. Along with lengthening final [ə] began to delete, ultimately leaving northern /ɔː/ and southern /aː/ fully distinctive.

At around the same time, various -VC sequences became the sources of a new set of diphthongs, in two ways: (a) sequences of vowel + [j w ɣ] ([ɣ] was an allophone of /g/ between back vowels) became diphthongs, i.e. [j] > [i] and [w ɣ] > [u]. That is, the consonant became 'vocalized'; or to look at it another way, it migrated from coda to peak of the syllable. Examples are OE *dæg* /dæj/ 'day' > ME *dei, dai* /dai/ (the same with /ej/ as in *weg* 'way'), OE *boga* [boɣɑ] 'bow' > ME *bowe* /bouə/, OE *grōwan* /groːwɑn/ 'grow' > ME *growen* /grouən/. (b) Vowels before /x/ developed offglides: [-u] after back vowels and /a/, [-i] after front vowels: OE *bōhte* 'bought' > ME *bouȝte* /bɔuxtə/, OE *hēah* 'high', later *hēh* /heːx/ > ME *heigh* /heix/, etc.

These various changes produced the diphthongs /ai iu eu ɛu ɔu au/, to which was added /ɔi/ from French (*poison, joy*, etc.). During the ME period /eu iu/ collapsed in /iu/, leaving /ai ɔi iu ɛu ɔu au/.

One important development in the consonant system remains to be discussed: the origin of the voiced fricative phonemes /v z ð/. Recall that in OE these were foot-medial allophones of /f θ s/, and occurred nowhere else. Two changes allowed them to become distinctive. First (cf. §2.7), the introduction of French loans with initial [v z], which for the first time placed these segments in the same foot-initial environments as [f s], thus creating the potential for contrast (English *ferry, seal* vs. French *very, zeal*). Second, the shortening of intervocalic long consonants. In OE the only medial contrast possible for fricatives was short voiced vs. long voiceless, as in *ofer* 'over' with [-v-] vs. *offrian* 'offer' with [-fː-]. Shortening of long fricatives (complete by c. 1400) leaves a medial contrast [-f-] vs. [-v-]. Thus the two classes can contrast now everywhere except finally. This last possibility was produced by the loss of final unstressed vowels mentioned above: e.g. OE *lufu* [luvu] 'love', early ME [lo:və], late ME [lo:v] vs. *luff*, ME [lo:f]. Finally at about the same time, initial /θ/ voiced in a small class of pronouns and determiners (the ancestors of *the*, *this*, *thou*, etc.), thus completing the pattern. (As far as I know these are the only forms in modern English with initial /ð/.)

By the end of the ME period (say c. 1400) we have the following vowel and consonant inventories (compare this with (3.36)):

(3.42)

(a) VOWELS:

	SHORT		LONG		DIPHTHONGAL			
	i	u	iː	uː	ai	ɔi		
	e	o	eː	oː	iu	ɛu	au	ɔu
	a		ɛː	ɔː				
			aː					

(b) CONSONANTS:

	Labial	Dental	Alveolar	Palato-Alveolar	Palatal	Velar
STOP	p		t			k
	b		d			g
FRICATIVE	f	θ	s	ʃ		x
	v	ð	z			
AFFRICATE				tʃ		
				dʒ		
NASAL	m		n			
LIQUID	w		r, l		j	

Note that modern /ʒ/, /h/ and /ŋ/ are still missing: we will deal with them in the next section.

For the most part the modern English key words for consonants in (3.3) can be assumed valid at this stage; very little has happened (phonetically) to the consonants since ME, and we will discuss the important individual developments below. But radical changes have affected the vowels: so as a guide to the next section, here is the ME vowel system with *modern* key-words, to make it easier to identify the particular rhyme-classes being discussed. At c. 1400, then:

(3.43)

i	bit	u	but	iː	bite	uː	out
e	bet	o	pot	eː	beet	oː	boot
a	bat			ɛː	beat	ɔː	boat
				aː	mate		

ai	day		ɔi	boy			
iu	knew	dew	au	law		ɔu	grow

3.10 Origins, 3: Early Modern to Modern English

If we compare (3.43) with the modern set-up, we see enormous changes, both in pronunciation and in the membership of particular classes. All the short vowels have shifted: /e o/ have lowered to /ɛ ɒ/, /i u/ have lowered and centralized to /ɪ ʊ/, and /a/ has raised to /æ/. And except for /ɔi/, all the long and diphthongal classes have shifted, so that e.g. the former /iː/ class (*bite*) is now /aɪ/, the former /ai/ (*day*) is now /eɪ/ which didn't exist in ME, etc. Further, some classes have fallen together: old /eː ɛː/ (*beet, beat*) have merged to create a new /iː/, /ɔː ɔu/ (*bone, grow*) have fallen together in /əu/, and /iu ɛu/ have fallen together in /(j)uː/. And – though it is not apparent directly from (3.43) – some classes have split: both *come* and *wool* have ME /u/, but now contrast /ʌ/ vs. /ʊ/.

The central set of alterations is due to a major systematic change called the Great Vowel Shift (henceforth GVS), which began probably in the 15th century, and reached completion in the late 16th or early 17th. Other changes have occurred, but the GVS is perhaps the central event in the post-ME history of English, and we will look at it in some detail. The GVS is responsible for the following historical relations:

(3.44)

ME		Mod E
iː	—— bite ——	aɪ
eː	—— beet ——	iː
ɛː	beat	
aː	—— mate ——	eɪ
uː	—— out ——	au
oː	—— boot ——	uː
ɔː	—— boat ——	əu

These relations aren't merely the results of individual changes, as one might guess from the display: they stem from a system-wide set of related shifts that affect all the long vowels – what is known as a chain-shift. Perhaps this is best illustrated before being explained. Taking the ME long vowel system in (3.42) as the starting-point, the position by the late 16th century is:

(3.45)

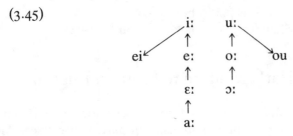

That is: each non-high vowel has raised one height; and the high vowels, being unable to raise any further, have 'got out of the way' by diphthongizing. The 'chain' aspect is this systematic inter-connection: it's not that one sub-change precedes another directly, but that there's a system-wide coordinated movement in which each change triggers or implies another. In the usual terminology, there is a mixture here of a push chain and a drag chain: the whole thing starts with the raising of the mid vowels /eː oː/, which had two effects: (a) it 'pushed' the high vowels /iː uː/ out of place, and (b) it left a space which in effect 'dragged' the lower mid /ɛː ɔː/ up to fill the vacated /eː oː/ positions. And the raising of /ɛː/ to /eː/ left the /ɛː/ slot open, so that /aː/ moved up into it.

This all took some time; by the mid-16th century, according to the testimony of contemporary phoneticians, everything except the raising of /aː/ was complete; this took place later on, and we can outline developments up to c. 1600 as:

(3.46)

	ME	1550	1600
bite	iː	ei	ʌi
beet	eː	iː	iː
beat	ɛː	eː	eː
mate	aː	aː	ɛː
out	uː	ou	ʌu
boot	oː	uː	uː
boat	ɔː	oː	oː

Later developments brought about a situation closer to that of modern SBE: /ai/ monophthongized to /aː/, so that *weight, mate* fell together in /ɛː/, later /eː/; before this /eː/ in *beat* raised to /iː/, so that the *beet/beat* classes merged. These developments began in the late 16th–early 17th century, but were not completed until well into the 18th: many words in the *beat* class still had /eː/ as late as the reign of Queen Anne – witness rhymes like this famous couplet from Pope's *Rape of the Lock* (III.7–8):

Here Thou, great *Anna*! whom three Realms obey
Dost sometimes Counsel take – and sometimes Tea.

(Indeed, the *beat* class has still not merged fully with *beet* in many dialects, particularly in Ireland: cf. §5.7.2; and in the standard some items like *great, steak, drain* escaped the merger completely.)

It should now be clear why the alternating vowels in forms like *divine/divinity, serene/serenity, profound/profundity, cone/conical*, etc. are so different. Recall that in late OE or early ME (§3.8) long vowels shortened in antepenultimate syllables; thus until the GVS the differences between the vowels would be only length: *divine* in ME was /diviːn/, *divinity* was /diviniti/. But the GVS affected only the long vowels, leaving the shorts unchanged: hence the extreme qualitative dissociation we find now – enhanced by quite separate developments of the short vowels (see below).

The modern SBE system results from the GVS plus a host of later changes. The raising of /ɔː/ to /oː/ left the /ɔː/ slot vacant, and a new /ɔː/ from monophthongization of ME /au/ (*law*) filled it – added to by later lengthenings before /r/ (*fort*). The other missing long vowel, /ɑː/, arose from a series of developments connected with short /a/, as we'll see.

At least up to the mid-16th century the ME short vowels seem to have retained their original qualities. But later on short /a/ raised to /æ/, while /e o/ lowered to /ɛ ɔ/, and /i u/ centralized and lowered to /ɪ ʊ/. The basic relations among the vowels remained, but they were now phonetically quite different. The primary phonological development was the present-day vowel in *but*, /ʌ/, which resulted (17th century) from a split in the old ME /u/ class: most ME /u/ became /ʌ/, but a certain number of items, especially in labial environments (e.g. *pull, bull, wool*) remained as /ʊ/. The /ʊ/ and /ʌ/ classes were further enlarged by developments of /uː/ from ME /oː/: most items in this class evolved normally and came down with /uː/, but there were a number of shortenings in particular ones. Those that shortened early, before the development of /ʌ/, fell in with this class (*blood, flood, glove*, etc.); those that shortened later, after the /ʊ/ > /ʌ/ change was no longer productive, simply remain as /ʊ/ (*good, book, hook*, etc.). As a general – but not exceptionless – rule, modern /ʌ/ or /ʊ/ words with -*oo*- spellings are from ME /oː/, those with -*u*- spellings from /u/.

Two other major changes are worth noting (though these do not, obviously, exhaust the list of important ones). In the later 17th century /æ/ lengthened in a number of environments: before voiceless fricatives (*laugh, path, pass*), before nasal + /s t/ (*dance, plant*), before syllable-final /r/ (*far, cart*). This new /æː/ developed into /ɑː/ in the course of the 19th century.

The other major change involves the merger of certain short vowels before /r/ in syllable codas (17th century): i.e. in the *bird* (ME /i/), *hurt* (ME /u/) and *fern* (ME /e/) classes. The merger here was to some kind of central vowel, probably rather like modern /ɜ:/. This clearly preceded the loss of postvocalic /r/ that now distinguishes rhotic from non-rhotic dialects – since all rhotic dialects except Scots (§5.7.1) and Hiberno-English (§5.7.2) have no distinction among these three historical classes.

Three more changes will wrap up this brief and over-concentrated history: the developments of /x/, of /n/ before /g/, and the origin of /ʒ/. As late as the mid-16th century /x/ in some form or other still occurred before consonants (as in *bought, night*: cf. §1.6) and finally, where it had not deleted or become /f/ (as in *through, rough*). During the next half-century or so this was lost, and the only remnant of the old /x/ phoneme was its foot-initial allophone /h/, which then contrasted with all other initial consonants, and hence became a new phoneme we can represent as /h/.

The velar nasal [ŋ] probably existed all through OE and ME as an allophone of /n/ before velars (e.g. in *think, sing*); but unlike the case in modern SBE, /g/ after [ŋ] was still pronounced as late as the 16th century: e.g. *sing* was [siŋg]. Beginning in the 1560s or so, /g/ deleted after [ŋ] in certain positions: word-finally as in *young, sing*, and before certain suffixes (e.g. in *singing, singer*); but it remained before others (e.g. in *younger, youngest*), and in disyllabic but morphologically simple words (*finger*). Deletion of final /g/ allowed [ŋ] to stand in contrast to other nasals: e.g. *sing* vs. *sin* – a state of affairs impossible while *sing* still had its final /g/. (The only dialects now that lack a phonemic /ŋ/ are those in the northwest of England where *sing* is still [siŋg]; here [ŋ] is still an allophone of /n/, since it only occurs before /k g/.)

Modern /ʒ/ as in *vision* arose in the 17th-century from palatalization of /zj/ clusters: thus [vɪzjən] > [vɪʒən]. At the same time the incidence of the other palato-alveolars was increased: new /ʃ/ from /sj/ (*vicious*), new /tʃ/ from /tj/ (*Christian*), and new /dʒ/ from /dj/ (*soldier*). This probably began as an allegro rule: the same one we see now across word-boundaries in *miss you* [mɪʃuː], *hit you* [hɪtʃuː], *kid you* [kɪdʒuː], and for some speakers within the word if they have distinctions like lento [ɛdjuːkeɪt] vs. allegro [ɛdʒəkeɪt] 'educate'.

Sections 3.9–11 have probably contained too much information, and very little tying together of developments. To help to rectify this, I append a chart showing the major sources of the modern vowel system in a rather diagrammatic and oversimple manner. The idea is to enable the reader to backtrack to some degree, and see where things come from. I have not done the same for the consonants, as the overall picture there is much simpler, and can be extracted from the text without too much trouble (I think):

(3.47)

OE	ME	GVS	Post-GVS	Mod E

æ:w _dew_ εu ————————— iu ————————— (j)u:

e:w _true_ eu —

ɑɣ _law_ au ————— ɔ: ————————— ɔ:

ɔi _boil_ ————————————————— ɔi

CHAPTER 3: NOTES AND REFERENCES

3.1 The approach to phonology introduced in this chapter is mostly somewhat conservative, with a rather concrete emphasis on distinctive units, their realizations, and systems: a version of what is sometimes called 'classical' phonology. For textbook introductions see Sommerstein (1977: ch. 2) and Lass (1984b: chs. 1–2). On phonological systems and their theoretical import, Lass (1984b: ch. 7 and references). The problem of delimiting phonology proper from morphology lies at the heart of the 'abstractness debate' in recent phonological theory: for discussion see Lass (1984b: chs. 4, 9) and the references there to the technical literature. The nub of the debate is whether e.g. a pair like *divine/ divinity* should be taken merely as phonemically distinct, i.e. /dɪvaɪn/, /dɪvɪnɪti:/; or whether the 'apparent' /aɪ/: /ɪ/ contrast in what are after all forms of 'the same' item should be derived from a common 'underlying form' different from both 'surface forms'. The usual suggestion is an underlying /dɪvi:n/, /dɪvi:n-ɪti:/, with rules deriving [aɪ] from /i:/ alone, and [ɪ] from shortened /i:/ in the third syllable from the end (cf. Chomsky & Halle 1968: ch. 2). Such analyses typically end up attributing to speakers of the current language something like earlier historical stages and processes (see §§3.8, 3.10); I will generally avoid such abstractness here, both in phonology and syntax.

3.2 For detailed descriptions of English phonological systems, with RP and related types as a reference point, see Wells (1982). This massive work treats all major dialect types; vol. I has a good introduction to phonological theory and treats many important historical and synchronic processes. My transcriptions and general approach are different from his, but not really incompatible, for the most part. The bulk of the details in this section come from my own observation and analysis, and don't rely on published sources.

3.2.1 On varieties of /r/ in different dialects, see Lass & Higgs (1984), which describes U.S. /r/s in detail, with some X-ray data. On general phonetic classification, see Appendix I and any standard phonetics text: Ladefoged (1975) is probably the best. On the rhotic/non-rhotic distinction, Wells (1982: §§3.2.1–3); on /h/-dropping, Wells (§3.4.1), and Milroy (1984) for the history.

3.2.2 For the analysis of English vowel systems proposed here, see the technical discussion in Lass (1976: ch. 1). This gives a historical summary of divergent views on the treatment of split systems of this kind. For further discussion Lass (1984c).

3.2.3 Aspiration: many texts misleadingly describe this as an 'extra puff of air' released after a consonant. Actually it's nearly exclusively a matter of timing: if a closure is released before the vocal folds start to vibrate for a following voiced segment, voiceless air passing through the glottis ([h]) is an automatic consequence – nothing 'extra' is involved. On glottalization of final /p t k/ see Wells (§§3.4.5, 4.2.10), Lass (1984b: §§2.7, 6.5, 12.3).

3.3 On the syllable in general and the model proposed here, Lass (1984b: §10.3) and references. On the heavy/light distinction, Lass (1984b: §10.3.2), and for technical discussion Lass (1984d). My analysis is controversial in parts.

3.4–6 The characterization of English stress is currently under intense debate; the model I have chosen here is a very simple kind of 'metrical' approach. For an accessible (if technical) introduction to metrical or 'SW' phonology, Giegerich (1985: ch. 1). On isochrony and stress-timing, Abercrombie (1963), which also introduces the notion 'foot'; the zero syllable is a nonstandard concept introduced by Giegerich. The original characterization of the MSR, NSR and CSR that much recent debate stems from is in Chomsky & Halle (1968). On English stress see also Fudge (1983).

3.7 On casual speech and its typical modifications, Brown (1977) is a classic; see also Lass (1984b: ch. 12), Lodge (1984).

3.8 The sketch of English historical phonology in this chapter, and the historical morphology and syntax in ch. 4, should be bolstered by further reading for anyone with a serious interest. A good beginning is to read one or two standard general histories of the language. For a bibliography on the history of English, Fisiak (1983). Among the general histories are Baugh (1957), weak on internal history and linguistically unsophisticated, but a good first book, Robertson & Cassidy (1954), Strang (1970). Strang is enormously detailed, more modern, and difficult, but is probably the best general history in English. More specialized and technical works, concentrating on phonology and morphology, are Wyld (1927, 1936). The standard and still irreplaceable historical phonology of English is Luick (1968); virtually all subsequent work stands in one way or another in Luick's shadow. On phonology, vol. I of Jespersen (1909–49) is also excellent. In a more modern vein, see the phonology papers in Lass (1969), Blake & Jones (1984), Davenport et al. (1983), Eaton et al. (1985).

For OE phonology, standard older grammars are Wright & Wright (1925), and Campbell (1959); Wright & Wright is more approachable and elementary. For a contemporary version, Lass & Anderson (1975); the characterization here is rather more conservative than that in Lass & Anderson.

The OE vowel system: there's a lot of controversy about both phonemic status and phonetic quality; my account here is fairly traditional. The most controversial topic perhaps is the assumption of long and short diphthongs, which has been strongly contested: for discussion and literature summary see Lass & Anderson (ch. III), and Lass (1984d). The account of the consonantal developments follows Lass & Anderson; there is a slightly less technical treatment in Lass (1984b: ch. 13). The names of the various sound changes except palatal softening are traditional; though some books refer to *i*-umlaut as *i*-mutation.

3.9 For ME phonology, standard scholarly sources are Luick, and Jordan (1968). For shorter but still copious treatments, Mossé (1950), Wright & Wright (1928), Fisiak (1968). For more modern treatment of some aspects of ME phonology in a 1970s generative model, Jones (1972), which is a good introduction to ME studies generally. The vowel systems I present are traditional in most respects: my /eː oː/ are equivalent to the older 'long close' mid vowels, often given as ẹ, ọ; my /ɛː ɔː/ to the 'long open' ẹ, ọ.

There is controversy about two main aspects of ME phonology : (a) the nature of the long vowels themselves (see Stockwell 1961), and (b) open syllable lengthening (see Minkova 1982). Both these issues are taken up in Stockwell (1985), which argues brilliantly against the traditional views. On the development of the /f/ : /v/ contrast, etc. see Kurath (1956).

3.10 For Early Modern English phonology see Luick, Horn & Lehnert (1954), Dobson (1963), Jespersen (1909–49, vol. I), Schlauch (1959), Ekwall (1965), Wyld (1927, 1936). The account of the Great Vowel Shift follows Luick and my own work (Lass 1976: ch. 2). The nature and stages of the GVS are controversial: for an overview, with excellent references, Wolfe (1972). See also the discussion of the social weighting of variant pronunciations in Dobson (1955), and Holmberg (1964).

4. MORPHOSYNTAX

4.1 Morphology, Syntax, Morphosyntax, Meaning

The study of 'grammar' is usually divided into two main areas: morphology (the inventory of word-forms in a language and the rules for constructing them) and syntax (the rules for combining words into higher-order structures like phrases or sentences). Thus it's a fact about English morphology that most verbs take -s in the present 3 sg; and a fact about English syntax that subject noun phrases (NPs) tend to precede verbs, and object NPs to follow them. So the facts of inflection and word-order in a sentence like *John like-s curry* (Subject + Verb-s + Object) belong to different components of a description of English.

But of course they're intimately connected. The -s on *like-s* is dependent on *John* being a singular NP (cf. *they like curry*); and it's independent of the number of the object (cf. *John like-s curry/curries*). That is: inflectional morphology generally can't be interpreted except in relation to the syntactic structures that it represents. To say that '-s is the present 3 sg ending of the English verb' is not to make a statement merely about verb forms; it is to make a statement about the connection between the forms of verbs and certain features of their subjects, and higher-level sentence-features like tense (which is not, despite what we tend to think, a property merely of verbs: see below and §§4.4, 4.5.2). And about the connection between forms and aspects of meaning, often very subtle ones, concerned with speakers' attitudes toward the sentences they utter.

Consider for instance the category 'past tense'. In traditional terms, every verb 'has' a past form or form(s), whose function is to mark a narrated state of affairs or event as prior in time to the 'zero-point' or moment of utterance. If I say *the cat is on the mat* as opposed to *the cat was on the mat*, I say something about the temporal relation of the cat's being on the mat to the moment I choose to talk about it.

But there's more to it. There are past tense uses in English (and many other languages) that either have nothing to do with time at all, or seem to represent something other than past time, e.g. a special kind of future, as in:

(4.1)

    a. What *will* you do if you *meet* a tiger in Adderley Street?
    b. What *would* you do if you *met* a tiger in Adderley Street?

We have two future conditional questions, one with a present verb in the *if*-clause, one with a past. But neither refers to present or past time. They appear rather to reflect a difference in the speaker's attitude to the likelihood of your meeting a tiger: in (4.1a) the encounter is assessed as more probable than in (4.1b). So here tense, as a morphological category, is being used to express a judgement of probability, i.e. not a location in time but a psychological state. (On the motivation for this use of the past see §§4.4, 4.5.2–3.)

The point is that word-form, syntax (the *if*-clause construction) and meaning may be inseparable parts of the description of a particular type of utterance. Another, rather different case:

(4.2)

    a. Mary *says* that she *is* tired
    b. Mary *said* that she *was* tired

Note that in both these cases, the statement reported in the subordinate (*that*-) clause can be the same: it is – from Mary's point of view, not the speaker's – a present-tense utterance. We can see this by translating from 'indirect' to 'direct' speech:

(4.3)

    a. Mary *says*: 'I *am* tired'
    b. Mary *said*: 'I *am* tired'

The tense in the *that*-clause is a purely mechanical matter of 'agreement' with that in the main clause, a phenomenon called 'sequence of tenses' (readers with a classical education may recall learning the *consecutio temporum* in Latin). That is, the verb in the object clause agrees in tense with the verb in the main clause in indirect speech. So the verbs in the object clauses in (4.2) carry no temporal meaning; their form is unconnected to the meaning of the utterance. Indeed, in other languages, like Yiddish, the verb in the subordinate clause in (4.2b) would be in the present as well: *Mary said that she is tired*. (This is at least marginally possible in my English as well, in informal speech anyhow.) Here then is another use of the past tense form that doesn't reflect either time of utterance or meaning in any direct way, but is merely a marker of concord, like the *-s* on a 3 sg present verb.

Cases like this suggest that it's unprofitable (at least in a book like this) to treat morphology and syntax as separate and autonomous topics; and further, that even the two together, under the hybrid term 'morphosyntax', are not independent of the representation of meaning. Some aspects of morphosyntax, like agreement, appear to have no communicative function; they are simply mechanical (if important) conventions of a particular language (but see the discussion of Latin case-marking in §4.2). But others have important communicative functions: they are intimately connected with the expression of meaning. Morphosyntax is a two-faced domain: partly pure 'structure', partly a 'carrier' or 'vehicle' for meaning. So in this chapter we will consider morphology and syntax and their interactions, i.e. the complex of properties concerned with the form of words, the grammatical and semantic categories encoded in these forms, the arrangements and interrelations of forms in larger structures, and the relation of all of these to meaning. Because the subject is so vast and complex, we will look at only some selected topics, both the current state and historical background; but this should give quite a useful picture of how English is put together.

4.2 English as a Grammatical Type

One device for ordering the mass of human languages is sorting them – at one structural level or another – into 'types'. Phonologically, for instance, English belongs to the class of languages with contrastive vowel length (like German, Latin as opposed to French, Russian), of stress-timed languages (like German but unlike French), of languages with moveable accent (like German and Russian but unlike Finnish and Polish), etc.

There are many more dimensions for grammatical than for phonological typology. We can talk of 'inflecting' vs. 'agglutinating' languages (see below), subject-verb-object vs. subject-object-verb vs. verb-subject-object, languages with and without case-marking, grammatical gender, tenses, etc. These features of 'language design' play an important part in technical theoretical debate in linguistics; but from our point of view they can also be useful classificatory devices, placing our subject language in the universe of possible language designs. In this section we'll look at some broad morphosyntactic features that give English its particular character – especially insofar as they contrast with features of closely related languages, and earlier stages of English itself.

First, morphological type. English hasn't much in the way of morphology, but what it has is of a specific kind. There is a problem of terminology here, which we must sort out to begin with. It is customary to distinguish between inflectional and derivational morphology; the former consists of suffixes and other items that form part of systems of agreement, category-marking, and the like; the latter of devices for word-formation. Thus under inflectional morphology come case-endings, markers of tense and number and so on; under derivational morphology come items like the suffixes that turn adjectives into nouns (*red→ red-ness*), nouns into adjectives (*nation→ nation-al*), etc. (see §4.8). But within inflectional morphology itself, the term 'inflecting' is used more specifically, to indicate a particular way of representing grammatical categories. Consider the forms meaning 'girls' (accusative pl) and 'I do' in Kannaḍa (a Dravidian language of SW India) and Latin:

(4.4)

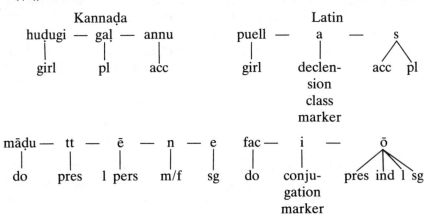

Kannaḍa is 'agglutinative': each morphosyntactic category is represented (normally) by a single independent item or morph. In Latin, an 'inflecting' language properly speaking, categories tend to 'cumulate' on single morphs. There is no place to 'cut' between case and number, or mood and tense and person. English in all its historical stages, in the typical Germanic (and ultimately IE) way, is predominantly inflecting. Even now at least some of the few endings that are left can mark more than one category, as in *walk-s = walk*-pres/3/sg. (Though the paucity of categories available makes some forms actually agglutinative: *walk-ed = walk*-past, simply because no other categories are marked in the past.)

Insofar as English has inflectional morphology, it takes three basic forms:

(i) *Suffixation.* Most noun plurals, one class of genitives, past and present of verbs are marked with suffixes: *boy/boy-s/boy-'s/boy-s'* (the last three of course phonologically identical), *walk/walk-s/walk-ed.*

(ii) *Internal Vowel Change.* Some noun plurals are formed by change of the stem vowel: *mouse/mice, man/men,* etc.; the same device (if with a different historical source) is used for the past forms of a number of verbs, either historical strong verbs (*write/wrote/written, sing/sang/ sung*), or weak verbs whose original suffixes triggered vowel changes (*buy/bough-t, leave/lef-t*).

(iii) *Suppletion*. Category differences are coded in pairs or larger sets of 'unrelated' forms: person and number in the verb *to be* (*am/are/is*), tense in some verbs (*am/was, go/went*), or case and number on pronouns (*he/him/they/them, I/me/we/us*). Of the three, only suffixation is regular and productive; the others are leftovers from times when the options were opener.

Three other types of inflectional marking that occur widely in other languages aren't used in English. Prefixation, as in Russian: *ja pro-čital roman* 'I read (and finished) the novel' vs. *ja čital roman* 'I read (and either finished or didn't finish) the novel'; infixation (where a marker is inserted inside a word) – e.g. certain Latin verbs, where a nasal is inserted in the present stem, like *ru-m-p-ō* 'I break' vs. past participle *rup-t-us*, root *rup-*; and reduplication, where a category is marked by a more or less exact copy of a syllable, among other things: Latin *can-ō* 'I sing', perfect *ce-cin-ī*, Gothic *haitan* 'be called', past *haí-hait*.

Considering the range of inflectional categories that were marked in IE, and still are in some related languages, English indicates very few: it lacks grammatical gender, case-marking on the noun, has a very reduced number and person system for the verb, and so on. We will look at some of these in detail later.

As far as word-formation goes, English is much richer in strategies; in addition to suffixation (*nation → nation-al-ity*), it has prefixation (*dress → un-dress*), and, perhaps the most widely used device, compounding. It's probably easier to create new vocabulary this way than any other (I've just invented *Emmenthal-flavoured, catworm*, and *tooth-cruncher*). English also, because of its general lack of inflectional morphology, makes extensive use of what is sometimes called 'zero-derivation'; since (for example) verbs aren't distinguished from other parts of speech by specific markers (like the German *-en* for infinitives), one can turn virtually anything into a verb. The same goes for nouns, which again lack specific markers of nounhood (except of course for derived nouns, like those in *-ness, -hood*, etc.). A good example is *but me no buts*, where the bare conjunction *but* is used as an imperative verb, and then is pluralized in the normal way and used as a noun. (For more on word-formation see §4.8.)

Inflectional morphological marking can have a number of functions. Perhaps the three most prominent are:

(i) Direct encoding of grammatical/semantic categories: e.g. G *war ich in Köln* 'was I in Cologne?' vs. *wäre ich in Köln* 'if (only) I were in

Cologne'. Here the same order of elements can signal quite different meanings: the 'subjunctive' or 'optative' mood is coded directly on the verb.

(ii) Establishment of concord or agreement: as in Ancient Greek *ho agath-ós anthrop-ós* 'the (masc nom sg) good-(masc nom sg) man-(masc nom sg)'. Here the members of a phrase are all marked for the categories of the head. Or L *host-ēs vēn-i-unt* '(the) enemy-(nom pl) come-(pres ind 3 pl)', where the number and person of a subject NP determine the ending of the verb.

(iii) Marking government. Certain case-forms of nouns or pronouns are 'governed' or controlled by verbs or prepositions: as in G *ich sehe ihn* 'I see him (acc)' vs. *ich hilfe ihm* 'I help him (dat)', or L *ab urb-e* 'from the city-(abl)' vs. *ad urb-em* 'to the city-(acc)'.

English, with its poor inflectional system, shows only traces of these three functions: (i) in oppositions like *if I were there* (contrary-to-fact: I wasn't there or am not there) vs. *if I was there* 'even though I (actually) was there' – for some dialects anyhow; or the marking of past on verbs, plural on nouns. For (ii), we have vestiges of verb-agreement with subjects in the present 3 sg (*I/you/they walk* vs. *he walk-s*); for (iii) we have the preverbal vs. postverbal and post-prepositional forms of some pronouns: *he saw him, he gave it to him*, etc.

A language like Latin or Greek can have a type of syntax that is rare in languages with poorer morphology. Since grammatical categories like subject, object, etc. are marked on nouns, and since items in NPs agree in case, number and gender, and verbs agree with their subjects, it's possible to have great freedom of word order. Thus the 'basic' or neutral word order (see below) of Latin is S(ubject) O(bject) V(erb): *lup-us puell-am parv-am ed-it* 'wolf-nom/sg girl-fem/acc/sg small-fem/acc/sg eat-pres/3/sg' i.e. 'the wolf eats the little girl'. But for stylistic effects the S, O, V relations can be shifted: *puellam parvam edit lupus* ('foregrounding' *the little girl*); even orders where the adjective and its noun are split are possible: *lupus parvam edit puellam, parvam edit lupus puellam*, etc. Grammatical relations are preserved: *parvam* must modify *puellam*; both, being accusative, must be objects of a verb; *lupus* being nominative must be subject, and so on. It doesn't matter, as far as basic propositional meaning goes, what's next to what, or on which side.

In English of course we could achieve some of these effects in different ways: e.g. foregrounding by clefting (§4.7.2), *it's the little girl that the wolf eats*, or fronting *the little girl* and leaving a pronoun 'copy' behind to show where she 'ought' to be: *the little girl, the wolf eats her*. The point is that English lacks the morphological machinery that would allow a (relatively) free word order. Hence grammatical relations are signalled primarily by linear order: *the wolf eats the little girl* vs. *the little girl eats the wolf*. In other instances, the functions of particular elements can be signalled either by word order or prepositions (which in this case are analogous to case-markers). Thus *I gave John the kitten* vs. *I gave the kitten to John*. In the absence of prepositional marking, the 'neutral' order Subject-Indirect Object-Direct Object is assumed; in the second version the preposition *to* signals the dative relation. Prepositions can also mark subjects that have been 'demoted' to non-subject positions, as in the passive: *the wolf ate the baby* vs. *the baby was eaten by the wolf*, where *by* marks a subject occurring in what is normally not a subject position (this is oversimple: see §4.7.1).

So in modern English, word order is the main – nearly the only – means of marking grammatical functions. But even languages that allow for considerable freedom of word order (and we'll see in §4.7 that English has more than one might think) generally have a basic or dominant order. This is the one that occurs, for instance, in the most neutral declarative sentences, and with the highest statistical frequency. To clarify the sense of 'neutral': compare *I hate this book* and *this book I hate*. The first is more natural and 'inexpressive', the less specialized of the two; one would tend to use the second only where there is some special emotive force behind the utterance, or in a so-called adversative construction: *this book I hate, (but) that one I like*. On these grounds, *I hate this book* would be taken as manifesting the basic order of English.

Discussions of basic order normally focus on the relations of three categories: subjects (S), verbs (V) and objects (O) in simple transitive sentences. The reasons for this are complex and technical, but it turns out that a number of interesting grammatical facts about a language can – to a large extent – be predicted from its basic order, particularly the relation of O to V: see below.

Taking these three major constituents, English is what we call an SVO language (verb between subject and object); as opposed to SOV languages like Turkish or Japanese, and VSO languages like Welsh or Biblical Hebrew. There are other order types as well, e.g. VOS, OSV, etc.; but these are rarer than the other three, and don't occur as basic orders within Indo-European. While SVO seems to be the commonest IE order nowadays, there are a good number of SOV languages (e.g. all the IE languages of India, like Hindi, Marathi, Gujerati, Bengali), and VSO (Welsh, Irish, Scots Gaelic). It's important to remember that just because a language is dominant SVO, this doesn't exclude other orders: e.g. OSV in English as in *this book I hate*.

Being basic SVO, English is similar to a number of other Germanic languages: Swedish, Danish, Norwegian, Icelandic and Yiddish. But German, Dutch, Afrikaans and Frisian have a 'split' order: SVO in main clauses vs. SOV in subordinate clauses. Compare *Jack says that he hates dogs* with Afrikaans *Koos sê, dat hy honde haat* 'Jack says, that he dogs hates'. (*Koos* is the diminutive of *Jacobus*, so it's close enough to *Jack*.) This is a bit oversimple: see the further discussion in §6.4.

Other important order criteria include the relation between modifiers and nouns, and genitives and their heads; and the type of adposition (preposition or postposition) a language has. Briefly:

(i) *Adjectives and Nouns.* English is an A + N language; adjectives precede their head nouns (as do numerals) except for a few fossils like *the Church militant, virtue triumphant.* If we want to consider certain participial and prepositional phrases as adjectives, then these as a class follow: *the man sitting on the rock, the book on the table.* But these might equally well be taken as 'reduced' relative clauses: *the man (who is) sitting on the rock, the book (that is) on the table.* All the Germanic languages are A + N; basic N + A (though with a lot of exceptions) occurs in French: *le livre rouge* 'the red book', *la sentinelle enceinte* 'the pregnant sentry'.

(ii) *Determiners and Nouns.* Determiners are items like definite and indefinite articles and demonstrative adjectives (*this, that*). It would seem (considering most familiar European languages) that determiners naturally come before nouns; but even some languages quite closely related to English have the opposite order. In the Scandinavian languages, for instance (cf. §1.4), the definite article follows its noun: Swedish *mann* 'man', *mann-en* 'the man', *hus* 'house', *hus-et* 'the house'. Though even in these languages, other determiners precede: *en mann* 'a man'; and in Swedish there is a construction with two articles, one in each position, as in *den stora mann-en* 'the big man'. English is thus uniformly Det + N.

(iii) *Genitive and Noun.* English has two ways of signalling 'possession' (cf. §4.3.1): by the genitive of the possessor (*John's brother*) or an *of*-phrase (*the roof of the house*). These are fixed: the *-'s* form precedes, the *of*-phrase follows. So English is Gen + N and N + Gen.

(iv) *Adposition Type.* English, like most SVO (and VSO) languages, has virtually only prepositions. SOV languages typically have postpositions (i.e. 'prepositions that follow their objects'). Thus English *outside the house* vs. Kannaḍa *maney-a-hōrage* 'house-of-exterior-to'. In general, the O,V relation will predict which adpositions a language has: VO (thus SVO, VSO) predicts prepositions, OV postpositions. There are however a few 'hidden' postpositional constructions in English: e.g. *hereof, thereof, therefore, hereunder, hereafter* – and even double postpositions, as in *hereinafter.* The first element in these is really a pronoun: *thereafter = after that,* etc.

If we take the various morphosyntactic features mentioned so far, and compare English with a number of related languages and one unrelated, the picture we get is as follows. (In the table below, + = possesses a feature, − = does not, ? = feature is marginal):

(4.5)

	Case-Marking	Gender	SVO	SOV	VSO	A–N	N–A
English	?[1]	−	+	−	−	+	?
Afrikaans	?	−	+	+	−	+	−
Dutch	?	+	+	+	−	+	−
Yiddish	?	+	+	−	−	+	−
German	+	+	+	+	−[2]	+	−
Icelandic	+	+	+	−	−	+	−
Swedish	?	+	+	−	−	+	−
French	?	+	+	−	−	+	+
Latin	+	+	+	+	−	+	+
Welsh	+	+	−	−	+	+	−
Kannaḍa	+	+	−	+	−	+	−

	Det + N	N + Det	Prep + N	N + Postp
English	+	−	+	?[3]
Afrikaans	+	−	+	+
Dutch	+	−	+	?
Yiddish	+	−	+	−
German	+	−	+	?
Icelandic	+	+	+	−
Swedish	+	+	+	−
French	+	−	+	−
Latin	+	−	+	−
Welsh	+	−	+	−
Kannaḍa	+	−	−	+

Notes

1. A '?' for case-marking indicates that nouns are not marked, but personal pronouns are.
2. German and other Gmc dialects have VSO in questions: *Sieht er den Mann?* 'Sees he the man?', etc. – but not as basic declarative orders.
3. Afrikaans has more prepositional than postpositional constructions, but I mark it '+' for the latter, since the type *ek gaan huis toe* 'I go house-to' = 'I'm going home' is common.

4.3 The Noun Phrase

4.3.1 INTRODUCTORY

In technical usage a phrase is a construction with a head – an obligatory and defining constituent. A phrase typically behaves like, and has the same overall distribution as, its head. So a noun (using the term loosely, to include pronouns) is the head of a noun phrase (NP), and a NP has the same distribution and function as a noun. Nouns can be defined by (among others) the following diagnostic features: (a) the ability to serve as subject or object of a verb; (b) the fact that they can be 'moved' by processes like passive-formation; and (c) the ability to serve as objects of prepositions. So for instance the noun *cats* meets the above criteria: (a) *cats eat mice/ mice dislike cats*; (b) *cats are disliked by mice*; (c) *fleas hang around on cats*. Likewise phrases with *cats* as head can be substituted for *cats* in the above examples: *the cats, the big hairy striped cats*. Or more complex phrases, even with sentences containing other noun phrases inside them, like *the big hairy cats who used to be fed by the old lady who said she preferred them to children*. (Note that in this case while *cats* is head of the whole phrase, there are other NPs 'inside' with their own heads, e.g. *the old lady ... children*, with *lady* as head.)

In the following sections we will look first at the morphology of typical NP constituents (nouns, pronouns, articles, adjectives), and some aspects of the meaning and history of certain categories; then at ordering relations within the NP.

4.3.2 NOUNS AND DETERMINERS

Many categories can in principle be represented on nouns: number, gender and case are perhaps the most common. How does one tell if a language 'has' a particular category? It's easiest where the category is explicitly marked: either on the form itself, or on some other item that obligatorily agrees with it. Thus in Latin virtually any noun with a nom sg in -*a* is feminine, and one with a nom sg in -*um* is neuter; in French or German, most nouns are not marked explicitly, but gender will be shown on an accompanying determiner (*la table* is feminine, *le pupitre* 'desk' is masculine, *der Mann, die Frau, das Kind* are respectively m, f, n). And even if a determiner is absent or ambiguous (in French both masculines and feminines take *les* in the plural), adjectives agree with the gender of nouns: *les tables brunes* 'the brown tables' vs. *les pupitres bruns*.

By these criteria it is clear that English doesn't have grammatical gender: it has neither gender suffixes nor obligatory agreement. An alert reader might however catch me on this: what about obligatory pronoun agreement? Just as *die Mann* is ungrammatical in German, so is *this *man – she died*. And there are gender-marking suffixes, like *-ess* which concords with feminine pronouns (**the tigress – he died*). And one might suggest that ships are characteristically feminine, as are (often) cars and motorcycles, since they are frequently referred to as *she*.

The answer to this is that while English has what we might call 'sex-sensitive' pronoun reference, if doesn't systematically partition its nouns into mutually exclusive gender classes: where there is apparent gender-concord, it reflects 'real-world' aspects of what nouns denote – either literally as in the case of animate beings, or metaphorically with ships, etc. It is not ungrammatical to call a ship *it*.

This leaves us with number and case. English nouns are systematically inflected for plural: mostly with *-(e)s* (cf. §1.5), though there are minor plural types as well, either native (*mice, oxen, sheep, children*) or foreign (*-a* on Latin or Greek neuters like *strata, phenomena*, *-im* on Hebrew loans like *kibbutzim*). Some of these borrowed plurals are increasingly yielding to *-(e)s*, as in *formulae ~ formulas*, and some more complex formations are levelling out: e.g. *appendix, index* have both old *-ices* and new *-xes* plurals.

Plural inflection however doesn't appear everywhere we might expect: some measure nouns in particular take singular forms when used adjectivally, as in *a three-mile run* (**a three-miles run*) – but *he ran three miles/*mile*. (Though some dialects will use the singular here too.) This construction is a relic of an old genitive plural, not historically a singular: measure nouns in OE used gen pl as a kind of partitive: *þrēo mīl-a brād* 'three miles-of broad' – cf. the French partitive in *je veux du pain* 'I want of-the bread' = 'I want some bread'.

There are also cases of number-ambiguity, or at least differing interpretations of inherent number: so called 'collectives' like *government, parliament, Tottenham Hotspur* (a better name might be 'team nouns'). These are generally taken as plural in British English (*parliament have decided*) and singular in American (*congress has decided*) – though British usage may vary according to whether the speaker wishes to emphasize the unity or the plurality. There are also nouns which are collective in sense and singular in form and concord (*furniture, equipment*), nouns representing uncountable properties that lack plural forms or concord (*redness, decrepitude*), and nouns with plural forms and concord but no singulars (*trousers, scissors*). Though in some dialects new singulars have been produced by back-formation: inferring from a formally plural-like item that there must be a singular: New York *a scissor*. This process led to *pea* from *pise*, *cherry* from *cerise*, and 19th-century coinages like *Chinee, Portuguee*.

Now to case. English nouns are not marked for nominative, accusative, dative, etc. – even though of course they enter into the relations denoted by these case-names in descriptions of languages with richer morphology. Older grammars often give 'the cases' of nouns in a format like: *O cat* (vocative), *the cat sleeps* (nominative), *I see the cat* (accusative), *to the cat* (dative), etc. But this simply says that the vocative, nominative, etc. of *cat* are *cat* – which means that English doesn't have case-marking. All languages have some means of expressing the relations that NPs contract with verbs and with each other; English is characterized by not marking these relations morphologically, but by word order, prepositions, and other devices.

But English does apparently have at least two 'case forms' for nouns: in the usual terms a 'common' and a 'possessive' or 'genitive' (*boy, boy's*). Whether these really constitute a case system in the usual sense is doubtful: on perhaps the most sensible interpretation, the *-'s* is no more a case-marker proper than the possessive particles in Dutch or Afrikaans (*Jan z'n huis, Jan se huis* 'John's house'), or the short-lived archaic *his*-genitive in English (*the king his throne*). The problem is made more difficult by the oddity of such a system cross-linguistically: normally case-systems encode, if anything, primary grammatical relations like subject and direct object (as to some extent the English pronouns still do: see §4.3.3). There is also a complication due to the alternative *of*-NP genitive and its relation to NP*'s*, and the vast number of functions served by the two forms. I will sketch this out briefly.

It's often assumed that the synthetic *-'s* genitive and the analytic *of*-NP are synonymous; but this isn't true – even if it appears so in simple cases like *England's Queen/the Queen of England*. Differences in head nouns however bring out differences in meaning: *the Queen's picture* doesn't necessarily = *the picture of the Queen*. In one sense, where the picture is in the Queen's possession, the equivalence doesn't hold: *the Queen's picture* can mean either 'the picture the Queen possesses' or 'the picture that portrays the Queen' (whether or not it's in her possession: cf. *the picture of the Queen in the National Gallery*). But *the picture of the Queen* can't mean 'the picture the Queen possesses'. So at least in 'picture-NPs', as we might call them, *-'s* and *of*-NP aren't fully equivalent.

In some cases there are either equivalences or mutual exclusivity. Many speakers restrict the *-'s* genitive to animates: *John's house, the dog's nose*, but *the roof of the house* only; others allow *–'s* for all nouns (I find *the house's roof* quite acceptable). Still other speakers make a distinction in terms of the length or complexity of the NP that is marked: some allow even NPs containing relative clauses to be marked by *-'s* (*the boy who used to live next door's sister*), others allow only simpler NPs. These variations seem to be personal, not systematic or regional.

As the case of *the Queen's picture* suggests, 'possessive' isn't a very useful name for -'s: it represents many other, often quite complex relations. Thus while *the PM's hat* is 'possessive', we would not normally say this of *the PM's assassination*, in that it is the PM who is assassinated rather than someone else whose assassination the PM has ordered. Similarly, *the Queen's picture* is less commonly used in the sense of a portrait of her; it could be used as in *the photographer took the Queen's picture*. (Note that *this of*-NP can't be possessive: for this sense we'd need a 'double genitive': *a portrait of hers*.) Many genitives, both -'s and *of*-NP, appear in fact to encode what might be called 'sentential' relations, i.e. to have implicit verbs. E.g. 'subject genitives' like *John's accomplishments* (= 'John accomplished X') or 'object genitives' like *the PM's assassination* (= 'X assassinated the PM'). The head noun is best construed as the subject or object of the verb 'underlying' the other noun. Such complex relations are even more striking in an ambiguous case like *the shooting of the hunters*: compare the continuations *was so bad they missed everything* vs. *was a cold-blooded act of terrorism*.

Other constructions that show no 'possessive' sense and also don't allow both -'s and *of*-NP are the type sometimes called genitive of respect or specification, like *a man of impeccable breeding* (**impeccable breeding's man*) or modifiers specifying what something is made of, like *the Man of Steel* (**Steel's Man*). This fragmentary discussion suggests (a) that if -'s is a case-form, it's a remarkably limited and at the same time hard to specify one, and (b) that it's not true that -'s and *of*-NP are two ways of saying the same thing. We can conclude that English lacks case-marking on the noun.

The class of items called determiners includes a number of forms, of which only the articles will concern us here. The English articles are uninflected: *the* for all cases sg and pl, and *a(n)* for all cases (obviously singular only). Both the articles have variant phonologically conditioned forms in most dialects: *the* is /ðə/ before a noun beginning with a consonant, and /ði:/ before one beginning with a vowel; the corresponding forms of *a(n)* are respectively /ə/ and /ən/. Some South African and southern U.S. standards however deviate from this pattern: both tend to have only /ðə/, even before vowels: perhaps because (at least in SA English) 'vowel-initial' words really begin with a glottal stop, which acts like any other consonant.

Things were not always this simple. The history of English noun-inflection, like that of much else in the language, is a story of simplification of forms: the earlier state was rather reminiscent of Latin. OE had three genders, maximally six distinct case-forms for any noun, plus distinct case/number/gender forms for the definite article. In addition, there were a number of noun-declensions, where the articles remained the same, but the noun-forms were different. Three of the commonest OE noun types (with definite article):

(4.6)

		'king' (m) (*a*-stem)	'ship' (n) (*a*-stem)	'gift' (f) (*ō*-stem)
sg	nom	se cyning	þæt scip	sēo gief-u
	gen	þæs cyning-es	þæs scip-es	þǣre gief-e
	dat	þǣm cyning-e	þǣm scip-e	þǣre gief-e
	acc	þone cyning	þæt scip	þā gief-e
pl	nom	þā cyning-as	þā scip-u	þā gief-a
	gen	þāra cyning-a	þāra scip-a	þāra gief-a
	dat	þǣm cyning-um	þǣm scip-um	þǣm gief-um
	acc	þā cyning-as	þā scip-u	þā gief-a

('*a*-stem', etc. are the traditional handbook designations of these classes, referring to the reconstructed PGmc morphology. A PGmc noun, like an IE one, generally had a root, to which was added some item to form a stem; and the endings were added to the stem. Thus the PGmc nom sg of 'king' was */kuninɣ-a-z/, where the stem was formed by */-a-/ added to the root, and the nom sg */-z/ was added to that.)

It's clear from these paradigms how complex case-marking in OE was. Even with this morphological richness (relative to modern English), many forms are ambiguous: e.g. *þā* can be nom/acc pl of any gender, or fem acc sg; an -*e* signals dat sg for masculines and neuters, but dat sg and gen sg for feminines. The situation is still more complex if we look at other major noun classes:

(4.7)

		'name' (m) (*n*-stem)	'son' (m) (*u*-stem)	'foot' (m) (consonant-stem)
sg	nom	nam-a	sun-u	fōt
	gen	nam-an	sun-a	fōt-es
	dat	nam-an	sun-a	fēt
	acc	nam-an	sun-u	fōt
pl	nom	nam-an	sun-a	fēt
	gen	nam-en-a	sun-a	fōt-a
	dat	nam-um	sun-um	fōt-um
	acc	nam-an	sun-a	fēt

Over the course of the ME period, unstressed vowels in the case-endings fell together in -*e* /ə/; in addition, more and more nouns began to move from other declensions into the *a*-stem type, which is of course the source of our modern -(*e*)*s* plural, and even neuter *a*-stems followed the masculine pattern: hence not only *king-s*, but *ship-s, gift-s, name-s, son-s*. The only simple relic of the *n*-stems is *ox-en*; and a handful of the consonant-stem (umlaut plural) type remains. (On loss of case-marking, see further §6.3.) The definite article system decayed completely, and modern *the* is probably not from any member of the original, but from analogical extension of initial *þ*- to the masc nom sg *se*.

In OE many relations that would now require prepositions or other syntactic means could be expressed by case-endings alone: thus the genitive could express specification (*mǣr-es līf-es mann* 'a man of glorious life'), instrumentality (*god-es þonc-es* 'by God's grace'); and the dative could be used like the Latin ablative for 'movement from' (*drēam-um bidǣled* 'of joys deprived'), the comitative (accompanying) relation (*lȳtl-e wered-e* 'with a small troop'), or the instrumental (*mund-um brugdon* 'with hands they waved'). These constructions could also occur with prepositions: e.g. *mid* 'with' in *mid lȳtl-e wered-e* (still governing dative), etc. When during the ME period the case-system began to collapse, the prepositional alternatives were gradually selected, and these have survived.

The other Germanic dialects show a spectrum from nearly full case-systems of the OE type (Icelandic) through reduced but still fairly rich systems (German), to ones even further advanced than English (Afrikaans). English is thus one step away from being the 'least Germanic' of the family in this respect – though in others (cf. §4.5 on the verb and §6.2) it's more conservative.

4.3.3 PERSONAL PRONOUNS

The only place where both gender and case show up in a fairly systematic way in English is in the pronoun system, which can be set out this way:

(4.8)

		1 Pers	2 Pers	3 Pers		
				m	f	n
	Nominative	I	you	he	she	it
Sg	'Genitive'	my/mine	your(s)	his	her(s)	its
	Objective	me	you	him	her	it
	Nominative	we	you		they	
Pl	'Genitive'	our(s)	your(s)		their(s)	
	Objective	us	you		them	

The pronominal genitive is different from that of the noun, in that it lacks an alternative simple *of*-form: *his hat*/*the hat of him* (but note *I* *don't like the look of her/ . . . *her look*). The system as a whole is a typical IE one, with gender marked only on 3 sg, and one plural set for all genders.

The case names need some discussion. The genitive is self-evident (but see below), and the nominative/objective dichotomy is traditional. Actually for this pair there might be better, if clumsier names: perhaps 'pre-verb case' vs. 'post-verb case'. The nominative is used for subjects, and the objective for all post-verbal and post-prepositional contexts. The pre-verb/post-verb terminology is designed to illustrate a (pseudo)problem concerning pronominal case after *to be*. Many normative grammars say that nominative forms are 'correct' in this position: *it is I, it is she*, etc. This judgement – rarely if ever supported by unselfconscious usage – seems to reflect the importation of a Latin rule into English by 18th-century grammarians, rather than a normal rule of English. For English the consensus of speakers' behaviour (if not their school-derived judgements) seems to be that only the objective forms are natural after *be*: *it's me, it's her*, etc. The pedagogical emphasis on the quite un-English nominative after *be* has led to a common hypercorrection: the use of nominatives after prepositions (*as for my wife and I*, and so on). The origin is simple: people have been taught that *me* is 'bad', so they avoid it except where they can't possibly (nobody yet says **give it to I*).

The syntactic point here is interesting: the hypercorrection occurs only if the first NP in the sequence is a noun or *you* or *it* – i.e. an item that can't be case-marked. The unmarked item as it were 'shields' the pronoun from the preposition, so that it's not felt to be a prep + object construction. A similar phenomenon can be seen in the speech of those who still use *whom*: it is most likely to occur if it is immediately to the right of a preposition (*to whom did you give it*), but not so likely in other situations (*who did you give it to*). The notion 'object of a preposition', that is, is based mainly on contiguity, not function.

With only one minor exception, all standard dialects have the same system. But some U.S. (southern) types have *y'all* /jɔːl/ as a distinct second-person plural. Otherwise, 2 pl formations are generally stigmatized (e.g. U.S., Scots, SA *yous(e)* /juːz/), and show no sign of getting into standard usage.

Even this system is much reduced from the original. OE not only had more case-forms, it had more numbers. It distinguished (an old IE feature) not only singular and plural, but for 1 and 2 persons singular vs. plural vs. dual (two and two only). The OE system was:

(4.9)

		1 Person	2 Person	m	f	n
Sg	nom	ic	þū	hē	hēo	hit
	gen	mīn	þīn	his	hire	his
	dat	mē	þē	him	hire	him
	acc	mē	þē	hine	hī	hit
Du	nom	wit	git			
	gen	uncer	incer			
	dat	unc	inc			
	acc	unc	inc			
Pl	nom	wē	gē		hī	
	gen	ūre	ēower		hira	
	dat	ūs	ēow		him	
	acc	ūs	ēow		hī	

A lot has happened, aside from obvious phonetic change. The dual is gone; the original 3 pl forms have been replaced by Scandinavian *they, their, them* (cf. §2.6); the neuter 3 sg has developed a new genitive *its* (17th c.), and its dative and accusative have merged in accusative – unlike masculine 3 sg, where the dative and accusative have merged in dative. And a new feminine nom sg has developed – *she*. This may be from a special phonetic development of *hēo*, but this is uncertain. In the second person, the old singular is now restricted to archaizing registers (religion, poetry), as is the old nom pl *ye*. And the dat/acc *ēow* has developed regularly to *you*, replacing the nominative, and the gen pl to *your(s)*.

The genitive forms have been listed as parts of the pronoun paradigms for both modern English and OE – though this is not appropriate for the present-day situation. Forms like *my*, etc. are now not really pronouns, but 'personal adjectives'. In OE, they were genuine case-forms, which could be governed by verbs, for instance, just like nouns: e.g. *fanda mīn* 'try me' (lit. 'try of-me'), or used in partitives as in *ān hiora* 'one of-them' (modern *one of them*/*one their(s)*).

The impossibility of *one their(s)* and the rest of the syntax of the genitives suggests that we take them as a kind of defective adjective. I.e. they function as attributes to nouns like other adjectives (*my horse*), occur in predicates after the copula (*this is mine*); but they can't undergo comparison (*his-er, *his-est*), and can't generally be qualified by *very* and the like (*this book is very his*). Though they can take analytic comparison (§4.3.4) under some conditions (*it's more mine than yours*) and some qualifiers (*very much her kind of music*).

The pronominal genitives also differ from other adjectives in having (some of them) different forms for prenominal or attributive position and predicate position: *your book, the book is yours*.

4.3.4 ADJECTIVES AND THE ORDER OF NP ELEMENTS

Syntactically adjectives are noun modifiers, i.e. constituents of NPs. Formally, they can probably best be defined as items that must follow determiners (*the red book/*red the book*), generally occur before nouns, and can be 'compared'. That is, degrees of an attributed property can be represented: either an unspecified degree (the positive form: *the big dog*), a degree greater than some other (the comparative: *the bigger dog*), or the highest possible degree (the superlative: *the biggest dog*). English has two mechanisms of comparison, which are partly complementary: a synthetic (morphological) one as above, and an analytic (syntactic) one, with *more, most*. The general rule seems to be that synthetic comparison is obligatory with monosyllabic adjectives (*bigger/*more big*); both occur with disyllables (*stupider/more stupid*); and analytic comparison is obligatory with adjectives of three syllables or more (*more beautiful/*beautifuller*). Comparison (like negation) is now obligatorily single: multiple comparison was however possible in earlier English, as in Shakespeare's *most unkindest cut of all*, etc.

Nouns are inflected for number, as are demonstratives; adjectives are unmarked. Therefore the only concord possible within the NP is of number between some determiners and the head noun: *this cat/these cats*, etc. But, as we might guess from the OE noun and article system, the situation was once very different: the OE adjective was richly inflected, and the NP as a whole was very much a concordial unit. The adjective had two sets of forms: a weak declension which occurred after inflected determiners, and a strong declension in most other situations. The weak declension was much less differentiated than the strong, being very much like the *n*-stem noun declension (see (4.7)): so 'the good man' would be *se gōd-a mann* (nom sg), *þæs gōd-an mann-es* (gen sg), *þone gōd-an mann* (acc sg), etc. – the main information was carried by the determiner. But where determiners were lacking, the strong declension endings were more like those of the article. Thus *sele mē mīn-ne dǣl* 'give me my-m/acc/sg portion', where the adjective ending *-ne* carries the concordial information (cf. the masc acc sg pronoun *hi-ne* (4.9) and the article *þo-ne* (4.6)). In other cases we could have 'of my portion' *mīn-es dǣl-es*, 'by means of my portion' *mīn-um dǣl-e* (note the dat sg pronoun *hi-m*, and the article *þǣ-m*).

English is now the only Germanic dialect without at least some relic of this old system. In some (like Icelandic) the whole system is virtually intact; in others it is reduced (German) or nearly absent (Afrikaans).

But even Afrikaans has a two-term system: inflected vs. uninflected (*die man is blind* 'the man is blind' vs. *'n blind-e man* 'a blind man').

Where the NP does become complex is in the matter of ordering of elements within it – beyond the obvious fact that determiners precede nouns, etc. On one analysis there are at least four distinct 'slots' before the head noun, each of which can be occupied by a member of one class of determiner or another, with the ordering relations remaining quite rigid. The first slot contains quantifiers (*all, many, both . . .*); the second articles, demonstratives, 'personal adjectives' (*a, the, my, . . .*); the third another set of quantifiers (*many, few*) and genitives (*father's, John's*); and the fourth contains adjectives and numerals. To illustrate:

(4.10)

Slot	I	II	III	IV	N
	all	the	many	fuzzy	kittens
	what	a		good	dog
	both	my	mother's	two	ears
	all	you	many	silly	communists
		the			Pope

There are of course complications: e.g. given (4.10), it's clear that *a few of* is to be treated as a single item, a complex determiner; it occupies as a whole only slot I, and allows all the slots after it to be filled (*a few of my uncle's many children*); and intensifiers or qualifiers like *very* seem to be able to occur as part of complex items in more than one slot (*all of the very many fuzzy kittens, all of the many very fuzzy kittens, all of the very many very fuzzy kittens*). But in general the orders are fixed, and slot-orders can't be reversed (**many the Ns*), and no items from one class can co-occur with another (**a my house*).

The adjective slot IV has a complicated internal structure of its own, partially sensitive to semantic categories. While it might seem at first that adjectives can simply be piled up before nouns pretty much at will (*fat pimply scruffy smelly little . . . boys*), on closer inspection this isn't so. Consider: *the big Victorian house* vs. **the Victorian big house, the old red barn* vs. **the red old barn*, etc. Without going into excessive detail, we can see that there is a fixed sequence 'size' + 'quality' + 'age' + 'colour' + 'style': *the big beautiful old red Victorian house*, etc.

There is actually a certain pragmatic method in this sequencing: the head noun and the adjective immediately to its left tend to form a head-like constituent themselves, with – in most cases – modifiers to their left taking this expanded head as a whole in their scope. The example above might be unpacked this way: What kind of house? A Victorian one. What kind of Victorian house? A red one. What kind of red Victorian house? . . . etc. We could represent the NP above graphically as:

(4.11)

[the [big [beautiful [old [red [Victorian [house]]]]]]]

(Reading inward from the outermost brackets, you get increasingly smaller constituents in the scope of the modifier immediately to the left.)

This suggests that there are both arbitrary and (communicationally) 'relevant' syntactic rules: i.e. some are not really informative (it doesn't matter whether verbs come before or after objects), while others seem to be connected in some way with meaning. In this case modifier order seems to represent the internal logical structure of propositions most likely to be reflected in normal discourse: *the Victorian red house* would normally have contrastive stress on *Victorian* (i.e. 'the Victorian one, not the Georgian one', in a discourse about more than one red house). (On more intimate connections between syntax and discourse, see §4.7.)

4.4 Deixis

The term deixis (from the Greek for 'pointing': the same root occurs in **digit**, **indicate**) is applied to the linguistic function of orienting and identifying participants and objects referred to in discourse. The main deictics are personal pronouns and demonstratives (spatial) and tense-markers (temporal). To clarify: a speech situation may be taken as having a speaker as a 'centre', with all temporal and spatial relationships defined according to him (language is essentially egocentric). Thus first person denotes speaker, second person addressee, and third person other objects or participants in the universe of discourse. Deictics are not – as such – 'parts of speech'; they are elements in a functional system that cross-cuts both nouns and verbs and their categories – hence the placement of this topic in a no-man's-land between the noun and the verb.

'Egocentricity' can be schematized this way:

(4.12)

> *Speaker-Centred*: I, here, this, now, come, bring
> *Non-Speaker-Centred*: you/he, there, that, then, go, take

Unlike 'ordinary' words like *John*, *cat*, *quickly*, *run*, deictics take part of their meaning from context. One could say for instance that there are circumstances in which *here* and *there* refer to the same place, while *I* refers to different persons, or *I*, *he* and *you* refer to the same person. Consider a conversation with three participants, with subscript numerals indicating identity of reference to places and persons:

(4.13)

a. Is he₁ there₂?
b. I₃ don't know. I₃'ll call him₁. Hey, are you₁ there₂?
c. Yes, I₁'m here₂. Where are you₃?

My *here* is your *there*, and his *there* as well. By the same token, *I* am *you* when *you* (who to *you* are *I*) are speaking to *me*.

The three main types of deixis, all of which are systematically coded in English, are: (a) **Person**: speaker vs. addressee, speaker vs. non-addressee, non-speaker; (b) **Space**: speaker's vicinity/direction vs. other vicinities/directions; (c) **Time**: speaker's moment of utterance vs. other times. These basically involve two speaker-centred dimensions, normally called proximal (toward-speaker) and distal (away-from-speaker). The main deictic systems in English can be outlined this way:

(4.14)

PERSON			LOCATION (Space/Time)	
Proximal	*Distal*		*Proximal*	*Distal*
		1 2 3	this	that
I, me, we, us	you	he, him, she, her, it, they, them	here now present	there then past

(Future is another kind of distal time-deixis: see §4.5.2.) The conflation of space and time as 'location' points to a very basic (perhaps universal) identification: time tends to be metaphorically construed as a locational category. E.g. *this* can refer to proximal space or time (*this book*, *this very minute*), we visualize time as having 'direction' (*forward into the future, the past is now behind us*); and we will see in the next section how verb-tenses can be used for subtle effects concerned not with time but with 'closeness' and 'distance'.

Except for person, most English dialects have a two-way deictic system, proximal vs. distal. In person, addressees are distinguished from other non-speakers (2 vs. 3 person); but demonstratives and locatives distinguish only speaker vs. all others (*this* 'near me' vs. *that* 'anywhere else', etc.). Some languages however, and even other dialects of English, make the same three-way distinction for space that standard English does for person: e.g. Scots, with *this* (proximal to speaker) vs. *that* (distal to speaker, proximal to addressee) vs. *yon* (distal to both speaker and addressee). This same distinction occurs in Latin (*hic* vs. *ille* vs. *iste*).

The Scots system seems to be a late development, capitalizing on the independent existence of *yon(der)* as a generalized distal term.

The neat present-day system of space deixis developed gradually during the Middle English period: in OE the *this*/*that* distinction did not exist as such, but there was a rather vaguer and more complex set of form/meaning pairings. The definite article (*se/sēo/þæt*: §4.3.2, (4.6)) served both as what we would now think of as an article and for distal deixis; but there was another form, *þes/þis/þēos*, which had a specifically proximal sense – though it was not used as commonly. It was only with the generalization in ME of the uninflected *þe* for the definite article (leading to modern *the*) that *that* (originally a neuter determiner) was free to be used as an all-gender counterpart to *this*.

All the Germanic languages have something like the English *this*/*that* contrast, but some do it more transparently; in Afrikaans for instance there are no simple forms, but *die*, the definite article, and the demonstratives *hierdie* 'this' (lit. 'here-the') and *daardie* 'that' (lit. 'there-the'). We might compare dialects of English that use *this here*, *that there*, or French *ce garçon-ci* vs. *ce garçon-là*, lit. 'specific boy-here' vs. 'specific boy-there'.

This and *that* are systematically connected with the locative adverbs *here*, *there*. More subtle deictic components are covertly represented in certain verbs as well, and can be teased out by tests involving the adverbs. Thus *come* and *go*, *bring* and *take* are inherently deictic pairs (proximal vs. distal), as we can see from the oddity of *come there/*go here, *bring it there/*take it here. (*Bring* is perhaps less clear for many speakers; it's not certain whether *bring* and *take* are really systematically opposed in my own dialect, since *bring it there* is quite all right, and *I'll bring it with me to London*/*I'll take it with me to London* seem to be largely interchangeable.)

4.5 Main Verbs and Auxiliaries

4.5.1 FORMS AND FUNCTIONS

In constructions like *I can swim*, *I am swimming*, *I have swum*, *I have been swimming*, the forms *swim(ming)*, *swum* represent the main verb of the predication ('swimming' is in one way or another predicated of 'I'). And *can*, *am*, *have been* are auxiliary verbs, in a way 'modifiers' of the main verb (further specifying it). It is clear that auxiliaries like *can* represent a subsystem distinct from *am*, *have*, *have been*; the latter can combine with members of the *can* class (*I can have been swimming*, etc.); whereas members of the *can* class ('modal auxiliaries': §4.5.3) do not in most standard dialects. (*I will can swim, *I can must swim). Though in other ways, as we'll see, the two classes pattern together: e.g. they all move to the head of the clause in question-formation (*can I swim? am I swimming? have I swum?* – cf. §4.5.4). We will look at the modal auxiliaries separately; this section and the next will be concerned with the main verbs of predications, and the *have, be* class of auxiliaries.

It's traditional to regard 'a verb' as a collection of forms, under two headings: finite (marked for tense, person, number) and nonfinite (not so marked). Taking the verb *write*, for instance, we have the following inventory:

(4.15)

FINITE	NONFINITE
Present: write, write-s	*Infinitive*: (to) write
Past: wrote	*Present Participle*: writ-ing
	Past Participle: writt-en
	Gerund: writ-ing

(On *have written, am writing, will write*, etc. see §4.5.2.)

These labels are functional rather than formal; the bare infinitive (without *to*, as in *he can write*) is the same as the present non-3rd-person, the present participle (*I am writing*) is the same as the gerund (*writing is hard*); and in weak verbs the past and past participle are generally the same (*I walk-ed/have walk-ed*). Functionally, the finite forms alone are 'verb-forms' proper; the nonfinite ones occur in complex sequences like *have written, am writing*, or act as non-verbal parts of speech: either adjectives (present participle: *a writing man*; past participle: *a written document*), or nouns (infinitive: *I like to write* (cf. §4.6.2 for justification of infinitives as nouns); gerund: *I like writing*).

4.5.2 TENSE AND ASPECT

The time-related forms of a typical English verb (here exemplified for the first person) might conventionally be given this way:

(4.16)

Present: I write	*Past*: I wrote
Present Progressive: I am writing	*Past Progressive*: I was writing
Present Perfect: I have written	*Past Perfect*: I had written
Present Perfect Progressive:	*Past Perfect Progressive*:
I have been writing	I had been writing

Future: I will write
Future Progressive: I will be writing
Future Perfect Progressive:
I will have been writing

(The past perfect is also called 'pluperfect'.)

We note first that there are two 'simple' forms (*I write, I wrote*), and a series of auxiliary + nonfinite verb constructions; these can be divided broadly into progressives (*be* + present participle, or *be* + V-*ing*) and perfects (*have* + past participle, or *have* + V-*en*); plus a form with *will* + infinitive, which itself combines with both perfect and progressive.

These are often lumped together as 'tenses of the verb'; but something else must be going on here as well, since under that definition we'd appear to have 'tenses of tenses'. But in fact the two terms 'past' and 'present' for instance don't combine with each other – though they do with 'perfect' and 'progressive'; and perfect and progressive must obligatorily be marked for tense as well, but past and present don't have to be marked for progressive or perfect. In modern terminology, past and present (and to some extent future) are grouped together as tenses, and perfect and progressive under another heading, as aspects. And the two categories, though similar in some respects (i.e. in being associated with 'time'), are really quite different.

We will begin with the more familiar, tense: this is a deictic category (§4.4) which relates the speaker's time of utterance to the time-location of the content of the utterance (the event, state etc. being described or narrated). The speaker's 'now' is the zero-point in terms of which the content is located. Thus *I was in Cape Town* could without too much nit-picking be paraphrased as 'I say [now] that [then] the proposition "I am in Cape Town" was true'. Similarly, *I am in Cape Town* claims the truth of the proposition at the moment of utterance. Diagrammatically:

(4.17)

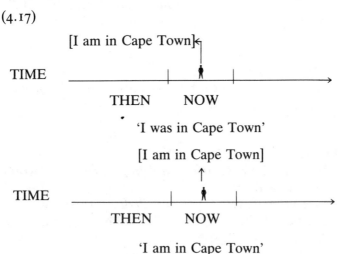

'I am in Cape Town'

There is of course another 'then': future. This is overlaid with yet another component, which we will look at in the next section; but from a temporal point of view we could diagram *I will be in Cape Town* as:

(4.18)

'I will be in Cape Town'

(The time-arrow in (4.17–18) is pointed in the direction of the future, as is conventional.)

Deictically, both past and future are distal (pointing away from the speaker): *at this moment* can only refer to present, while *at that moment* can refer to past or future (*at that moment I was eaten by a bear/I will be eaten by a bear*). So for tense proper, the primary function appears to be one of 'positioning' a speaker *vis-à-vis* what he's talking about.

There are however extended (largely metaphorical) functions of both present and past, more or less distantly related to their deictic status. Thus present is used to express 'timeless' and 'generic' truths (*the sun rises in the East*; *a poor workman blames his tools*; *lions are carnivores*). Note that the typical tense of proverbs and other 'gnomic' utterances is present. The extension can probably be construed in terms of either timelessness or recurrence, both of which presuppose that at all moments of utterance, a proposition will be true: thus lions are always carnivores, while the sun rises in the East only once in 24 hours; but given our expectation that the solar system will keep on working as it does now, it is (overall) 'always' true, and this is as it were 'good enough for human language', i.e. within the bounds of acceptable (unconscious) metaphor. The use of present for future (*I leave for Johannesburg tomorrow*) is rather more complex, and we will look at that below.

In a similar metaphorical way the past, as a distal deictic, can be used to signal 'distance from' the present in non-temporal senses, i.e. 'imaginative' or 'psychological' distance, distance from 'reality': thus the distinction between *what will you do if you meet a tiger* and *what would you do if you met a tiger* discussed above (§4.1). Other extensions, coupled in a complex way with the perfect, occur in expressions of doubt (the present statement is 'distant' from what I think is the case): e.g. *I would have thought that leprechauns are Irish* in response to someone's statement that they're Jewish. Note also that this statement is 'distant' in another way: it is somehow 'softened', made less direct and challenging, by use of the past (compare the tone of *I think leprechauns are Irish* in the same dialogue, where the statement of disbelief is more direct, represents a less ambiguous commitment on the speaker's part). This same softening of challenge or direct address is also mediated by the past in requests: *will you get me a drink* vs. *would you get me a drink*, and in a more complex and even more indirect way in a construction like *I was wondering if you'd be so good as to get me a drink*.

So much for simple present and past. The third apparent 'straight' tense, the future, is more complex, since there seem to be many more ways of expressing it than there are for the others. Enough so that there's reason to doubt whether it's really appropriate to talk of a 'future tense' in English, as a genuine morphological (rather than semantic) category. Is there really a grammatical category 'future', or merely a conceptual one (as is the case in all languages, of course), and a collection of constructions that mark it in one way or another? The answer here is as usual 'yes' to both alternatives.

The 'standard' future is *will* + infinitive; but there is also a *go*-future (*I'm going to do it later*) and a 'present-future' (*I leave tomorrow*); and the *will*-construction is used for purposes other than future (*that will be John at the door*) – though this can be related to simple futurity, as we'll see. Overall, the following seems to be true:

(i) The *will* (or for some speakers *will/shall*) future is probably the most general.

(ii) The *go*-future (either full *going to* or the reduced and probably more common *gonna*) is widespread, and seems to be subtly different in meaning from *will*: it carries a nuance of 'intention' (neutral *I'll do it later* vs. 'intentional' *I'm gonna do it later*); it is also used in questions when a proposed or predicted future action has been (to the speaker) inordinately delayed: *When are you going to clean up your room?* implies that you ought to have done it already, whereas *when will you . . .?* is a more neutral request for information.

(iii) The present-for-future correlates in some uses with avoiding redundancy: e.g. with an unambiguous future adverb, present obviates double tense-marking (*I leave tomorow*). It is also used – probably as a result of the use of present for 'timeless' truths – where the certainty of a future event is institutionalized, as in schedules or timetables. Thus *Sam will pick me up at 10.00 and drive me to the station; then I catch the 10.33 to Scunthorpe*. A time-tabled train-departure is, like the sunrise, effectively 'timelessly true' (in an ideal world); but someone picking me up by car is subject to unpredictable contingencies (*Sam picks me up at 10.00* is odd unless he does it every day, and my future statement simply singles out one of a repeated series). Similarly one doesn't normally ask **When will the train to Scunthorpe leave?* unless it's been delayed.

The future also has a component of modality (§4.5.3): it reflects not only time, but a speaker's mental state, the certainty of his knowledge of events, etc. Future, unlike present or past, involves prediction of as yet unrealized events, hence assessment of degrees of likelihood. This probably accounts for uses like *that will be Joe at the door*, or *Ahmed? Oh he'll be Maurice's son* – the future allows a degree of potential indeterminacy and possibility of error that wouldn't be carried by a bald present: any prediction, however likely, can still be wrong.

So English might best be seen as having a two-way 'core' tense system: present (or better 'non-past') vs. past; with future a slightly ambiguous, not fully grammaticalized category, essentially tense-like but with modal overtones. And the whole system – core + future – interacts with the second main time-related dimension, that of aspect. The two main explicitly marked aspects in English are progressive and perfect; we will begin with the progressive, which is rather simpler.

Aspect is an essentially non-deictic category that (roughly) specifies the relation of an event or state represented by a verb to the passage of time, or specifies its internal temporal structure. Aspectual markings typically answer questions like: Is the action complete or incomplete? Is it once-only, or repetitive? Is it just beginning, or do we catch it at some (unspecified) point in the middle? To take a Latin example, the infix *-sc-* marks an inchoative aspect (becoming, but not having fully become): *rub-ē-ō* 'I am red', *rub-e-sc-ō* 'I redden'.

In English, aspect is normally marked by an auxiliary + V construction. The progressive (*be* V-*ing*) can be unpacked by looking at a pair of 'present' forms: say *I write* vs. *I am writing*. The first appears to state habitual or typical activity (*I write for a living/with a quill pen*); the second an activity currently in progress (*I am writing now/these days*). Thus the simple present covertly encodes a 'habitual' aspect (cf. the use of present for 'timeless truth' or 'recurrence'); the progressive overtly encodes the notion 'being in process of doing X'. Note that progressive normally occurs only with verbs of 'action', rather than 'state': hence the oddity of **I am knowing the answer* vs. *I am learning the answer*. The same is true of predicate adjectives: *I am being careful* (taking care is arguably an 'action') vs. **I am being pregnant* (except as a joke, e.g. as an answer to *why are you throwing up?*).

Every non-past utterance in English must be marked for progressivity or its lack, in contrast to other Germanic languages where the simple present is aspectually ambiguous. Swedish *jag skriver*, Afrikaans *ek skryf* can mean either 'I write' or 'I am writing'; the aspect is interpretable from the situation of utterance, or from other linguistic items: *ek skryf nou* 'I write now' can only be progressive, *ek skryf boeke* 'I write books' only habitual. But both Swedish and Afrikaans have optional progressives, used where for some reason progressivity is particularly important, or the speaker feels it should be marked: Sw *jag håller på att skriva* 'I am occupied in to-write', Afr *ek is besig om te skryf* 'I am busy with to-write'. The same is true in French: *j'écris* is ambiguous, but *je suis en train d'écrire* 'I am in process of to-write' is progressive. If Swedish or Afrikaans or French wanted to develop obligatory progressive marking, the material would be there; and in fact English developed its progressive from a formerly optional construction (see §4.5.4).

The other marked aspect in English, the perfect, is less 'purely' aspectual: it has a modified deictic component that puts it on a cline somewhere between a simple tense like past and a true aspect like progressive. The deictic component is perhaps easiest to describe: perfect can function as a kind of second-order tense, encoding the notion 'prior-to' – but in relation to something other than the speaker's zero-point. This function is especially clear in the past and future perfect: take a sentence like *Mary had fed the cat when I got home*. Here the primary temporal orientation is the past-tense *got*: getting home is past with respect to my moment of utterance. The past perfect *had fed* locates the feeding as prior to my arrival home – but in relation not to my zero-point, but to the other event related to my zero-point by the past tense. Similarly with the future perfect: *Mary will have fed the cat when I get home*. Here again the feeding occurs before my arrival – but this time both events are future with respect to my moment of utterance. Diagrammatically:

(4.19)

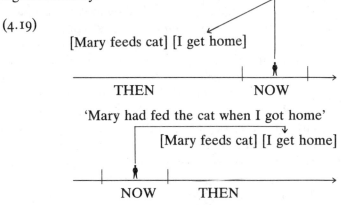

'Mary had fed the cat when I got home'

'Mary will have fed the cat when I get home'

This 'anteriority' relation is often said to give the perfect an element of 'completion': the event marked by it is finished before some other one. This is not so clear when perfect is combined with progressive, however: *Mary had been feeding the cat when I got home* (does this imply that she stopped when I arrived?); *Mary will have been feeding the cat when I get home* (same question). This is one of those cases (commoner than many linguists like to believe) where even a native speaker isn't sure what a construction means, though he may be able to use it perfectly appropriately.

The present perfect is rather harder to pin down: *I have eaten* expresses anteriority, but so does *I ate*. The difference is multifaceted; the perfect does seem to have an element of 'completion', but more significantly, what is sometimes called a 'prospective aspect', or a dimension of 'present relevance'. This aspectual component establishes a narrated past content as having some particular importance for the moment of utterance: compare *I lived in Scotland for ten years* (*at some time or other*) with *I have lived in Scotland for ten years* (*as of now*).

This component is reinforced by the normal cooccurrence of perfect, but not simple past, with 'present-relevant' adverbs like *yet*, *already*: *have you eaten yet?*, *I haven't eaten yet*, *I've eaten already*, etc. Most dialects have a fully grammaticalized perfect, in which the above restriction is rigid: **I ate already*, **did you eat yet?* (on *do* as a tense-marker in questions see §4.5.4). But some, notably east coast U.S. ones like mine, appear to be losing the distinction: the aspectually unspecified past (or aorist, to borrow an appropriate term from Greek grammar) can be used instead of the perfect in many cases: *did you eat* (*yet*)?, *Yes, I ate* (*already*) are quite acceptable for me – though only in less formal spoken contexts. (On the significance of this development see §6.4).

We can sum up the discussion of modern English tense and aspect with a diagram illustrating the relative 'purity' of the different categories: closeness to a category label = closeness to that category type (on modality see the next section):

(4.20)

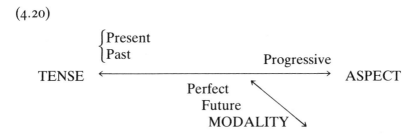

4.5.3 Modality

In addition to expressing some proposition or basic conceptual content, a normal English utterance also contains deictic (spatial and temporal) and aspectual elements, the latter usually coded on the verb. So a simple utterance like *leprechauns are Jewish* could be said to consist of:

(4.21)

> PROPOSITION: leprechauns be Jewish
> SPACE-DEIXIS: Distal to Speaker (3rd person)
> TIME-DEIXIS: Proximal to Speaker (Present)
> ASPECT: Habitual

But there's still another component: the kind of utterance it is. We can see the point of this distinction by comparing (4.21) to another utterance: *Are leprechauns Jewish?*

(4.22)

> PROPOSITION: Leprechauns be Jewish
> SPACE-DEIXIS: Distal to Speaker
> TIME-DEIXIS: Proximal to Speaker
> ASPECT: Habitual

But clearly the two are not the same. The first is a statement or assertion, the second a question. And if we compare others like *leprechauns may be Jewish, leprechauns must be Jewish*, we will still find the same proposition, deixis and aspect. The differentiating component is what is generally called modality. This is a complex dimension involving (roughly) the 'speaker's attitude' to a proposition expressed, some aspect of his mental state or state of knowledge with regard to it, or certain obligations or similar constraints that may be said to exist or be imposed on some participant(s).

To illustrate in greater detail:

(i) *leprechauns are Jewish.* [An assertion: Jewishness is timelessly predicated of them.]

(ii) *leprechauns: be Jewish!* [A command: speaker wishes to impose an obligation].

(iii) *leprechauns can be Jewish.* [A statement of speaker's knowledge that leprechauns have a certain ability; or of his assessment that their being Jewish is not improbable; *or* a granting of permission.]

(iv) *leprechauns may be Jewish.* [A statement of speaker's view that a state is possible or not improbable; *or* a granting of permission.]

(v) *leprechauns will be Jewish.* [A prediction, i.e. an assertion of knowledge of some kind that a future state of affairs will come to pass; *or* imposition of an obligation.]

(vi) *leprechauns ought to be Jewish.* [A statement of speaker's view that their behaviour or other properties conduce to knowing that they are Jewish (they are frequently seen in synagogues); *or* an imposition of an obligation – if a weaker one than that imposed by *will* or the form of (ii).]

(vii) *Are leprechauns Jewish?* [A statement of speaker's lack of knowledge about the predicated state of affairs; another way of looking at this is as a desire to impose an obligation on an addressee, i.e. that he furnish information.]

Let p = 'leprechauns be Jewish'. Then we could represent these various modalities as operators (the logical term) which add certain information to (modalize) the proposition. Thus:

(i) FACT (p)
(ii) COMMAND (p)
(iii) ABLE (p) *or* PERMITTED (p)
(iv) POSSIBLE (p) *or* PERMITTED (p)
(v) PREDICT FACT (p) *or* OBLIGED (p)
(vi) PROBABLE (p) *or* OBLIGED (p)
(vii) QUERY (p)

Modality is closely connected but not identical to the traditional grammatical category of mood. Thus (i) above is an indicative mood, (ii) is imperative, (vii) is interrogative. Other languages have mood-forms that express other modalities: e.g. the Latin subjunctive form can express wishes (optative modality) as in *viv-a-t rex* 'may the king live' vs. indicative *viv-i-t rex* 'the king lives'; or exhortations (hortatory modality) as in *ador-ē-mus tē* 'let us adore thee' vs. *ador-ā-mus tē* 'we adore thee'. But even in a language with elaborate verb morphology like Latin, there is no necessary one-to-one connection between mood (a formal category) and any particular modality – even if many of the modalities expressed by a single mood are related. To keep our terminology neat, we should say that English does not (except for a marginal set of 'subjunctives': cf. §4.5.5) encode mood in its morphology. As the glosses to the Latin examples suggest, it expresses different modalities through different lexical items and syntactic constructions.

But one central group of modalities is encoded in a small, idiosyncratic but important group of verbs: the modal auxiliaries (or modals). These constitute a closed class, whose members now are *can/could*, *shall/ should*, *may/might*, *will/would*, and *must*; and a small group of 'semi-modals', mainly *ought*, *dare* and *need*. The true modals have a number of odd properties in common, some of which they share with all auxiliary verbs, and some of which are unique. The general auxiliary properties (shared with *be*, *have*, and auxiliary *do*) are: (a) no '*do*-support' or *do*-periphrasis (§4.5.4) in questions or negation: *I can swim/I can't swim/ can I swim?* but **I don't can swim*, **do I can swim?*, etc.; (b) ability to take the negative clitic *-n't*: *he can't* (like *he hasn't/isn't*), but **he goesn't*, etc.

The uniquely modal properties are: (a) lack of non-finite forms: no participles (**I am canning swim*), and for most dialects (but see §5.7.1) no *to*-infinitive (**I want to can swim*); (b) lack of aspectual forms (tied in with (a)): **I have canned swim*; (c) no marking of 3 sg present: *I/you/he can*, **he cans*'; and (d) no true past tense.

The last point needs some comment. It seems at first as if *can/could*, *will/would*, etc. are present/past pairs: isn't *I could speak French* the 'past of' *I can speak French*? But compare *I can speak French (if I want to*) with *I could speak French* (*if I wanted to*). The latter might be a past (*I could speak French in 1950, but I've forgotten it*); but it's at least as likely to be something non-past: *I could speak French if I wanted to – but I don't want to*. The time-reference (if any) is hypothetical future. The literal past of *can* is probably *used to be able* or a similar periphrasis; or sometimes *could* with a past adverb (*I once could speak French*); only the latter use of *could* is unambiguously past. Similar tests can be done with the other pairs.

Historically of course the *-d* forms are pasts; but the main relic of this that they retain is the 'softening' or 'distancing' effect of the metaphorical extension of pastness (§4.5.2): compare the tone of *will you be so good as to leave* with that of *would you be so good . . .*, or *can you lend me a pound* with *could you . . .*, and so on. Similarly with the 'possibility' sense of *may* (see below); *might* isn't its past, but either a synonym or a different form with a slightly different degree of probability and/or doubt implied: for me anyhow *it may be true* and *it might be true* seem to be the same. If *might* is to be an unambiguous past of *may*, it is used with a perfect: *I may go/I might have gone*.

The English modals, like those of the other Germanic languages, typically code (ambiguously) two different types of modalities:

(i) Epistemic (Gr *epistēmē* 'knowledge'): modalities reflecting speaker's assessment of degrees of likelihood, doubt, certainty, possibility; the modality of prediction (future with *will*): i.e. those modalities concerned with his 'state of knowledge' with respect to a proposition.

(ii) Deontic (Gr *deon* 'that which is binding'): modalties of obligation, permission, command, etc. – those that reflect speaker's desire to 'bind' someone to a course of action. Sometimes also called the 'root' sense.

If this all seems rather abstract, we can give some concrete illustrations:

    (i) Mary *can* speak French
        (a) because (I know) she knows how [epistemic]
        (b) because it's now legal [deontic]

   (ii) You *may* leave the room
        (a) though I don't know it you will [epistemic]
        (b) because I give you permission to [deontic]

  (iii) You *must* drink a lot of beer
        (a) because (I know) otherwise you wouldn't have a belly like that [epistemic]
        (b) by tomorrow, if you want to get the Gluttony Prize [deontic]

  (iv) Herman – Oh he *will* be Maggie's husband

(a) judging from the fact that he married her in 1967 [epistemic]
(b) because I'll see to it, with a shotgun if necessary [deontic]

(In (iv) we see *will* as a true modal, in addition to its semi-modal function as a future marker.)

The verbs *ought, need, dare* have some auxiliary-like properties, but their status is not clear-cut. They all take clitic *-n't* (*you needn't/oughtn't (to)/daren't do that*), and in some dialects (though this is recessive) can be fronted in questions (*need you/dare you do that?*). They don't however take bare infinitives in assertions, but require *to*: *I need to do it/ *I need do it*, etc. In most U.S. dialects *ought* doesn't occur in the negative: *you ought to* is negated as *you shouldn't* (though some do have *you hadn't ought to*). *Ought* alone in this group has both epistemic and deontic senses: *that man ought to be the ratcatcher* (a) *because his van says 'Rodent Control'* [epistemic]/(b) *because he looks like the sort who likes killing rats* [deontic].

It's perhaps worth mentioning that at least three other verbs in some varieties of English have developed some auxiliary-like properties: *help*, and *come, go*. The two cases are rather different, and neither is identical to the other auxiliaries. *Help* can occur freely in constructions with unmarked infinitives, e.g. *I helped wash the dishes, he helps feed the chickens*. It does however still retain, even in auxiliary function, its nonfinite forms and past and present 3 sg inflections (above and *I'm helping feed the chickens, he helped eat the zucchini*), and it does not move in questions (**Helped I wash ...*) or take a postposed full or clitic negative (**I helped not/helpedn't*), but takes *do*-support like any other verb (*Did I help feed ..., I didn't help feed*).

Come and *go* have a more limited distribution as what we might call 'quasi-auxiliaries'. In some dialects (mainly or solely U.S.) they can occur in constructions like *let's go eat Chinese (food) tonight, they come sleep over at our house on Fridays*. What's interesting here is that this usage is apparently patterned after the morphology of the modals: *come, go* as auxiliaries not only have no nonfinite forms (**we're going eat Chinese*), but the only grammatical uses involve present non-3rd-person. Thus *I/you/we/they go eat Chinese every week*, but **I went eat ...*, **He goes eat ...*, etc. That is, only those forms that are like the modals, i.e. that lack the *-s* inflection or marking for tense, can take on the auxiliary function. Like *help*, however, these take *do*-support: *Do you go eat ..., we didn't come sleep over ...*, and so on. As far as I know, this construction, unlike that with *help*, is strictly informal, and does not occur in the written language; certainly in my dialect it is very casual and exclusively spoken.

4.5.4 THE SYNTAX OF THE AUXILIARY: TENSE, ASPECT, QUESTIONS, NEGATION

The auxiliary + main verb construction has some interesting properties. To begin with, it furnishes an excellent example of the possibilities of disparity between grammar and meaning. Even though aspect (§4.5.2) is a semantically unitary category, its syntactic representation is discontinuous. That is, the main verb intervenes between two halves of a 'split' aspect marker:

(4.23)

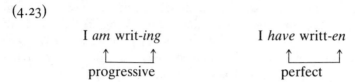

When both progressive and perfect occur in the same construction, the discontinuities are 'nested':

(4.24)

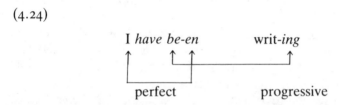

Here *been* is a double aspect marker: its left half (*be-*) connects with a suffix to its right (*-ing*), and its right half (*-en*) with an auxiliary to its left (*have*); the two realizations 'cross', as it were.

A perfect syntax-meaning match would be **I have-en be-ing write*; the modern discontinuities reflect the historical sources. The progressive derives syntactically from an OE construction with a present participle as predicate adjective (type: *ic eam wrīt-ende*), parallel in meaning to a simple copula + adjective sequence like *I am tall*; it also apparently involves some semantic influence from an old locative construction, with the preposition *on* 'in' plus the dative of a verbal noun, e.g. *on fiscap-e* 'in fishing' (which remains as a relic in archaic and local *a-fishing*). The old participial form has been lost and replaced by the gerund. Locatives for progressives are quite natural; after all, progressivity represents a 'state-in-which' one is – hence the optional German progressives of the type *ich bin am Schreiben* 'I am in-the-dat to-write' = 'I am writing', with the infinitive as verbal noun serving as object of the preposition.

The perfect probably originates from an adjectival construction in which the past participle represents an 'achievement' or 'completed state' into which something has been brought. Consider the difference between modern English *I have cornered him* and *I have him cornered*. The latter (in essence 'I have got him into a state of being cornered') is the older type, and the main contributor to the modern perfect: the participle here modifies *him*, and is not in construction with *have* – though it's easy to see how it came to be interpreted as a perfect. To clarify (perhaps), the difference is between *I have [him cornered]* and *I [have cornered] him*; in OE the first type could apparently have both meanings.

The first position in any auxiliary sequence, no matter how complex, has certain unique properties: (a) it's the only place in the sequence where tense is marked; (b) it's the position whose occupant moves in the formation of questions; and (c) the negative marker normally goes immediately to its right. E.g.

(4.25)

    i. John *is* writing a book
       Is John writing a book?
       John *is*n't/*is* not writing a book

    ii. The book *could* have been being written
       Could the book have been being written?
       The book *could*n't/*could* not have been being written

The rules look simple: for questions, move the first auxiliary to the beginning of the clause; for negation, insert *not* or clitic *-n't* to the right of the first auxiliary.

But what happens where there is no auxiliary at all, in simple present and past sentences without modals? If the above rule applied, *John wrote* would give **wrote John?* and **John wrote not*. But of course we get ***did** John write?* and *John **did** not write*. This construction is called *do*-periphrasis or *do*-support. English is unique in Germanic in having this obligatory 'supportive' use of *do*. In the other languages, the rules as above operate on the first verb, whether it's main or auxiliary: G *schrieb Johann?*, *Johann schrieb nicht* (as well as *hat Johann geschrieben?* 'has J. written?', *Johann könnte nicht schreiben* 'J. couldn't write'). English once had very much this system: see below.

The 'rationale' of *do*-support is quite simple: note that *do* appears only when there's no other auxiliary (modal or aspectual); and that it appears where the auxiliary would go if there were one. It also appears in the appropriate form: it takes on the tense and agreement features of the 'absent' auxiliary: *John writes/does John write?*, *John wrote/did John write?*, *they write/do they write?* This suggests that we might interpret the question rule this way: move tense and number, along with whatever they're attached to, to the front. If the sentence has an overt auxiliary, that moves; but if there isn't one, something has to 'carry' the tense and agreement features. And it seems not to be an accident that the choice is the maximally empty or 'meaningless' verb *do*. In questions and negations it's a kind of 'dummy', a piece of phonological material there by default, to provide a stem to attach endings to.

So auxiliary *do* has no lexical meaning, only a grammatical function – unlike the aspectual or modal auxiliaries, or the main verb *do*. That there is a main verb *do*, different from if related to the auxiliary, is clear from cases like *what do you do for a living* (**what do you for a living?*), *I don't do anything* (**I don't anything*). But even main *do* means 'less' than other verbs (note that it's also used as a 'pro-form' substituting for verbs or whole predicates: *John got sick and so did Mary, Lincoln started the Civil War and Jefferson Davis did too*). This makes it a natural candidate for the default case.

Other verbs as well can be both main and auxiliary: *have* is a clear case. In my own dialect at least possessive *have* behaves like any other verb: *do you have a match?/I don't have one*, etc. And with both auxiliary and main *have*: *I haven't had any in a long time*. In many British dialects, however, possessive *have* is treated like an auxiliary too: *Have you a match/I haven't any*, and so on. (These would be ungrammatical – or at least 'foreign' – to most Americans.)

The history of *do*-support is complex and controversial. OE had a verb 'do', which among other things had the same general meaning as modern *do* (*dōð swā ic bidde* 'do (imp pl) as I bid'); during the course of ME there was an increase in its use as a 'filler' (often for metrical purposes) but also as an emphatic, an affirmative, etc. These other senses began to 'bleach' out during the 16th century, and for a while we had e.g. *I believe it* and *I do believe it* as virtual synonyms. As time went on, the *do*-forms were retained mainly for negatives and questions, and except in a few archaisms (note that *I think not* as a strong expression of scepticism still occurs), the modern negative and question forms were established – at least in the spoken language – during the 18th century. In 'high' styles of course the old forms (*Say not the struggle nought availeth*) remained much longer, in part reinforced by Biblical and Shakespearean usage (*And lead us not into temptation . . .*).

The modern negative system is also the result of a long and complex development. In OE the unstressed negative particle *ne* usually occurred before first auxiliary, otherwise before the main verb: *ac hie ne dorston þær on cuman* 'but they neg dared there on to-come' = 'but they dared not come there'. There was also a stressed emphatic negative *nāht/nōht* < *ne-ā-wiht* 'not-ever-thing' which occurred after the auxiliary or verb: *ne con ic nōht singan* 'neg can I nothing sing' = 'I can't sing anything'. This is the origin of modern *not*.

In OE and ME, and well into the early Modern period, multiple negation was more or less the norm: Chaucer's *He never yet no vileynie ne seyde/In al his lyf unto no maner wight* (CT A7of) is not unusual. It was only during the 18th century (see §2.10) that such constructions were barred from the standard. In outline, the development can be seen as loss of the unstressed preverbal *ne*, with the previously emphatic *nōht* in postverbal position taking over its functions, loss of the ability to have more than one negative in a clause, and stabilization of *do*-support. (The generalization about one negative per clause fails in certain specialized cases, which always have an identifiable intonation pattern: *I don't want **not** to go there* = 'I don't really want to, but on the other hand . . .').

4.5.5 THE VERB AND AUXILIARY: HISTORICAL BACKGROUND

The finite and nonfinite verb forms (§4.5.1) have quite disparate origins. Only the finites are properly 'verbal'; the others are old nouns or adjectives.

The gerund is a noun-formation of the type called a 'feminine abstract': the Germanic suffix */-inɣ ~ -unɣ/ formed feminine nouns off verbal roots. The *-ung* form occurs in German, as in *schreib-* 'write', *Schreib-ung* 'spelling'. In most other Germanic languages, however, the old verbal abstracts are used rather differently from the way they are in English: a construction like *I like writing* would normally use the infinitive, not the gerund: Sw *jag tycker om att skriv-a* 'I like to to-write', or English *smoking prohibited* vs. G *Rauch-en verboten*.

The infinitive, as these examples suggest, is also a noun: specifically a neuter noun derived from a verb stem. The original type can be seen clearly in Sanskrit: the root *bhṛ-* 'carry' yields both finite forms like *bhár-a-mi* 'I carry' and the verbal noun *bhar-aṇ-am* '(the) carrying', where *-aṇ-* is the noun-forming suffix and *-am* the nominative singular neuter ending. This type was the basis for the Germanic infinitive; but the nom sg ending was lost in prehistoric times, and the oldest texts show only *-an* (Gothic *baír-an* 'to carry'. The ending survives in various forms: in some WGmc dialects the nasal remains (G *schreib-en*, Yi *šrajb-n* 'write'); elsewhere we get the old vowel minus the nasal (Sw *skriv-a*), or some reduced [ə]-like vowel (Danish *skriv-e*, Dutch *schrijv-en* /sxrɛivə/). English and Afrikaans alone have lost the ending entirely (*write, skryf*).

The participles are adjectival in origin. The present participle in OE is *-ende*, which continues an old formation in */-nt-/ (cf. L *fer-e-nt-ēs* 'bearing' (nom pl)); this, or a related form with a different vowel, remains in the other dialects (G *schreib-end*, Sw *skriv-ande*), while English has lost the old form and replaced it with the gerund in *-ing*.

The past participles of weak and strong verbs have different sources. The strong ending is *-en* (OE *ge-word-en* 'become'), from an IE formation in */-no-/ (cf. Skr *vart-ā-na-ḥ* 'having become'); the weak ending is normally *-ed*, and continues IE */-to-/ (OE *ge-dēm-ed* 'judged';

cf. Latin 'supine' participles of the type *cap-tu-s* 'captured'). Both these had a perfective or completive sense, so they were natural candidates for the formation of a perfect.

Old English had the standard two verb types, strong and weak, distinguished by their mode of tense-formation (cf. §1.3). The strong verbs had a set of differing vowel-qualities or grades, the weak formed pasts with a suffix. But the tense-structure of the strong verbs is more complicated, and intersects with the marking of mood (indicative vs. subjunctive) and number, as we will see below.

The OE strong verbs formed a coherent and quite regular system, with six major classes, each with a clear-cut set of principal parts or stems, from which all other forms can be derived (see (4.27) below for an example). To illustrate the system and show something of what happened to it, here are typical examples of the first six classes, with expected modern developments; forms marked * either never developed or were short-lived. The present stem is represented by the infinitive, and non-existent modern forms are given in the spellings they would most likely have if they'd survived:

(4.26)

Class		Present	Past Sg	Past Pl	Past Participle
I	OE	bīt-an	bāt	bit-on	ge-bit-en
	ModE	bite	*bote	bit	bitt-en
II	OE	frēos-an	*frēas	frur-on	ge-fror-en
	ModE	freeze	*frease	*froor	*fror-en
III	OE	drinc-an	dranc	drunc-on	ge-drunc-en
	ModE	drink	drank	*drunk	drunk-*(en)
IV	OE	ber-an	bær	bær-on	ge-bor-en
	ModE	bear	*bar	*bear	bor(e)n
V	OE	brec-an	bræc	bræc-on	ge-broc-en
	ModE	break	*brack	*break	brok-en
VI	OE	stand-an	stōd	stōd-on	ge-stand-en
	ModE	stand	stood	stood	*stand-en

Note first that no modern strong verb has four distinct vowel-grades; in particular, none distinguish past sg and pl. And if we look at more members of each class, we see that no class has survived intact; many verbs have gone their idiosyncratic ways, redistributing vowel grades, taking them from other classes, turning weak, etc. The strong verbs now do not constitute a system of well-defined, historically transparent classes. There has been quite radical remodelling, whose domain is largely the individual verb.

Take class I for example. In OE it contained among others *drīfan* 'drive', *rīdan* 'ride', *strīdan* 'stride', *scrīfan* 'shrive', *rīsan* 'rise', *smītan* 'smite', *wrītan* 'write', *scīnan* 'shine', *scītan* 'shit', *grīpan* 'grip', *slīdan* 'slide', *slītan* 'slit', *glīdan* 'glide', all with the same vowel-set as *bītan* (4.26). Of these, *drive, ride, shrive, rise, smite, write* show the expected three-way development (*drive/drove/driven*, etc.); others have quite different patterns. E.g. (a) two grades, pres and past sg: *shine/shone*; (b) two grades, pres and past pl or participle: *slide/slid*, likewise *bite*; though *bite* has retained the *-en*, which *slide* has lost; (c) past pl grade generalized: *slit/slit/slit*, likewise *shit* (though in some dialects *shit* has a class V type past *shat*, and weak *shitted* is also attested); (d) verb has become weak: *glide/glided*; (e) past pl grade extended to present and verb is weak: *grip/gripped*; here the expected present would be *gripe* – which in fact has survived, but as another (also weak) verb. Similar examples could be multiplied for the other classes, including types not represented for class I: e.g. migration of present-stem consonants into the past participle (*freeze/frozen*: the *-r-* in OE is due to Verner's Law (§1.3)); development of a weak past, but retention of a strong participle: *swell/swelled/swollen*; and variable verbs with a weak past and both strong and weak past participles, like *hew/hewed/hewed ~ hewn*, also *show, sow, sew, saw*.

The kind of development shown here is not uncommon: what might be called 'dissolutive change' – the apparently near-random destruction of a tight system, leaving a host of 'irregular' alternations. Such developments had already begun in OE: a number of verbs were part-members of more than one class. This is the result of the strong verb type of conjugation simply becoming unproductive: with very few exceptions (among them *strive* < OF *estriver*), no new strong verbs have been created since OE times, and all new verbs are weak.

The weak verbs also fell into a number of distinct classes, though these have had much less impact on the present shape of their descendants. The most common was class I with infinitive usually in *-an*, and past in *-(e)de*, participle in *-(e)d* (e.g. *dēm-an* 'judge', *dēm-de*, *ge-dēm-ed*); class II had infinitive in *-ian*, and *-o-* rather than *-e-* in the past forms (*luf-ian* 'love', *luf-ode*, *ge-luf-od*); there were also class I verbs with consonant alternations like *bycgan* 'buy', *sēcan* 'seek', *bringan* 'bring', pasts *bōh-te*, *sōh-te*, *brōh-te*, and important because of its use as an auxiliary, the class III verb *habb-an* 'have', pres 1 sg *hæbb-e*, 3 sg *hæf-þ*, participle *ge-hæfd* (which is still irregular, though not in precisely the same way).

The morphology of the verb as a whole was complex, and the inflections were different for strong and weak verbs. One category (the 'subjunctive') was uniformly marked, though it has now disappeared as a distinct inflection (or rather lack of inflection) except in fossil phrases like *long live the Queen* (cf. *the Queen live-s long*), and in some dialects in constructions like *I demand that he leave tomorrow* (with the unmarked relic of an old subjunctive pres 3 sg), rather than *I demand that he leave-s*. This distinction is still made in some U.S. dialects (which tend to be morphologically conservative), but seems to be becoming less common in British English; the same is true of *if I were* vs. *if I was* (cf.§4.2).

Characteristic OE strong and weak verb paradigms: strong class IV *beran*, weak class I *dēman*:

(4.27)

STRONG: *beran* 'to bear'

		Pres Ind	*Past Ind*	*Pres Subj*	*Past Subj*
	1	ber-e	bær	ber-e	bǣr-e
Sg	2	bir-st	bǣr-e	ber-e	bǣr-e
	3	bir-þ	bær	ber-e	bǣr-e
Pl	1–3	ber-aþ	bǣr-on	ber-en	bǣr-en

Pres Part ber-ende   *Past Part* ge-bor-en

WEAK: *deman* 'to judge'

		Pres Ind	*Past Ind*	*Pres Subj*	*Past Subj*
	1	dēm-e	dēm-d-e	dēm-e	dēm-d-e
Sg	2	dēm-est	dēm-d-est	dēm-e	dēm-d-e
	3	dēm-eþ	dēm-d-e	dēm-e	dēm-d-e
Pl	1–3	dēm-aþ	dēm-d-on	dēm-en	dēm-d-en

Pres Part dem-ende   *Past Part* ge-dem-ed

Note (among other details) that the past sg and pl of strong verbs have different vowels, except that the past pl vowel appears in the 2 sg pres indicative and throughout the subjunctive; there is a set of distinct person endings in the indicative sg but not in the subjunctive; and -þ marks both 3 sg pres and all plurals for the indicative, while -n marks all past plurals, indicative and subjunctive being distinguished by the preceding vowel.

The prefix *ge-* marking the past participle is apparently an old perfective or completive marker, retained in all the WGmc languages except English; it does not occur in NGmc, which had lost it in prehistoric times. The OE prefix was pronounced /jə/, and often comes down into early southern ME in a reduced form spelled *i-*, *y-*; this remained well into modern times in a few archaisms, like Milton's *yclept* 'called' (*l'Allegro*, 12) < OE *ge-clip-od*, past participle of *clipian* 'call'.

One oddity in the modern auxiliary system can now be understood in the light of the difference between present and past inflections in OE: the formal peculiarities of the modals (§4.5.3). Their ancestors in OE belonged to a group called preterite presents – verbs which (roughly) had old pasts or perfects as their present-tense forms, with the form retained but the meaning changed. This is an old IE pattern: L *nov-ī* 'I know', *od-ī* 'I hate' are the same type (*-ī* is a perfect ending: cf. *am-ā-vī* 'I have loved'). In OE terms, the presents of the 'pre-modal' verbs like *cunnan* 'can', *sculan* 'shall', *magan* 'may' are identical in form to strong pasts: *ic cann, þū cann-st, hē cann*. So these verbs now lack endings for pres 3 sg because they never had any – the OE strong past is marked only for second person, unlike the present where all three persons are distinct. (Obviously other properties of the modals are due to later developments, e.g. the loss of infinitives and the special details of their syntax.)

Since these verbs had formal pasts for presents, they developed new pasts, weak ones: *cū-ðe* 'could', *sceol-de* 'should', *meah-te* 'might' (hence *could, would, might*: the *-l-* in *could* is probably by analogy with that in *should*, but was never pronounced).

Perhaps the most complex of the OE verbs was 'to be', which was not actually a single verb, but a collection of fragments of different older paradigms. The present indicative forms *eam, eart, is* (later *am, art, is*) are cognate to Latin *sum, es, est*; the infinitive *bēon* (later *be*) and its forms like the alternative presents *bēo, bist, biþ* (1–3 sg) are from another verb related to L *fiō* 'make', Skr *bhū-* 'dwell'; and the other infinitive *wesan*, and its past sg *wæs* and pl *wǣron* (now *was, were*) are from yet another verb, an incomplete class V strong verb with somewhat dim relations to an IE root meaning 'exist, dwell': Old Irish *feiss* 'remain' and Tocharian *wašt* 'house' are cognate. The imperative of *wesan* remains buried in *wassail*, a contraction of *wes hāl* 'be healthy'. (For paradigms and more on the history of *be*, see §5.4.)

The entire verb morphology was greatly simplified during the ME period. Unstressed vowels fell together in *-e* /ə/, obliterating distinctions like *-an/-on/-en*; the past plural and singular of strong verbs tended to collapse under one vowel or the other, so that old four-vowel verbs like *bear* (see above) had only three or two qualities. Thus in Chaucer's English, *bear* would have infinitive *ber-en*, past singular *bore*, past pl *bor-en*, with the sg/pl distinction in the past signalled only by the ending, instead of twice (ending and vowel) as in OE. By the 14th century, the dialects ancestral to the modern standards had a system of verb endings like this:

(4.28)

		Pres (Weak/Strong)	Past (Weak)	Past (Strong)
	1	-e	-(e)d-e	-∅
sg	2	-est	-(e)d-est	-(e)st

		Pres (Weak/Strong)	Past (Weak)	Past (Strong)
	3	-eþ/-eth	-(e)d-e	-Ø
pl	1–3	-en	-(e)d-en	-en

By the 16th century, all the vocalic endings had gone, as had the infinitive marker; in Shakespeare's English we would have a system like this:

(4.29)

		Pres (Weak/Strong)	Past (Weak)	Past (Strong)
	1	-Ø	-(e)d	-Ø
sg	2	-(e)st	-(e)d-(e)est	-(e)st
	3	-(e)th/-(e)s	-(e)d	-Ø
pl	1–3	-Ø	-(e)d	-Ø

I.e. essentially the modern system, except for a distinct 2 sg inflection, which dropped (except for poetic and religious use) during the 17th–18th centuries, and the coexistence of the old and new 3 sg forms (On the origin of the -(e)s 3 sg, see §2.9.)

4.6 Subordination

4.6.1 SUBORDINATION IN GENERAL
Grammars traditionally talk about main or independent vs. subordinate or dependent clauses. Oversimply, a main clause can 'stand alone': i.e. it normally has at least a verb, and no overt marker of dependence. If we take possession of a verb as the minimal requirement for clause-hood, then *stop!*, *Sam stopped*, *Sam stopped the car* count as main clauses, and *that Sam stopped*, *whose car stopped* count as clauses on the verb criterion, but as subordinate on the 'standing alone' criterion.

We can however define subordinateness less vaguely: a subordinate clause serves some kind of dependent or non-sentential function (acts as another part of speech) in relation to another clause. E.g. in *the girl* [*who(m) you molested*] *was a WPC*, the bracketed clause is an adjectival modifier of *the girl*; in *the girl said* [*that you molested her*], the bracketed clause has a noun function – direct object of the verb *said*.

Both these examples show a specific marker of subordination: *who(m)*, *that* (conventionally a relative pronoun and a subordinating conjunction respectively); but this is not always the case: cf. *the girl* [*you molested*] *was ...*, *the girl said* [*you molested her*]. Even without the subordinator, the grammatical relations between the two clauses remain clear: they are still respectively an adjectival modifier of the subject of the main clause and an object of the verb of the main clause. If this analysis is not fully convincing, compare examples with non-clausal modifiers and objects: *the girl [in green]*, *the girl said [something]*.

In the usual terminology, clauses of the first kind are relative clauses, and those of the second type noun clauses, or as we will call them here, complement clauses or simply complements. We will discuss complements first, as they raise some interesting general issues, and have a bearing on an important distinction between two rather different types of relative clauses in English. The discussion in the next three sections may appear to be excessively detailed; but there's a reason for this. Not only are subordination phenomena of considerable interest in themselves, and a central part of syntactic description; but they are particularly complex, and their analysis can shed a good deal of light on more general problems of grammar-meaning relations, and the nature of syntactic structure. In addition, the relative and complement systems are reasonably self-contained, and can be easily studied as systems; and the amount of scholarship in these areas is enormous, especially over the past twenty years or so, so that a lot of interesting problems have come to light.

4.6.2 COMPLEMENTATION
There's no difficulty in identifying the complement in *the girl said [that you molested her]* as a clause; but there are other constructions that don't appear at first sight to be subordinate clauses, but can – on a slightly looser definition of 'clause' – be insightfully included. Consider the 'infinitive phrase' in *Sam wanted [to eat the porridge]*. On the face of it, *to eat* is simply an infinitive, acting in its expected noun-like way (cf. §4.5.5) as object of a verb. But it also has its own direct object: *the porridge*. So the 'infinitive phrase' is at least a quasi-clause, since it has a verb (if not a finite one) with an object; and the sequence infinitive + NP is itself a direct object, so that it functionally falls into the same category as full sentential complements like *that you molested her*. The only standard clause-member that seems to be missing is a subject.

But is it? Consider *Sam wanted [Ayesha to eat the porridge]*. *Ayesha* is subject of *eat* (who is to eat the porridge?), and *the porridge* is object of *eat*. Despite the lack of tense/person/number marking on *eat*, the relations it contracts with the two NPs are those typical of any transitive clause: there is a 'complete predication'. (We could paraphrase: 'Sam wanted it to be the case that the proposition [Ayesha eat the porridge] was true'.) The bracketed material is a kind of clause where the marker of subordination is in fact the lack of tense, etc. on the verb, plus the *to* before it. The normal S-V-O relations are all there.

By extension, *Sam wanted [to eat the porridge]* also contains a kind of subordinate clause; this time without an explicit subject. (Which is no problem: imperatives like *eat that porridge*! don't have explicit subjects either. Though they do have recoverable ones, which is the key to the analysis here.) Who does Sam want to eat the porridge? Obviously, Sam. Therefore the two infinitive constructions are essentially the same: *Sam wanted [(Sam) to eat the porridge]* like *Sam wanted [Ayesha to eat the porridge]*. There are various ways of describing this: we could say that in an infinitival complement, if the subject of both clauses is the same, the infinitive subject is 'deleted under identity' to that of the main clause; or, looked at from the other end, the 'zero-subject' of the infinitive is interpreted as being the same as that of the main clause.

We could construct a parallel argument from a pair like *Sam hates [reading Kafka]* and *Sam hates [Ayesha('s) reading Kafka]*; once again the constructions with nonfinite verbs (here gerunds rather than infinitives) display S-V-O relations: explicitly in the second case, and implicitly in the first (*Sam hates [Sam('s) reading Kafka]*).

It's also clear that infinitive and gerund complements are often interchangeable: *Sam hates [(for) Ayesha to read Kafka]* alongside *Sam hates [Ayesha('s) reading Kafka]*. And we could relate both constructions to 'full' subordinate clauses, like *Sam hates (it) [that Ayesha reads Kafka]* or *Sam hates (it) [when Ayesha reads Kafka]*. All three constructions have in common the property of involving subordinated predications (whether or not they have the superficial form of full clauses).

The three kinds of complements do not however have identical distributions. Certain verbs take only certain complements. Thus *want, desire, allow* normally take only infinitival complements (*I want him to go/*that he goes/*his going*); *hope, insist, demand* take only finite *that*-complements (*I hope that he leaves/*him to leave/*his leaving*); whereas *believe, consider*, take both *that*- and infinitive (*I believe that he is stupid/ him to be stupid/*his being stupid*).

With certain verbs (of the last-mentioned class) there is an interesting relation between the structures of *that*- and infinitive complements, reflecting an ancient and widespread IE construction. Consider a pair like *I believe (that) Mary is pregnant* vs. *I believe Mary to be pregnant*. If we translated these into Latin, we'd get: *Credo quod Maria gravida est* (with subordinator *quod, Maria* and *gravida* both nominative, and finite *est*). And *Credo Mariam gravidam esse* (with *Mariam, gravidam* both accusative, and infinitive *esse*). English sentences with nouns don't reflect all the details (since nouns aren't case-marked); but substitution of pronouns will show the same pattern as Latin: *I believe (that)* **she is** *pregnant* vs. *I believe* **her to be** *pregnant*.

The source of this distributional oddity seems to be the ability of a single NP to function simultaneously in more than one way in a single complex sentence. Plus a quite rigid rule that says in essence that a transitive verb governs a non-nominative in its own clause. This should be a little disturbing; in the notational system I've been using, both *her* and *she* are 'in' the complement, not the main clause. As is often the case, yes and no. From the point of view of semantic interpretation (*Mary* is the subject of *is*), she is 'in' the complement in both cases; but in the infinitival one, she is treated morphologically as if she were also in the main clause, i.e. as the object of *believe*. Thus at the level of description at which case-forms are assigned, the structures are:

(4.30)

[I believe [that *Mary* is pregnant]]

vs.

[I believe *Mary* [to be pregnant]]

One analysis is that in the infinitive case, the subject of the subordinate clause has been 'extracted' or 'raised' into the main clause. (If you take a subordinated structure to be 'under' what it's subordinated to, as the Latin grammatical tradition did: hence *sub-ordinate*.) Thus it serves as a syntactic object in the main clause, while being interpreted as a subject of the subordinate clause in terms of meaning. (Another 'mismatch' between syntax and meaning: cf. §§4.5.4, 4.7.)

This perhaps surprising analysis can be supported by the behaviour of reflexive pronouns in the same construction. The usual rule is that if two coreferent NPs are in the same transitive clause, one as subject and the other as object, the second must be realized as a reflexive pronoun. So (with subscripts indicating identity of reference):

(4.31)

   i. Mary$_i$ saw herself$_i$ in the mirror.
   ii. *Mary$_i$ saw she$_i$ in the mirror.
   iii. *Mary$_i$ saw her$_i$ in the mirror.
   iv. *Mary$_i$ saw Mary$_i$ in the mirror.

The same restrictions hold for infinitive complements:

(4.32)

   i. Mary$_i$ believes herself$_i$ to be pregnant.
   ii. *Mary$_i$ believes she$_i$ to be pregnant.
   iii. *Mary$_i$ believes her$_i$ to be pregnant.
   iv. *Mary$_i$ believes Mary$_i$ to be pregnant.

In a finite *that*-complement, type iv is also excluded (on the general grounds that nouns are replaced by anaphoric pronouns within the same sentence – simple or complex); otherwise the restrictions are reversed:

(4.33)

i. Mary$_i$ believes that she$_i$ is pregnant.
ii. *Mary$_i$ believes that herself$_i$ is pregnant.
iii. *Mary$_i$ believes that her$_i$ is pregnant.
iv. *Mary$_i$ believes that Mary$_i$ is pregnant.

From a purely syntactic point of view, the subjects of infinitive complements can be taken to be 'outside' the boundaries of the complement – even though they are interpreted as acting also within them; while the subjects of *that*-complements must be taken as syntactically 'inside'.

The gerund complement is more complex, since there are two acceptable forms: one with the subject of the gerund unambiguously outside the complement in the sense above, and one where it is probably inside. If the subject of the complement gerund is an object-form pronoun, it must – by the criteria above – be taken as the object of the main clause verb: *I hate him/*he doing that*, etc. When the subject of the gerund is genitive, as in *I hate his doing that*, there may be no real morphological grounds for making a decision; though since the genitive is an adjectival modifier of the gerund (as well as a subject), it can probably be taken as being within the same NP, and hence within the complement.

Each complement type has one or more characteristic construction markers or subordinators – or as they are now more commonly called, complementizers. But there are some problems in deciding exactly what should be taken as primary. For the *that*-complements, the data is unambiguous: *that* or zero (*He said (that) S*). Whether 'zero' is a complementizer in its own right or a 'deleted *that*' is a technical issue that will not concern us here. There is in fact a third possibility: that a construction like *He said he was tired* does not involve true subordination at all, but is paratactic: i.e. it consists of two loosely associated clauses, rather than being hypotactic (having one in clear subordination to the other). The fact that only *that*- and zero-complements have finite verbs however suggests that the constructions are related.

The only case I know where one can make a clear distinction between paratactic and hypotactic complements is in languages where there is some marker of subordination other than a complementizer; e.g. in Afrikaans (or German, Dutch, Frisian), where the word-order in subordinate clauses is different from that in main clauses. Thus in Afrikaans *He said that he was tired* is *Hy het gesê, dat hy moeg was*, i.e. 'He has said, that he tired was': the complementizer *dat* marks a subordinate clause, which is verb-final, unlike the verb-second main clause. But the version without the complementizer is *Hy het gesê, hy was moeg*, with main-clause order in both clauses: hence the construction is paratactic, with neither clause subordinated to the other.

For the infinitive complement, the construction marker is apparently the *to* before the infinitive; though it is worth noting that if we look at complements in subject position (rather than objects, as we've been doing), the situation is different. If the infinitive is subjectless, the marker is simply *to*: as in *to kill a hippo bare-handed isn't easy*. But if there's a subject, the complementizer is a discontinuous *for ... to*: *for a midget to kill a hippo is even harder*, **a midget to kill a hippo*, etc. And indeed in some dialects the *for ... to* sequence appears in object position as well; many U.S. dialects have *I'd like for you to do this*, etc.

Similarly for the gerund complement: in some analyses the complementizer is taken to be the *-'s* ending on the subject: *Ayesha's reading Kafka* as above. The problem is that for many speakers the genitive marking is not obligatory: *I hate Ayesha reading Kafka*. Even an accusative may appear: *I hate him reading Kafka*. In subject position, however, the genitive is much more likely, and the accusative excluded: *Ayesha's reading Kafka depresses me/?Ayesha reading Kafka.../*Him reading Kafka....* (Many pedagogical grammars stigmatize the non-genitive forms, but this appears to be merely a prejudice.)

The reader who has managed to keep alert through this exposition may wonder about the notion 'complement in subject position'. In what sense are things like *for a midget to kill a hippo, Ayesha's reading Kafka* (*depresses me*) 'complements'? And to what? It's reasonable to see an object as a complement ('that which completes') to its verb; but what can a bare subject be a complement of? A partial answer (or at least a justification for talking this way) emerges from data like the following:

(4.34)

i. (a) *For a midget to kill a hippo* isn't easy
   (b) *It* isn't easy *for a midget to kill a hippo*.

ii. (a) *That Mary is pregnant* surprises me
   (b) *It* surprises me *that Mary is pregnant*

When a subject whose structure is the same as what in object position is clearly a complement is 'moved to the right' of its predicate (or extraposed, as the technical term is), a 'place-holder' *it* appears – obligatorily. Forms without it are generally unacceptable, e.g. **isn't easy for a midget...*, **surprises me that Mary....* (At least in written language and formal spoken styles: the starred forms appear in normal speech in many dialects, including my own.) In the days when complex transformational analyses of such phenomena were popular, it was often suggested that the 'underlying' structure was of the type [*it* [*for a midget*...] *isn't easy*], i.e. that we had an infinitive sequence as complement of *it*; or that there was a 'dummy' noun △ in subject position, which was 'replaced by' *it* of the complement was extraposed: [△ [*for a midget*...] *isn't easy*].

Both these accounts capture the fact that we do indeed have a subordinated structure: subordinated to some kind of 'latent' or 'unspecified' noun. However we actually interpret this, such a claim allows us to use the sensible terms 'complement' and 'subordination' to cover all occurrences of the same kind of construction, in obviously nominal function. And indeed in many cases even subject complements are explicitly subordinated to nouns (usually abstract): *the fact/claim/ idea* [*that cholesterol is an aphrodisiac*]..., etc. I am not saying that all the items I've discussed are 'really the same thing', or even that nonfinite complements are 'really reduced sentences' – only that the similarities are striking, and worth taking seriously. At least this way of looking at things brings together under one descriptive heading a set of phenomena so similar that we would lose something if we described them as being radically different.

4.6.3 RELATIVE CLAUSES

A relative clause is an adjectival modifier subordinated to an NP: in the simplest case with a pronoun inside the clause coreferent to the outside NP (the head of the clause). So in *the man* [*who eats fruitcake*] *dies a horrible death*, the clause [*who eats fruitcake*] is embedded inside the main clause *the man... dies a horrible death*, as a modifier of *the man*; and the relative pronoun *who* is coreferent with *the man*; it also happens to be the subject of its own clause, as *the man* is of its own. But the head and the relative pronoun do not have to have the same grammatical function in their clauses: in *the man* [*who(m) I saw*], *was obese*, *the man* is subject of the main clause, while the coreferent *who(m)* is the object of *saw* in the subordinate clause. Referential and grammatical identity are not the same thing.

Keeping the grammatical relations in a main clause constant for illustration, we can see that there is in fact quite a wide range of grammatical functions that can occur within the relative clause. Given the same main clause – say *the man* [...] *was obese* – we can have not only subject and object relatives as above, but also genitives: *the man* [*whose trousers split*]...; indirect objects: *the man* [*to whom I gave anti-fat pills*]...; other 'oblique objects' like locatives (*the man* [*on whom the flea sat*]...), comitatives (*the man* [*with whom I was dancing*]...); and in some (normally only written) styles objects of comparison like *the man* [*than whom nobody was grosser*]..., etc. It is clear – a point we'll return to – that not all of these relative types are equally usable in all styles, and that some are commoner than others.

Cross-linguistically in fact, there is evidence that there exists an 'accessibility hierarchy' with respect to the syntactic functions relativizable in human languages: i.e. the categories that can serve as the heads of relative clauses. It looks like this:

(4.35)

Subject > Direct Object > Indirect Object > Oblique Object > Genitive > Objective of Comparison

The claim made by this hierarchy is that any language will relativize only a continuous subsequence; and that relativization of any category preceded by '>' will imply relativization of all categories above it. And that if a language relativizes only one category, this will be subject. Thus English, which relativizes genitives, also does all categories above; whereas Icelandic, which does not relativize genitives, nonetheless does do subject through oblique object. (Thus what in English would be *the man [whose house was sold]* would in Icelandic be *maðurinn, [sem átti húsið] [er selt var]*, i.e. a sequence of relativizations on higher positions: literally *the man [that owned the house] [that was sold]*. That is, the first clause is a subject relative, and the second a direct object.) With minor exceptions, no language will relativize a discontinuous subsequence of the hierarchy – e.g. subjects and indirect objects but not direct objects.

In general, as the Icelandic material suggests, the further down the hierarchy you go, the more 'complex' or 'difficult' relativization becomes, apparently; we will see (§4.6.4) that this distinction is reflected in the history of the English relative clause system in a quite interesting way, and to a minor extent (this section) in current usage in at least some dialects.

English is traditionally said to have two 'relative pronouns': a *wh-* set (*who, whom, which, whose*), and another form *that*; and there are also zero relatives, like *the man [I saw]* ..., which on some analyses would have an 'empty' relativizer slot, i.e. *the man [Ø I saw]*. But if the *wh-* forms are pronouns, and merit the name 'relative pronoun', this is not the case with *that*; there are good arguments for calling it something other than a pronoun in this context, as its syntactic behaviour is quite different from that of the *wh-* set.

The *wh-* forms are typically pronoun-like in two ways: (a) they can be marked for case (*who* vs. *whom* vs. *whose*); and (b) they can be objects of prepositions (*the man [to/with/at whom ...]*). The subject/non-subject distinction does not of course show up formally with *that*: *the man [that saw me]* vs. *the man [that I saw]*; but we note one discontinuity immediately in that in standard non-Scots dialects there is no genitive:

*the man [**that's** daughter I married] (many varieties of Scots do have this construction).

But most strikingly, if we look at indirect and oblique objects, we find *that* impossible as a (contiguous) prepositional object: *the man [to whom/with whom...]*, but **the man [to that/with that...]*. If ability to serve as a prepositional object is one of the diagnostics of nominal-ness, then *that* as a relativizer is something else. It is a marker of a relative construction, to be sure, but not a pronoun. (The fact that we can get *that* as a prepositional object in discontinuous constructions is not to the point here: *the man [that I talked to/with...]* does not have *that* immediately to the right of a preposition, in canonical object position; this construction is in fact parallel to the zero relative *the man [I talked to]*.) And note that both *that*-relatives and zero-relatives on indirect and oblique objects can only occur if the preposition is stranded at the end of the clause: **the man [to that I was talking]*, **the man [to I was talking]*. *That*-relatives are more like zero-relatives, and distinctly unlike *wh*-relatives.

So we reserve the term 'relative pronoun' only for the case-marked *wh*-set; *that* is simply a complementizer or 'subordinating conjunction' – which ties in nicely with its use as a marker of complementation as well (§ 4.6.2). We have in English then, on one interpretation, two lexical items with the shape *that*: a deictic pronoun/adjective (§4.4) and a complementizer. (Note that deictic *that* can be a prepositional object: *do it with this, not with that.*)

Rather than talking about forms themselves, however, it is better to talk about relativization strategies; English thus has three, let's call them P(ronoun)-strategy, C(omplementizer)-strategy, and zero-strategy. A fourth 'mixed' type, C-P, will be discussed in §4.6.4. Within any given dialect, these strategies may interact in complex ways, according to style, syntactic position being relativized, and the nature of the head. Rather than aiming for an overall survey, I will concentrate on one dialect (my own), which is I think typical enough to illustrate what English relativization in general is like.

In my own speech, the following regularities seem to hold:
(i) C-strategy or zero is preferred in normal spoken styles, except for genitive (though zero is rare with subjects). The lower positions on the accessibility hierarchy, e.g. indirect objects, locatives, etc. are characteristically handled with a stranded preposition: *the man [(that) I gave the book to/(that) the knife was stuck in]*. For human heads, the P-strategy is fairly frequent (*the man [who was there]*), but its behaviour suggests that the *wh*-forms are being treated rather like complementizers: since I don't have (in spoken styles) the case-marked *whom*, all non-subject human-head relatives except genitives take the invariable *who* (with

stranded prepositions for positions below direct object): *the man* [*who I saw*], *the man* [*who I gave it to*], etc. An indication that *who* is really acting like *that* is the ungrammaticality of **the man* [*to who I gave it*], and so on (see above on *that*).

The use of unmarked *who* in non-subject positions is often stigmatized; unreasonably, it seems to me, since as far as I can judge my speech is standard, and educated usage in my own and many other dialects follows this pattern. But – and here is the source of the stigmatization – in formal speech, and especially in writing, the normal case-marked P-strategy takes precedence. I can (and in fact must) write *to whom*, or *whom . . . to*, with both case-marking and stranding; though I find such things virtually impossible to say except in a pompous and stilted style – even if my sociolinguistic competence dictates that I use it sometimes. The point is that written language typically represents a more archaic variety than spoken; and the normative judgements of certain kinds of 'purists' are based on yesterday's spoken form, embodied in today's written. But every fully literate user of English who is also a competent speaker is at very least bidialectal.

(ii) The only genitive relative – for all heads, human or not, animate or not – is *whose*: *the man* [*whose daughter I knew*], *the house* [*whose roof is leaking*]. But even the last example isn't optimal: the only relative-clause alternative is *the house* [*the roof of which is leaking*], which I can barely write, much less say. Genitive relatives on inanimate heads are in fact quite rare; a more normal version would be *the house with the leaky roof*, or some other (non-relative) paraphrase. It seems that the low positions on the hierarchy are disfavoured: cf. the Icelandic example above, which is another way out.

(iii) C vs. Zero. In ordinary speech the zero-relative seems to be preferred (see (i)) for all positions except subject. Zero-subject does however occur in very casual and rapid speech, e.g. *the guy* [*came to see me*] *wanted a job*. But in this case we may be dealing not with a genuine syntactic zero-variant – rather a phonological deletion under low prominence. I.e. since the forms [ðæt], [ðət] and even [ət] occur for *that* in increasingly casual styles, it may be that an utterance like the one above is 'really' a *that*-relative, with 'deleted [ət]'. That is, parallel to pronunciations like *clothes* as [kləʊz] which could be taken as '[kləʊðz] with deleted [ð]'.

The relative clauses discussed so far are of the type traditionally called restrictive (or defining); they contrast with a less common but interesting type called nonrestrictive (non-defining). This distinction holds for certain ordinary adjective constructions as well, and provides further evidence of the adjective-like properties of relative clauses. I will illustrate before defining.

Consider a sentence like *the industrious Japanese will take over the car industry*. The phrase *the industrious Japanese* is ambiguous; it can be unpacked in two ways:

(4.36)

a. The property 'industrious' can be attributed to all the members of the set {Japanese}: i.e. 'the Japanese, all of whom are industrious'.

b. The property 'industrious' can be attributed to only some members of the set {Japanese}: i.e. 'those particular Japanese who are industrious'.

So with a set-referring definite noun, an adjective can either attribute a property to the whole set (nonrestrictive modification (a)), or only to some subset of its members (restrictive modification (b)). But in the adjective + noun construction there's no overt marker of the distinction.

Relative clauses show the same contrast, this time with an explicit marker. The ambiguous phrase above has two clausal paraphrases, one for each reading:

(4.37)

a. The Japanese, who are industrious, will ...
b. The Japanese who are industrious will ...

The commas setting off the nonrestrictive clause are the normal way of indicating the intonation-break that would occur with this type in speech: though it's worth noting that nonrestrictive relatives are much rarer in speech than in writing (unlike nonrestrictive adjectives).

They also show another difference from restrictives: they admit only P-strategy (*wh*-form) for all syntactic positions. So *the Japanese, that are industrious ...*, *the Japanese, that the Ainu went to war with ...*, etc. And they do not allow zero: *the Japanese, the Ainu went to war with*. Thus nonrestrictives stand out as a separate, somewhat marginal subsystem; their exclusive use of P-strategy for all hierarchy positions is a sign of this (see next section).

It has been suggested that nonrestrictives are not in fact true subordinate clauses, but a modified kind of coordination. Indeed, they tend to have quite reasonable 'parenthetical' paraphrases with introductory *and* rather than a *wh*-form: *the Japanese ((and) they're industrious) ...*, and so on, with the same type of intonation break before the modifying clause as in the relative proper.

4.6.4 THE EVOLUTION OF RELATIVIZATION STRATEGIES

Old English had a quite different relative system from the modern one. In particular, it had no distinctive relative pronoun as such (which seems to be an inheritance: neither did PIE or PGmc). It rather had a complex of strategies involving the definite article, complementizers, and personal pronouns. The major types were:

(i) P-Strategy: a definite article form, concording in gender with the head noun, and carrying the case-marking appropriate to its function within the relative clause (see §4.3.2 for the article forms):

(4.38)

a. ān   *wif*   [*sēo*   wæs hāten   Eurydice]
   one   woman   def-nom-   was called   E.
                   sg-f
   'a woman [who was called Eurydice]'

b. intō ān-um   *sēaþ-e*   [on *þām*   wǣron seofon lēon]
   into one-dat- pit-dat-   in def-   were   seven lions
        sg   sg   dat sg
   'into a pit [in which were seven lions]'

(In (4.38a) the relative *sēo* does not actually concord with *wīf*, which is grammatically neuter; it agrees in 'natural gender'.)

(ii) C-Strategy. The complementizer *þe* is the sole marker:

(4.39)

þā   *englan*   [*þe* ēower   gymdon]
def   angel-   C   you-   care for-
nom pl   pl   gen pl   past pl
   'the angels [who cared for you]'

(iii) 'Mixed' Strategies:
(a) C + 'Shadow pronoun': *þe* marks the clause-type, but there is also a coreferent pronoun inside the clause:

(4.40)

Ēadig   bið   se   *wer* [*þe his* tohopa bið   tō Drihtne]
blessed   be   def   man   C   his   hope   be   to God
                3 sg m nom   3 sg   dat sg
                pres sg   pres
   'blessed is the man [whose hope is in God]'

(b) P + C: an article form coreferent to the head occurs inside the clause, case-marked for its function, but with the complentizer *þe* following:

(4.41)

to	þām	*tūngerēfan*	[*se*	*þe*	his	ealdorman	wæs]
to	def	sheriff	def	C	his	alderman	be
	dat sg	dat sg	nom sg				past sg
			m				

'to the sheriff [who was his alderman]'

The zero relative also occurred, as in *Ælfred, wæs at Baðum gerēfa* 'Alfred, (who) was reeve at Bath', but less commonly.

The 'shadow pronoun' type has vanished in most dialects of English; though it remains in many Scottish varieties, mainly for genitives: *the man [that his wife's here]*, *the dog [that its leg got broken]*, etc. It is also the normal strategy for anything below direct objects in some other Germanic dialects, e.g. Yiddish: e.g. *der man [vos ix ken zajn vaib]* 'the man [what I know his wife]' (i.e. 'the man whose wife I know').

One point worth noting is the absence of *wh*-forms in Old English (actually *hw*-forms: *hwilc* 'which', *hwā* 'who', etc.). The descendants of these do not begin to appear in relatives until quite late, and in a way that ties in with the accessibility hierarchy and the structure of nonrestrictives. In the ME period, we find a gradual transformation of the OE system: *þe* still occurs in early ME as a complementizer introducing relative clauses, but is lost during the 13th century. During this early period the old relatives with *se/sēo/þæt* vanish, and *that* gradually becomes the primary relativizer.

Now in OE *þæt* was already used occasionally in places where the basic grammatical rules suggest it shouldn't be: *þæt* was the neuter nom/acc form of the definite article (cf. §4.3.2), and hence should have been used only with neuter singular heads. But as early as the 9th century we find occasional non-concording uses, e.g.

(4.42)

centauri	[*þæt*	sindon	healf	hors	healf	men]
Centaurs	def	be	half	horse	half	man
	n sg	pres pl		(pl?)		pl

'Centaurs [that are half horse, half man]'

Why *þæt*, rather than some other form? The answer seems to be that there was 'another *þæt*' in OE, a non-pronominal complementizer that normally introduced complements of the type of the modern *that*-S ones:

(4.43)

cwædon	[þæt	he	wǣre	manna	mildust]
say	C	he	be	man	mildest
past pl			pres	gen pl	
			subj		

'(they) said [that he was the mildest of men]'

We seem to have an identification of the pronoun *þæt* with its homo-phonous complementizer, and the beginnings of an extension of *þæt* to the role of all-purpose subordinator. This is further borne out by the fact that when *that* appears as a relative marker in ME, it does not serve as a contiguous prepositional object – just like modern relative *that* (cf. the previous section). Under circumstances like this it becomes possible to argue that 'one particular *that*' is being selected – even though it is phonetically identical to 'the other one'.

The ancestors of the modern *wh*-relatives were indefinite or interroga-tive pronouns in OE. These do not occur in relative clauses until well into the ME period, and when they do, they start at the bottom of the accessibility hierarchy (4.35). That is, the first appearances of *wh*-relatives are in oblique object or genitive positions (in constructions like *to which, of which*); *which* in this usage is established in the 14th-15th centuries. The animate/human *who* begins to be used in the 15th century, but only in very formal styles; it becomes fairly well established in the 16th, but the nominative is the last form to appear: *whose* and *whom* are established earlier.

There is an interesting correlation here: the *wh*-strategy first appears (a) in the lower positions of the hierarchy, and (b) in more formal or elaborate styles. I.e. the presumed 'complexity' (in terms of being disfavoured for relativization) of the lower hierarchy positions correlates with 'complexity' in the stylistic sense: the more elaborate Latinate registers were the first to introduce the new *wh*-forms. (There may also be some Latin influence: use of *wh*-forms in 'high' styles may have been encouraged by knowledge of the Latin P-strategy, using the pronoun *qui/quae/quod*; as well as perhaps by the French *qui/que*. But it is doubtful if the construction as such is 'borrowed'; more likely encour-aged by the prestige, in a multilingual community, of the more traditional literary languages.)

4.7 Grammar and Meaning

4.7.1 SEMANTIC VS. SYNTACTIC ROLES

The discussion of the English verb in §4.5 dealt with tense, aspect and modality, but omitted one category normally included in grammars under the heading of the verb: voice. Traditional descriptions often deal with the two 'voices' of the verb, active and passive (*the cat ate the mouse* vs. *the mouse was eaten by the cat*). This particular phenomenon is actually something quite different, concerned only incidentally and accidentally with the form of the verb. It really has to do with such things as discourse-structure, focus of speaker's interest, and the like; and the passive does not stand alone, in a unique relation to the active, but is part of a family of processes, all with similar or at least related effects.

We can approach this by looking at sentences which are essentially synonymous, but grammatically different. I'll operate here with a simple definition of 'synonymy': two sentences are synonymous (or 'mean the same') if (a) their truth-conditions are the same (i.e. it is impossible for one to be true while the other is false), and (b) their entailments are the same (i.e. the class of other sentences that they logically imply). So: given an active/passive pair like the one above, there's (a) no way that one could be true while the other was false; and (b) both entail other sentences like *the felid consumed the rodent, some small mammal ended up inside some larger mammal*, . . . etc. There's no entailment of one that isn't an entailment of the other.

So in that case what's the passive for? Is it simply 'another way of saying' an active? In a sense yes; but explicating this will take us further afield. If we look at an active and a passive in terms of the grammatical functions of the NPs, we find:

(4.44)

The	cat	ate	the	mouse
	Subject	V		Object

The	mouse	was	eaten	by	the	cat
	Subject		V		Adverbial (?): non-Subject	
					anyway	

That *the mouse* is a grammatical subject is clear from the fact that the leftmost NP in a passive controls verb-agreement, as we would expect from a subject: compare *the mice were eaten by the cat*. So the grammatical roles of the NPs (as well as their positions) are changed by passivization. But the semantic roles remain the same; *the cat* is still the agent (doer of the action), and *the mouse* still the patient (animate 'recipient' of the action). If we look at both grammatical and semantic roles:

(4.45)

	The	cat	ate	the	mouse
Grammatical:	Subject		V	Object	
Semantic:	Agent			Patient	

	The	mouse	was	eaten	by	the	cat
Grammatical:	Subject			V	Non-subject		
Semantic:	Patient				Agent		

That is: the semantic roles are not necessarily paralleled by the grammatical roles; the function of passivization appears to be to put an agent in a non-subject position – to 'demote' it, as it were, while at the same time 'promoting' the patient. The neutral or 'unmarked' case is for agent-role and subject-position to coincide; the passive does whatever it does by virtue of not observing this coincidence. We also note that the 'displaced' agent is marked with a preposition (*by*) which in fact shows its semantic role: the equivalent of say an ablative case-marking in Latin (in the corresponding Latin active, the subject would be nominative *felis*; in the passive, it would appear in the ablative as *felid-e*).

We can see better how this works by looking at a more complex case: here including not only agent, but object (non-animate 'recipient') and beneficiary (someone for whom something is done). In this example I will indicate only which role player or participant is grammatical subject:

(4.46)

(i) John played Mary a Mozart sonata

Gramm:	Subject		
Sem:	Agent	Beneficiary	Object

(ii) John played a Mozart sonata for Mary

Gramm:	Subject		
Sem:	Agent	Object	Beneficiary

(iii) A Mozart sonata was played for Mary by John

Gramm:	Subject		
Sem:	Object	Beneficiary	Agent

(iv) A Mozart sonata was played by John for Mary

Gramm:	Subject		
Sem:	Object	Agent	Beneficiary

(v) Mary was played a Mozart Sonata by John

Gramm:	Subject		
Sem:	Beneficiary	Object	Agent

Each of the three participants can be made into a subject by passivization; the function of the process seems to be to extract a non-agent, non-subject NP and make a subject of it. But the rule works only on the assumption that the order with Agent-as-Subject is the unmarked case; English is not only a subject-initial language, but in terms of 'basic' order an agent-initial one too.

Syntactically, then, passivization is a subject-forming rule: it creates grammatical subjects out of non-subjects, while leaving their semantic roles unchanged. But the interesting question is why: what function does this rather complex procedure have? The examples in (4.46) provide a clue. The state of affairs being described is the same in all five cases – player, playee and music are unchanged; but what is different is the focus of the speaker's interest – in simple terms, 'what he's really talking about'. In the neutral (i–ii) the focus is either on the event as a whole (what happened?) or (less likely) on John; in (iii–iv) we seem more to have an answer to a question like 'What did John play (and for whom)?'; and in (v) an answer to 'Who got a Mozart sonata played for her?'

On the assumption that leftmost position in the sentence is a focus-position, and that (all things being equal) subject is a peculiarly focal category, it becomes clear that the passive foregrounds or highlights that NP in a sentence closest to the focus of the speaker's (or in his judgement, the hearer's) interest.

This is further borne out by the use of another kind of passive – one where the agent is unexpressed: *dinner is served, Mahmoud was arrested, the dog was run over*. Here the focus is on the recipient of the action – to such an extent that the agent is of no interest, or is so obvious (pragmatically) that it can be left out. That is, on the basis of the speaker's and the hearer's knowledge of the world, *dinner is served* (by whoever is host), *Mahmoud was arrested* (by the relevant law-enforcement agency), etc. Specification of the agent would in many cases be quite odd: *Mahmoud was arrested by the police* would be normal only if the *by*-phrase were genuinely informative: e.g. if you'd expected him to be arrested by Military Intelligence.

In addition to passives with and without agents, English has another kind, with *get* rather than *be* as auxiliary: *Mahmoud got arrested, the dog got run over*. This is somewhat different from the *be*-passive, in that it does not usually have a fully synonymous active counterpart. *Mahmoud got arrested by the police* for instance does not relate to the active *the police arrested Mahmoud* in the same way as *Mahmoud was arrested by the police*. The *get*-passive carries a special nuance: normally that the state of affairs is in some way the 'fault' of the grammatical subject, due to some action of his, or is deliberate. Continuations like *of his own volition, deliberately, because he was careless/stupid/clumsy* and the like are normal for *get*-passives – much less so for the *be*-type.

4.7.2 MORE ON FOCUSSING

In the light of the last section the passive can be seen as one of a family of processes whose function is to bring normally non-subject NPs into initial position – either making them subjects or not (see below), or otherwise to focus, foreground or highlight them. There are also some processes serving related functions that move items to the right: we will look at them briefly below.

In the last section and elsewhere I talk, in a manner prompted by years of immersion in transformational grammar, of rules that 'move' items, etc.: the passive is thus a process that (a) moves an original subject into object position and attaches *by*; (b) moves the original object into subject position; and (c) changes the verb to *be* + past participle. Such talk is not (necessarily) to be taken literally; a perfectly reasonable alternative is to say that for a given active sentence there exists a passive related as above (subject in a postposed *by*-phrase, etc.) – and that in a given discourse situation the speaker can choose either format for expressing a given proposition, depending on what he wants to focus. For the purposes of this discussion I take the two formulations to be equivalent, and I'll use the simpler (or at least more vivid) 'movement' terminology, without implying any serious belief that it represents a 'reality'.

Focussing rules that move NPs to the left are of two types: those that change grammatical function, and those that don't. Passive clearly does change grammatical role; so does the rule involved in the following set:

(4.47)

    (i) It's hard to park cars in Cape Town
   (ii) Cape Town is hard to park cars in
  (iii) Cars are hard to park in Cape Town

This rule (called '*tough*-movement' in the literature of the 60s and 70s) effects a complex change in grammatical relations – though it is still subject-forming, like passive. Assuming (i) to be the most semantically transparent and neutral version (ii) is produced by shifting a locative object to subject, and (iii) by shifting the direct object of a verb. I.e. what is 'hard' is 'parking-cars-in-Cape Town': clearly neither Cape Town nor cars are literally 'hard'. But the speaker's focal interest overrides literal interpretation, and determines what becomes subject: (ii) is appropriate as a comment on Cape Town, (iii) as a comment on cars (as against horses or bicycles).

Movement without change in grammatical role can be illustrated by:

(4.48)

    a. I like her, but I can't stand him
    b. Her I like, but him I can't stand

The fact that the case forms of the pronouns remain unchanged shows that even though they've been moved to leftmost position, they're not subjects: they have been positionally promoted without (as in passive or *tough*-movement) becoming subjects. The result is the (for English) unusual sequence OSV, whereas passives and similar constructions are still subject-initial. But the function is the same: focus on a non-subject by moving it to the front.

It's even possible, paradoxical as it may seem, to focus a subject: as in

(4.49)

      (i) John, he's a good guy
     (ii) This book, it's one of the worst I've read

At least this seems the best explanation for such ('left-dislocated') structures. Since the primary focus position is the extreme left, left of that is even more focal – and if you move a subject to its left you create a 'hole', which is then filled by a pronoun agreeing with the moved NP. This construction also often goes along with a heightened intonational emphasis on the moved subject – another indication of its function.

Another way of focussing – though semantically more complex – involves the opposite strategy: postponing mention of a focussed item rather than introducing it earlier than would be done in the neutral case. To illustrate:

(4.50)

      (i) a. *John*'s a good guy
         b. He's a good guy, (is) *John*
          ['right dislocation']

     (ii) a. *The bear* ate *my sister*
        b. It was *the bear* (that) ate my sister
        c. It was *my sister* (that) the bear ate
         ['clefting']

    (iii) a. Herman detests *spinach*
        b. What Herman detests is *spinach*
         ['pseudo-clefting']

These three processes appear to serve somewhat the same rhetorical function: introducing a (less informative) pronoun before its antecedent, or providing some introductory item that tells you what kind of thing to expect – but making you wait for the actual item. Thus in a way it's a kind of heightening of expectation, or a strategy for gaining audience-attention to make sure a focal item won't be lost, or will be attended to perhaps more carefully than in the neutral case.

Pseudo-clefting in particular can also be used as a kind of 'placeholder' strategy in planning discourse: variants like *what I really want to say is* ... and the like can give a speaker time to organize the utterance to follow – as well as creating expectation or gaining attention. These postposed-NP strategies, then, focus in the opposite way from left-movement: by introducing relatively uninformative material that asks the hearer to wait for something, and tells him roughly what kind of thing he's waiting for.

Note that all of these devices depend on the existence of neutral counterparts: focus, like stress (cf. §3.4), is relational. In a similar way, violation of the 'norms' for placement of sentence or constituent stress can have a similar effect: e.g. *John's reading in the study* normally has its highest prominence on *study* by the NSR, but *John's **reading** in the study* shows an implicit contrast (he's not having erotic fantasies . .), as does ***John's** reading in the study* (not Mary . . .). Any device that foregrounds a constituent can be used for focal effect, and syntactic and phonological devices are both available.

The emphasis in this section on 'strategies' for achieving expressive or communicational ends is deliberate; I've tried to indicate that the question 'what does construction X mean?' is often unanswerable outside a discourse situation, and that even constructions with the same propositional meaning (like actives and passives) do not have the same uses. The meaning of a construction partially depends on its use; 'meaning' in this sense includes speaker intention, discourse context, and many other pragmatic factors. Obviously languages need determinate structures if they are to be learnable, and function as codes for communication; but some aspects of the code at least are strictly communication- or discourse-centred, and can't sensibly be treated in isolation (e.g. discussion of the passive isn't a matter of 'syntax').

4.8 Word-Formation

4.8.1 LEXICAL EXPANSION
When language needs or wants a new word for something, it can get one in three basic ways: (i) create the item from scratch, using available phonological material; (ii) create it by combining already existing items into new units, or otherwise using native resources; (iii) borrow an item from another language. Strategy (i), creation *ex nihilo*, is (at least at present) rare and specialized: though at some point in the prehistory of language it must have been the rule rather than the exception – when language was invented, all lexis must have been made from scratch, since before language there were no linguistic forms.

But in historical times this is not a preferred strategy; virtually the only creations of this type are trade names: from George Eastman's *Kodak* (1888) through modern ones like *Dreft* (an American detergent) or *Jik* (a South African bleach); slang terms like *barf* 'vomit' (onomatopoeic?), *zilch* 'zero, nothing'; or adoption of acronyms, like RADAR 'RAdio Direction And Ranging', UNESCO 'United Nations Educational Scientific and Cultural Organization', SAAAPEA /sá:pi:ə/ 'South African Association Against Painful Experiments on Animals'.

Strategy (ii), usually called Word-Formation (WF), consists of at least three sub-strategies:

(a) Compounding: putting two (or more) otherwise independent items under one stress contour: recent examples are *sit-in*, *call-girl*, *car-park*, *massage-parlour*.

(b) Derivation (Affixation): using prefixes or suffixes that create new words from old either by changing part of speech (*nation-al*, *solid-ify*, *en-code*), or that change meaning without affecting grammatical class (*un-clear*, *pre-owned*, *green-ish*).

(c) Zero-Derivation (Conversion): taking advantage of the lack of inflexional morphology in a language like English, and simply (say) using a noun as a verb: recent examples are *to access*, *to input*.

Strategy (iii), as we have seen (ch. 2), has played a considerable part in the growth of the English vocabulary; and it still goes on, especially for representing items characteristic of or invented by other cultures (since the 1940s we can instance *strafe*, *blitzkrieg*, *apartheid*, *sputnik*, *ombudsman*).

The structure of the lexicon also changes constantly through sense-shifts of various kinds, some apparently unmotivated, others 'designed'. The first type can be exemplified by 'upward' or 'downward' shifts on the parameter of 'status' (*steward* < *stȳ-weard* '(pig)sty guardian', *knight* < *cniht* 'servant' moving up, *silly* < *sǣlig* 'blessed', *crafty* < *cræftig* 'strong, ingenious' moving down). Or by expansion (generalization) and contraction (specialization) of denotation: *pen* < L *penna* 'feather' now meaning any writing implement with liquid or semisolid fuel showing expansion, *meat* < *mete* 'food' now meaning only food made out of pieces of dead animals (cf. *baked meat(s)*) showing contraction. Each such change – in a rather trivial sense – 'creates new words'.

The second type of internal structural change involves the deliberate use of terms with particular kinds of senses in a 'political' way, i.e. by some group wishing to redefine public attitudes. A classic recent case is *gay* for 'homosexual', where the intent is clearly to create an attitude. Whether this one has had its effect is another question: what's probably happened is that the word has simply changed status and become restricted in use. Now derivatively, phrases like *gay young thing*, *gay abandon*, have irrevocably changed nuance.

The changes just discussed do not really affect lexical resources in any serious way; they represent rather a reapportionment of lexical items among available senses – or perhaps the other way round. Their interest is in most cases more social than linguistic. But the major word-formation processes are deeply embedded in grammatical structure, and often highly productive. In the rest of this section we will look at some of the more important WF processes in English, and the kinds of words that result from them.

4.8.2 COMPOUNDING

We distinguish two major WF strategies – derivation and compounding. The latter is one of the most productive in English (as in Germanic generally). It can be defined roughly as putting together two or more independent lexical items so that they form 'one word' – i.e. take a single (usually SW) stress contour, and can be inputs to the appropriate inflectional rules: e.g. a noun compound like *call-girl* can be marked for plural in the usual way (*call-girl-s*), a compound verb like *bad-mouth* can take 3 sg and past inflection, has participles, etc. (*bad-mouth-s, -mouth-ed, -mouth-ing*). Compounds may be made up of simplex lexical items (e.g. *gastank*: N + N); or one or more members may be morphologically complex, e.g. *gas-guzzler*, where *guzzl-er* is itself a derived – but non-compound – form consisting of Verb + -*er*. Thus compounds will typically have a complex morphological representation, where the labelling of the compound as a whole may be different from that of its component parts:

(4.51)

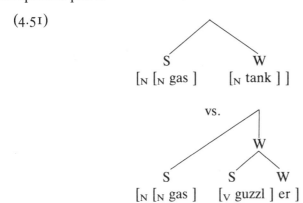

Note that – pretty much regardless of the complexity of internal structure – the basic compound rule (§3.4) assigns an SW contour to the whole.

Perhaps the bulk of English compounds are two-member; but the process allows for potentially much larger (if rarer) types, and there is enormous freedom for new production (the point, after all, of WF processes). Thus a device for removing paint from large American cars could be a *gas-guzzler-paint-coat-remover*: here two compound nouns, one of two members, and one of three containing another two-member one. And we could have a *gas-guzzler-paint-coat-remover-sales-representative-supervisor* . . . though it's not likely we would. But the principle should be clear. In the rest of this section we'll look at some major compound types in terms of their semantics and grammatical structure.

Compounding is an ancient WF strategy, dating back to Proto-IE. The older IE dialects used it freely, and in fact we owe one useful classification to the pre-Christian Sanskrit grammarians' own analysis of Sanskrit compounds. This will serve as the basis for my treatment here, as it casts some light on the semantic relations between compounds and their members – which are not always as straightforward as in the above examples.

(i) Dvandva (Skr 'pair'). Also 'copulative'. These are of the form $[_N N + N]$ or $[_A A + A]$, and their meaning is basically (Unit composed of (X & X)). These were common in early Germanic, e.g. OS *gisun-fader* 'son-(&)-father'; obscured dvandvas remain in the numerals 13–19, which historically were additive: E *fourteen* is opaque, but cf. Gothic *fidwōr-taíhun* 'four-(plus)-ten' = 14. Non-obscured ones remain in the numeral system as well in the types *twenty-one*, *twenty-two*, . . . though these do not have compound stress. Other dvandvas occur in place-names like *Alsace-Lorraine* 'the unit consisting of Alsace & Lorraine', *Schleswig-Holstein*, and company names like *Rowntree-Mackintosh*. The type is not very productive, but there are more recent formations in fields like colour-names (*blue-green*, *red-orange*), ladies' underwear (*panty-hose*, *panty-girdle*, *cami-knickers* (partly a 'clipping': see §4.8.6)) and musical instrument names (*banjo-mandolin*, *banjo-ukulele*).

(ii) Tatpuruṣa (Skr 'his servant') or 'Determinative'. These are compounds of the forms $[_N N + N]$ (*earring*, *rat-catcher*), $[_A A + N]$ (*superstar*), $[_A N + A]$ (*sex-mad*), $[_A A + A]$ (*ever-ready*). In these, one element is either in a modifying relation to the other (*superstar* 'star (who is) super'), or in a kind of 'prepositional' or 'case' relation: thus *earring* 'ring (for an) ear', *rat-catcher* 'catcher (of) rats' (in the last case the relation is actually verb/direct object, as usually in *-er* compounds). The internal relationship between members of tatpuruṣas is likely to be idiosyncratic: thus *milk-bottle* 'bottle (for containing) milk', *milkman* 'man (who delivers) milk', *milk-tart* 'tart (made with) milk', *milk-fever* 'fever/disease (caused by lack of calcium in mothers giving) milk', *milk-float* 'float (for carrying bottles of) milk', *milk-tooth* 'tooth (present – typically – while young mammal is still drinking) milk', *milkweed* 'weed (with sap like) milk', etc. The interpretations of many of these are given pragmatically: *milkman* is not likely to mean 'man (made with) milk'. But many, perhaps the majority, have to be learned as individual items, or at least as members of characteristic sets (*milk-bottle* like *soda-bottle*, *medicine-bottle*, *wine-bottle*, . . .).

(iii) Bahuvrīhi (Skr 'much rice') or 'Exocentric'. These are usually of the form [$_N$N + N] (*shithead*) or [$_A$A + N] (*barefoot*). They have the peculiar property that their sense is not strictly 'compositional', i.e. derived from a relation between their constituents; or to put it another way, the head is in fact 'outside' the compound. Thus a *milk-bottle* is a kind of bottle; but *barefoot* does not refer to a kind of foot, rather a person having such a foot: not 'foot (which is) bare', but '(property of a person having) foot/feet (which is/are) bare'. Similarly – and in a rather more complex way – *shithead* does not mean 'head (made of) shit', but '(person having) head (describable as/reminding one in some way of) shit'. That is, the structure as a whole is predicated of some 'third party'. This type seems particularly productive in informal compounds like the one above, and similar ones like *clever-clogs*, *smart-ass* (where the semantics are even more complex, and the metaphorical extension greater).

What follows is a brief overall description of the main English compound-types, classified first by the final grammatical category of the compound (e.g. compound N, etc.), and then by the categories of the constituents (N + N, etc.).

(i) *Compound Nouns*

Perhaps the most common group is N + N: this includes tatpuruṣas like *boyfriend*, *manservant*, *fishing-rod*, dvandvas like *Alsace-Lorraine*, *owner-occupier*, and bahuvrīhis like *skinhead*. One of the most productive types is N + V-*er* (*ratcatcher*, *party-pooper*, *piano-player*); these are interesting because the N and V are in object-verb relation, and the normal order for this construction in English is VO, not OV. The type *pooper-party* seems not to exist; though there are VO compounds (if less common) where the first constituent is a V, not an N: *pickpocket*, *kill-joy*, *dreadnought*.

There are also a few compounds interpreted by some writers as N + V: *nosebleed*, *sunshine*, *nose-dive*; but these may well be N + N, since *bleed*, *shine* and *dive* occur as nouns (if zero-derived from verbs). Probably the only clear case of a compound noun whose second element is a verb is *make-believe*.

Among the more productive other types are A + N (*software*, *underwear*, *redskin*); Prep + N (*in-crowd*, *outgroup*, *overbite*); and V + Prep (*cop-out*, *sit-in*, *fuck-up*, *fallout*, *pullover*). Note by the way that whether or not an item is written with a hyphen has nothing to do with its status as a compound: that is purely a matter of stress and morphological behaviour. The conventions for hyphenation are inconsistent and linguistically unrevealing.

(ii) *Compound Verbs*

On the whole, verb compounding is less productive than noun compounding; verbs tend to be formed more often by conversion or by backformation: e.g. chopping off the *-er* or similar endings on what is assumed to be (but in fact isn't) a noun derived from a verb: classic cases are *edit* < *editor*, and *burgle* (a facetious coinage of W.S. Gilbert that caught on) from *burglar*, interpreted as *burgl-er*.

Perhaps the most common verb compounds are N + V (again, note, with OV order): *carbon-date, colour-code, sky-dive, breath-test*: though these may be complete or partial back-formations from nouns like *colour-code* or participial adjectives like *colour-coded*, etc. A + V compounds also occur: *double-book, fine-tune, free-associate*, as do A + N: *brown-bag* 'carry food or liquor for consumption on premises not your own', *bad-mouth*. There are also Prep + V examples like *over-achieve, undergo, offload*; their status as true compounds, i.e. lexical items distinct from their component parts, can be seen from sense differences: *undergo* is not the same as *go under*. There are also a few V + V compounds, like *test-market, typewrite* (if not a back-formation from *typewriter*), *freeze-dry*.

(iii) *Compound Adjectives*

These are much more productive than compound verbs, approaching noun compounds in this respect. We have N + A (*labour-intensive, waterproof, machine-readable, card-carrying, species-specific*); A + A: *bitter-sweet, open-ended, ready-made, blue-green*; and some Adv + A like *overqualified, up-tight*. There are also N + N adjectives, which tend to be bound to specific nouns or classes of nouns: *back-street* (affair, abortion), *coffee-table* (book), *turtle-neck* (sweater); the less common A + N types also behave this way: *red brick* (university), *solid-state* (physics, circuitry). The same is true of Prep + N adjectives: *in-depth* (analysis, investigation), *before-tax* (profits), and A/Adv + V like *high-rise* (block), *quick-change* (artist). A final type consists of V + Prep: *see-through, tow-away, wrap-around* – again with a limited class of possible modified nouns.

There is another, increasingly productive class, that falls somewhere between true compounds and forms derived by affixation. In a true compound, both members are generally independent words (aside from exceptional cases like *cranberry*, where though *cran-* doesn't exist independently, parallelism with *strawberry, loganberry*, etc. assigns it to a 'word-like' class, sometimes called a 'bound word'). This special class has been called 'neoclassical compounds' by Bauer (1983): one – or even both – of the elements are Latin or Greek, do not occur as free words, but carry what Bauer calls a 'higher density of lexical information' than mere prefixes or suffixes. Examples of these neoclassical formatives are *astro-*, *hydro-*, *photo-*, *gastro-*, *eco-*, *tele-*, *hyper-* for first elements, and *-crat*, *-cide*, *-ology*, *-scope*, *-phile*, *-phobe*, *-ectomy*, *-aemia* for second elements. These can occur compounded with 'ordinary' lexical items: *eco-freak*, *biosphere*, *astrodome*, *lumpectomy*; but most often with other members of the same class, as in *biocide*, *gastroscope*, *hyperaemia*, *photophobe*, *gastrectomy*.

If these items were taken as affixes, we would be in the odd situation of having words made up only of affixes, with no lexical roots; we can see their different status by contrasting the impossibility of making acceptable words out of prefixes and suffixes of the ordinary kind: **non-ity* 'property of not being', **pre-al-ity* 'property of coming before', etc.

4.8.3 PRODUCTIVITY

Not all derivational types are equally productive; we saw earlier in our discussion of dvandva compounds (4.8.2) that a formerly productive process can become obsolescent. Not all derived forms, then – even uncontroversial ones that are morphologically complex, with the boundaries visible – will be usable for new formations.

For instance *warm-th*, *streng-th*, *heal-th*, perhaps less clearly *thef-t*, all contain a base plus a nominalizing suffix *-th*/*-t*; it takes little reflection to see that the bases are respectively *warm*, *strong*, *heal*, *thief*. And that at least some of the vowel alternations are types duplicated elsewhere in English (*thief*/*theft* is the same as *leave*/*left*, *keep*/*kept*, etc. – due to late OE or early ME shortening before consonant clusters: cf. §3.8). All the forms cited above show reflexes of the OE suffix *-þu* (earlier **/-iθu/*), which formed feminine abstract nouns from verb and adjective bases, with the /i/ causing umlaut of the stem vowel (cf. §3.8): hence *strong*/*strength* go back to OE *strang*/*streng-þu*, etc.

But we can no longer produce new forms this way: **big-th*, **small-th*, **red-th* (though for some speakers the later analogical *cool-th* is acceptable). Thus even though these forms contain a WF suffix with a determinate grammatical function, the complexes have been lexicalized – frozen into independent words – and are members of a closed and unproductive set.

At the opposite extreme we find suffixes like *-ette*, *-esque*, which have virtually no restrictions on their use in forming new words. *-ette* can be used as a 'feminizer' (*usher-ette*, *author-ette*, even *undergradu-ette* – though this use is receding), as a diminutivizer (*super-ette*, *launder-ette*);

or in the sense 'inferior/cheaper imitation' (*leather-ette*, even *plastic-ette*). Similarly, *-esque* can be attached to virtually any proper name to yield an adjective with the sense '-like' or 'in the characteristic style of': *Stalin-esque*, *Churchill-esque*, even – assuming a reason to do it – *Lass-esque*.

Most of the other derivational affixes come somewhere in between; their productivity is limited in one way or another. For instance, there seems to be a restriction on even very productive affixes like *-er* 'agent' if there exists another word (preferably simple) with the same sense that the derivative would have: thus **stealer* because of *thief*. The same would be true of **un-big* because of *small*, **un-pretty* because of *ugly*. (Though the *un-* type can often be used idiosyncratically for nuance: *unpretty* is not a 'standard' word, but the formation is at least marginally available for special purposes, e.g. as an intermediate point on the *pretty* . . . *ugly* scale.)

4.8.4 DERIVATIONAL MORPHOLOGY: PHONOLOGICAL IMPLICATIONS

Some derivational affixes are phonologically neutral: they have no effect on the bases they're attached to. But others have effects either on stress or segmental properties of their bases, or both; still others are constrained by rhythmic factors.

With respect to stress, English suffixes (see below on prefixes) fall into three major classes:

(1) Stress-neutral. The suffixes are unstressed, and do not affect the stress-pattern of their bases. Examples are *-able*, *-hood*, *-ish*, *-ment*, *-ist*: *pérish/pérish-able*, *nátion/nátion-hood*, *yéllow/yéllow-ish*, *estáblish/estáblish-ment*, *phýsic/phýsic-ist* (on the consonant alternation in the last pair see below).

(2) Stress-reducing. These suffixes bear primary word-stress in derivatives, and reduce all stresses in the base. Examples are *-esque*, *-ee*, *-itis*, *-ese*, *-ette*: *pícture/pictur-ésque*, *detaín/detain-ée*, *tónsil/tonsil-ítis*, *jóurnal/journal-ése*, *léather/leather-étte*.

(3) Stress-attracting. These suffixes (unlike those of class 2) do not bear stress; but unlike class 1, they affect it: they attract the main stress to the syllable immediately to their left. Examples are *-ic*, *-ity*, *-ian*, *-ia(c)*, *-ial*. Thus *sýmbol/symból-ic*, *módern/modérn-ity*, *hístory/históri-an*, *régal/regál-ia*, *démon/demón-iac*, *círcumstance/circumstánt-ial* (On the vowel and consonant alternations see below.)

In the case of a form with more than one suffix, it's the last one that determines the stress of the whole word. Thus:

(4.52)

nátion

nátion-al   [class 1 suffix]

nátion-al-ist   [class 1 suffix]

nation-al-íst-ic   [class 3 suffix]

Note that the effect of the class 3 suffix is to shift the stress onto another suffix – but one that by itself would be unstressed. Thus it's clear that *nation-al-ist* is in fact being treated by *-ic* as if it were a simplex word like *symbol*: we are dealing with structures like [[symbol]ic], [[[[nation]al]ist]ic].

If it were possible in this case to add another suffix, the stress could shift again, e.g. onto *-ic*: if a scholar specializing in the study of independence movements could be called a *nationalistician*, we would have *nation-al-íst-ic → nation-al-ist-íc-ian* (since *-ian* is also a class 3 suffix).

Actually I have deliberately misled the reader for the sake of a simple illustration: *-al* is not in fact a class 1 suffix, though from forms like *nation-al*, *comic-al*, *statistic-al* one might think it was. It is in fact class 3, but behaves like class 1 (hence its utility in the above example) under certain conditions. That is, the normal English Main Stress Rule (cf. §§3.4–5) interacts with suffixes, and may take priority. If you recall, the MSR stresses a heavy penultimate syllable; if the penult is light, stress moves back to the antepenult. In a disyllabic word, the MSR skips a light final syllable and stresses the initial, regardless of weight. Thus in *nation* /néɪʃən/ the first syllable is heavy and the second light; hence the S W pattern. In *national* /næʃənəl/, both the final and the penult are light; hence the stress goes back to the antepenult.

To see *-al* in its 'true' class 3 light, we must look at cases where it does not come into conflict with the MSR: i.e. where the base has a heavy final or penult. Thus in *ánecdote/anecdót-al*, *díalect/dialéct-al*, *áncestor/ancéstr-al*, the stress is attracted to the syllable immediately to the left of *-al* because the MSR does not disallow it. Cases like *national* are 'failures' of *-al* to exhibit its class 3 properties because of the precedence taken by the more general stress rule.

A different kind of connection with stress is exhibited by one highly specialized derivational process – the only productive example of infixing in English. This is the rule allowing (in certain styles) the insertion of disyllabic expletives inside words (mainly *-fucking-*, *-frigging-*, *-bloody-*). Typical instances are *im-bloody-possible*, *three-o'-fucking-clock*, *propa-fucking-ganda*, *kanga-bloody-roo*.

These infixes are tied to stress in the following way: (a) they must normally be inserted immediately to the left of the main word stress: *propa-fucking-gánda*, *kanga-bloody-róo*; (b) they must not be inserted before an unstressed syllable: *three-fucking-o'-clóck*, *impóssi-bloody-ble*; (c) because of this the only disyllabic words allowing insertion are those with a stressed second syllable: *ur-fucking-báne*, but *éar-fucking-ly* (the *urbane* type does not work for me, but some speakers use it); (d) therefore the preferred insertion sites are in words of three or more syllables, without initial main word stress.

Note incidentally that these restrictions seem to apply – if perhaps not quite so strictly – in the use of the 'free' forms of these words. Thus *he was fucking rúnning around like a madman*, but not *he was rúnning fucking aroúnd like a madman*, *what are you bloody dóing*? but not *what bloody are you dóing*? The general constraint seems to be avoidance of a dactylic (SWW) foot consisting of an expletive plus anything else. (Note that this only applies to expletives, not e.g. the ordinary verb: *fucking aroúnd* itself is prosodically well formed.)

Expletive-insertion may seem a marginal case of word-formation: it seems more to add an affective nuance than create new words. But 'affective' WF is a legitimate and productive type; we also get it in affectionate diminutives like *kitty*, *doggie*. Actually, *kanga-bloody-roo* might be said to be synonymous with *bloody kangaroo* – a lexicalization of the phrase; just as in a sense *doggie* might be a more radical lexicalization of something like *cute/nice/dear little dog*.

So far I have dealt only with suffixes, not with prefixes; one of the reasons is that their behaviour is overall more complex and less regular – and linguistically more interesting. Though we can point out a few major features of prefixes. For one thing, there appear to be no stress-attracting prefixes, like the class 3 suffixes: though there are stressable prefixes. But even some of these are problematical: thus *sub-* is stressed in *súb-committee*, *súb-division*, *súb-way*; but unstressed in *sub-sístence*, *sub-júnction*, *sub-júnctive*. In general, prefixes tend to be stressed on nouns, and unstressed on adjectives and verbs: hence *sub-cutáneous*, *sub-jóin*, *sub-síst*; but they may fail to get stressed in nouns derived from verbs or adjectives, as in *sub-júnction*, *sub-sístence* above. (The differential stress on complex nouns and verbs is fairly general: cf. *díscharge/dischárge*, *pérmit/permít*, *réfill/refíll*.) Derivational prefixes are also generally stressed if they have two or more syllables: *ánti-frèeze*, *ánte-dàte*; though here we have only secondary stress if the base is not monosyllabic: *ànti-aírcraft*, *ànti-rábies*, *ànte-nátal*.

While most of the rules for stress in affixes hold across all dialects, there is at least one prefix that varies. *Con-* (or its variant *com-*) is unstressed in most southern English varieties, in forms like *convert*, *converse, compel, compare*; but in northern English and (somewhat surprisingly, on historical grounds) in South African English, it carries secondary stress and an unreduced vowel: RP *convert* /kənvɔ́ːt/ vs. SA /kɔ́nvø̀ːt/.

Derivational affixes are also involved in a number of important segmental (morphophonemic) alternations. Some of the most wide-ranging are:

(i) '*Vowel-Shift*'. Because of the effects of the Great Vowel Shift (§3.10) and other rules, there are a large number of items in which a long or diphthongal nucleus in a non-derived form alternates with a short vowel in a suffixed one. The most common pairings are:

(4.53)

    (a) aɪ ~ ɪ   d*i*vine/d*i*vinity, s*i*gn-s*i*gnify, cr*i*me/cr*i*minal
    (b) iː ~ ɛ   ser*e*ne/ser*e*nity, cl*e*an/cl*e*anliness
    (c) eɪ ~ æ   s*a*ne/s*a*nity, hum*a*ne/hum*a*nity, gr*a*in/gr*a*nary
    (d) aʊ ~ ʌ   prof*ou*nd/prof*u*ndity, pron*ou*nce/pron*u*nciation
    (e) əʊ ~ ɒ   c*o*ne/c*o*nical, verb*o*se/verb*o*sity

And there is a rather marginal /ɔɪ/ ~ /ʌ/ as in *joint/juncture, point/ punctual/(contra)puntal*. These alternations are in general not productive: new formations do not exhibit them. Experiments with nonsense-words (what's the *-ity* derivative of *spline*?) and the behaviour of many real words (*spice/sp*[aɪ]*ciness*, not **sp*[ɪ]*ciness*, etc.) suggest that these are fossils; but they are a very basic part of the Latin/Romance stratum of the vocabulary.

(ii) *Reduced/Non-Reduced Alternations*. There are many instances where a /ə/ in one member of a derivational set appears as an unreduced vowel in some other(s):

(4.54)

g á l a x y	g a l á c t i c
æ ə	ə æ
h í s t o r y	h i s t ó r i a n
ə	ɒ
t é l e g r a p h	t e l é g r a p h y
ɛ ə æ	ə ɛ ə
p h ó t o g r a p h	p h o t ó g r a p h y
əʊ ə æ	ə ɒ ə
c r é m a t e	c r e m á t i o n
iː	ə
J ó h n s o n	J o h n s ó n i a n
ə	əʊ

These alternations between /ə/ and full vowels have led many linguists to posit underlying forms containing only full vowels, with one or the other reduced if unstressed. Thus the stem underlying *galaxy/galactic* is /gælæk-/, that for *telegraph/telegraphy* is /tɛlɛ-græf/, and so on. Even if no form with all full vowels ever appears on the surface, such 'constructed underlying forms' do predict – in cooperation with stress and vowel-reduction rules – the actual phonetic forms. This is no place to go into the arguments for and against such abstract analyses (see notes to §3.1); but it's worth observing that similar issues arise for the vowel-shift forms, and for the consonantal alternations discussed below.

(iii) *Palatalization Alternations.* The English inheritance from the Classical languages and Romance includes a number of consonant alternations taken in along with borrowed lexis, as well as some more recent developments based on the original forms of borrowed items. The most important of these involve velars or alveolars in base forms, and /s/ and palato-alveolars in derived forms. Some paradigms contain both types. Examples:

(4.55)

	/t/	/s/	/ʃ/
i.	educa*t*e	–	educa*t*ion
	par*t*	–	par*t*ial
	democra*t*	demo*c*racy	–

	/d/	/s/	/ʒ/
ii.	eva*d*e	eva*s*ive	eva*s*ion
	divi*d*e	divi*s*ive	divi*s*ion

	/s/	/ʃ/
iii.	convul*s*e	convul*s*ion

	/d/	/z/	/ʒ/
iv.	vi*d*eo	vi*s*ible	vi*s*ion

	/k/	/s/	/ʃ/
v.	logi*c*	–	logi*c*ian
	criti*c*	criti*c*ize	–

The forms in the middle column mostly go back to original Greek, Latin or Romance alternations: cf. L *divīdō* 'divide', past participle *divīsus*, or Gr *krítikos* 'judge', *krísis* 'judgement'; those in the last column are from the 17th-century palatization of /sj zj/ (§3.10): the original /j/ that triggered the change to /ʃ ʒ/ is still visible in French forms like *vision* /vizjõ/, *éducation* /edykasjõ/.

4.8.5 DERIVATION BY AFFIX: BASIC TYPES

Derivational affixes can be divided into two main types according to function: class-maintaining and class-changing. The former 'modify' meanings in some way; the latter (whatever other effect they have on meaning) also change grammatical class. This section is a brief overview of both types, with no pretence at completeness.

(i) *Class-Maintaining*

Perhaps the bulk of these are prefixes; it is in fact characteristic of prefixes not to change grammatical category (though there are a few exceptions like *en-*: see below). There is a wide semantic range, including negativizers for verbs and adjectives (*de-, un-, a-, in-* and its variants *im-, il-, -ir*: *destabilize, unseat, apolitical, inedible, impossible, illegal, irreverent*). For nouns, the negativizer is *non-* (*nonentity, nonperson*). We also have broadly aspectual prefixes for verbs like *re-* 'do again' (*recycle, remould*), *be-* 'spread, cover with' (*besmirch, bespatter*), *dis-* 'reverse' (*discover, dismount*). There is also a (relatively new) diminutive/augmentative pair *mini-/maxi-* (*miniskirt, minicomputer, maxiskirt*); and the quantifying prefixes for multiplication (*kilo-* 'thousand', *mega-* 'million' (*kilowatt, megawatt* – though *mega-* often just means 'big' as in *megatherium, megalith*) and division: *centi-* 'one-hundredth', *milli-* 'one thousandth' and the newer *nano-* 'one millionth' (*centisecond, millisecond, nanosecond*; though *centi-* and *milli-* can simply indicate (supposed) total count as in *centipede, millipede*).

Among the class-maintaining suffixes are the diminutives *-(l)et, -ling, -ie, -ette* (*owlet, birdlet, duckling, drinkie, kitchenette*); the feminizers *-ess, -ette* (*Jewess, usherette*); *-ette* in its 'ersatz' sense (*leatherette*); and a group that while not changing class as such, convert concrete nouns into abstracts or collectives: *-dom, -hood, -ship* (*Afrikanerdom, nationhood, authorship*).

(ii) *Class-Changing*

(a) *Noun-Forming.* One of the most productive is the 'agentive' *-er*, which forms deverbal ('from a verb') nouns with the general sense 'one/thing that Vs' for any verb V: *bak-er, scrap-er, gather-er, blackmail-er*. One productive subclass (cf. §4.8.2) is formed by attaching *-er* to an OV verbal 'pseudo-compound' – i.e. a compound which, as an independent verb, does not occur: *truck-driver* (no verb **truck-drive*), *motherfucker, party-pooper, pig-sticker*. Nouns are also formed from complex derived verbs in *-ate* or *-ize* by *-ion* (*fractionation, catheterization*). Still other deverbal nouns are formed with *-al* (*arrival, betrayal, survival*), or *-ure* (*licensure, candidature*). A special case of deverbal noun is that where a verb (usually transitive) becomes the patient of its own action with *-ee*: *blackmailee, deportee, employee*.

Nouns are also formed from adjectives: with *-cy* (especially if the stem ends in *-ent/-ant* (*permanency, expectancy*)); though here *-ce* is now more productive (*excellence, elegance* – but not **pregnance*). Deadjectival nouns are also formed with *-ity* (*divinity, conformity*), and perhaps most productively with *-ness*, (*redness, grottiness*).

(b) *Verb Forming.* There are not many verb-forming processes currently productive: perhaps the most widespread is denominal or deadjectival formation with *-ize* (*catheterize, containerize, Africanize, pedestrianize*). Verbs are also formed with *-ate* (*fractionate, calumniate*), and with *-ify*, which occurs most frequently with 'neo-classical' roots (cf. §4.8.2), and often has a somewhat specialized sense: X-*ify* = 'make into X' (*petrify, calcify, acidify*).

The one verb-forming prefix that seems to be at all productive is *en-*: *encode, encircle, enshroud.* This is normally only for denominal formations, but there are archaic deadjectivals like *empurple* (*em-* is the normal variant of *en-* before labials), *encarnadine.*

(c) *Adjective- and Adverb-Forming.* There are two main classes of adjective formations: denominal and deverbal. Among the denominal suffixes are *-al* (*educational, anecdotal*), *-ic* (*demonic, algebraic, Arabic*). Others are rarer, like *-iac* (*paranoiac, demoniac*); a few items show the fossil *-en* (*wooden, brazen, earthen*) in the sense 'made out of N'. Among other productive ones are *-y* (*crappy, sunny, handy*) and the specialized *-esque* (*Hitleresque*).

Deverbal adjectives are formed mainly with *-able* (*believable, countable, kickable, squeezeable*); though some are in *-ful* (*resentful, careful*), and in *-ive* (*generative, concatenative*).

Other parts of speech can be made into adjectives, to a limited degree: prepositions (*uppish*), and even conjunctions (*iffy*); the *-y* suffix here covers quite a large range (*woody, crawly, creepy*).

Adverbs are formed most often with *-ly* (*quickly, happily*); though there are many in *-ward(s)*, *-wise* (*westward(s), cross-wise*).

4.8.6 SOME OTHER WF PROCESSES

There are a few unsystematic but highly productive WF processes that deserve mention:

(i) 'Pseudo-Suffixation'

Essentially a kind of back-formation: the second part of a word which is not actually a suffix in the derivational sense is used as the base for forming a new class of words. Perhaps the classic case is *-burger*: originally of course the second element of *Hamburger* (*steak*) 'steak in the Hamburg style/from/of Hamburg', *-burger* became abstracted in the sense 'patty of meat, etc. served on a bun'. Thus *cheeseburger,* *steakburger*, *fishburger*, *soyaburger*: and eventually by a process of 'clipping' (see (ii) below) *burger* moved from pseudo-suffix to simple noun. (The fact that the *ham-* in *hamburger* is known not to refer to ham creates a problem: what would you call a burger made of ham?)

Other items that have developed combinatorial freedom like this are *-teria* (from *cafeteria* to *washeteria*, etc.), *-rama* (from *panorama*) to *photo-rama* (camera-store), *rand-a-rama* (discount sale at a Cape Town supermarket), *-torium* (*auditorium* to *lubritorium*), and *-tique* (*boutique* to *boy-tique* – a children's clothing store in Cape Town). I have also come across *monokini* for a topless bathing suit: really a one-off pun on a possible interpretation of *bi-* in *bikini* – but a nice illustration of the process.

(ii) *'Clipping'*

A common way of producing neologisms is by chopping off some part of a word (usually on the right, but not always): early examples are the 18th-century *mob* < *mobile vulgus* 'fickle crowd', and *phiz(z)* 'face' < *physiognomy*. Other standard clippings are *piano*(forte), *miss*(tress), *gas*(oline), (peri)*wig*, (de)*fence*, and the multiply clipped (di)*still*(ery). In our time we have, among innumerable others, *homo*(sexual), *hetero*(sexual), *deli*(catessen), *narc*(otics agent), *porn*(ography), *prom* (enade concert), *op*(tical) *art*, *sci*(ence)-*fi*(ction), *lit*(erary)-*crit*(icism), *sit*(uation)-*com*(edy).

(iii) *Blends*

Also called portmanteau words, after Lewis Carroll's pioneering analysis of the type in Humpty-Dumpty's glosses to 'Jabberwocky' (*Through the Looking-Glass*, ch. VI). When Alice asks him what *slithy* means, he says:

> Well, *'slithy'* means 'lithe and slimy'. 'Lithe' is the same as 'active'. You see it's like a portmanteau – there are two meanings packed up into one word ... Well then, *'mimsy'* is 'flimsy and miserable' (there's another portmanteau for you).

Humpty-Dumpty also clearly recognizes clippings of the more usual sort in the text: after agreeing with Alice that *the wabe* is the grass plot around a sun-dial, he says 'It's called "*wabe*" you know because it goes a long way before it and a long way behind it'; and for *mome* he says 'I think it's short for "from home"' '.

Among more recent portmanteaus are *chunnel* < *ch*(annel t)*unnel*, *motel* < *mot*(or hot)*el*, *cremains* 'what's left after a cremation', *Reaganomics*, *liger*, *tiglon* (lion-tiger crosses). It's clear (and Humpty-Dumpty of course saw it as well) that the distinction between clippings and blends is really not one of principle: a blend is normally a pair of mirror-image clippings set back-to-back.

CHAPTER 4: NOTES AND REFERENCES

4.1 The approach to grammatical description in this chapter is 'post-traditional', in that it's influenced by various modern schools of grammatical thought; but it's also 'traditional', in that it is very much concerned with relations between grammar and meaning, and is rather informal in conception. For introductions to contemporary grammatical theory of various kinds, Lyons (1968: chs. 4–8), Atkinson et al. (1982: chs. 5–6), Brown & Miller (1980), Matthews (1981). Brown & Miller is the best introduction for the reader with little linguistic background; Matthews is rich and sophisticated, but difficult – though it is to my mind the best single book on syntax there is. For English morphology and syntax, both historical and descriptive, the older grammars are indispensable: Sweet (1891) and Jespersen's monumental seven-volume grammar (1909–49) are two works that belong in the library of anybody interested in English grammar. Of modern accounts of English structure, perhaps the best are Strang (1968), Quirk et al. (1972), Quirk & Greenbaum (1973), and Huddleston (1984). The analyses presented here are in general my own, though they are of course indebted to the works mentioned, and others.

4.2 On grammatical typology, Comrie (1981) is probably the best introduction; on word order see Greenberg's famous paper of 1966, which is still worth reading. For morphology, the best general text is Matthews (1974); see also Brown & Miller (chs. 11–16), Atkinson et al. (ch. 5), and Lyons (ch. 5).

4.3 On the noun and noun phrase, Jespersen vol. II (chs. II–VII); on gender vol. VII (ch. V), and on case vol. VII (chs. VI–IX). On pronouns, Jespersen II (chs. XVI–XVII). See also Strang (chs. VII–VIII), and Huddleston (chs. 6–8). On grammatical categories and 'parts of speech' in general, Lyons (§7.6), and Huddleston (ch. 3); for number, gender and case in general, Lyons (§§7.3–4).

Most of the standard histories of English give good accounts of the development of morphology; Moore (1964) is particularly useful for an overall view of the history of inflections. Morphology is also well covered in Wyld (1927, 1936), and in the OE and ME grammars cited in the notes to ch. 3. I will not give further references to general accounts of the history of morphosyntactic categories per se except when special issues are involved; the standard handbooks are well-organized, and the data is easily accessed. For more recent and more specialized work on historical morphosyntactic topics, see the papers in Lass (1969), Blake & Jones (1984), Davenport et al. (1983), Eaton et al. (1985).

For uses of the case-forms in OE, Quirk & Wrenn (1957) is particularly clear. For later developments of the case forms and their uses, Traugott (1972: 121ff). Despite being cast in a now somewhat outmoded theoretical framework, Traugott is an extremely useful book for an overview of the history of English syntax, particularly because of her concern with meaning; there is probably no better one-volume history of English syntax available.

4.4 On deixis, see the introductory account in Lyons (1968: §7.2); for a more technical treatment, Lyons (1977: ch. 15) – difficult but immensely rewarding, and Levinson (1983: ch. 2).

4.5.1 On the English verb, Palmer (1974), Strang (ch. IX), Huddleston (chs. 4, 9). The last is a particularly useful account of the nonfinite forms. See also Jespersen V (chs. VIII–XX).

4.5.2 On tense and aspect in general, Lyons (1968: §7.5, 1977: §§15.4–6), For more specialized cross-linguistic studies, Comrie (1973) on aspect, (1985) on tense. On English tense and aspect see Palmer, and Jespersen IV (Chs. I–XIV); Sweet (1891: §§271–98); For the perfect, also McCoard (1978). This section bears the impress of many discussions with Susan Wright, who made me get rid of a lot of wrong ideas and gave me some right ones.

4.5.3 On modality, Lyons (1977: ch. 17); on mood as a category in English, and the functions and history of the modal auxiliaries, Jespersen IV (chs. XV–XXII), VII (ch. XVIII). On the development of the senses of the modals, and their complex and controversial history, Goossens (1984), Plank (1984).

4.5.4 On auxiliaries and main verbs as categories, Matthews (1981: 155f, 164); on the syntax of the auxiliary see Huddleston (ch. 4, and ch. 13 on negation); also Brown & Miller (ch. 8). On questions and negation Jespersen IV (chs. XXV, XXIII). For the origins and development of *do*-support, Traugott (137–42) and Ellegård (1953). On the 'semi-modal' status of *ought*, see Harris (1986).

4.5.5 For the history of the verb phrase in English, the primary source now is Visser (1963–9); there is also much information scattered throughout Jespersen under headings like tense, etc. See also Traugott under part B of chapters 3–5.

4.6.1 On subordination in general Brown & Miller (ch. 9), Matthews (1981: chs. 4, 8); on English subordination Huddleston (ch. 12).

4.6.2 The English complement system has long been a focus of interest for transformational grammarians: for a recent account see Radford (1981: chs. 5–6). For a historical study of the origins of the modern complement system, Warner (1982).

4.6.3 On relative clauses, Jespersen III (chs. III–X); the *wh*- forms are treated in detail in ch. VI, and *that* in ch. VII. The accessibility hierarchy was first proposed in Keenan & Comrie (1977). The general treatment of relativization here owes a good deal to that in Romaine (1980, 1984).

4.6.4 On the history of English relativization, Jespersen as above, Traugott, Romaine (1984). OE examples here and elsewhere are unattributed, as they are often taken from standard grammars where they are also unattributed.

4.7 On semantic and syntactic roles, Brown & Miller (chs. 17–19), Lyons (1977: ch. 12). On the general question of the role of the passive, focus, etc., Huddleston (ch. 14). The material covered here impinges on the related areas of discourse analysis and pragmatics, both of which are fields under intensive development. For excellent textbook introductions see respectively Brown & Yule (1983, especially chs. 4–5) and Levinson (1983). There is an influential and accessible treatment of many related issues in Halliday (1978); and for an interesting contrastive study of focussing processes in English and Polish, with a valuable bibliography, see Grzegorek (1984).

4.8 The basic work on English word-formation is Marchand (1969), which covers both history and synchronic structure. For a more recent treatment, setting English WF in the context of current debates in phonological, morphological, syntactic and semantic theory, see Bauer (1983). This is a full, sophisticated and quite accessible discussion, and I have depended quite heavily on it for this section. There are also treatments of WF scattered through most of the standard histories listed in the notes to chs. 2–3, and a very full discussion in Jespersen VI (chs. VIII–X on compounding, XI–XXIX on other WF types).

5. DIALECTS OF ENGLISH

5.1 Criteria

On the face of it, there ought to be as many 'dialects of English', in the usual sense of the term, as there are geographically distinct speech communities. We could for instance define Cape Town by map coordinates, and set a boundary beyond which we're out of it and into another region with its own dialect. Thus 'Cape Town dialect' seems to be a regional term. But like any other reasonably sized community, Cape Town is a complex entity, with social stratification, ethnic differences, and other features with potential linguistic implications. 'Cape Town dialect' does not in fact identify anything very precise; the place label must at least be prefixed by a class label: say 'Working Class Cape Town'.

But any regional/social dialect will have subdialects defined by age: if the language of the community changes (as it will), and if at least some of its speakers remain in it, the older and younger ones will to some extent speak different dialects – since the language of one age-group will show changes that the other hasn't undergone. And within any age/class group there will probably be differences based on sex, ethnicity, religion, etc. Preliminary work in Cape Town, for instance, suggests that an accurate pinpointing of a dialect type will require up to five categories: e.g. 'Coloured Working-Class Female Muslim Teen-Age' would define a distinctive variety different from 'Christian' with all other variables held constant, or 'Male' or 'White', and so on.

But a survey like this is no place for such finesse. We need some relatively simple criteria for classification – that will be empirically justified, easy to handle, and above all reasonably predictive. By a 'predictive' classification I mean a maximally informative one, in which assignment of a label will predict as many properties as possible. Consider classifying human beings by hair-colour vs. by sex. Hair-colour tells us little about anything except hair-colour: though 'blonde' will be a good predictor of 'not Chinese'. Whereas classification by sex will predict ability to grow a beard, suitability for vasectomy – and as we'll see, some linguistic features as well. Both classifications are 'true'; but one is more useful.

So what criteria do we choose for English dialects? We might select class, sex, age, religion; and in some cases these would yield interesting results – but normally only in specific regional settings. Thus 'Christian dialect' and 'Muslim dialect' would be meaningful in Cape Town (where indeed 'Jewish dialect' would also be – as it would in New York or London or Leeds); but it's unlikely that there's much to say about Christian dialects of English generally. There may be something to be said about Jewish dialects, but this will normally be a matter of lexical or other Jewishness imposed on a clear regional base: Cape Town or New York Jewish English are recognizable Cape Town or New York varieties.

With the social caveats above (and see below for refinements), the most richly predictive categories are regional: there is a lot in common among all Scottish or southern U.S. or South African dialects. This isn't surprising: regional features usually belong to an older historical stratum than social ones, and the basis for social variation is generally a regional 'given' (if often with some tension between it and a standard which may come from another region: cf. §§5.5–6). Indeed, there are modern regional boundaries in England that can still be seen as reflections of medieval ones (see §5.2).

But which regional types should we treat (since we can't do all of them)? And what social varieties do we take as typical for a region? An answer to the second question (for the first see §§5.2–3) grows out of certain properties of languages that have extensive regional variety, social stratification, and a set of more or less standard dialects. This can be summed up in the following diagram (complicated and modified after Hughes & Trudgill 1979: 6):

(5.1)

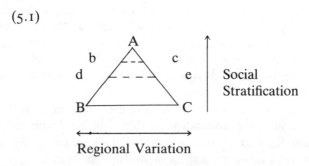

If the length of the base of the main triangle ABC (or any of the subtriangles Abc, etc.) represents difference between dialects, and the vertical dimension a social-class hierarchy, then the higher up the social scale you go, the less striking regional differences are likely to be. And vice versa. The greatest structural diversity (even to some degree of mutual incomprehensibility) will be found at the extreme points of BC or AB or AC.

Let's assume we have criteria for establishing a set of points along BC representing typical regional varieties, as well as a set of social categories of proven predictive value. E.g.

(5.2)

Upper Class
Upper Middle Class
Middle Class
Urban Working Class
Older Rural Working Class

(On the urban vs. rural working class distinction see below.)

If B–C are regional types, any line AB, AD etc. represents the social stratification for a given region; and we can choose any level to locate our description. But if the general claim about regionality and class is valid, the lower we make our intersection, the more different the dialects will be. So there's a *prima facie* justification – at least at the outset – for focussing on the lowest level: this should give us the maximal set of differences, and hence the richest variety of dialect types.

Now urban and rural working class dialects are both likely, with respect to the standard, to be markedly 'individual'; but there are reasons for beginning our survey with the rural ones, and indeed paying special attention to them. By and large the urban ones are more innovative; since they are more recent developments they tend to show newer structural features, and to have lost certain older ones. The older rural varieties, on the other hand, what I will call after Wells (1982) 'traditional dialects', represent a greater continuity in many respects with earlier stages of English, and are differentiated in such a way as to provide a context and background for later developments. That is, the traditional dialects may show us things about the history of the language obscured in the more modern ones; and in a book like this, with a general historical bias, the richness of information there is worth sampling.

5.2 Regional Dialects and Boundaries: An Example

Obviously any teatment of dialects of English starts with England, where they all came from (even Scots, as we'll see: §5.7.1). The first cut then will be between 'home' or 'Mainland' and 'Extraterritorial' dialects. Within the Mainland category I will adopt a quite traditional Anglocentric classification, based largely on historical phonology; the development of the phonological system (especially the vowels) seems to be the most distinctive regional feature, and represents the oldest stratum of differences. After treating England in some detail, we'll turn to the 'Celtic countries' (Scotland, Ireland and Wales), and then to the Extraterritorial dialects, where again the treatment will be regional, since each new settlement area has developed a distinctive (cluster of) dialect(s).

If we look at a map showing the major OE dialect boundaries, we find that they are roughly in line with the basic political divisions of the time: compare map I (§2.4) with the one below:

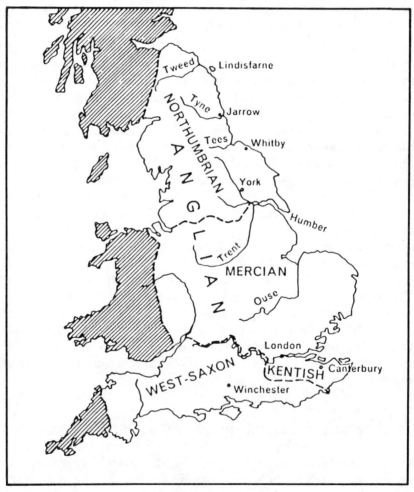

Map 3. Old English Dialects
[From Bourcier 1981: 53]

And if we compare this with a map of the major ME dialect boundaries (say c. 1300, in a rather simplified version), we note that while details differ, there are still basic continuities: a northern dialect area (descendants of Old Northumbrian), a Midland group (largely Mercian, divided into East and West), and a southern group, consisting of SW (West Saxon) and SE (Kentish):

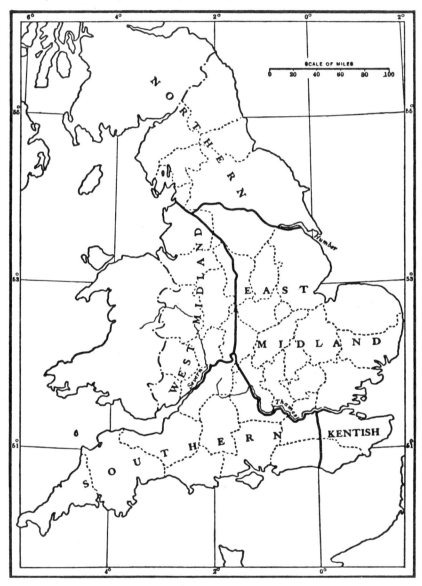

Map 4. Middle English Dialects
[From Baugh & Cable 1978: 190]

And a modern regional map would show a similar – if more complex – picture; but we will get to that later.

The precise boundary lines on dialect maps are obviously idealizations; dialects are actually divided in most cases by rather fuzzy transition zones, in which features belonging to one dialect or another will coexist, or speakers will use forms from two neighbouring dialects (so-called 'mixed lects'), or even have forms intermediate between those of two dialects ('fudged lects': *lect* is a back-formation from *dialect*, used as a combining form). That is, dialect boundaries of the type conventionally shown on maps are constructs – if generally justifiable ones.

Traditionally, they come about this way: dialect geographers will map occurrences of particular forms, on the basis of sampling of texts (for written dialects) or speakers; then lines can often be drawn separating the areas where two different forms, or variants of the same form, occur. These lines are called isoglosses (or with specific reference to phonological features, isophones). A boundary between two dialect areas is usually defined as a zone where a number of isoglosses 'bundle' or run (roughly) together.

This is rather abstract; we can illustrate the general procedure (and some interesting properties of boundaries) with a specific example. One of the most striking features of the older rural dialects of the SW of England is the presence of voiced initial fricatives where other dialects have voiceless ones: /v z ð ʒ/ instead of /f s θ ʃ/ in *farmer, six, thumb, shilling*, for instance. This is one of the features of the 'Zummerzet' (= Somerset) stereotype, probably familiar to non-English readers from Hardy's southwestern rustics. (Scattered through the first three chapters of *Tess of the D'Urbervilles* are forms like *zaid* 'said', *volk* 'folk', *vlee* 'fly'.) On the basis of the *Survey of English Dialects* (SED) materials, the isoglosses for this voicing are shown in map 5. Note that the isoglosses don't coincide: for instance the [z] in *six* and [ð] in *thumb* lines cut north of the [v] in *farmer* line and the *thumb* line cuts northeast. Similarly, the [v] line runs furthest east of all of them, extending to the western edge of Surrey; and so on. Yet clearly the lines do delimit a general area: if we disregard the fine details, we can 'average out' the northernmost and easternmost extensions of isoglosses, and turn the bundle into a general SW/SE boundary; see map 6.

The area inside the boundary (which itself is an abstraction from the isogloss bundle in map 5) 'has voiced fricatives' – whatever else it may have, and whatever the details are. And from a historical point of view it's interesting that this area coincides roughly with both SW ME and West Saxon OE (cf. maps 3, 4).

But why is there that small area out east in Sussex with only [v] in *farmer* and none of the others? And why don't all the isoglosses

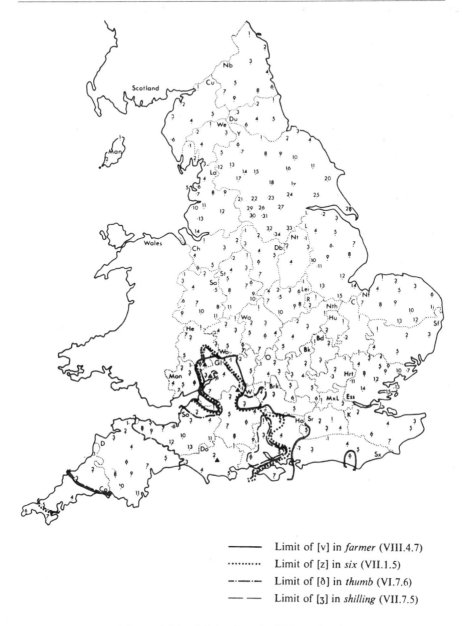

—————— Limit of [v] in *farmer* (VIII.4.7)
·········· Limit of [z] in *six* (VII.1.5)
—·—·— Limit of [ð] in *thumb* (VI.7.6)
— — Limit of [ʒ] in *shilling* (VII.7.5)

Map 5. Voiced Fricatives in SW England
[After Wakelin 1972(a): 93]

The notations *'farmer* (VIII.4.7)' etc. refer to the responses for a particular item
in the SED materials. E.g. the '[v] in *farmer*' line encloses (to the South and
West) those areas where informants have this particular feature.

Map 6. A possible SW/SE Boundary

coincide? It seems in the first place that today's distribution is a reduced relic of a formerly much wider one: in ME a general voicing of at least /f s/ occurred throughout the whole South, including both original West Saxon and Kentish territory. E.g. the *Aʒenbite of Inwit* ('Remorse of Conscience'), written in Kent in 1340, shows spellings like *vor* 'for', *veste* 'fast', *verst* 'first', *zenne* 'sin', *zigge* 'say', *zuyn* 'swine'. We assume that the other fricatives were voiced as well, but the spelling doesn't help here: both [θ ð] were then as now written the same, and /ʒ/ hadn't arisen as an independent phoneme, and had no unique spelling.

Since ME times, then, the isoglosses have been receding toward the West, i.e. speakers have gradually been adopting forms of a Midland type, probably under the influence of London. The isolated [v]-enclave in Sussex is what's called a relic area: the retreat of the [v]-forms has passed it by. This differential recession of isoglosses isn't in fact surprising; we have already seen (§1.5, and cf. §5.5) that change tends to enter a language in the form of variation, gradually diffusing across different environments. The picture shown by the static placement of isoglosses on these maps is a reflection of a long historical dynamic: in a sense, the image of the extending influence of London.

The SW/SE boundary in map 7 also delimits other features as well. Our line seems to define a set of 'core' SW counties: (part of) Cornwall, Devon, Somerset, Wiltshire, Dorset and Hampshire, as opposed to the SE counties of Berkshire, Surrey, Kent, Sussex and southern East Anglia. Some other features reflecting this division:

(i) /iː/ in *mice*, *lice* and other OE /yː/ words, where in late OE there was a change /y(ː)/ > /e(ː)/ in the SE and later /eː/ > /iː/ by the Great Vowel Shift (§3.10): Berkshire, Surrey, Kent, East Sussex, East Anglia.

(ii) /ɛ/ for /æ/ < ME /a/: Surrey, Kent, Essex, Sussex, and parts of East Anglia, as well as non-standard London.

(iii) *en* [ən ŋ] for *him*, *it*, (objective): probably a retention of OE *hine* (masc acc sg, as opposed to dat *him*: §4.3.3, (4.9)): Somerset, Wiltshire, Cornwall, Devon, Dorset, Hampshire and the very west of Sussex.

(iv) Loss of /w/ before rounded back vowels (e.g. in *wool*, *wood*): Somerset, Wiltshire, Devon, Hampshire.

These partly reflect a larger and vaguer E/W division throughout the Midlands and South (see §5.4). However loose a 'boundary' may look, the notion still is important: there are clearly major dialect areas, if with fuzzy and complex transition zones between them. It is in this historically broad sense that I use the term 'regional dialect': the sum of the criterial features that cluster around a major isogloss bundle.

5.3 Traditional Dialect: Some Remarks

Both the previous section and the following one deal with a very specific dialect type. The material is derived from the published records of the SED; and the SED was biased in a particular way. The bulk of the fieldwork was done in the 1950s, and the intention was to record 'the kind of dialect ... normally spoken by elderly speakers ... belonging to the same social class in rural communities'; specifically agricultural workers, 'for it is amongst the rural populations that the traditional types of vernacular English are best preserved today' (Orton 1962: 14).

The SED informants ranged in age from the 50s to the 90s, with the mean age in the mid 70s. Thus what its records provide is really a picture of the most conservative rural dialects of the late 19th century (on the assumption that – overall – a person's speech represents not the time he is recorded, but broadly the speech of his community in his childhood). Dialects, that is, as devoid as possible of influences from the southern (or other) standard, or other urban developments. And, significantly, the sample was not stratified: the SED furnishes no information on class or age variation within the communities studied. (Except incidentally, in informants' comments about particular items: thus a Yorkshire speaker's remark that *back end* is the 'older' way of saying *autumn* (Area 6.5, *autumn* VII.3.7).)

Obviously the SED is aimed at the 'purest' form of rural vernacular; but such purity (ideally a historical development uncontaminated by outside influences, showing a socially isolated regional type) is rarely attainable – there is always some interdialect communication. And there is – from the investigator's point of view – a problem in that speakers of non-prestigious dialects will normally know something of more prestigious ones, and will often attempt to accommodate to standard speakers, whether out of politeness or a desire to appear higher up the social scale (cf. §5.5).

We can see this difficulty cropping up in dialect investigation even at the end of the 19th century; the following passage from Joseph Wright's *English dialect grammar* (1905: vi–vii) is worth looking at in this connection (transcriptions changed to accord with practice in this book):

> As I did not learn to read until I was practically grown up, the knowledge of my own dialect [Yorkshire West Riding: RL] – uninfluenced by the literary language – has been of considerable use . . . and has enabled me to avoid mistakes which would certainly have been made by anyone who had not spoken a dialect pure and simple in his youth. The working classes speak quite differently among themselves, than when speaking to strangers or educated people, and it is no easy matter for an outsider to induce them to speak pure dialect, unless he happens to be a dialect speaker himself. An excellent example of this came before me the other day in a Westmorland village. A man said to me: [ðə roːdz ə dəːtɪ], and I said to him: [dʊənt jə seː ʊp ɪər ət trɪɛdz ɪz mʊkɪ]? With a bright smile on his face he replied: [wɪ dɪʊ], and forthwith he began to speak the dialect in its pure form.

(In case of problems, the first utterance is *the roads are dirty*, with standardized [oː] in *roads*, non-northern *are*, and the standard word *dirty*; the second is *don't you say up here that t'roads is mucky?*, with northern vowels, /t/ for *the*, northern *is* for plural, and the more typical local form *mucky*; the third is *we do*, with northern [ʊ] in *do* rather than southern [uː].)

So eighty or more years ago we see even the most conservative rural speakers at least partly bidialectal; Wright remarks that he knew an old Yorkshire woman who used to say [deə, ʊəm] for *day, home*, and who now says [deː, oːm] (with vowels obviously standard-influenced).

Even in Wright's day there was a feeling of urgency about recording the older dialects; he says (vii) that

> There can be no doubt that pure dialect speech is rapidly disappearing even in country districts, owing to the spread of education, and to modern facilities for intercommunication. The writing of this grammar was begun none too soon, for had it been delayed another twenty years I believe it would then be quite impossible to get together sufficient pure dialect material to enable any one to give even a mere outline of the phonology of our dialects as they existed at the close of the nineteenth century.

We will see in the next section that old forms are more tenacious than Wright thought, and that he may have been a shade too pessimistic; nonetheless the process of attrition through contact was well under way in his time, and has gone much further now. We will also see (§5.5) that the tension between local and more prestigious forms is still an important determinant of speakers' behaviour.

So even the 'purest' traditional dialects are likely (more so now than in Wright's time) to show at least some standard(ized) forms. For instance, in a study of Scotswood (Newcastle upon Tyne) in 1954, Sara Hepher reports that while /uː/ for ME /uː/ in the *house, out* class (a typical northern feature: see §5.4) was 'basic', even her oldest informants showed both alternations and replacements in some lexical items. Thus /uː/ in *bounce, brown, crowd, down, house, out, mouse, now, thousand, mountain, crown, sour*; both /uː/ and newer /aʊ/ in *cow, hour*; and only /aʊ/ in *shower, glower*. That is, non-local forms are percolating in; some show their relatively new status by alternating with older pronunciations, while others have become established in the new form, and ousted the old. Still, it's proper to call this a '/uː/-dialect' – noting however that the traditional forms are beginning to recede.

Dialect speakers of the type recorded in the SED are becoming thinner on the ground these days, and some of the older dialects may be nearing extinction. But the basic regional features are still quite stable; if we want to have an idea of where the modern dialects come from, and explore as much as possible of the regional variety of English, we must take what we do know of these older, 'purer' types as a starting point. If nothing else, this will help us establish some of the major overall continuities in the history of English. We will look in §5.5 at some of the more complex patterning that emerges from dialect study in non-homogeneous, highly stratified urban settings, and from newer kinds of research methodology. The point to remember is this: even if none of the traditional dialects had survived into the present, they would still be indispensable for any kind of coherent picture of the modern dialects: they furnish the historical input to newer developments, and many of their major diagnostic features are still basic to the classification of English dialects.

5.4 The Traditional Dialect Regions of England

We have established rough SW and SE regions (though not yet a distinct South). We now turn to the major divisions in England as a whole. The first important one is between broadly 'Northern' and 'Southern' (we'll look at Scots later – §5.7.1; it's basically northern, but has enough special features to be treated separately). The most obvious criteria here are the reflexes of ME /u/ (*some*, *but*) and ME /a/ before voiceless fricatives (*chaff*, *bath*, *pass*). The North (which includes the North Midlands – see below) has a vowel of the general type [ʊ] (sometimes unrounded [ÿ]) in *some*, and short [a] in *chaff*; whereas the South has [ʌ] in *some* and a long vowel [aː] or [ɑː] in *chaff* (cf. §3.10 for these developments in the South). The isoglosses for these features run as shown in map 7 (p.228). The isoglosses in map 7 divide England into two major areas: South vs. North & Midlands. Within this broad framework, it's customary to divide the North proper from the North Midlands as follows:

(i) N [uː] in *out* (< ME /uː/) vs. NML [aʊ] or monophthongized [aː]; N [ɪə] in *boot* (< ME /oː/) vs. NML [uː]. These are related. In the North, ME /uː/ never diphthongized in the Great Vowel Shift (§3.10), but remains as a high back monophthong (occasionally fronted to [yː]). And ME /oː/ has not raised to [uː] as elsewhere, but comes out with a front nucleus, most commonly [ɪə]. The relation is this: the 'chain' property of the GVS (cf. (3.44)) was dependent on the top three heights in back being 'occupied' by vowels. I.e. in order for the high vowels /iː uː/ to diphthongize, there had to be a lower one to 'push' them out of place, in a 'push chain'. Outside the North, ME /eː oː/ had this function. In the North, however, before the GVS, /oː/ fronted to /øː/, thus leaving a gap in the back vowel series:

(5.3)

iː	uː		iː		uː
eː	oː		eː	øː ←	□
ɛː	ɔː		ɛː		ɔː
aː			aː		
Before Fronting			After Fronting		

Hence /ɔː/ was able to raise to /oː/, but there was no /oː/ to raise to /uː/; hence there was no diphthongization. The new /øː/ later unrounded, giving [ɪə] or something of the sort. There were however no dialects in which ME /eː/ was uniformly 'displaced'; hence no dialects with unshifted ME /iː/ (*bite*). Comparing the reflexes of ME /uː/ and /oː/ in the N, NML and S, we get:

(5.4)

ME	N	NML	S
/uː/ *out*	uː	aʊ	aʊ
/oː/ *boot*	ɪə	uː	uː

(ii) In Northern ME (§3.9) OE /ɑː/ (*stone, boat*) became /aː/; outside the North (including the NML) it became /ɔː/. Hence, by the GVS we would expect the North to have /eː/ or some other front nucleus (as it happens, most often /ɪə/: see below) in words of this class, and the NML and the rest of England to have /oː/ or some later development with a back (or at least non-front) nucleus. The oldest type of NML reflex here is [ʊə], often replaced by a newer [oː], probably under standard influence; the South typically has [əʊ]. Thus for *stone* we get the following history:

(5.5)

OE stān /stɑːn/ →
{
NME /staːn/ → [stɪən]

non-NME /stɔːn/ → NML [stʊən]
                  ↘ S [stəʊn]
}

(iii) In the North and South, ME /e/ lengthened in open syllables (*eat* < OE *etan*) falls together with the reflexes of ME /ɛː/ (*wheat* < *hwǣte*) and /eː/ (*feet* < *fēt*) in /iː/; in the NML the lengthened forms stay

227

Map 7. ME /u/; ME /a/ before Fricatives
———— General southern limit of [ʊ] in *some* (V.8.4)
----------- General southern limit of [a] in *chaff* (II.8.5)
[After Wakelin 1972(a): 87]

separate, with *eat* having [ɛɪ], thus distinguishing the NML from both North and South. Similarly /o/ lengthened in open syllables (*throat* < *protu*) remains separate in some areas as [ɒɪ], not falling in with the *stone* class. In addition, ME /a:/ in the North (*mate*) usually falls together with the fronted reflexes of ME /o:/ (*boot*). Perhaps this can be clarified by a diagram showing the vowels in the items mentioned above:

(iv) In late OE (§3.8) short vowels generally lengthened before a

(5.6)

	N	S	NML
eat			ɛɪ
wheat	iː	iː	iː
feet			
mate	ɪə	eɪ	eː
stone		əʊ	ʊə
throat	ʊə		ɒɪ

nasal or liquid and a voiced consonant at the same place of articulation: hence modern long nuclei in *blind*, *ground* (OE *blind*, *grund*). This lengthening did not take place in the North: hence [ɪ] in *blind*, [ʊ] in *ground*.

(v) OE /aŋ/ (*song*, *wrong*; OE *sang*, *wrang*) shows up as /ɒ/ in non-northern dialects (sometimes as /ɔː/); in the North it has not undergone lengthening or rounding, hence modern /a/ in these forms.

The Main N/NML isoglosses run as shown in map 8 (p.230).

It is very difficult to define a clear E/W division in the Midlands; the major E/W isoglosses (except for those in the South, discussed earlier) seem to disregard the S/ML division, and run through both Midlands and South. A case in point is the forms for the feminine nominative pronoun; most dialects in the East and North have *she*, but in the West we find *hoo* (a normal development of OE *hēo*: cf. *you* < *ēow*, *choose* < *cēosan*), and *shoo* in the northern part of the area; and the original objective *her* in a large part of the WML, extending down into the SW; see map 9 (p.231).

East and West are further divided by a number of other features, which are interesting in themselves, and tell us something about the enormous variety of things that can happen when a morphologically complex language embarks on a programme of simplification, as it were. The first of these is the retention of some form of the old singular second person pronoun (OE *þū*). This occurs normally as *thou* (N /ðuː/, non-N /ðaʊ/ or the like), as a reduced form often spelled *tha* (/ða/), or replaced by the old oblique *thee* (see below). *Thou* is retained over a large part of the country: the SED records some variety of it from all the northern counties, Yorkshire, Lancashire, Cheshire, Derbyshire, Staffordshire, Herefordshire, Worcestershire, Gloucestershire, Oxfordshire, Lincolnshire, Somerset, Wiltshire, Berkshire, Dorset, Devon, Hampshire, and Cornwall. Thus both northern and southern, eastern and western counties.

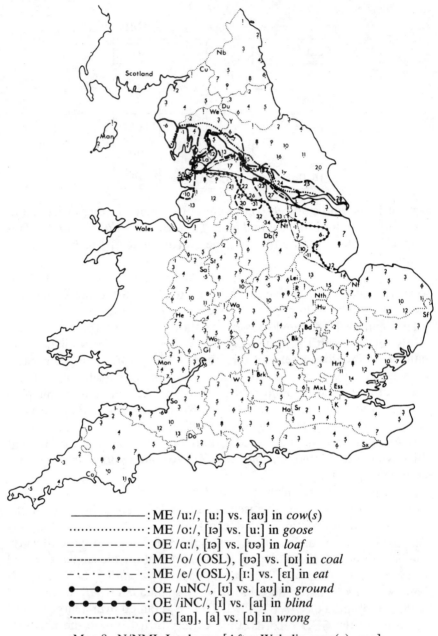

-------------------- : ME /uː/, [uː] vs. [aʊ] in *cow(s)*
····················· : ME /oː/, [ɪə] vs. [uː] in *goose*
- - - - - - - - - : OE /ɑː/, [ɪə] vs. [ʊə] in *loaf*
--------------------- : ME /o/ (OSL), [ʊə] vs. [ɒɪ] in *coal*
—·—·—·—· : ME /e/ (OSL), [ɪː] vs. [ɛɪ] in *eat*
●—●—●—● : OE /uNC/, [ʊ] vs. [aʊ] in *ground*
●●●●● : OE /iNC/, [ɪ] vs. [aɪ] in *blind*
·—·—·—·—·— : OE [aŋ], [a] vs. [ɒ] in *wrong*

Map 8. N/NML Isoglosses [After Wakelin 1972(a): 103]

But a look at this list shows that while *thou* covers the whole North
and NML (Northumberland in the East to Cumberland in the West,
Lincolnshire in the East to Lancashire and W. Yorkshire in the West),

there is a clear E/W division in the South and Midlands: *thou*-forms do not occur in the East south of Lincolnshire. But which *thou*-forms occur is also geographically restricted: the old nominative *thou* occurs throughout the N and NML, but *thee* appears only in the West: Shropshire, Herefordshire, Worcestershire, Gloucestershire, Oxfordshire, Berkshire (the eastern limit), Somerset, Wiltshire, Devon, Dorset and Cornwall. Furthermore, *thou* does not extend south of Derbyshire. So the substitution of *thee* for *thou* is a SWML and SW innovation. And one that coincides largely with *her* for *she*, suggesting a general western tendency to substitute obliques for nominatives. This has been carried further in a few places: *us* for *we* occurs in Berkshire and Cornwall, and is general for Devon. (This phenomenon occurs elsewhere in Germanic: thus Afrikaans has *ons*, an old oblique form, for both 'we' and 'us' – cf. Dutch *wij* vs. *ons*; and *hulle* (also oblique) for both 'they' and 'them': cf. Dutch *zij* vs. *hulle*.)

Map 9. Forms of the Feminine Nominative Pronoun
[From Duncan 1972: 186]

231

A further E/W division shows up in the forms of the present of the verb 'to be'. In OE, this was (cf. §4.5.5) a complex 'hybrid' verb, with two distinct present systems, built on different stems, as well as a past with a completely different stem. This was simplified everywhere – but in very different ways – and many of the resulting paradigms differ markedly from the modern standard. The OE presents were:

(5.7)

		A		B
Sg	1	ic eam		1 ic bēo
	2	þū eart		2 þū bist
	3	hē is		3 hē biþ
pl	1	wē	sindon,	1 wē
	2	gē	sint,	2 gē } bēoþ
	3	hīe	earon	3 hīe

Infinitive: bēon
Subjunctive sg bēo, pl bēon

A fully 'normal' evolution (allowing for Scandinavian *they* for *hie*) would lead to the following in modern English:

(5.8)

		A		B
Sg	1	I am		1 I be
	2	thou art		2 thou bist
	3	he is		3 *he bith
	1	we	*sind,	1 we
	2	ye	*sint,	2 ye } *beeth, been
	3	they	are	3 they

(Starred forms do not seem to have come down: on the ones that have survived in rural dialects, see below.)

In the North, inflections (as in the verb in general) have been reduced: the typical case for the N and part of the NML is generalization of *is* to all persons sg, and *are* to plural: thus *I/thou/he is, we/you(thou)/they are*. (*Are* is specifically an Anglian form, probably originally Northumbrian, and moves south during ME.)

What has happened elsewhere is more complex. In the standard, the original *am/is* are retained, and *are* is extended to 2 sg as well as retained for all plurals. The *bēo-* forms survive in the standards only in the infinitive and participles (*be, being, been*), and in some now old-fashioned styles in 'subjunctives' (*Though I be defeated ..., I insist that he be removed ...*). But the *bēo*-paradigm has played a much more important role in other dialects: again, only in the West (except for parts of Buckinghamshire, which is pretty much a border area). To give some idea of the richness of the developments, we can survey some of the major types of 'be' paradigms:

(i) *bin* /bɪn/ (< the OE infinitive or subjunctive pl) generalized to all persons/numbers: *I/you/she ~ her/they bin*: apparently restricted to Cheshire and Shropshire.

(ii) *bin* generalized, but *bist* /bɪst/ for 2 sg: *I bin/thee bist/you/he/they bin*: again Cheshire and Shropshire.

(iii) *be* (either < *bēo* or reduced infinitive) generalized to all persons/numbers: Oxfordshire, Buckinghamshire, Somerset.

(iv) *be* generalized, except for 3 sg *is*: *I be/you be/her is/they be*: Warwickshire, Somerset.

(v) *be* generalized, but *bis(t)* for 2 sg, *is* for 3 sg: *I be/thee bis(t)/her is/ they be*. Herefordshire. Monmouthshire, Buckinghamshire, Somerset. Some dialects of this general type (mainly in Worcestershire) have *bin* for plural, and some for 3 sg. Another version has *be* everywhere except 2 sg: Gloucestershire, Oxfordshire, Somerset, Wiltshire, Berkshire.

(vi) *be* for 1 sg and pl, otherwise *art*, *is*: *I be/thee art/her is/they be*: Somerset, Cornwall, Devon, Dorset, Hampshire.

There are actually more individual types, but this will give an idea of the main ones. As usual, forms with consonantal endings (*art*, *bis(t)*, *bin*) tend to remain distinct, while others merge. What's interesting about this material is that is shows us how a language can 'dismember' a complex paradigm. When a trend towards simplification sets in, it's rather as if all the older forms are up for grabs, and the whole system can be restructured in a large number of ways.

A quick review of the major isoglosses that have emerged so far shows that with a few exceptions (*en*, *her*, *thou*, *be*) the features involved are phonological: and of these, all but one (voicing of initial fricatives in the SW) are vowel features. (We could have added a few relatively minor consonantal isoglosses as well, e.g. a uvular /r/, which sets off parts of Northumberland and Durham as a distinct NE area, or retroflex /r/, which generally characterizes the West; but these are of much less overall importance.) We could also have distinguished rhotic from non-rhotic dialects; but this is much more indicative for modern than older types, rhoticity being pretty much restricted to the SW and part of Lancashire.

The reasons for this limitation are in part principled, and in part due to defects in our data base. The principled reason is that overall phonological change is probably more frequent than (major) syntactic change (and to some extent than morphological change). Small phonetic changes occur continuously, because of their physical basis: that is, it's easy to miss an articulatory 'target' – get a vowel higher than you wanted, a stop less voiced, etc.; but there's not the same kind of continuum in (say) where a verb goes in a given utterance: it's either before or after the object, not somewhere in between. Of course things like this change too, as we've seen; but less frequently, and to some extent in a different way. And both old and new forms seem to have a tendency to coexist longer than is the case with phonological variants.

As for the importance of vowel rather than consonant developments, this is merely a parochial fact about English – and perhaps recent Germanic in general. After the widespread consonantal changes in early Germanic (e.g. Grimm's Law: §1.3) and OE (§3.8), the English consonant system has remained quite stable: little else of importance can be added to the voicing of initial fricatives, the development of /ʒ/ (§3.10), the loss of initial /h/ in most non-standard dialects, and the development of the rhotic/non-rhotic distinction through loss of post-vocalic /r/. There have been no consonantal changes of the size and structural coherence of the GVS.

The lack of major morphosyntactic isoglosses is another matter. It may be that English morphosyntax has remained relatively stable (in respect of word-order and features of that depth it certainly seems to have, since about the 18th century). On the other hand, with regard to many features we lack detailed information of the kind we have for phonology: there is as yet no survey of English dialect syntax or morphology. We do know of many constructions that appear to be geographically limited: e.g. modal infinitives (*you have to can drive*) seem to be only Scots, as is the non-animate genitive relative *that's*; 'positive *anymore*' (*things are tough anymore* = 'nowadays') appears to occur only in Northern Ireland and the U.S., and there are special features of the aspect system restricted to Ireland (see §5.7.2). But for the most part we don't really know. Most of the available information is scattered, anecdotal and unsystematic. Structural units like tense/aspect systems, relativization, the modals, etc. have been well described for some areas, but as far as I know never systematically mapped even for the U.K. – let alone the whole English-speaking world. We will look at some of the more striking regional characteristics in later sections – though with the warning that detail of description doesn't necessarily provide an index of the actual spread of differences or the richness of dialect differentiation: it rather reflects available information.

It also seems that certain features are not in fact regional, but either 'generally old', or simply 'nonstandard' (whatever that exactly means). For example, the genitive relative with shadow pronoun (*the man that his brother drowned*) occurs, according to SED data, in all parts of the country except a scattering of counties in the SE and SW: in the SED data it is absent only from Sussex, Kent, Hampshire, Surrey, Berkshire, Worcestershire, Dorset and Cornwall. This group of counties appears to lack (at least for the informants interviewed) other nonstandard relative types as well, which are otherwise very widely distributed: relative *what* (*the man what his₂brother* ...) occurs in Derbyshire, Lincolnshire and Suffolk (as well as being very widespread in the South in more modern dialects), and relative *as* occurs everywhere except in the far North. But the organized information is tantalizingly incomplete: to my knowledge, as I said above, relative *that's* is Scots; but one occurrence of *what's* in Somerset makes me suspect that this type is more widespread.

Taking the major isoglosses or semi-isoglosses we've discussed so far, we can set up a kind of checklist of major dialect features in England:

(5.9)

Major Features of the Older English Dialect Types

	SBE	SE	SW	WML	NML	N
1. /ʊ/ in *some*	−	−	−	+	+	+
2. /ʌ/ in *some*	+	+	+	−	−	−
3. *eat/wheat* distinct	−	−	−	−	+	−
4. /uː/ in *house*	−	−	−	−	−	+
5. /ɪə/ in *boot*	−	−	−	−	−	+
6. *throat/goat* distinct	−	−	−	−	+	+
7. /ɑː/ in *chaff*	+	+	+	−	−	−
8. /a/ in *chaff*	−	−	−	+	+	+
9. /iː/ in *mice*	−	+	−	−	−	−
10. /v/ in *farmer*	−	−	+	+	−	−
11. *her* for *she*	−	−	+	+	−	−
12. *en* for *him*	−	−	+	−	−	−
13. finite *be*	−	−	+	+	−	−
14. *thou*	−	−	−	+	+	+
15. *thee* (nom)	−	−	+	+	−	−

5.5 Regionality and Social Variation

Britain, like most of Europe, has undergone major social and demographic changes in recent times, especially since World War II. Small farms have been replaced by 'Agribusiness' with loss of rural employment and extensive urbanization of former rural pupulations; communication and mobility have improved, mass education has spread (even – for better or worse – to tertiary level); the electronic media have vastly increased any individual's potential exposure to different varieties of English, both regional and non-regional – especially the access of nonstandard speakers to various kinds of standard speech.

One result has been a reduction in the fine regional differentation we looked at in the last section; the more 'extreme' rural dialect types are becoming increasingly restricted to older speakers. But this has not led to overall 'homogenization' and loss of regional character; rather the whole country has become increasingly characterized by highly distinctive broad regional types, with focal points in the great conurbations that form the regional population centres: e.g. Edinburgh and Lothian Region, Clydeside, Tyneside, Leeds-Bradford, Birmingham-Wolverhampton, Merseyside, London, Bristol, Belfast. Perhaps the best way to look at the modern dialect picture is in terms of these broad groupings, with their internal social and age stratification.

In a recent study, John Wells (1982) suggests abandoning, for contemporary description, such divisions as the dialectologists' North vs. North Midland, and coming closer to popular terminology. For most Englishmen, for instance, both Liverpool and Newcastle are 'in the North'; to use one stereotype, 'the land of flat caps and flat vowels' (a reference to the peaked workman's cap and the 'flat *a*' [a] in *bath*, etc.). Both cities are 'northern' in this folk-linguistic sense – even though (at certain social levels) they're on different sides of the major North/North Midland isoglosses (e.g. Tyneside has [uː] in *house*, Liverpool [aʊ]). In modern urban terms, however, there's something to be said for the view that anyone with the same vowel in *put* and *putt* and /a/ in *bath* 'is a Northerner'.

The SED and other studies in the older tradition of rural historical dialectology give us a vast amount of valuable – if at times unsystematic – information about traditional dialect. There have unfortunately been no surveys of comparable breadth dealing with the total urban (and suburban) picture. Nor have rural dialects again been surveyed in the same detail, with coverage of younger speakers to allow us to detect basic trends of change, and with sophisticated use of the tools developed in modern urban sociolinguistics (see below). We are faced with the odd situation of knowing more in some ways about archaic rural dialects than we know about modern urban ones: but, as we will see, knowing less about their social structure and its interaction with linguistic behaviour. In fact we know rather different things about each of the two domains, which makes comparison difficult.

The SED type of dialectology emphasizes one-word citation-form (§3.7) answers to items on a questionnaire, elicited by a field worker through direct questions. Here is an example of the kind of question asked, and responses for two counties, Somerset (So) and Berkshire (Brk):

(5.10)

IV.8.4 FLEAS

Q. *What do you call those little black insects that jump about and bite you?*

31 So   1–2 fliːz   3–8 vliːz   9 vləɪz   10 vliːz
      11 fliːz   12–13 vliːz
32 Brk   1 fliːz   2 flɪiː   3–4 flɪiz   5 mɪdʒɪts [pref.],
                                                  flɪiz

(31, 32 are SED county codes; 1, 2 etc. are area numbers.'[pref.]' = 'preferred response', i.e. the informant normally calls them *midgets* but knows *fleas* as well.)

The initial [v] forms in Somerset are unsurprising, since this is well within the voicing area (§5.2); but what about the [f] forms? We know they're more 'standard', 'newer'; yet if we look at other words with standard initial [f] we find something curious. Take Somerset 3, which shows the following initial consonants in the same speakers:

(5.11)

fleas	fox	flies	frogs	fern	fire	flour	flood
v	f	v	f	v	v	f	f

The informants show a mixture of older and newer; standard versions seem to be encroaching item-by-item on the old ones.

For the SED this distribution is simply a static 'fact'; but there are other kinds of questions we'd like to ask, which modern research shows are worth asking. For instance, do all speakers have [f] and [v] in the same words? Or at least all speakers of (roughly) the same age? Or is there variation, younger speakers perhaps showing proportionately less [v] and more [f]? And do speakers with [v] in *fleas* have it on all occasions, in all speech styles and tempi? Do they give the same response in unreflecting casual speech as in the formal interview situation? E.g. would some speakers with [f] in citation forms perhaps show (at least some) [v] in casual speech? How far up the social and down the age scale does any use of [v] go?

These questions embody some important assumptions: that speech communities may have a stratified class structure that is reflected in their language; that different speech styles may show significantly different properties (perhaps not the same for all social classes and ages); that chronological and social stratification may interact; that it's not necessarily the case that any speaker (or collection of similar speakers) will show only one form for a particular item. In other words, the SED doesn't give us a picture of linguistic variation; and variation as an essential element of linguistic structure in particular communities has become an important element in linguistic description.

Sociolinguistic work done since the pioneering studies of William Labov in the 1960s indicates an often intimate connection between social variables like age, class, sex, style, even attitudes, and choice of linguistic forms (both categorical choice and frequency of use); and we now have a huge amount of data from well-studied British and American communities that shows this in striking detail. We will look in this section at a few typical results of this kind of research, as a complement to the material we've examined so far.

Perhaps the most important concept to emerge is that of the linguistic variable: a feature with social and stylistic evaluation attached to it, that varies systematically in the usages of a given speech community. An examination of one typical variable will give some idea of how variation is tied into social structure. In a study of Norwich English, Peter Trudgill (1974) looked, among other things, at a variable he called (ng): the pronunciation of unstressed *-ing*, e.g. in *walking, seeing, Woking, Dorking*. (Variables are conventionally put in ( ).)

In Norwich, as in many other places, this variable has two values: [-ɪŋ] and [-ŋ] (the latter often called in lay language 'dropping one's *g*'s' – though of course nothing is dropped: it's simply substituting an alveolar for a velar nasal). In general, the [-ɪŋ] pronunciation is standard, and the [-ŋ] nonstandard and stigmatized. But the actual situation isn't so simple: even educated standard speakers have some [-ŋ], and Lower Working Class speakers have some [-ɪŋ]: it's how they're distributed that's interesting and complex.

If we look not only at social class, but at style as well, we find an intricate but revealing pattern. Trudgill elicited material in four increasingly casual styles: his informants read word-lists (WLS, Word-list style), read a passage (RPS, Reading-passage style), responded to formal questions (FS, Formal style), and just talked casually (CS, Casual style). The assumption is that the further down the scale of formality speakers go, the less attention they pay to their speech. There is a technique (whose details will not concern us here) for calculating an 'index score' for a speaker's use of a variable, which works out in Trudgill's study as follows: consistent use of standard [-ɪŋ] produces a score of zero, and consistent use of nonstandard [-ŋ] produces a score of 100. Therefore the higher the score, the more 'vernacular' and less standard a speaker is. The actual results (typical for this kind of variable in a stratified community) show some interesting patterns of variation; using a five-class layout, we find the following index scores (Hughes & Trudgill 1980: 71):

238

(5.12)

	WLS	RPS	FS	CS
Middle Middle Class	0	0	3	28
Lower Middle Class	0	10	15	42
Upper Working Class	5	15	74	87
Middle Working Class	23	44	88	95
Lower Working Class	29	66	98	100

Index Scores For (ng) in Norwich

Note that in each case the lowest (most standard-like) scores are in the more formal styles; and that in each style scores go up as we go down the social scale.

The pattern may be clearer if we take three classes from the list above, and graph the results:

(5.13)

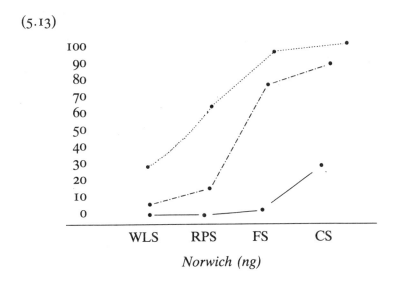

Norwich (ng)

It's important to interpret this properly: except at zero and 100 levels, the pattern does not predict which variant will occur in any particular utterance. Only that over a good sized stretch of speech, a given speaker will approximate to the group average for a particular style. (The scores here are averaged over a group of informants from each social class.)

Another pattern emerges if we break the total scores down by sex (based on figures in Hughes & Trudgill 1980: 72). In the histogram below, the average for each social class is given in the dotted bar (A), and next to it the scores for males (♂) and females (♀):

(5.14)

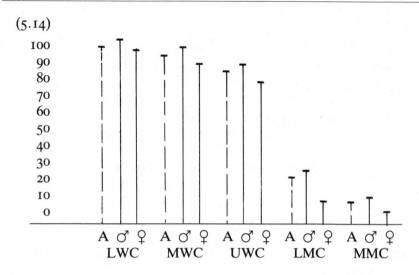

This shows a characteristic pattern (at least for western industrial societies): in general women appear to be more status-conscious than men, and to approximate more to the 'overt prestige' standard norms, while men tend to approximate more to the 'covert prestige' nonstandard norms. It's also clear here that the sexual differentiation is smallest at the lowest and highest points of the social scale, and most striking at the Middle Class/Working Class 'border': the points where the possibilities of realising upward aspirations are respectively least and greatest.

Such variation can be a major input to linguistic change: the different values of a variable provide a pool of forms that can be capitalized on over time by increasing the proportion of one variant at the expense of others (cf. §1.5). We can in fact see this happening in many cases if we look at age-graded samples: this has become a standard technique for dealing with cases of apparent change in progress.

For instance: an old feature of Belfast Working Class speech, stigmatized as early as the 19th century, is the use of dental [t̪] rather than the usual alveolar [t] in the neighbourhood of /r/ (as in *tree, butter*). A graph of the percentages of [t̪] in a recent Belfast sample (Milroy & Milroy 1978) shows the pattern in (5.15), p.241. This can be interpreted in two ways: (a) statically, it represents the distribution of variation patterns over the age-cohorts and sex-groupings in a community; (b) dynamically, as an image of a process, it represents the recession of an older variant with the sharpest drop in the 42–55 generation, apparently spearheaded by women. The pattern in (5.15) shows a change in what is called 'apparent time', projectible onto 'real time' on the assumption that such a distribution must show the results of a genuine process of change.

(5.15)

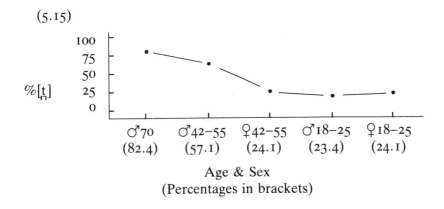

Age & Sex
(Percentages in brackets)

If we average out the male and female scores in each age-cohort, the overall pattern becomes even clearer: the apparent levelling out in the graph above is due to the fact that the sharpest individual drops are in the 42–55 women, and then in the 18–25 men; if this 'sex-lag' is ironed out, we get:

(5.16)

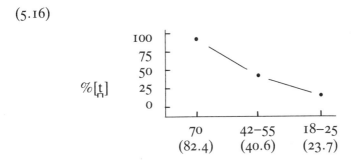

It's important to note that these group-correlations of language behaviour with social variables like age, class, sex, do not show the whole picture. Individual personal factors and aspects of actual discourse situations (even if associated in the end with larger social variables) can also produce highly specific patterns of variation. We've already noticed that there's a common tendency for women in vernacular-speaking social groups to be more standard-like than men; but within one social group there can be differences independent of sex, but related to attitude, which even override 'normal' group behaviour.

Let's look at one final example of the interplay between linguistic behaviour and social variables. This will give some insight as well into the complex role played by individual attitudes; we will be concerned here with the behaviour of individual speakers, not group averages. In a study of variation in the Northern Irish village of Articlave (Co.

Londonderry), Ellen Douglas-Cowie (1978) investigated the relation between use of standard-like forms by nonstandard speakers and two other factors: social ambition, and the other participants in a conversation. Articlave is a kind of microcosm of the general rural situation in Britain: a formerly isolated agricultural village that is slowly opening up to the 'outside world', due to the collapse of local agriculture and the industrialization of the nearby town of Coleraine, which is drawing an increasing number of inhabitants away. Added to this is growing exposure to non-local English via the media, and the movement of 'outsiders' (often English) into the village. As local rural communities lose their indigenous economic base, non-agricultural people from outside tend to move in to the 'idyllic' village setting; we can see this most clearly around cities like London, where former farming villages have become dormitories for urban commuters.

In Articlave, whose inhabitants normally speak a Northern Irish vernacular, there is a distinct awareness of RP and other standard varieties as prestigious: upwardly mobile natives attend elocution classes where RP-like norms are taught, and they even have them in the schools. Douglas-Cowie's study was designed to explore the relation between speakers' shifting from local to more standard norms, and their social attitudes and the speech situation they were engaged in. The basic task was assigning to each of ten speakers an index for a set of non-standard variables; this was correlated with a scale of 'social ambition', and their behaviour in different speech situations. Social ambition was defined as the speaker's desire to 'better himself', or to 'get on in the world' – as assessed not by himself, but by the rest of the speakers in the sample, all of whom were well acquainted with each other.

The variables included such things as (ng) – the same as in Norwich; (ɪ), the pronunciation of the vowel in *bit*, ranging from standard-like [ɪ] to very local [ʌ]; the use of *yes* or local *aye*; and others. As in Trudgill's Norwich study and much other work of this kind, the index scores were calculated so that zero represents a fully standard profile, and 100 a fully local one. The ten informants were ranked in four divisions according to social ambition: (1) Not ambitious; (2) Quite ambitious; (3) Ambitious; (4) Very ambitious. A correlation of ambition-groups with index-scores for (ng) gives the pattern shown in (5.17) on p.243 (after Douglas-Cowie 1978: 50; A–J are individual informants). While there isn't a 100% correlation (F in group 1 and H in 2 have the same scores, and C in group 3 is higher than D in group 2), the overall trend is clear: loyalty to the home vernacular tends to relate inversely to social ambition.

Another aspect of this emerges from a situation set up by the investigator, in which groups of informants were interviewed by an RP-speaking English 'outsider'. The interviews were recorded, and index-

(5.17)

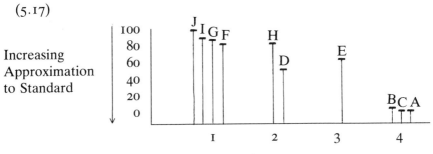

Increasing
Approximation
to Standard

Increasing Ambition →

scores were calculated for the informants in two situations: (a) their speech to the outsider, and (b) their speech to each other. Taking the variable (ng) again, look at the scores for two informants: 'very ambitious' C, and merely 'ambitious' E:

(5.18)

	Overall Index	Conversation between C & E	C, E to Outsider
C	5	7	3
E	42	74	30

Not only is C more standard than E in general, and when the two are conversing; but both their scores drop when they're speaking to the prestigious outsider. What's exhibited here is called 'convergence' or 'accommodation': the tendency of speakers to shift their speech in the direction of their interlocutors. Here we have 'upward convergence', the adoption of more prestigious patterns in the presence of a prestigious speaker.

This section has not been designed as a mini-course in sociolinguistic variation; just an indication of the kind of things that happen in the actual use of language, and the enormous complexity of living speech communities. We can assume that patterns of these general kinds hold for all English-speaking communities; and the descriptions to follow, even when not directly concerned with variation, should be assumed to reflect details of complex pictures somewhat like the ones we've been looking at.

5.6 Modern Dialects in England

5.6.1 REGIONAL VERNACULAR, REGIONAL STANDARD, AND RP

The last section suggests that talking about a 'regional dialect' is a pretty complicated business: a question like 'how is *-ing* pronounced in

243

Norwich?' has a lot of answers, depending on what class, age, etc. you happen to be interested in. But it's still true that there are stable broad regional characteristics, and that quite different types of speakers can easily be identified as coming from the Home Counties or Yorkshire or the West Country.

In the U.S., the relation between regionality and standardness is relatively simple: for every linguistically distinguishable region there is a range from vernacular to standard, and everyone speaks some form of his regional dialect (just as in ME times everyone also wrote one). Movement from vernacular to standard, say, is change within a regionally defined set of parameters – since there is no supraregional or 'national' standard. A New York nonstandard speaker who moves up the social scale ends up speaking a New York Standard: there's no other place to go. Every American can pretty much be identified as coming from someplace. Though there is a tendency for Americans with certain very marked regional accents to accommodate to a more widespread type under certain conditions: especially for Southerners and Northeasterners to adopt certain 'General American' features, such as being rhotic. This is particularly so in the media, where up until recently anyhow, newsreaders speaking southern standards for instance have tended to drop some very local features. It's worth noting that in the U.S. strong regionality is not negatively related to political success: at least four recent presidents (Roosevelt, Kennedy, Johnson and Carter) were markedly regional in speech; in my memory the only British Prime Minister of whom this could be said is Harold Wilson – unsurprisingly a Labour politician, who made political capital of his Yorkshire accent.

In England however (and to some extent elsewhere in the U.K., and in South Africa) there is an added complication. In addition to regional standards, there is another, non-regional one (at least phonologically) – the system of RP. Now RP happens, historically, to be a southern dialect type (cf. the discussion of the rise of the standard in §§2.8–9); and to a large extent it still has a special status, as a kind of class-bound 'superstandard'. In other words, a speaker of a fully standard regional variety still has somewhere to go: he can (try to) get rid of all features of his original region.

The point about RP is that even though it's regional in type, it isn't in detail: it's not the accent of London or any other place, but the accent of a (non-localized) class. Since in many connections RP still has special prestige, and since it can be identified as 'southern' (see below), we have the odd situation that a non-southern speaker wishing to become upwardly mobile beyond the confines of his regional standard must in effect end up speaking a 'foreign' dialect-type. (It's even odder in South Africa, where one crosses a national boundary.) But this foreign dialect is just different enough from the local versions of its regional type for us to get a very different situation from what holds in the U.S.: an RP speaker can't be identified as coming from anywhere. This in fact is the rather strange ideal cherished by many Englishmen: the 'best' way of speaking is the one that gives no information about where you come from.

The essential southernness of RP, and the derivative prestige of RP-like southern accents, leads to problems for Northerners. The northern dialects (in the broad sense that includes much of the Midlands) are structurally different from the southern ones in two important respects (cf. §5.4): the lack of a /ʊ/: /ʌ/ (*put*: *putt*) distinction, and a short /a/ or /æ/ rather than a long /aː/ or /ɑː/ in *grass*, *bath*, etc. Diagrammatically:

(5.19)

	South	North
put	ʊ	ʊ
putt	ʌ	
bath	ɑː	a
cat	æ	

This is problematical because the southern distinctions are phonemic, not (except in part) conditioned. A non-native learning the southern system in effect has to memorize arbitrary word-lists. Imagine a northern speaker faced by RP distributions like these:

(5.20)

/ʊ/	/ʌ/	/æ/	/ɑː/
put	putt	tassel	castle
foot	but	mass	mask
room	rum	cancel	chancel
butch	touch	gas	grass
		ant	aunt

Since 'deregionalization' for a Northerner involves becoming 'southern' (on the way to RP as it were), and these two lexical sets are important shibboleths, it is often quite easy to detect the speaker in process of shifting. A Yorkshire-born acquaintance of mine produced, in addition to the common hypercorrections /kʌʃn̩/ 'cushion' and /bʌtʃə/ 'butcher', the double inversion /gɑːsmæsk/ 'gasmask'. And why not? Historically the assignment of words to one set or the other is partly arbitrary; even a historian could only calculate the odds for a given word belonging to one or the other.

The RP/regional situation is of interest as a major aspect of the sociolinguistic structure of British (mainly English) society; it's also historically interesting, in that it shows how long a shadow an old sociopolitical situation can cast. In a sense the status of RP and the whole 'North'/'South' division stem directly from the choice of SEML dialects as the basis for a nascent standard in the 14th century.

5.6.2 SOME MODERN ENGLISH REGIONAL TYPES

To set both the preceding and following material in context, we will look at some diagnostic features of major urban dialects, with emphasis on phonology (for justification see §5.4). The example dialects will be from six regions, with RP for comparison. I have chosen four broadly northern regions (Tyneside, Bradford, Merseyside, Birmingham), and two southern (Norwich, London). The chart below shows the major vowel contrasts in 'broad' (highly local, non-standard) varieties; for comments see below:

(5.21)

	Tyneside	Bradford	Merseyside	Birmingham	Norwich	London	RP
bit	ɪ	ɪ	ɪ	ɪ	ɪ	ɪ	ɪ
bet	ɛ	ɛ	ɛ	ɛ	ɛ	e	ɛ
bat					æ	æ~ɛ	æ
fast	a	a	a	a			
part	ɑː	aː	aː	ɑː	aː	ɑː	ɑː
out		aʊ	aʊ	æʊ	æʉ	æʊ	aʊ
boot	uː			uː	ʉː	ʉː	uː
book		uː	uː				
foot				ʊ	ʊ	ʊ	ʊ
but	ʊ	ʊ	ʊ				
one					ʌ	ä	ʌ
pot	ɒ	ɒ	ɒ	ɒ	ɒ	ɒ	ɒ
feet	iː	iː	ɪi	ɪi	iː	ïi	iː
mate	ea	eː	eɪ	ʌɪ	æɪ	äɪ	eɪ
fair	ɛː	ɛː		ɛː	ɛː	eə	ɛə
hurt		3ː	ɛː	ø̈ː	3ː	3ː	3ː
bought	ɔː						
walk	aː	ɔː	ɔː	ɔː	ɔː	oː	ɔː
boy	ɒɪ	ɒɪ	ɒɪ		ɔɪ	ɔɪ	ɒɪ
bite	ɛɪ	aɪ	aɪ	ɒɪ	ʌɪ	ɑɪ	aɪ
oat	ʊə	oː	əʊ	ʌʊ	ʌʊ	äʊ	əʊ
thing	ŋ	ŋ	ŋg	ŋg	ŋ	ŋ	ŋ
city	iː	ɪ	iː	iː	iː	iː	ɪ

(More 'advanced' RP varieties, e.g. that of the younger Royals, show a fronting of *boot* toward [ʉː]: this is a general tendency in many Extraterritorial Englishes as well: §§ 4.8.3–4.)

We can see that 'being northern' isn't a simple yes/no matter: despite the similarities there are distinct differences between what Wells calls the 'Far North' (Tyneside) and the 'Middle North' (Merseyside, Bradford); and between them and the WML (Birmingham), which shows a mixture of southern and northern features. The broad regional diagnostics are:

(i) The North: /a/ in *fast*, /ʊ/ in *but/foot*, which we're already familiar with; lack of shortening in *-ook* words (< ME /-oːk/) like *book*, *look* (homophonous with *Luke*). Note that here Birmingham agrees with the South. Within the northern group, Tyneside shows an unusual merger of the *hurt*, *bought* classes in /ɔː/ (due to the former uvular /r/ in *hurt*), and a three-way low-vowel contrast /a/ vs. /aː/ vs. /ɑː/ (the latter mainly before historical /r/) – as opposed to the two-way /a/ vs. /aː/ in the rest of the North, and southern /æ/ vs. /aː/ or /ɑː/. Merseyside in contrast shows a *fair/hurt* merger. Only Tyneside is far enough north to show unshifted ME /uː/ in *out*. We also note that final /ŋg/ in *thing* occurs only in the western reaches of the northern areas; these also show a special development in *one*, *once*: the vowel here goes with *pot* rather than *but*. Hence *won* and *one* are distinct as /wʊn/ vs. /wɒn/, as opposed to /wʊn/ for both on Tyneside and /wʌn/ for both in the South.

(ii) The South: Clear separation of *foot*, *but*, with the latter vowel lower and unrounded; long vowels in both *fast* and *part*, vs. N length only in *part*. (Though some northern dialects have length in *half*, *calf* and similar words with lost historical /l/.) The South in general requires, from the standard (or non-British) point of view, less comment than the North, because of the general familiarity of the system types (cf. §3.2.3); most Americans for instance will have virtually the same set of vowel contrasts as London or RP (except for no contrast or length only in *bat* vs. *fast*, and in some areas no *pot/bought* contrast: cf. §5.8.2). Note also that at least in the broad dialects, the North typically has /a/ in *bat*, as opposed to southern /æ/. We might say in fact that the 'typically English' vowel quality [æ] is really only a typically southern one, not 'generally English' at all; though the more standard a non-southern speaker is (cf. §5.6.1), the more likely he is to have it.

The 'transitional' status of the Midland dialects generally is illustrated by Birmingham: e.g. northern *fast*, *but/foot* distributions, but southern (London-like) vowels in *out*, *bite*, shortening in *book*. The *bite* class is particularly diagnostic: the farther north, the closer and fronter the first element of the diphthong; the farther south, the opener and backer. Thus Tyneside /ɛɪ/, Bradford /aɪ/, Birmingham and London /ɑɪ/ or /ɒɪ/. (See below on Birmingham.) Similarly, monophthongal *boot*, *beet* in the North, diphthongal with lower onsets in the South. (Recall Trevisa's comment on the 'syde longages' of the Midlands in the 14th century

(§2.8); something of this seems to hold today for areas north of London but south of 'true North'.)

Some comments on the individual areas:

(a) Tyneside: Local name *Geordie* for both people and dialect. Throughout the U.K. speakers of local varieties are often conscious of – and make capital of – the differences between their dialects and the standard (especially southern) types. A classic Geordie story hinges on the difference between Geordie *work* /wɔːk/ (the same as southern *walk*) and *walk* /waːk/. A Geordie workman is recovering from a broken leg, and his (non-Geordie) doctor tells him: 'You're doing fine, you'll soon be able to [wɔːk] again.' The workman answers: '[wɔːk]? I can't bloody [waːk].'

Other local features: (i) final /iː/ rather than /ɪ/ in *city* (also SA, USE, Aus/NZ); (ii) retained /h/ even in broad varieties (rare in vernacular speech outside of East Anglia); (iii) clear /l/ in all positions; (iv) very open final unstressed vowels, often approaching [ä], as in *letter, China*; (v) glottal stop with audible release after foot-medial /p t k/, e.g. [lɛtˀä] *letter*. Less broad speakers, as expected, modify the most local features in a SBE-like direction: e.g. [aɪ] rather than [ɛɪ] in *bite*, [əʊ] or [aʊ] in *out*, [øː] or [ɜː] in *hurt*, [eː] in *mate*.

Grammatically Geordie has one distinctive and as far as I know unique feature: a special negative form *divn't* /dɪvnt/ for *didn't/doesn't/don't*. There are also a number of specifically northern lexical items, normally associated by Southerners with Scotland rather than the North of England: e.g. *bairn* 'child', *greet* 'cry', *message* 'errand, shopping'; as well as general northern items like *aye* 'yes', *road* 'way' (*get out of my road*), *stop* 'stay temporarily' (e.g. *I'm stopping in Newcastle for a month*), and plural *yous* /juːz/.

(b) Bradford: For some speakers there are extra contrasts: e.g. cases where ME diphthongs have failed to merge with long vowels before the GVS: thus /ɛɪ/ in *weight* vs. /eː/ in *mate*, /ɔʊ/ in *know* vs. /oː/ in *nose*. A specifically Yorkshire and Lancashire feature is the realization of *the* as an unreleased /t/ or [ʔ] (cf. the stereotype *trooble at t'pit*): thus *in the garden* as [ɪn tgaːdn̩] or [ɪn ʔgaːdn̩]. This area is also characterized by what Wells calls 'Yorkshire Assimilation', a general devoicing of voiced obstruents before voiceless ones, as in [bratfəd] *Bradford*, [ɛtkwɔːtəz] *headquarters*. The same process of course occurs in most dialects of English in *have to* [hæftə], *used to* [juːstə] (vs. *used two* with [juːzd]); but in W. and S. Yorkshire it's general, not lexically restricted.

This area also shows 'secondary contraction' in negatives: i.e. the further contraction of already contracted forms like *isn't, doesn't, aren't, weren't, won't*. The first consonant in the final cluster deletes: thus forms in consonant + *n't* lose the consonant, as in *isn't* [ɪnt], *doesn't* [dʊnt]; and those in vowel + *n't* lose the /n/, as in *aren't* [aːt], *won't* [woːt]. Bradford also shows general *were* for all past of *be* (*I/he were*); and the nearly stereotypical Yorkshire *owt* and *nowt* for *anything* and *nothing*.

(c) Merseyside: The speech of the Merseyside conurbation, locally called *Scouse*, is probably the most familiar northern variety to non-Britishers, at least since the Beatles' films. It is overall North Midland, like Bradford, with some western features (final *-ng* as [ŋg], *one/won* distinct), as well as a number of local specialities. One of the most characteristic is the merger of the *fair/hurt* classes. The most typical local version is [ë:~ë:] for both (*fair, fur* as [fë:]), though in less conservative speakers the merger may be to [ɜː], i.e. in the original (and southern) *hurt* direction, rather than to *fair*.

The consonantal phonetics of Scouse are also distinctive: the voiceless stops in particular are frequently affricated or become fricatives: [tˢɒp] *top*, [kˣɪɬ] *kill*, [bakˣ ~ bax ~ baχ] *back*. Final /t/ may also be a voiceless tap [ɾ] (also typical of Hiberno-English: §5.7.2): the acoustic quality is rather [s]-like, but with lower-frequency frication noise. It is possible that this is at least partially due to Irish influence; Liverpool also shows frequent substitution of [t d] for [θ ð], which again is found in Hiberno-English. Merseyside does have a large Irish immigrant population, and the latter feature is particularly marked among working class Catholics, which may support the Irish connection.

(d) Birmingham represents the speech of the West Midland conurbation (e.g. the Wolverhampton-Birmingham-Coventry complex). As we've seen, this area shows some London features as well as northern ones. Note particularly the first element in the *mate, oat* classes, and a peculiarity of the *bite, out* diphthongs. In *mate* and *oat*, the first element is quite open, a feature found not only in London, but in the less standard forms of extraterritorial dialects with a strong London input (Australian and South African: §§5.8.3–4). The situation with *bite, out* is this: in the North (and in RP) either the first elements of both are the same, or that of *bite* is slightly fronter than that of *out*: e.g. [baɪt], [äʊt]. This can be seen as adjustment or assimilation to the frontness of the second mora – the first is fronter before front(ish) [ɪ] and backer before back(ish) [ʊ]. But in Birmingham, as in London, the two values seem to be reversed (Wells calls this 'the *price/mouth* crossover'): the back-gliding *out* nucleus has a front first element [æ], and the front-gliding *bite* nucleus has a back first element [ɒ] (here leading to merger with *boy*). This same feature, in modified form with no merger, occurs also in standard New York English, and in many Australian and South African varieties, as well as being widespread throughout non-northern England.

The defining features of 'northernness' seem to have different social values. In particular, having the same vowel in *foot/but* is much more stigmatized or at least perceived as nonstandard (by Southerners or RP speakers) than having a short [a] or 'modified' [æ] in *fast*. Northerners who 'standardize' without going all the way to adopting RP or a general SBE profile will normally 'correct' the *foot/but* identity (sometimes with a 'compromise' [ə] in *but*); they will however often retain the short front vowel in *fast*, perhaps as a mark of regional loyalty.

(e) Norwich and London: The southern systems in (5.21) look rather more similar than they in fact are; there are both phonetic and phonological differences obscured by the rather idealized transcriptions there. Though in an important sense the picture is a true one: RP and London have had a significant influence on East Anglian urban speech, and London features have for a long time been radiating out and eclipsing local ones.

Broad Norwich speech, however, has a number of special features worth noting: (i) retention of /h/, unlike London; (ii) dropping of /j/ in /Cj-/ clusters as in *cute, beautiful* /kʉːt, bʉːtɪfəl/: thus *Hughes, whose* are homophones; (iii) a number of vowel-distinctions and mergers that are not typical of SE English in general. The most important ones are: (a) ME /ɔː/ and /ɔu/ (*moan: mown, nose: knows*) are still to some extent separate (as in the North) – the former with [ʊu] and the latter with [ʌu]; this distinction is well-entrenched in WC dialects in major cities like Norwich and Kings Lynn, but decreases further up the social scale and/ or closer to London (e.g. it is now absent in places close to London like Colchester). (b) Some members of the *boot* class vary between the expected /ʉː/ and the /ʊu/ typical of particular words in the *oat* class: thus *soup, moon, boot* may have /ʊu/, and fall in with *soap, moan, boat*.

The broadest forms of London speech, generally known as *Cockney*, are familiar and stereotyped; one of the easiest kinds of 'eye-dialect' is having Londoners say *fice* for *face*, *noice* for *nice*, *bovver* for *bother*, *abaht* for *about*. These reflect some criterial features: (i) a very open and often retracted onset to the *mate* nucleus, often the same as the (rather front) vowel in *but*: thus [bät], [märt]; (ii) a very back and sometimes rounded first element in *bite*, giving [ɑɪ] or [ɒɪ]; (iii) frequent nondistinction of /θ ð/ from /f v/, giving *three/free* as homophones beginning with /f/; (iv) a very front first element in *out*, frequently monophthongized to [æː].

But it isn't the case that Cockney 'has no /θ ð/'; current research suggests that the distinction is always at least potential, regardless of how broad the speaker is. Thus while *fought* is always [foːt], *thought* will have two possible versions, [foːt] and [θoːt]. The use of one or the other is a matter of style and situational appropriateness. This feature is quite widespread in the South of England.

Two other features of London phonology are worth at least a brief mention: the distribution of glottal stops, and the development of vowels before historical /l/. Glottal stop for /p t k/ in codas is extremely widespread in England and Scotland, both word-medially (*butter* as [bʌʔə(ɹ)]) and finally (*cat* as [kæʔ]). Probably the majority of mainland vernaculars have at least some [ʔ] for /t/, and this also occurs in standard varieties as well (see §3.2.2), though in more limited environments. In London however the distribution is wider than in most other areas: since voiceless stops in codas are usually preceded by [ʔ], it's easy to delete the following stop, so that for instance *sap, sat, sack*, citation forms [sæʔp sæʔt sæʔk], can all be [sæʔ]. Though the frequency of [ʔ] alone is much higher for /t/ than for /p k/, sometimes the process of reduction goes further, and the glottal stop is deleted: thus *batter* can have the variants [bæʔtə], [bæʔə], [bæə] (as well as others with medial [tʰ tˢ ɾ] for /t/). Unusually, [ʔ] can substitute for other consonants as well: e.g. /f v/ in [dɪʔrən] *different*, [gɪʔəm] *give 'em*, and /θ ð/ as in [sæːʔend] *Southend*, [äʔə] *other*. (Though since glottal-stop substitution is as stigmatized as /f v/ for dental fricatives, the latter two could also be taken as examples involving /f v/.)

In much of the South, syllable-final /l/ is 'vocalized', i.e. the secondary articulation of dark [ɬ] is split off from the lateral, which deletes, leaving a vowel: thus *fill* [fɪo], *fall* [foʊ], etc. This can lead to homophony e.g. of *fault/fought/fort* as [foːʔ(t)]. Because there are changes of vowel quality in this context, other contrasts as well can be lost: *fill/feel* as [fɪo]. This occurs only before what would be a dark [ɬ] in citation form: e.g. though *fill* and *feel* fall together, *filling* and *feeling* are still distinct as [fɪlɪŋ] and [fïilɪŋ].

5.7 The Celtic Countries

5.7.1 SCOTLAND
Scotland has had a peculiar and in some ways unique history, which has led to radical discontinuities between its speech and that of the rest of the English-speaking world. This section will be rather longer and fuller than those on some other areas, since the details do not seem to be well-known outside of Scotland.

Until the 17th century Scotland was an independent, mainly Celtic-(Gaelic) speaking nation. The English presence was at first restricted to the South; the territory they inhabited, roughly between Forth and Tweed, was originally part of Northumbria, ceded to Kenneth II by King Edgar in 973. This cession established pretty much the boundaries of present-day Scotland, and brought a sizeable Anglophone population under the Scottish crown. Thus indigenous Scottish English was from the beginning northern; until about the 14th century there is virtually no major difference between texts from north and south of the Border.

Before the Norman Conquest, however, there had already been some contact with non-northern English; Malcolm III Canmore, for instance, spent three years in Wessex at the court of Edward the Confessor, and married an English princess. After the Conquest, large-scale contact with both southern English and French began; refugees from England poured north in the 11th century, followed by Normans and their English retainers.

The English and Norman influx had much the same effect on the native Celts – or at least their language – as the Saxon Conquest had on the Britons (§2.3): English (and French at court) became the 'establishment' languages, and Gaelic 'was forced into the hinterlands' (Romaine 1982: 57). Gaelic remained the language of the Highlands and Islands (except Orkney and Shetland, which were Scandinavian speaking) until the 18th century; but English was introduced along with the military occupations following the Jacobite Risings of 1715 and 1745. (Though here southern English was brought in directly: Scots in the usual sense has never been a Highland language.)

Scotland spent much of the Middle Ages formally or informally at war with England over the latter's territorial ambitions; this, plus Scotland's autonomous nationhood, led to there being two independent Anglophone nations, with very different standard languages, separated only by the Tweed. (The main thing they had in common was a Frenchified high literary culture; they were, that is, two European nations that both happened to use dialects of English.)

One consequence of this was the elaboration of a fully functional standard Scots; while the English of England began to look more and more toward the Southeast Midlands and London as a centre of gravity, Scotland remained fundamentally northern, and Scots continued to develop in its own way. By the end of the 15th century the term *Scottis* appears as a replacement of the older *Inglis*, and Scottish writers increasingly use it as the name of their language. Certainly from the 15th to the late 16th century, Scots was the only non-SEML variety of English with the status of a full literary standard on its own territory, and a major prose and verse tradition.

All through the period, however, there were extensive and increasing contacts with southern English; the two nations had diplomatic and cultural relations, and the linguistic fashions of London made their way to Edinburgh. During the 16th century Scotland, as a less powerful English-speaking nation in contact with a more powerful one, began to take on some of the features of a 'province' as well – though without loss of its national character. We can see this mixture of nationalist and 'provincial' elements in some comment on language choice by Gavin Douglas, who translated the *Aeneid* into Scots verse c. 1515; he is clearly aware of the differences between Scots and what he calls *sudron* 'southern', and unambiguous about the status of both as 'languages'. He says (prologue to Book I, 103) that he writes 'in the language of Scottis natioun', and that he tries to avoid southern English; but at times he admits being forced to borrow (113ff):

> Nor yit sa clene all sudron I refus,
> Bot sum word I pronunce as nyghtbouris doys:
> Lyke as in Latin beyn Grew termys sum,
> So me behufit quhilum or than be dum
> Sum bastard Latyn, French or Inglys oys
> Quhar scant was Scottis ....

[*sa* 'so'; *doys* 'does'; *beyn* 'are', *Grew* 'Greek'; *quhilum* 'at times'; *or than* 'rather than'; *oys* 'usage'; *quhar* 'where']

The phonology, spelling and grammar are Scots; but there is a trace of English influence (southern *bey-n* 'are' vs. N *do-ys*: cf. §2.9); the past participle shows Scots *-it*, and we have northern *sa* (< OE *swā*) – as well as southern *so* (perhaps a scribal inadvertence).

This is slightly self-conscious Scots of the early 16th century; but even at the end of the century we still find poets writing a fully native Scots, e.g. this sonnet by Mark Alexander Boyd (1563–1601), in standard literary Scots of Shakespeare's time:

> Frae bank to bank, frae wood to wood I rin,
> Owrhailit with my feeble fantasie,
> Like til a leaf that fallis from a tree,
> Or til a reed owrblawin with the wind.
> Twa gods guides me: the ane of them is blin,
> Yea, and a bairn brocht up in vanitie;
> The nixt a wife ingenerit of the sea
> And lichter nor a dauphin with her fin.

Aside from S *from* ~ N *frae*, the lexis and syntax are Scots: like *til* rather than *to*, both sg and pl verbs in *-is*, *twa*, *bairn*, *wife* 'woman', *nor* 'than', etc.; and the rhymes of N *rin* 'run': *blin* 'blind': *fin* (loss of final /d/ is normal in Scotland, and short vowels didn't lengthen before /nd/ in the north (§5.4)).

The 'provincialization' really began with the Reformation: major English influence was entrenched via the official translation of the Bible (the Geneva version of 1560). This became the basis for Scottish liturgical language, and – most significant – was used in teaching children to read. Printers also began to print largely in English, and even translated Scots manuscripts into *sudron*. Thus by the late 16th century a kind of bidialectalism was beginning: literacy skills came increasingly through the medium of a foreign dialect.

This led to a polarization: Scots proper began to be relegated to the 'homely' end of the register spectrum, and English occupied the 'elevated' and public end. Written Scots came to be used increasingly for jocular topics, and English for 'serious' ones.

In 1603, on the death of Elizabeth, James VI of Scotland became James I of England, the crowns of two nations were joined, and the cultural and political centre moved from Edinburgh to London. Until the Union of Parliaments in 1707 Scotland still had its own legislature; the loss of this was perhaps the final blow to Scots as an independent standard language. As David Murison says (1979:9), 'Scots ... lost spiritual status at the Reformation, social status at the Union of the Crowns, and political status with the Parliamentary Union'.

But Scots did remain – to one degree or another – the normal spoken language, even though educated people began increasingly to speak a more 'Anglicized' (i.e. southernized) variety. During the 18th century things became exceedingly complex, with the vogue for 'ascertaining the language' and 'correctness' (§2.10) militating against 'Scotticisms', and the whole armory of Augustan linguistic attitudes moving north, helping to sap Scottish self-confidence in the value of the indigenous forms of English. But at the same time a resurgent romantic nationalism led to an increased attention to Scots. One result was a kind of schizoid poetics, with writers using as many as three 'languages': relatively pure Scots, Scots mixed with southern English, and pure southern English. Three passages from poems by Robert Fergusson (1750–74) will illustrate this:

(a)   Upo' the tap o' ilka lum
            The sun began to keek,
        And bid the trig made maidens come
            A sightly joe to seek;
        At Hallowfair, where brousters rare
            Keep gude ale on the gantries,
        And dinna scrimp ye o' a skair
            O' kebbucks frae their pantries
              Fu' saut that day.

[*tap* 'top'; *ilka* 'every'; *lum* 'chimney'; *trig* 'true'; *joe* 'sweetheart'; *brousters* 'brewers'; *gantries* 'trestle-tables'; *dinna* 'don't'; *skair* 'share'; *kebbucks* 'cheeses'; *fu* 'full'; *saut* 'salt(ed)'.]

(b)   On Scotia's plains, in days of yore,
        When lads and lasses tartan wore,

Saft music rang on ilka shore
In hamely weid;
But harmony is now no more,
And music dead.

[*saft* 'soft'; *hamely* 'homely'; *weid* 'weed'.]

(c)   Who would not vindicate the happy doom
To be forever numbered with the dead,
Rather than bear the miserable gloom,
When all his comforts, all his friends are fled.

Extract (a) is full of Scots lexis, and Scots spellings (often indicating Scots pronunciations) of words common to both Scots and English (*gude, o', saut*); (b), while in a 'classical' English style, has some Scots forms (*ilka*) and pronunciations (*saft, hamely*); it also has Scots rhymes (*weid: dead*, presumably in /id/ as would be the case now in broad varieties; in much of the North ME /ɛː/ did not shorten in *head, dead, deaf*, etc.). But it also has a southern English rhyme (*more: shore* – the Scots would be *mair*, rhyming with *share*). Extract (c) not only has no Scots forms, it rhymes *dead* in southern fashion with *fled*.

By the 19th century Scots was pretty much restricted to the speech of 'low' characters in fiction, and to certain lighter styles of verse; except in some experiments by John Galt, there were no real attempts to use anything but standard English for serious literary purposes. In this century however, notably in verse, there have been attempts to revive Scots as a serious national literary language. To get some idea of what is involved, consider Fergusson: if we assume that he would have read these poems in a middle-class, university-educated Edinburgh accent, and that he would have spoken more or less like any of the three extracts (with some accent adjustments) depending on company and subject, we can see that even in the 18th century the dividing line between 'Scots' and 'English' was, except at the poles, quite fuzzy – at least from the observer's viewpoint. To be an educated Scot, then as now, is to command a subset of this continuum: though one can command only the Anglicized end now, it's doubtful if this would have been so for Fergusson.

As a reaction against the 'Anglicization' of public language in Scotland, poets, spearheaded by Hugh McDiarmid (C.M. Grieve, 1892–1978), began in the 1920s to evolve a poetic diction based on eclectic use of contemporary Scots regional and class dialects, plus a wholesale pillaging of earlier writers, from the Middle Ages on. They created a 'language' divorced from both modern spoken vernaculars and standard varieties of Scottish English – but one that was unmistakeably both literary and Scottish. It's difficult for an outsider to pass judgement on the success of this kind of work (which is still done); on the one hand, one is tempted to echo Ben Jonson's comment on Spenser's diction ('In affecting the Ancients, he writ no language'); on the other, one must admire the power of some of the verse. Here is McDiarmid on his own language choice:

> Mony's the auld hauf-human cry I ken
> Fa's like a revelation on the herts o' men
> As tho' the graves were split and the first man
> Grippit the lates wi' a freendly han'
> ... And there's forgotten shibboleths o' the Scots
> Ha'e keys to senses lockit to us yet
> – Coorse words that shamble thro' orr minds like stots,
> Syne turn on's muckle een wi' doonsin emerauds set.

[*hauf*, 'half'; *ken* 'know'; *fa's* 'falls'; *ha'e* 'have'; *coorse* 'coarse'; *stots* 'oxen'; *syne* 'then, afterwards'; *on's* 'on us'; *muckle* 'great'; *een* 'eyes'; *doonsin* 'glinting'.]

There have also been attempts to 'revive' the older literary language as an all-purpose prose standard; here is Alexander Scott writing in 1974 in the journal *Lallans*:

> Fergusson is less taen up wi himsel, and mair taen up wi ither fowk, nor onie o the makars sen the Union. Whan we see Fergusson in his ain poems, it's through the reflection o what he sees o the warld roun about him. First and foremaist, he is a tounsman ... it is when he scrieves anent the toun, the burgh that he cried "Auld Reikie" that he finds the maist to say and the maist mindable weys to say it.

[*makars* 'poets'; *scrieves* 'writes'; *anent* 'about'; *cried* 'called'; *Auld Reikie* 'Old Smoky', i.e. Edinburgh.]

It's most unlikely that any educated Scot would seriously say *taen up wi himsel* [ten ʌp wi hımsɛl]; though *cried* for *called* is normal; there is something here of a rescue operation on the vernacular, embedded in a traditional orthography, often with no phonological import (*fowk* is [fok], the normal way of saying *folk*; what *is* very Scottish is using that instead of *people*). It's not clear what the market for this kind of language would be, outside of a small group of enthusiasts; but what is interesting is that the attempt should be made at all. It's hard to imagine educated English speakers anywhere else trying to treat serious or academic topics in anything but a fairly 'international' standard language.

The linguistic repertoire in Scotland ranges from local 'broad' Scots varieties that may be close to incomprehensible to speakers of other dialects, to 'Standard Scottish English' (SSE) – what some writers think is 'standard English spoken with a Scottish accent' – though this is an exaggeration, as any Scot who doesn't speak RP is likely to have Scots lexical and grammatical features. I will, following a trend among 'foreign' dialectologists, use 'Scots' loosely from now on to mean any clearly Scottish variety of English, from the broadest local to the most standard.

But I will focus on SSE, as it is widely spoken, and is sufficiently distinctive to make the main points. If we compare a typical SSE stressed vowel system with RP or any form of SBE, we find:

(5.22)

	SSE	RP
beet	i	iː
bit	ɪ	ɪ
mate	e	eɪ
met	ɛ	ɛ
(never	ë)	
bat	a	æ
palm		ɑː
pot	ɔ	ɒ
bought		ɔː
boat	o	əʊ
boot	ʉ	uː
book		ʊ
but	ʌ	ʌ
bite	ʌi	aɪ
out	ʌʉ	aʊ
boy	ɔe	ɒɪ

A number of things are immediately obvious: (i) SSE does not have distinctive vowel length (on allophonic length see below); (ii) it may have an extra vowel /ë/ in *never* and some other items (the brackets around /ë/ indicate that not all speakers have it); (iii) the inventory is smaller (12 or 13 vowels as against RP's 15); certain classes normally distinct in all SBEs are not in SSE (*pot/bought, boot/book*: for most Scottish speakers, therefore, *not/nought, pull/pool* are homophones). There are also some notable differences in phonetic realization, e.g. short monophthongs in the *oat, mate* classes, and most often a central vowel in *boot*.

Perhaps the most striking structural feature of all varieties of Scots (SSE included) is the distribution of vowel length; this pattern (often called 'Aitken's Law') is unique to Scots and Scots-derived Ulster dialects (§5.7.2). Basically, all vowels are short in most environments, and all except /ɪ ʌ ɛ̈/ are predictably long in others. The 'long' environments are: before /r/, before the voiced fricatives /v ð z/, and before major boundaries. The diphthongs /ʌi ɔe/ also undergo lengthening, but with quality-changes as well. To illustrate:

(5.23)

/i/: $\begin{cases} \text{[i]} & \text{in } beet\ bead\ bean\ leaf\ east \\ \text{[i:]} & \text{in } bee\ fear\ leave\ wreathe\ breeze \end{cases}$

/e/: $\begin{cases} \text{[e]} & \text{in } mate\ made\ main\ safe\ face \\ \text{[e:]} & \text{in } may\ mare\ grave\ lathe\ graze \end{cases}$

/ʉ/: $\begin{cases} \text{[ʉ]} & \text{in } boot\ mood\ moon\ roof\ loose \\ \text{[ʉ:]} & \text{in } sue\ moor\ move\ smooth\ lose \end{cases}$

/ʌi/: $\begin{cases} \text{[ʌi]} & \text{in } bite\ bide\ line\ life\ lice \\ \text{[a·e]} & \text{in } buy\ fire\ strive\ lithe\ rise \end{cases}$

The fact that vowels are long at boundaries leads to the possibility of a special type of length contrast unique to Scots. If for instance a verb ends in a vowel (e.g. *agree, brew*), the addition of the past tense or participial suffix /-d/ does not shorten the vowel. Thus *brewed* /brʉ-d/ will have a long vowel, and *brood* /brʉd/, with no internal boundary, a short one. So:

(5.24)

greed	[grid]	agreed	[əgri:d]
brood	[brʉd]	brewed	[brʉ:d]
staid	[sted]	stayed	[ste:d]
road	[rod]	rowed	[ro:d]
tide	[tʌid]	tied	[ta·ed]

Not all speakers will have all these distinctions; they are commonest for /i/, /ʉ/ and /ʌi/.

The extra vowel /ë/ (often called '4a' after a conventional numbering of Scottish vowels) is unevenly distributed; about half of Scots speakers appear to have it, though not necessarily in the same words. If it does appear, it will be most likely in *never, ever, seven, leopard, leaven, next, bury, herd* (see below).

All Scots dialects are rhotic; but unlike American or SW English rhotic varieties, they may retain a full set of contrasts before historical /-rC/ (e.g. *bird, word, heard*: on the loss of this distinction see §3.10). Thus in comparison with RP, a maximal Scots subsystem:

(5.25)

	Scots	RP
first	ɪr	
heard	ɛr	3ː
herd	ër	
word	ʌr	

(The symbol [r] here stands for whatever the realization is for a given speaker; for most standard speakers the norm is an approximant, often retroflex, though this may vary with a tap. In general, non-approximant /r/, either tap or trill, is older and less standard.)

Some speakers lack /ë/ in this set (*heard*/*herd* are the same); others – especially upper-class – may tend toward an English norm, using [3r] for some or all of this group (if one remains distinct it's most often the *heard* class).

The 'basic' system in (5.22) is often augmented or varied: some speakers may have an /a/: /ɑ/ contrast (*Sam*: *psalm*). If they do, they will likely use /ɑ/ also in *salmon, alpha(bet), value, parallel* as well.

Scots consonant systems are fuller than the SBE 'archetype' in §3.2.2: they virtually all have a /w/: /w̥/ contrast (*wail*: *whale*), and /x/ (*loch*, placenames; also in local vocabulary like *och* /ɔx/ 'oh').

Some individual pronunciations stand out as peculiarly Scots: e.g. /n/ rather than /ŋ/ in *length, strength*; a trisyllabic *Wednesday* with pronounced /d/, i.e. [wɛdn̩zdeː]; *December* as [dɪzɛmbʌr]; and *tortoise, porpoise* with compound stress and unreduced final syllable, e.g. [tɔ́rtɔ̀ɪs].

The discussion of phonology has centred on standard Scots; but of course there is an enormous range of dialect types, including not only local 'traditional dialect' (§§5.3–4) but a fine urban stratification as well. It's notable that the system described so far is not – surprisingly perhaps in the light of my remarks at the beginning of this section – particularly northern. Except for short /a/ in *fast*, it in fact looks southern (a diphthong in *out*, *but* distinct from *foot*). But this is only the 'Anglicized' standard, which phonologically different as it is from SBE, still has a rather southern distribution pattern – the result of long-term historical bilingualism. If however we look at either rural traditional dialects or urban vernaculars, we find most of the other main northern features: undiphthongized ME /uː/ (*out*), and in many varieties a front ME /oː/ (*boot*). But as far as I know all Scots dialects make a *foot*/*but* distinction, which has not been satisfactorily explained: the otherwise fully northern vernaculars shouldn't.

Within a stratified community like Edinburgh, for instance, the *out* vowel is a potent social indicator – but a complex one. First, monophthongs in *out*, *house* of the type [ʉ] or [y] are stigmatized, and people wanting to 'talk proper' or 'posh' will (variably) use diphthongs like [əʉ] or [ʌʉ]. I remember once hearing a status-conscious working-class mother trying to get her teenage daughter to talk proper in my presence, saying 'Och Debbie, stop messin' [əbʉt] ... eh ... [əbəʉt] like that'. Interestingly, and not unusually, she didn't correct the equally noticeable [ëi] in *like*, or the glottal stops replacing /k t/ in *like that* [lëiʔ ðaʔ] – both of which are also social markers.

For speakers with a monophthong in *out*, this class is or may be homophonous with *boot*, i.e. /ʉt/, /bʉt/; and here another social marker comes into play. For the *boot* vowel, the fronter the realization is, the less prestigious: thus very upper-class speakers may have a back [u], though the norm is roughly central. But very front realizations like [ʏ] or [y] are stigmatized (and unrounded ones like [ɪ] even more so). Thus a socially conscious speaker may have not only monophthong/diphthong variation in *out*, but frontness/backness variation in *boot* as well.

Things are made even more complex by the fact that even those with a stable monophthong in *out* also have a diphthong /ʌʉ/ in items like *loup* 'run', *howk* 'dig' and often *loose* (< On *lauss*, not OE *lōs* as in the South). So it's not that the broad speakers 'lack /ʌʉ/': they have it (nonvariably), but in different words. Hence patterns of overlap like this are possible:

(5.26)

i.e. *loup*, *boot* have only one pronunciation, but *out* has two.

The phonological systems of the traditional regional dialects are more complex; one striking example of possible correspondences can be taken from an Angus dialect:

(5.27)

	Angus	SSE	RP
book	u		
bull	ʌ		ʊ
foot	ɪ		
boot	ø	ʉ	
lose	o		uː
loose	ʌu		

One would expect that a speaker of this type would also have – under appropriate conditions – a dialect much closer to SSE; but not that an SSE speaker would have a more traditional one, even if he came from Angus.

So far the material has been phonological; but there are a number of lexical and grammatical features characteristic of most varieties of Scots, including SSE, and some of these are worth noting.

(i) Lexical items unique to Scotland: *gean* 'wild cherry', *jag* 'prick (n, v), injection', *whin* 'gorse', *rones* 'eaves-troughs, gutters', *roup* 'public auction', *haar* 'sea-mist', *aye* 'always' (*aye* 'yes' is general northern), *gey* 'very', *swither* 'hesitate', *blether* 'chatter', *weans* 'children' (general N *bairns* is also common), *thole* 'bear, endure', *peelie-wallie* 'under the weather'.

(ii) Scots senses for General English items: *bramble* 'blackberry' (the fruit, not just the canes), *sort* 'mend', *while* 'until', *messages* 'shopping' (*do the messages* 'go to the shops' – also occurs in the far North of England), *cry* 'call (by a name)', *clap* 'pet (an animal)', *stay* 'live in a place' (e.g. *I stay in Edinburgh*; the American sense of *stay* (have temporary accommodation) would be *stop*).

(iii) Idiomatic features: one notable one is a kind of 'third person' self-portraiture (for want of a better term), in narration and comment: e.g. *there's me sitting on the floor after the chair broke, that's me away home* (= 'I'm leaving now'); *what like* 'what kind' e.g. *that's what like it is; the cat needs/wants out; the now* 'now'; *back of* 'just after' e.g. *I'll be there the back of ten.*

(iv) Grammatical features: perhaps the two most notable are the structure of the negation system and the modals. Scots negation allows the usual English patterns; but there are a number of special ones as well. Overall there's a general tendency to avoid cliticizing *not* onto *will*, shared with much of the North: thus *I'll not go* rather than *I won't go*, *will you not do it?* rather than *won't you do it?* But in more local varieties, there is a quite different negation system, in which English *not* is absent, and the two forms are clitic *-na/-nae* /-na/-ne/ and *no* /no/. The rules for their use are complex, but they can be illustrated by *I cannae do it* vs. *I'll no do it, can you no do it?* The verb *do* takes on a reduced form before /-ne/, giving /dɪzne/ *disnae* 'doesn't'. Since the normal form of final *-y, -ey, -ie* in Scots is /e/, this gives rise to a Scots children's riddle: *Q*: 'What's the difference between Mickey Mouse and the man that invented him?' A: 'Mickey Mouse got big ears and Walt Disney.'

The modal system shows two distinct features, one unique to Scotland as far as I know, and the other occurring in N. Ireland and the U.S., but probably under Scots influence. The first is the existence of *to*-infinitives for modals (*you have to can drive a lorry*: cf. §1.1); the second is the use of modals in series, e.g. *will you can go?* 'will you be able to go?' and the like.

5.7.2 IRELAND, SOUTH AND NORTH

English has had a complex 700-year history in Ireland, quite different in the South (the Republic) and the North (Ulster). The current political division dates from a treaty of 1921, in which three of the nine original Ulster counties (Donegal, Cavan, Monaghan) were ceded to the Irish Free State as it then was, while the other six (Antrim, Armagh, Down, Fermanagh, Londonderry and Tyrone) stayed under British rule. The current linguistic border between the North and South doesn't follow the political one: characteristic Ulster speech extends into much of Co. Monaghan and parts of Cavan, and all of Donegal.

English came to Ireland in 1169, with a Norman settlement established by Henry II in the south of what was then a Celtic-speaking island. From the beginning these settlers (unlike later ones) tended to see themselves as put-upon colonists, and identified with the native Irish population, rather than with England. This led them not to try to impose French or English, but to learn Irish, and eventually assimilate – very different from most English-Celtic contacts, including later ones in Ireland. Edward III's Statutes of Kilkenny (1366) attempted to impose English on the Irish living in English settlement areas – and failed. During the 14th–15th centuries English steadily receded, and except for a strip along the east coast ('The Pale') and a few rural areas it was virtually extinct by the 16th century.

Ireland remained isolated in many ways; it's significant that it was virtually untouched by the Reformation, so that by Tudor times, in addition to being once more Irish-speaking, it was effectively a Catholic province of a Protestant kingdom. So during the Tudor and Stuart reigns the English began the first of their attempts to deal with 'the Irish problem' – i.e. to Anglicize Ireland. In the 16th–17th centuries they established 'plantations' or settlements of English (later Scots, in the North) in rural areas to combat the Irish/Catholic influence. By the 17th century the major east-coast ports like Limerick and Dublin were English, and there were large settlements in Ulster. Cromwell in particular, as part of his jobs-for-the-boys programme, gave extensive lands to loyal followers, displacing Irish landowners.

Thus English was introduced twice to Ireland: the first (medieval) introduction aborted, leaving behind only some archaic rural dialects; the second, however, was ultimately successful, and led to the near-total extirpation of Irish. By the mid-17th century English was solidly established in the East, the middle of the country was mixed English-Irish, and the West alone still firmly Irish-speaking. Around 1800, perhaps 50% of the population had English as mother tongue; according to the 1851 Census, the proportion had jumped to nearly 75%; and in 1861 it was reported that only 2% of children were monoglot Irish.

This radical change was brought about in a number of characteristic ways: first, Irish faced the problems of any minority language confronted by a 'world language' spoken by an unsympathetic occupying power; second, the English took positive steps to destroy Irish, e.g. in setting up the National Schools in 1831, which discouraged Irish; and third, in the hard economic times and famines of 1830–50, nearly two million people – mostly from the Irish-speaking West – died or emigrated.

So the basis for southern Hiberno-English (HE: the usual term now for the varieties of English spoken in Ireland), which is where we will begin, is essentially 17th-century Mainland English. But developments in Ireland, partly because of somewhat restricted contacts, were different. HE remained rhotic, and some 17th–18th-century SBE vowel-changes failed to affect it, or did so only partially. It also remained to some degree in contact with Irish, and there are (more in nonstandard than standard varieties) some clear Irish influences. The standard view is that HE derives its basic features from the confrontation of 17th-century SBE with Irish: that its phonology is a 'compromise', and that it shows many morphosyntactic features of Irish origin. I take a rather more sceptical view, and assume that except for a few clear cases the direct influence of Irish is marginal, and that we have in all forms of HE basically an indigenous and independent development of English.

The range of dialect-types in current HE is large; we will be concerned here mainly with the phonology of a standard (but not upper-class or Anglicized) type, to illustrate the main features. For historical and comparative purposes I include RP and 17th-century SBE in the display:

(5.28)

	17th-c.	HE	RP
bit	ɪ	ɪ	ɪ
bet	ɛ	ɛ	ɛ
bat	a~æ	a~æ	æ
foot	ʊ	ʊ	ʊ
but	ʌ	ɔ̈~ʌ	ʌ
pot	ɔ	ɑ	ɒ
beet	iː	iː	iː
beat	eː~iː	iː~eː	
mate	eː	eː	eɪ
fast	æː	aː	ɑː
boot	uː	uː	uː
boat	oː	oː	əʊ
bought	ɔː	ɑː	ɔː
hurt	ʌr	ɔ̈r~ʌr	3ː
pert	ɛr	ɛr	
bite	ʌɪ	ʌɪ~aɪ	aɪ
out	ʌʊ	ʌʊ~aʊ	aʊ
boy	ɔɪ	ɔɪ	ɒɪ

(Many speakers, not only nonstandard ones, also have [ʊ], at least variably, in the *but* class.)

A number of quite conservative features are displayed here. Note first the variation of /eː/ and /iː/ in the *beat* (ME /ɛː/) class. As we saw earlier (§2.10), the merger of ME /eː/ and /ɛː/ in the aftermath of the GVS was late, not fully stabilized in SBE even in the 18th century. The partial separation, with some *beat* items going with *mate* rather than *meet*, is now recessive in the South, and occurs mainly in provincial and urban nonstandard varieties. The non-merger is regarded as old fashioned, and tends to be restricted in those dialects that have it to a small set (*leave, meat, eat, tea, beat*), and *Jesus* (as a swear-word, not the name).

The *foot/but* quality split is there, but aside from the common rounded

/ɔ̃/ (which probably represents an older stage than unrounded /ʌ/) is distributed differently from the SBE set-up: in conservative speech there is no contrast before /l/, while /ɔ̃/:/ʊ/ contrasts can appear in pairs like *pub/sub*, *nut/cut*, which would, all rhyme in /ʊ/ in the North of England, and in /ʌ/ in SBE. This suggests that the ME /u/ split was partly independent in Ireland, i.e. it arrived in its early and variable stages (§3.10). As far as other archaisms go, note the monophthongal *boat*, *mate*, and the distribution of vowels before /rC/ (rhoticity itself of course is conservative). The HE system is somewhere between the full retention of the ME /i e u/ here in Scots and the complete merger in Mainland English, U.S. and other extraterritorial varieties (§§3.10, 5.7.1). It's usual, as (5.28) suggests, for at least ME /e/ and /u/ to be separate, as in *prefer*, *earn* with /ɛr/ vs. *fur*, *urn* with /ɔ̃r/; educated Dublin often shows full merger under /ɔ̃r/, sometimes with rather English-sounding realizations like [ɜr] (cf. Edinburgh, §5.7.1).

Note that *pot* (ME /o/) and *bought*, *law* (ME /ɔu, au/) are typically unrounded. This is often attributed to the lack of a 'matching' back rounded vowel in Irish, but is in fact duplicated elsewhere: cf. *tap* for *top* in the Fergusson extract in §5.7.1, and the usual unrounded vowel at least in *pot* in U.S. English – which may be partly due to early HE influence (§5.8.2).

Some dialects show a potential merger of *boy* and *bite* – though the more standard the speaker, the less likely. Apparently early HE speakers merged 17th-century SBE /ɔɪ/ and /ʌɪ/ under /ʌɪ/, supposedly because Irish lacked an /ɔɪ/ diphthong. But the HE version of /ʌ/ was [ɔ̃] or [ɔ] – so the *boy*, *bite* diphthongs both came out with the *but* vowel as first element. Nowadays older and rural speakers still merge *boy* and *bite*; but in the standard these classes are normally separate.

The rather complex developments of ME /a au ɔu o/ can be illustrated by comparing HE and RP:

(5.29)

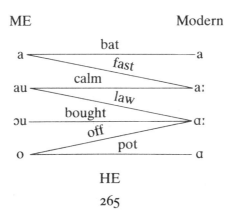

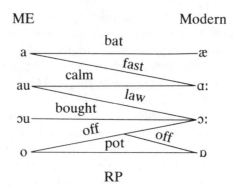

The same number of categories, but quite different phonetic realizations; in addition, RP has generally re-merged lengthened /o/ before /f s θ/ (*off, loss, moth*) with the rest of short ME /o/; though in some SBE dialects, as in South Africa and generally in the U.S., some of these items (the result of a 17th-century lengthening) are still long.

HE consonants show a number of local features, perhaps due in part to the early partitioning of the complex Irish consonant system by the first HE speakers. Irish has about 33 consonant phonemes as opposed to SBE's 23. It has an opposition of plain vs. palatalized consonants, so that when the first Irish speakers learned English, they had in many cases two choices for one English category. E.g. should E /p t k/ be associated with Irish plain /p t̡ k/ or palatalized /p′ t′ k′/? For /l/, for instance, the choice seems to have been palatalized /l′/ in all positions – hence the extremely clear syllable-final /l/ so noticeable as a feature of HE.

The palatalization opposition may be involved in another HE characteristic. Irish lacks the dental fricatives /θ ð/, but has two sets of stops, palatalized /t′ d′/ and non/palatalized /t̡ d̡/ – the plain stops are dental and the palatalized ones alveolar. It looks as if the dental /t̡ d̡/ were used for E /θ ð/, and the alveolars for /t d/. This leads to what sounds to non-HE speakers like mergers of /t θ/ (*tank: thank*) and /d ð/ (*dough: though*). But this is primarily a function of non-HE speakers not being very good at hearing dental/alveolar contrasts; the actual situation is more complicated. For most HE speakers (except the most standard), both sets do in fact begin with stops – but with dentals and alveolars distinct. Thus *tank* [tʰaŋk] vs. *thank* [t̡ʰaŋk], *dough* [do:] vs. *though* [d̡o:]. (Though there are some who generalize one set of stops for both.)

This is complicated further by the fact that in the vicinity of /r/, the dental/alveolar contrast is merged in favour of dentals: *three, tree* are [t̡ri:], *breather, breeder* are [bri:d̡ər]. Before /l/, on the other hand, the merger is to alveolars, so that one speaker may oppose a final dental in *faith* [fe:t̡] with an alveolar in *faithless* [fe:tləs] – which then becomes identical to *fateless*, while *fate* [feːt] is distinct from *faith* [feːt̪]. This may be obscured in some cases by the frequent fricative-like realizations of /t/ in weak (non-initial) positions in the foot, usually a voiceless tap [ɾ̥]. Thus *thought* can be not only [t̪ʰɑːt], but also [t̪ʰɑːɾ̥], with the same consonant as in the middle of *butter* [bɔ̈ɾ̥ər] and the end of *but* [bɔ̈ɾ̥]. In connection with this weakening of /t/ to [ɾ̥], it's interesting that in certain (usually foot-medial) contexts it's carried a step further, and we get substitution by /h/: one very common form in which this occurs is *Saturday* /sáhərdeː/.

Southern HE also shows some prosodic differences from SBE and other dialects, e.g. in the distribution of stress. There is a strong tendency for stress to move toward the end of the word, and for suffixes like *-ate, -ize, -ess, -ite, -ment, -ute* to be stressed: *educáte, organíze, hostéss, expedíte, complimént, persecúte*. This also applies to further derivatives, e.g. *administrátor, educáted*. (This is also reported for some Coloured speakers in the Cape, but any HE connection is dubious.) In general, while U.S. English tends toward initial stress, and SBE is fairly well balanced between initial and end-stress, HE tends where possible to shift stress to the right. Comparatively:

(5.30)

U.S.	SBE	HE
rótate	rotáte	rotáte
mígrate	migráte	migráte
éducate	éducate	educáte
órganize	órganize	organíze

Most of the characteristic morphosyntactic features of HE are shared by both North and South. The most important of these relate to the aspect system, and are commoner the less standard the speaker is.

(a) A transitive perfect construction, often called 'PII' in the literature, in which the object comes between the auxiliary and participle, is in:

(5.31)

    i. Aston Villa have the league won.
    ii. I've a loaf not touched.
    iii. I haven't even it made yet.

These are different from the usual perfects of the type *Aston Villa have won the league*, *I've not even made it yet*, in that they refer to a state brought about as the immediate result of past action. This is shown by the exclusion of most past adverbials: while non-HE allows e.g. *I've only read Ulysses once*, HE would not permit **I've only Ulysses read once*.

That is, the sense of PII is 'having the object of the verb in some present state'. This is clearly an archaism, since it reflects an old type that is probably the original of the standard perfect (cf. §4.5.4), and was common in 17th-century SBE (cf. Shakespeare's *Have you the lion's part written?*, *Midsummer Night's Dream* I.ii.68).

(b) A very characteristic type of HE perfect, of the 'hot news' (past with immediate present relevance) type, is apparently built on an Irish model:

(5.32)

    i. She's after telling him the news.
    ii. I was after getting married.

The Irish model can be illustrated by:

(5.33)

    Tá sí tréis an bád a dhíol
    was she after the boat selling
    'She has just sold the boat'

This reflects the characteristic use of perfect for anteriority (§4.5.2): the speaker's moment of utterance is just 'after' the event being reported. There is also an Irish analogue to PII, e.g. *Tá an bád díolta aici* 'Was the boat sold at-her' = 'She has sold the boat'; but the existence of the same type in English suggests that this isn't a borrowing, but at most the similar Irish construction 'encouraged' the retention of the English one.

(c) HE makes certain aspectual distinctions using *do* and *be* that do not occur in the same form elsewhere (though similar constructions exist in the SW of England and in U.S. Black English):

(5.34)

i. Well, there *be's* games in it and there *be's* basketball, darts and all.

ii. He's the kind of person that you would never know when he was drunk, but he *does be*, if you know what I mean.

iii. Well, when you put them on the barrow you *do have* them in heaps and then you *do spread* them...

iv. Then *be shooting* and fishing out at the forestry lakes.

In (i) and (ii) we have a HE habitual form, simple in (i) and in (ii) with *do*. *He's* suggests a general (timeless) state (the kind of person he is), but *does be* is habitual (he is normally, at time x and time y and ...) drunk.

Here is a standard MUE system, compared with its relatives southern HE and Standard Scots, and RP: a few extra items have been added to the usual list to throw contrasts and similarities into relief:

(5.35)

	MUE	SSE	SHE	RP
bit	ɪ	ɪ	ɪ	ɪ
bet	ɛ	ɛ	ɛ	ɛ
bat	a	a	a	æ
fast		a	aː	ɑː
father	aː			
foot	ʉ	ʉ	ʊ	ʊ
boot			uː	uː
pot	ɔ	ɔ	ɑ	ɒ
bought	ɔː		ɑː	ɔː
but	ɵ̈	ʌ	ʌ~ɵ̈	ʌ
beet	i	i	iː	iː
mate	e(ə)	e	eː	eɪ
boat	o	o	oː	əʊ
pert	ɛr	ɛr	ɛr	ɜː
hurt	ɵ̈r	ʌr	ɵ̈r	
bite	əi	ʌi	ʌɪ	aɪ
out	əʉ	ʌʉ	ʌʊ	aʊ
boy	ɔeː	ɔe	ɔɪ	ɒɪ

This is clearly a 'hybrid' system. It shows some characteristic HE qualities (e.g. /ɵ̈/ in *but*), and phonetic Scots features (e.g. the non-back vowel in *boot* /ʉ/ vs. HE, RP /uː/). Structurally, however, it is Scots in type: Aitken's Law, in a modified form, controls much of the distribution of length. But there are limitations; in addition to the invariable shortness (as in Scots) of the vowels in the *bit*, *but* classes, there are also invariant long vowels: that in *boy*, which has no short allophones, and the nuclei of *bought* /bɔːt/ which ≠*pot* /pɔt/, and *father*, *rather* with /aː/ as opposed to the /a/ of *gather*.

In (iii) we have what is called 'iterative perfective', i.e. 'a plurality of events, each of which is viewed as a self-contained whole' (Harris 1984b: 306); and in (iv) an 'iterative imperfective', indicating again a plurality of events, but each of them viewed 'with regard to its internal structure (e.g. duration)'.

Northern HE as a whole is the result of a 'meeting' of Ulster Scots coming down from the North and southern HE coming up from the South, and thus shares characteristics of both. The usual account posits a three-way division into Ulster Scots (US), essentially a conservative form of Scots, Mid Ulster English (MUE), which is structurally Scots-like, but has southern features, and South Ulster English (SUE), which is much closer to southern HE. 'Core' Ulster Scots is essentially rural, and is concentrated in the North (NE Down, N. Antrim, Derry, E. Donegal), MUE covers the bulk of the province including Belfast, and SUE is the speech of S. Armagh, Fermanagh and Monaghan, along the border with the Republic. MUE is the dominant type.

This classification is based mainly on the vowel systems: the further south, the more the systems are 'split', with phonemic length (§3.2.3); the further north the more Scots-like, with vowel length controlled by some version of Aitken's Law (§5.7.1). In view of the enormous complexity of the Ulster dialect picture, both regionally and socially, I will confine myself here to a general picture of MUE, with some comments on one of its major varieties, Belfast Vernacular (BV).

In the less standard systems of the type generally called Belfast Vernacular, however, things get much more complicated:

(a) Many items in the ME /u/ and /oː/-shortened classes which in SBE have /ʊ/, in BV alternate between a conservative SUE /ʌ/ and an innovative /ʉ/. Items like *pull, bush, foot, took* can appear either with the vowels of the (invariant) *but* class, or that of the (invariant) *boot* class. This distribution appears to be individual to each word, and socially and attitudinally stratified: pronunciations like [fʌt] for *foot* are highly vernacular, and tend to be most common in the speech of younger WC males. The pattern can be illustrated this way: in a sample of conversational speech in a Belfast survey (J. Milroy 1980), the following percentages of [ʉ] and [ʌ] occurred:

(5.36)

	ME /u/			ME /oː/	
	%[ʉ]	%[ʌ]		%[ʉ]	%[ʌ]
bullet	20	80	stood	59	41
pull	26	74	foot	65	35
full	53	47	took	67	33
put	61	39	could	69	31

This displays yet another aspect of the kind of variation discussed in §5.5. Here it's not just variation within a phonological category – the shifting of items from one class to another is word-specific, and each word has its own statistical profile. E.g. *bullet* is less firmly established in the new class than *put*, and both *bullet* and *put* than any member of the ME /oː/ class except *stood*. This is also stratified by age and sex, with women 18–25 showing the most transfer. A similar pattern occurs with the non-merger of *meet/mate*, rather like southern HE.

(b) The Aitken's Law length alternations have been interfered with and restricted by a number of other rules. The phonetics of the system are extremely complex, but we can illustrate the general pattern by looking at three vowels that don't follow the Scots rule – /ɛ a ɔ/. These are short before voiceless stops and affricates /p t k t ʃ/, or before a nasal or liquid followed by a voiceless consonant, or a stressed syllable followed by an unstressed one within the morpheme; otherwise long:

(5.37)

	Short			Long		
/ɛ/ pet	bent	tenor	bed	bend	tenner
/a/ pat	pant	Bannon	pad	band	banning
/ɔ/ pot		robin	pod	pond	robbing

There are many more interesting and complex features, but these will illustrate the general situation.

Northern HE also has, in addition to the aspectual features discussed above for HE generally, some other syntactic peculiarities, at least two of which show up in U.S. English as well. These two are (a) *for to* as a complementizer (*He went up the street for to buy a paper*), and (b) 'positive *anymore*' (*I'll be getting six or seven days' holiday anymore* 'from now on/nowadays'). Other features which seem to be restricted to the North are sentence-final *but* in the sense 'however' (*I never seen him, but*); *from* = 'since' (*She's living here from she was married*); and *whenever* = 'when' (*My husband died whenever I was living in the New Lodge Road*).

5.7.3 WALES

Wales is yet another English colony on Celtic territory – though the ultimate results of English colonization have, partly because of different attitudes, been rather different from what they were in Scotland and Ireland. Until quite some time after the Norman Conquest, the English presence in Wales was small; but in 1284 the English conquered the country, and established an English political and legal system (though Welsh was still the language of government). As the Middle Ages progressed, cultural and political ties increased, reaching a first climax under the Tudors, who were themselves of Welsh ancestry. In 1536, after Henry VIII split with Rome and declared himself head both of the English nation and church, the Act of Union was passed, which incorporated Wales under the English crown. By the Wales and Berwick Act of 1746, Wales was officially defined as 'part of' England.

As in the other Celtic countries, there has been a gradual replacement of the indigenous language by English – not only through attitude change and demographic shift, but through official policy. Until the mid-19th century, most attempts at spreading education in Wales encouraged the use of Welsh; but from 1870 on policy became strongly Anglocentric, discouraging Welsh. This was further supported by a typically bureaucratic attempt at 'uniformity': if Wales is 'English', then English ought to be the official (and only) language. A commission of enquiry into Welsh education reported as early as 1847 that the 'Welsh language is a vast drawback to Wales ... it dissevers the people from intercourse which would greatly advance their civilization, and bars the access of improving knowledge to their minds' (cited in Price 1984: 103). The 1870 Education Act made no provision for the educational use of Welsh, and it was not until the 1890s that it was reintroduced, first as a medium for teaching English to monoglot Welsh speakers, and later as an optional schools subject (in effect a 'foreign language' in its own nation).

The situation has been improving in recent times, with the establishment of Welsh medium schools; but the overall speaker figures, even with the rise of an often aggressive Welsh nationalist movement, have been dropping. According to census data. Welsh speakers as an overall percentage of population dropped from 43.5% in 1911 to 20.9% in 1971. Still an impressive showing compared to the roughly 1.8% of Scots Gaelic speakers – though of course most of Scotland had not been Gaelic-speaking since medieval times. (The 28% reported competence in Irish in the Republic has to be viewed against the fact that it's now a compulsory school subject: the average outside the core Irish-speaking areas is probably about 4%.)

The regional picture for Welsh English (WE) is not clear, but scholars agree that there are at least two major types, northern and southern, the northern showing more Welsh influence and the southern 'more evolved' (Thomas 1984: 178), less Welsh-influenced and more akin to the English dialects of the West Midlands and SW. The southern type could be said to represent the last stage of a process of language-shift, as most of its speakers are monolingual; the northern one is spoken largely by Welsh-English bilinguals. We will look at a southern variety here.

If we compare a typical southern WE vowel system (Swansea Valley) with RP, we find:

(5.38)

	WE	RP
bit	ɪ	ɪ
bet	ɛ	ɛ
bat	a	æ
fast		ɑː
palm	aː	
foot	ʊ	ʊ
but	ə	ʌ
pot	ɔ	ɒ
bought	ɔː	ɔː
oar	oː	
boat		əʊ
slow	oʊ	
mate	eː	eɪ
eight	eɪ	
boot	uː	
blue		uː
blew	ɪʊ	
beet	iː	iː
hurt	əː	ɜː
bite	əɪ	aɪ
out	əʊ	aʊ
fair	ɛː	ɛə
boy	ɔɪ	ɒɪ

We note first one typical N/ML English feature – lack of lengthening in *fast*, etc. – though there is a long vowel from ME /arC/ and /alC/ (*cart*, *palm*). The central vowel in *but*, characteristic also of SW England (e.g.

Bristol), may be an influence from that area, or an original /ʊ/-dialect approximation of SBE /ʌ/.

There are also a number of archaic distinctions that represent (cf. §5.6.2 on W. Yorkshire and East Anglia) non-implementation of mergers that occurred in general SBE. The SBE /əʊ/ class, for instance, is often reflected in WE by /oː/ < ME /ɔː/ and /oʊ/ < ME /ɔu/ (*boat* vs. *slow*); similarly the SBE /eɪ/ class shows up as WE /eː/ < ME /aː/ vs. /eɪ/ < ME /ai/ (*mate* vs. *eight*). There is also lack of merger of some earlier /iu/ diphthongs with /uː/ as in *blew*, *threw* with /ɪʊ/ vs. *blue*, *through* with /uː/. WE /ɪʊ/ is also used for those items that in SBE have /juː/ (*tune*, *few*, *music*).

Some other phonological features include (a) frequent non-reduction of unstressed vowels that appear in SBE as /ɪ/ or /ə/: e.g. /ɛ/ in the final syllables of *helpless*, *ticket*, often with what to non-WE speakers sounds like secondary stress; (b) lengthening of consonants in foot-medial position after a short vowel, as in [sɪtːi] *city*, [fɪlːə] *filler*; (c) interpolation of [j w] after certain long vowels and diphthongs, giving clear disyllabic forms where SBE often has (nearly or totally) monosyllabic ones: e.g. [fɔ́ɪjə] *fire*, [sloʊ́wə] *slower*, [díːjə] *deer*. Except for a few rural varieties, WE dialects are non-rhotic, and /r/ is usually a tap [ɾ]; /l/ is clear in all positions.

The consonant inventory contains two extra members: a velar-to-uvular fricative /x/ and a voiceless lateral fricative / ɬ /, both of which occur primarily in Welsh proper names and other loan words: e.g. /bax/ *bach* 'term of endearment', /ɬəwélɪn/ *Llywelyn*.

There are a few noteworthy grammatical features as well: (a) use of *some*(*thing*) in negative rather than positive contexts (*I wonder if we've got some books*; *he hasn't got something to wear*); (b) what in other varieties are progressive forms used for habitual aspect (cf. §4.5.2), e.g. *I'm going to chapel every Sunday* = 'I go . . .'; (c) use of *isn't it* as a tag, regardless of person agreement (*you're going home now, isn't it?*); and topicalization of predicates other than NPs (cf. §4.7.2), a device probably taken over from Welsh, which allows this quite freely: e.g. *coming home tomorrow he is*, or *loud he was singing*.

5.8 Extraterritorial English

5.8.1 BASIC DIVISIONS: 'AMERICAN' VS. 'BRITISH'
The exportation of English in the 17th–19th centuries (§2.12) created a host of new varieties which I will call Extraterritorial Englishes (ETEs). There seem to be three main types:

(a) Mother-Tongue ETEs: normal developments of transported Mainland varieties, of much the same type as the development of

Mainland English itself from ET North Sea Germanic: e.g. North American, South African, Australian English.

(b) Foreign-Language ETEs: varieties arising where English is not the mother-tongue, but for one reason or another (often as a colonial legacy) is used as an administrative, trade or educational language. These show a marked degree of interference from other languages: e.g. Indian, Singaporean, West African English.

(c) Creolized ETEs: varieties developed from the adaptation and elaboration of English-based pidgins that arose in colonial or semi-colonial contact situations: e.g. Jamaican Creole, Sierra Leone Krio, New Guinea Tok Pisin.

Obviously a 'complete' treatment of all these types is impossible in the compass of this book; I will confine myself to discussion of the main Mother-Tongue ETEs, in keeping with my general 'Mainstream' bias.

Despite the fact that ETE speakers originally came from all over the British Isles, all of the major ETEs, even those with a large Scots, HE or Northern English input, are essentially southern in type (cf. the criteria in §§5.4, 5.6). As far as I know there is no ETE that doesn't distinguish the vowels of *put* and *putt*, for instance, and none that does distinguish those of *bird/heard/word*. Non-southern features that do occur are generally unabsorbed relics; they tend to be sporadic, largely matters of lexis or the survival of local constructions (e.g. the type *my hair needs washed* in Scots-Irish settlement areas in the U.S., or Scots *pinkie* 'little finger' in the U.S. and South Africa).

There were two major waves of ETE formation: the first in the late 17th–early 18th centuries, the second in the late 18th–mid 19th. The timing is crucial with respect to two developments in Mainland Southern English: the loss of postvocalic /r/ leading to the rise of the rhotic/non-rhotic distinction, and the qualitative change in the lengthened vowel in *fast* (§3.10). Post-vocalic /r/ begins to drop in the SE in the 17th century, but the change was not complete until well into the 19th; lengthening of /æ/ in *fast*, etc. had begun in the 17th century, but the retraction to [ɑː] was nonstandard at first, and stigmatized until well into the 19th century. Hence, to oversimplify a bit, we might expect the earliest ETEs to show a tendency to be rhotic, and to have no more than (at most) a length distinction between the vowels of *cat* and *fast*; and the later ones to be non-rhotic, and to show both length and quality distinctions of the SBE type. This is generally the case; though there are complications having to do with the nature of cultural and political ties to the Mainland, and the character and timing of particular waves of migration, as we'll see. (If we take Hiberno-English (§5.7.2) as an ETE proper rather than a 'Celtic Country' development – which is probably correct – then it furnishes an excellent example of how these predictions work for an early ETE.)

As it happens, the timing distinction correlates with a geographical one: the early settlements were in Canada and the U.S., and the later ones in Australasia and South Africa. So we have a division between Northern Hemisphere and Southern Hemisphere ETEs, as follows:

(5.39)

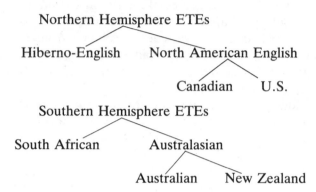

It may be that Southern African requires finer treatment; it's not clear to what extent the English of white mother-tongue speakers in Zimbabwe, for instance, is distinct from South African, though recent work suggests that it has enough individual properties to deserve treatment as a distinct, if related variety.

The differences between the two groups stem largely from political and social history. The U.S. (in the process of becoming the U.S.) severed its political ties with Britain in the late 18th century – though cultural ties between the Mainland and the eastern coastal areas remained fairly strong (cf. §5.8.2). And even though Canada is still a member of the Commonwealth, the U.S./Canadian border is in many ways more of an administrative convenience than a genuine national or cultural divide – at least for English-speaking Canadians. Canada and the U.S. are certainly more of a cultural and linguistic unit than Canada and Britain. Australia, New Zealand, Rhodesia and South Africa, however, retained an intimate contact with Britain from the time of settlement onward – until South Africa's exit from the Commonwealth in 1960, and Rhodesia's UDI in 1965. But by this time the damage, as it were, had been done: for Australia, New Zealand and even South Africa, Britain continues, though with its influence undercut by that of the U.S., to be the external cultural centre; the dialects of these areas have remained much closer to SBE than have those of the Americas.

The Southern Hemisphere ETEs, while different from each other, share certain major features – some general SBE, others reflecting something rather like what London English might have done if it had developed without contact with RP and similar standards. E.g. they all have long vowels in *fast* and are non-rhotic (general SBE); and they all show markedly raised vowels in the *bat* and *bet* classes (in the vicinity of [ɛ] and [e~ë] respectively) – a feature notable in popular London speech as early as the beginning of the 19th century.

Australasian English is distinguished from South African by, among other things, the *fast* vowel: in Australia and New Zealand it is the older front [aː], in South Africa a back [ɑː], sometimes rounded to [ɒː]. And South Africa and New Zealand share a vowel shift that has resulted in a very central quality [ï] for the *bit* vowel (cf. §§5.8.3–4).

It's usual for books on English to say something about what are customarily described as differences between 'British' and 'American' English: everyone knows about 'American' *gas(oline)*, *elevator*, *monkey-wrench*, *flashlight*, *diaper* vs. 'British' *petrol*, *lift*, *spanner*, *torch*, *nappie*. These differences do exist, but 'British' must be understood in a special sense. While 'American' is reasonable, 'British' ought to refer not just to the Mainland, but to the Southern Hemisphere ETEs as well. This is an expectable reflection of the cultural and political relations described above. The fact that many of these characteristic differences, especially in vocabulary, are modern reinforces the point: even in this century the presence or absence of a British 'centre of gravity' has continued to have a strong effect. This is true even in South Africa, after nearly 40 years of government by Afrikaans speakers in an officially bilingual nation.

I'll look briefly here at some of the major differences in the two basic types, across what from a Northern Hemisphere perspective we might call the 'Mid-Atlantic Border'; with the caveat above, I will continue to use the terms 'British' and 'American'.

(i) *Item-Specific Pronunciation Differences*. Typical examples are Br initial /h/ vs. Am lack of it in *herb(al)*; Br *leisure* with /ɛ/ vs. Am /iː/; Br *tomato* with /ɑː/ vs. Am with /eɪ/, thus rhyming with *potato*; Br *clerk* with /ɑː/ vs. Am with /ər/, so that Am rhymes *clerk* with *Burke* (though the Br pronunciation survives in the name *Clark(e)*); Br /lɛftɛnənt/ vs. Am /luːtɛnənt/ *lieutenant*; Br *arse* with /ɑː/ distinct from *ass* 'donkey' with /æ/ vs. Am /æ/ in both, even in rhotic dialects; Br /iː/ (also Canadian) in *been* (rhyming with *bean*) vs. Am /ɪ/ (rhyming with *bin*); frequent Br /iː/ in *evolution* vs. Am /ɛ/.

(ii) *Stress and Vowel Reduction in Polysyllables*. A large number of items are differently stressed in typically Br and Am varieties; this often involves a different treatment of vowels, the unstressed ones reducing to [ə] or deleting. Thus for *attaché* we have Br /ætǽʃeɪ/ vs. Am /ætəʃéɪ/, for *margarine* Br /mɑːdʒɑríːn/ vs. Am /mɑ́ː(r)dʒərɪn/, for *research* Br /rɪsɔ́ːtʃ/ vs. Am /ríːsərtʃ/. In words with suffixes like *-ary*, *-ory*, the differences are quite striking:

(5.40)

	Br	Am
secretary	sékrətrɪ	sékrətèriː
dictionary	díkʃənrɪ	díkʃənɛriː
capillary	kǽpílərɪ	kǽpɪlèriː
laboratory	ləbórətrɪ	lǽbrətɔ̀ːriː

In general, Am pronunciation tends to avoid reduction in suffixes, giving them a secondary stress; BrE tends typically to delete or reduce the first vowel.

(iii) *Grammatical Features*. There are not many clearly defined by the Br/Am divide, but there are some clear tendencies.

(a) Br *got* vs. Am *got/gotten* (cf. §1.2). AmE typically has *gotten* as the past participle of *get* in the sense 'obtain' vs. *got* in the possessive sense, while BrE only has *got*. This leads to a common error on the part of British writers attempting to characterize Americans in some more elaborate way than giving them names like Cyrus X. Hoophammer and having them say 'I guess' a lot (Agatha Christie and John Galsworthy are two notable offenders); giving them lines like *you haven't gotten any brains* = 'You're stupid'. An AmE speaker could only naturally interpret this as meaning. 'You haven't obtained any brains (e.g. from the butcher)'.

(b) Another verb difference is in Br pasts and past participles in *-t* where AmE has *-ed* (with the expected phonetic difference): Br *burnt*, *smelt, split, spoilt, leant* (with /ɛ/, not the /iː/ of *lean*). This is restricted to weak verbs with a stem ending in a nasal or liquid. AmE may have some *-t* forms, but they normally have a specialized (often fossilized) sense: e.g. *burnt offering*, which is not the same as *burned offering* (one that has accidentally caught fire).

(c) Modals (§§4.5.3–4) and other auxiliaries. *Shall* is rare in AmE, except in fossils like *shall we dance?* Normally AmE has *should* where BrE has *shall* (e.g. *should I open the door?* – this does not apply to South African English, where many varieties would have *must* in this connection: §5.8.4). Likewise *should* is often represented by Am *would*: *I should like to come* would be at least odd for most Americans, except in written styles. With *used to* and *need (to)*, some BrE varieties can still treat them syntactically like other auxiliaries, e.g. *used you to do that?*, *you needn't come*; AmE would extend *do*-support to these verbs, giving *did you use to ...* , *you don't need to ...*

Do is also used differently when it functions as a 'pro-verb' replacing a predicate. In (mainly southern) BrE it has a more extensive range:

(5.41)

A. You should have washed the dishes

BrE	AmE
B. Yes, I should have (done)	Yes, I should have (*done)

A. Are you going to read that book?

BrE	AmE
B. Yes, I might (do)	Yes, I might (*do)

(d) Tag-Questions. A tag-question is a construction of the type *He didn't go, did he?* or *He did go, didn't he?*, where the appended tag generally presupposes a particular answer (negative in the first case, positive in the second). In AmE, the tag implies that the speaker acknowledges the likelihood, approaching certainty, that the addressee actually knows the answer. BrE has this, but also another reading. In many (mainly nonstandard) varieties, there is what might be called a special 'aggressive' tag, in which pragmatically the addressee can't possibly know the answer, but is presumed for the sake of a discourse effect to be stupid or otherwise inadequate for not knowing it. Thus *I was here, wasn't I?* in response to a question about your whereabouts on a particular night is an aggressive assertion of your not being elsewhere. (This appears to be restricted to Mainland English.)

(e) Prepositional Constructions. BrE typically omits the article in phrases like *in hospital, in future, at university*, where AmE will have *in the hospital*, etc. With indirect objects, many BrE varieties allow deletion of *to* with pronominal objects (e.g. *give it me*), which AmE would exclude.

(iv) *Lexis.* There are two major types of vocabulary differences:

(a) Different word for the same item. Some of the commonest, aside from those listed earlier, are:

(5.42)

BrE	AmE
Autumn	Fall (Autumn is 'poetic')
compère	M.C.
bum ~ arse	ass
hire purchase	instalment plan
flat	apartment
dustbin	garbage-can
car park	parking lot
chemist	drugstore
dinner jacket	tuxedo

ironmonger	hardware store
silencer	muffler
wing (of car)	fender

(b) Items existing in both varieties, but with different meanings – the popular source of the 'two nations separated by a common language' idea. E.g. Br *vest* = Am *undershirt*, but Am *vest* = Br *waistcoat*; Br *suspenders* = Am *garters*, but Am *suspenders* = Br *braces*; Br *knickers* = *(ladies')* *underpants*, but Am *knickers* = Br *knickerbockers, plus-fours*.

Some of these differences can lead to amusing misconstruals, the best of which are mildly obscene. E.g. in BrE *pecker* is used in the sense of 'spirits' (perhaps originally from something like 'beak' or 'chin'), so *keep your pecker up* is a reasonable exhortation to be of good cheer. But in AmE it has only the meaning 'penis', casting a somewhat different light on things. Similarly BrE *to knock up* means simply 'awaken', but in AmE the only meaning is 'to make pregnant'. Hence *knocking up the doctor at 3 a.m.* is a different activity in different places.

5.8.2 NORTH AMERICA: CANADA AND THE U.S.A.

Despite some differences, Canadian and U.S. English are similar enough so that it's fair to view them as regional variants of a single type, North American English (NAE); the reasons for this lie in settlement history. There was a small English presence in Canada as early as 1583 (Newfoundland), but there was little formal colonization until much later. Canada was a French possession until it came into British hands in its entirety in 1763; until the 18th century most of the English-speakers living there were either in small enclaves in the east-coast Maritime Provinces, or scattered throughout the vast wilderness areas as trappers or hunters, many employed (from 1670) by the Hudson's Bay Company. The first large wave of English speakers came in the mid 18th century; in 1713, by the Treaty of Utrecht, England received from France Newfoundland, the Hudson's Bay Territory in the North, and the French colony of Acadia (Nova Scotia and New Brunswick). Later on (1755–58), the English deported around 6000 French nationals, and replaced them with British settlers.

The second – and most important – influx, which gave Canadian English its essentially American character, came in the 1780s. The end of the American Revolution led to a mass migration of 'United Empire Loyalists' – refugees of pro-British sympathies who were not pleased with the new dispensation. Most of these were from New York and New England, with a small group from the South. Within a generation Ontario alone had c. 90,000 settlers, mostly from the U.S. In the 1830s–

40s, in common with the U.S., there was extensive immigration from the British Isles, but this population was, as it was in the U.S., linguistically absorbed. (About the only exception to this is a group of Irish and SW English origin in Newfoundland, which still shows HE features like [d] for /ð/ and syllable-final clear /l/.)

Thus the basis of Canadian English (CE) is essentially U.S. English of the 1780s–90s (we'll see shortly where that comes from); with – subsequently – just enough separation and loyalist feeling to guarantee a certain amount of continuing British influence. There has also been, as usual, a good deal of independent development on both sides of the border, but contact has remained intimate and intensive. CE and USE are still more like each other than like anything else. (Most British speakers can't tell the difference, and even some Americans have trouble.) In a historical if not political and patriotic sense, CE is in fact a regional dialect of USE, even if built partly on the speech of an original independent Mainland settlement. In terms of the framework of this chapter it's a 'secondary' ETE, growing out of the movement of one ETE onto the territory of another.

U.S. settlement history is quite different. The first major colonies were established before the end of the 17th century, beginning with Jamestown, Virginia (1607), and including Plymouth, Massachusetts (1620), Boston (1630), Delaware (1638), Maine (1641), Charleston, South Carolina (1670), and Pennsylvania (1681). Thus by the time the Hudson's Bay Company began to exploit the Canadian north in 1670, the east coast of the U.S. was colonized from Maine to South Carolina. And by the time the British began to settle in French territory in the 1750s, there had been a large Ulster influx into Pennsylvania (1720 on), and there were English-speaking enclaves in New York State, New Hampshire and Connecticut. By 1790 settlement of some sort had reached as far west as Kentucky and Illinois, and as far south as northern Florida in the East and central Louisiana in the West.

The greater part of the early migration – until the Ulster immigrants of the 1720s – was from SE England. One study of 17th-century New England towns showed the following profile, which appears to be typical: North of England 7%, WML 4%, SW 9%, SE 5%, EML 75% (mainly East Anglia and London). Later migrations – after the coast had been settled – tended to move inland, and we find the greater part of the Ulster, northwestern and southwestern English settlements away from the coasts. Later population movements continued this trend, with the bulk of the Midwest and West being settled from the inland North and Mid-Atlantic states. Thus at quite an early stage the east coast was distinct in origin from much of the interior – a point we will return to below when we look at some major regional features of U.S. English.

Since ETEs tend in their early stages to be somewhat isolated from Mainland developments, it's not surprising that they are in some respects, from a historical point of view, 'conservative': they often retain features that have been lost in their sources. (They are of course also frequently innovating – we will look at this below.) The presence of such archaisms is often given a kind of romantic tinge in media folk-linguistics; Americans are familiar with reports that isolated settlements (especially in the southern Appalachians) 'speak pure Elizabethan English'. This is of course nonsense, but there certainly are very old features retained in some of these areas: e.g. initial /h/ in *it* (< OE *hit*: cf §4.3.3), and the old progressive type *a-fishing, a-hunting* (cf. §4.5.5). But even in more standard NAE there are archaisms at all grammatical levels.

Some of these are lexical: e.g. *loan* 'lend' (common but often stigmatized), an old usage replaced in the 17th century by *lend*; *druggist*, which in 17th-century Britain replaced older *apothecary*, but was itself replaced c. 1750 by *chemist*; *sick* in the general sense of 'ill', rather than specifically 'nauseated'/'vomiting' (Americans (and South Africans) are often *sick in bed*, which to (non-Scots) British speakers would be a disaster); *tariff* meaning only 'customs duty', whose sense was extended in Britain during the 18th century to 'price list' in general (e.g. in a restaurant, as still today); and *jack* 'knave' (in cards), now the only NAE term, but one that had become distinctly lower-class in Britain by the 19th century.

Phonologically, the most archaic features are widespread rhoticity (but see below for some complications); the general lack (except in some east coast areas) of a quality contrast in *cat* vs. *fast*, *ant* vs. *aunt*; retention over much of the area of the old /w̥/:/w/ contrast (*whales* vs. *Wales*: §3.2.2); and retained secondary stress in *-ary/-ory* and the like (*díctionàry, láboratòry*: cf. §4.8.1). The currency of this pattern in older Mainland English is clear from early dictionaries, and from metrical practice; a familiar example of the latter is *Hamlet* I.ii.77–8:

> 'Tis not alone my inky cloak, good mother,
> Nor customary suits of solemn black,

where the metre requires *cústomàry*. Other archaisms include old present subjunctives (*I demand that he leave*, rather than innovating BrE *leaves*), and *gotten* as a past participle of *get* (§4.8.1: *get* is originally a strong verb with an *-en* participle).

The extensive rhoticity of NAE looks as if it should be a simple archaism, since as we know (cf. § 3.10) postvocalic /r/ was at least in the early stages of loss in SBE in the 17th–18th centuries; but it is not, in NAE, simply a local ETE retention. The picture is more complex: the earliest colonies are in fact non-rhotic, and seem to have been at least partly so at the time of settlement; the history suggests that rhoticity may be a kind of 'secondary archaism' – i.e. a later import by speakers of more conservative Englishes (largely Ulster Scots and HE – themselves archaizing ETEs), which had no /r/-loss at all. What we know of population movements in the early U.S. confirms this: the rhotic interior was settled mostly from the 'Scots-Irish' 1720s colonies, while the non-rhotic coastal areas – at any rate the 'primary' early ones down to the Carolinas – had predominantly SE English inputs. Those later settlements populated mainly from the early coastal colonies (Alabama, Mississipi, Georgia, Louisiana, E.Texas) are still basically non-rhotic. The current picture is shown in map 10 (p.284): non-rhotic areas shaded. This is complicated in a number of areas – e.g. New York City and parts of the coastal South – by social factors: even though an area may be traditionally non-rhotic, postvocalic /r/ may be a sociolinguistically relevant feature, carrying either prestige (New York) or its opposite (North Carolina). More on this below.

Canadian English, then, being mostly rhotic, is continuous with that of the northern inland U.S., as we expect on historical grounds; the Canadian border in fact runs across the whole northern U.S., touching eleven of the original states (plus now of course Alaska). Before looking at the regional layout of the U.S., it's worth comparing some features of USE and CE, to see what the main differences – and similarities – are.

(i) Differences between USE and CE. Most of these are relatively unsystematic, and reflect pronunciation differences for individual lexical items, different lexical choices for the same referent, or uniquely Canadian lexis.

(a) Pronunciation. In many cases CE chooses BrE variants: e.g. *been* with /iː/, *again* with /eɪ/ (vs. U.S. /ɪ ɛ/); *evolution* with /iː/ (~ /ɛ/, against U.S. /ɛ/); *lieutenant* with /lɛft-/ (U.S. /luːt-/); *Z* /zɛd/ rather than /ziː/; *-ile* generally /-aɪl/ rather than U.S. /-əl/ (except in *missile, futile*); *zebra* with /ɛ/ rather than /iː/; *schedule* with /ʃ-/ rather than /sk-/ (though /sk-/ does occur, as does the 'compromise' /ʃk-/); *fungi* as /fʌŋgiː/ rather than U.S. /fʌndʒaɪ/; *senile* with /sɛn-/ not /siːn-/; *semi-* /sɛmiː-/ (non-Eastern U.S. /sɛmaɪ-/), the same with *anti-*.

(b) Lexical Choice. CE is basically American, but there are some BrE lexical items, most often as alternants of AmE ones. These are frequently more prestigious or 'finer': thus *lavatory/toilet, luggage/baggage, porridge/oatmeal, tie/necktie* are all in use, but upwardly mobile or status-conscious Canadians are reported to prefer the first (BrE) members of each pair.

(c) Canadian Lexis. As with any ETE, CE has a large number of local items, both new coinages and borrowings. Among the more typical

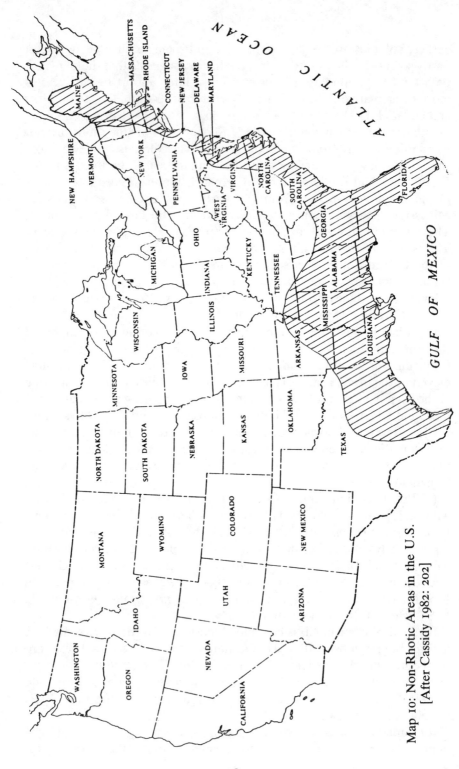

Map 10: Non-Rhotic Areas in the U.S.
[After Cassidy 1982: 202]

Canadian novelties are: *bush* 'wilderness' (definitely not U.S., but used in Australia and South Africa; probably a Canadian development (the adjective *bushed* 'crazy, lost' certainly is); *chesterfield* 'sofa'; *Quebec heater* 'tall cylindrical stove'; *corduroy road* 'road made with logs' (apparently also known in the U.S., but the verb *to corduroy* 'make such a road' is not); *acclamation* 'election without opposition'; *stanfields* 'long underwear' (from the name of a New Brunswick company); *frost boil* 'eruption on a road surface'; *silver thaw* 'frost on trees after a thaw'.

Because of the long and intimate contact with French, there are quite a number of French loans in CE that are not used elsewhere: examples are *bateau* 'large boat', *Métis* 'half-breed', *tuque* 'wool cap', and calques like *dead waters* 'stagnant pools' (< *eaux morts*), *strong woods* 'wilderness areas' (< *bois forts*).

But perhaps the sharpest difference, at least the one most apparent to most Americans, is a set of diphthong alternations commonly called the 'Canadian Diphthong Rule' (or, incorrectly, the 'Canadian Raising'). This affects the *bite* and *out* classes: the first elements of the diphthongs are closer and more central before voiceless consonants, opener and a bit more peripheral before voiced consonants and in final position. Thus:

(5.43)

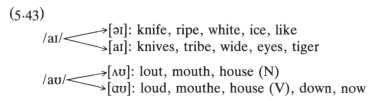

The term 'Canadian Raising' derives from the idea that the [ə-, ʌ-] beginnings are raisings of (input, non-Canadian) open vowels [a-, ɑ-]; but they're more likely retentions of earlier values, related to similar qualities in Scots and HE (cf. §§5.7.1–2). It seems clear that onsets of the [ə] or [ʌ] types were normal in SBE in the 17th–18th centuries, and that the modern open vowels are a good deal later. Rather than 'raising' we have 'non-lowering': an archaism (restricted to a small set of contexts), not an innovation. Similar alternations occur elsewhere; CE [əɪ ~ aɪ] is very like the Aitken's Law alternation [ʌi~aˑe] in Scots (§5.7.1); and alternations nearly identical to the CE ones occur in northern Michigan, the Virginia Tidewater, and parts of New England.

(ii) Similarities between USE and CE. Aside from rhoticity and the archaisms mentioned earlier, there are a number of shared innovations as well. Among them are:

(a) The Status of Vowel Length. The long/short contrast is much less clear-cut in NAE generally (outside perhaps of the east coast of the U.S.) than in other English-speaking areas. In at least one case (see (b) below) there has been a merger of short and long categories in many dialects. Overall, the durational contrasts in pairs like *bit/beet*, *foot/boot* are less clear than in most BrE varieties. The tendency in much NAE is to lengthen short vowels in many or all environments, often quite considerably, and for long vowels often to be rather longer than in many BrE varieties – but not all that much. To a British ear the effect is to make much American speech seem 'slow' or 'drawling'; while to American ears SBE for instance sounds 'clipped'. These lay terms often correspond to something measurable; as an example, consider these measurements (in centiseconds) for average peak durations in the *bit* and *beet* clauses in RP and one variety of USE:

(5.44)

	bit	*beet*
RP	10.2	22.3
USE	18.0	24.0

The *beet*: *bit* ratio in RP is over 2:1 (i.e. the long vowel is more than twice the duration of the short one), while that in USE is 3:4; and USE /ɪ/ is over half-again as long as RP /ɪ/, while /iː/ – though longer – is only marginally so. The differences between the two are small in USE, but they're there, even if their perceptual effect is different. The distinction seems to me clear enough in most varieties so that claims (as in Wells 1982) that NAE generally 'lacks vowel length' are untenable. Even in doubtful cases, the vowel sets distinguished as long vs. short in most BrE dialects are phonologically distinct: a /-VC/ rhyme with a member of the *bit/bet/bat/but* set is light, and one with *beet/boot/mate/out* is heavy, a foot-initial syllable can't terminate in a member of the first class, etc. (cf. §§3.2.3, 3.3–4).

(b) The *cot/caught* Merger. Over a large part of North America the ME /o/ and /au/ classes (SBE /ɒ/, /ɔː/) have merged, so that *cot/caught*, *collar/caller*, *hock/hawk* etc. are homophones. The merger is generally to a short(ish) low back vowel, either rounded [ɒ] or unrounded [ɑ]. The merger covers all of Cánada, and a belt in the U.S. beginning in western Pennsylvania and extending through central Ohio, Indiana and Illinois into Missouri and Iowa, then westward in a widening band to include Nebraska, Kansas, Wyoming, Colorado and all states west except northern Washington. The very northern inland U.S., including New York State and New England (except for a small coastal strip), keeps the distinction intact.

The history of this change doesn't appear to have been properly worked out, but it's probably not an accident that except for a small New England enclave it is wholly contained within the rhotic, partly Scots and northern HE influenced portion of the U.S. Recall that this same merger (though usually to a closer value [ɔ]) is also characteristic of modern Scots and many Ulster dialects as well (cf. §§5.7.1–2). It's at least possible that this is a heritage from that settlement.

(c) The *Mary/merry/marry* Merger. With the exception of Canada and parts of the U.S. all English dialects have a three-way contrast in this set of forms: RP /mɛərɪ/ ╪ /mɛrɪ/ ╪ /mærɪ/, etc. The three words are cover-terms for sets including quite a large number of items: thus '*Mary*' means *fair, square, staring, fairy, hairy, tearing* ...; '*merry*' means *very, bury, ferry, herald, Jerry, herring, ferro-* ...; and '*marry*' means *carry, Harry, Harold, farrow, barrow, Clara* .... The three-way contrast, usually as [ëə] vs. [ɛ] vs. [æ], is stable in the northeastern U.S., but reduced in one way or another in most of the rest of the country. There appear to be three basic merger patterns:

(1) *Mary* vs. *merry/marry*. Most commonly the vowel of *fair* in *Mary*, and that of *bet* in *merry/marry*. This occurs in western New England, upper New York State, and a good deal of the West.

(2) *marry* vs. *merry/Mary*. The last two merge under the vowel of *bet* or *fair*, while *marry* retains /æ/. This appears to characterize older Canadian speakers; younger ones show the total merger (3).

(3) *Mary/merry/marry*. Normally with the vowel of *fair* for all three, or in some areas that of *bet*. This one is widespread through much of the U.S., probably more in the West than further east.

In terms of vowel height:

(5.45)

Distinct	Merger 1	Merger 2	Merger 3
Mary	Mary	Mary ⎱	Mary ⎫
merry	merry ⎱	merry ⎰	merry ⎬
marry	marry ⎰	marry	marry ⎭

(d) The *do/dew* Merger. The later developments of ME /iu, ɛu/ have tended to be unstable, and to merge with /u:/ in a number of environments. In SBE and most other British and ET varieties (except East Anglia: §5.6.2) /iu/ has remained as /ju:/ in certain cases, so that *do/dew* are distinct as /du:/ vs. /dju:/, and the /j/ is also retained after /h/ (*hue*), after labials and velars (*music, cute*), and after /t d n/ (*tune, due, new*). Virtually all dialects have lost it after palatals (*chew*), after /r/ (*rude*) and after /Cl-/ (*blue, flew*: an exception here is Wales, §5.7.3). In many SBE varieties there is variation after /θ s l/, e.g. *enth*[ju:]*siasm* ~ *enth*[u:]*siasm*, the same with *suit, lute*. In most parts of the U.S. and Canada (except the U.S. South) /j/ is retained only after labials and velars; though there is something of a school-based normative attempt to promote /tj-/ in *tune, Tuesday* and the like. The loss of /j/ is very much, from a British point of view, an American stereotype: one useful way of representing Americans in fiction is to have them read *noospapers* and sing *toons*.

Comparing the length of English settlement in the U.S. (a bit over 350 years) with that in Britain (half a millennium or so), we might expect that U.S. dialect differentiation would be much more restricted. It's not surprising that we don't get the enormous typological range we saw in Britain (§§5.2–7); nor that by and large the isoglosses cluster most thickly in the East and become fuzzier and more diffuse toward the West, where major settlement did not begin until well into the 19th century.

There is however no easy consensus on U.S. regional dialectology, of the kind we have for Britain; scholars are not agreed even on what the major areas are and how they're divided, and there are at least two conflicting regional pictures. Until the 1940s, the received model was one with three basic regions: Eastern (basically the Northeast), Southern, encompassing both coastal and inland areas as far north as southern Ohio, Indiana and Illinois, and west to East Texas; and a vast 'General American' area covering the rest of the country:

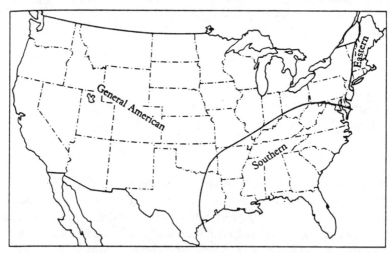

Map 11: The Older U.S. Dialect Model
[Bronstein 1960: 44]

Research in the 1940s by Hans Kurath and his collaborators suggested a radically different and more highly elaborated picture, with major isoglosses running east/west, and no 'General American'. The U.S. on this view is divided into three roughly horizontal belts, North, Midlands and South, with a NML rather more akin to the North and a SML akin to the South. This is now generally accepted in the U.S. (though with some dissenters); the older one, with its 'General American', seems to be more popular outside the U.S.: Wells (1982: ch. 6) has argued strongly for its reinstatement, though few Americans are likely to be convinced. The isoglosses in this model define differences rather smaller than the British ones, and many more of them are lexical (see below). The picture suggested is:

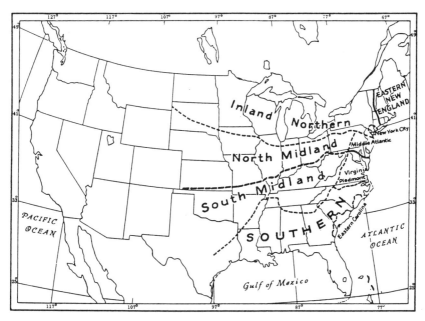

Map 12: The Newer U.S. Dialect Model
[Baugh & Cable 1978: 370]

The areas west of the main isoglosses, where the more clearly defined regions begin to peter out, show complex mixtures, due to hetero-geneous inputs from later population movements, when improved transport brought people from many different areas to the West. The westward continuations are suggested by map 13 (p.290), which takes as its point of departure the eastern seaboard and shows the main migration routes. Thus, to take one example, the extreme south of Indiana is not just SML, as map 12 shows, but more specifically a westward extension of SML area 12 – i.e. its speech is more or less continuous with that of parts of West Virginia and Kentucky.

KEY

North: 1 E New England; 2 SE New England; 3 SW New England; 4 Inland
        North; 5 Hudson Valley; 6 Metropolitan New York
Midland: (a) NML: 7 Delaware Valley (Philadelphia); 8 Susquehanna Valley;
        10 Upper Ohio Valley (Pittsburgh); 11 N West Virginia
        (b) SML: 9 Upper Potomac & Shenandoah; 12 S West Virginia & E
        Kentucky; 13 W Carolina & E Tennessee
South: 14 Delmarva (E Shore); 15 Virginia Piedmont; 16 NE North Carolina;
        17 Cape Fear & Peedee Valleys; 18 South Carolina Low Country

Map 13: A Refined Dialect Map of the Eastern U.S.
[Francis 1958: 580]

It's clear from other dialectological work that areas like the Southwest, Northwest, California, Upper Midwest, etc. also have their own
specific features; but the distinctions are not as great as in the East, and
in many cases boundaries are difficult or impossible to fix. It is in fact, I
think, this progressive dilution of strong regional character as we move
westward that accounts for the persistence of the notion 'General
American': it's not so much a dialect-type proper as an image produced
by much non-eastern, non-southern American speech in the perception
of hearers with no clear idea of the more subtle regional diagnostics.
There are no more speakers of 'General American' than there are of
'Northern English' in England; but there are enough features in common
among the local types in the area to allow the construction of a
stereotype: and 'General American' is harmless – perhaps even useful –
in this sense, as long as we don't take it as an actual variety spoken by
anybody. (I.e. it's probably a good deal less accurate than the

abstraction 'Southern British English' that we've been using throughout.)

The major U.S. regional diagnostics are complex and subtle, and I will only sketch out a few major ones here. More of them appear to be morphosyntactic or lexical than in Britain; this is probably an artifact, due to the more extensive focus on these distinctions in U.S. dialectology.

Some of the main features of the N, ML and S and the more distinctive subregions are:

(i) *North*. Here *morning*, *horse* are often distinct from *mourning*, *hoarse* (as occasionally in the coastal South), the former with the vowel of *bought*, the latter with that of *boat* (e.g. /ɔ(ː)/ vs. /oʊ/); *wash*, *wasp*, *log*, *hog* (but not *dog*) have an unrounded vowel, usually that of *calm* (normally [ɑː] or [ɑə]); *pot*, *cot* have a shorter and normally fronter nucleus [ä]. This lends to a very complex kind of distribution, with the ME /o/ category split in an entirely different pattern from anything normally observable in Mainland (or southern hemisphere ETE) dialects. Comparing RP as a Mainland representative with New York standard (my own), we find:

(5.46)

	RP	NYC
pot	ɒ	ä
pod		ɑə
calm	ɑː	

This is further complicated by the developments of ME /a/: in New York, for instance (rather typically for the North and much of the ML), it is lengthened in (generally) the same environments as in SBE (e.g. before /s θ ns/ as in *pass*, *path*, *dance*); but lengthening has failed in certain items and classes. Thus in my own dialect *can* (Aux) and *can* (N) are phonemically distinct, /kæn/ vs. /kæːn/, as they typically are in South Africa as well. The same applies to *have* with /æ/ and *halve* with /æː/. Adding this category to the above pattern, we get (5.47) on p.292.

While this general pattern of distinctions in the North is quite stable, the phonetic realizations of two of these categories have changed extensively, in a chain process generally known as the 'Northern Cities Shift' (e.g. Buffalo, Chicago, Detroit). Here the vowel of the *bat* class has raised and diphthongized, to [ɛə] or even [ɪə], and that of the *pot* class has fronted, to [a] or even [æ]. In the speech of the younger residents of Detroit and Chicago, the extent of the shift is great enough

(5.47)

	RP	NYC
pot	ɒ	ä
pod		ɑə
calm	ɑː	
fast		æː
can (N)		
can (V)	æ	æ
bat		

so that outsiders can have distinct comprehension problems: for a New Yorker, advanced Chicago *lock* is virtually identical to his *lack*, and *lack* has a vowel virtually identical to what he has in *fair*. In addition, the vowel of *bought* in the Northern Cities has been lowering and fronting, moving into the position originally occupied by *pot*. Taking the New York values as representing an older, more conservative system, the two can be related as follows:

(5.48)

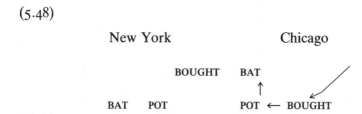

(Arrows indicate the direction of vowel-shifting.)

Other Northern features include /s/ in *grease* (V), *greasy* (S, ML /z/), final /ð/ in *with* (S, ML /θ/). The past *dove* for *dive* is also restricted to the North. Among lexical features are *pail* (S, ML *bucket*), *angleworm* 'earthworm', *clapboards* 'wooden siding' (S, ML *weatherboards*), and *darning-needle* 'dragon-fly' (older ML *snake-feeder*, S *mosquito-hawk*).

There are both rhotic and non-rhotic dialects in the North (see Map 10); the non-rhotic ones usually have linking /r/ (/r/ retained in *far and wide*) and sometimes intrusive /r/ (as in *law-r and order*: cf. §3.2.2). Among the distinctive northern subareas are:

(a) Eastern New England. Here we have frequent /a(:)/ in *fast*, *bath*, etc. (contrasting with /æ/ in *bat*), and regularly the same quality before (lost) historical /r/ in codas, as in *yard*, *car*. In this area word-final intrusive /r/ also occurs (very unusually for non-rhotic English dialects) as in *China* [tʃaɪnər], etc. (A good example of the speech of this area is that of the Kennedy family.)

(b) New York City. This is one of the most intensively studied English-speaking communities – in part because it was the site of Labov's pioneering studies in the 1960s, and has continued to be worked on intensively. Here rhoticity is variable and socially significant, with older and lower-class speakers tending to be non-rhotic, and the pronunciation of postvocalic /r/ following the typical prestige patterns of a sociolinguistic variable with respect to class and style (cf. §5.5). Non-rhoticity is older, and /r/ pronunciation seems to have begun accumulating prestige after World War II. For older and lower-class speakers, again, the *hurt* class is diagnostic: this often has [əɪ] or [ɜɪ], leading to the (erroneous) stereotype of New Yorkers merging *bird* and *Boyd* (actually [bəɪd] vs. [bɔɪd]). New York also shows marked raising and diphthongization of /ɔ:/ (*off, bought*) and the long allophones of /æ/ (*fast*) – often to the (stigmatized) extremes of [ʊə], [ɪə]. There is also variable loss of /θ ð/, with partial or complete merger with /t d/, or distinct realization as dental [t̪ d̪] as in Hiberno-English (§5.7.2).

(ii) *Midland. Morning/mourning* are never distinct; *wash, watch, hog, log* have a rounded vowel /ɒ/, sometimes raised to [ɔ] before /ʃ/, and often with inserted /r/, e.g. *wash* as /wɔrʃ/, rhyming with *Porsche; Mary/merry* merger in /ɛ/ is common. Among typical lexical items are *blinds* 'window-shades', *green beans* (N *stringbeans*, S *snap-beans*), *hull* 'to shell (beans)'; the construction type *all the further/bigger ...* etc, 'as far/big as ...' is ML, as is *a quarter till* (*the hour*), vs. N *quarter to/of* and *wait on* (N *wait for*). 'Positive *anymore*' (*things are tough anymore*: cf. §5.7.1) also occurs at least in the southern parts of the ML area.

The SML shows a number of features akin to southern ones: e.g. monophthongization of /aɪ/ (*bite*) to [a:] or lowering and shortening of the second mora, giving [a:ᵉ], [a:ᵊ]. Specifically SML lexis includes *French harp* 'harmonica' (S (*mouth*)*harp*), *redworm* 'earthworm'.

(iii) *South.* Coastally non-rhotic; the non-rhotic varieties (unusually) generally lack linking or intrusive /r/: thus [fɑ: ən nɪə] *far and near*. Some varieties even tend to delete /r/ between vowels, thus [vɛ:ɪ] *very*. In most parts of the South diphthongization of /æ/ is common, especially before alveolars: [kʰæɪnt] *can't*, [pʰæɪs] *pass*. In Eastern Virginia, the Charleston area, and parts of Georgia there is an alternation like the Canadian Diphthong Rule, giving [əɪ] in *white* vs. [ɐɪ] in *wide*, [ʌʊ] in *house* vs. [ɐʊ] in *down*; these areas also show occasional [ɜɪ] for *bird*, as in New York. Rhoticity in the South tends to have the opposite prestige value to what it has in the North, e.g. in New York: in non-rhotic areas pronunciation of postvocalic /r/ tends to be identified with rusticity or nonstandardness.

Syntactically, the South is the home of double modals and other double auxiliary constructions, e.g. *might could, used to could, used to didn't*. These are generally stigmatized except among some upperclass coastal speakers, who also have *ain't, he don't*.

For a partial summary of the complex developments sketched out in this section, we can compare two NAE vowel systems with SBE (represented by RP): a New York (NYC) and a Canadian (CE):

(5.49)

	NYC	CE	RP
bit	ɪ	ɪ	ɪ
bet	ɛ	ɛ	ɛ
bat	æ	æ	æ
can (N)	æː		
fast		æː	ɑː
calm	ɑə	ɑ(ː)	
pod			ɒ
pot	ä	ɒ	
bought	ɔə		ɔː
foot	ÿ	ʊ	ʊ
but	ə	ə	ʌ
beet	ɪi	ɪⁱ	iː
boot	ÿʊ	ʊu	uː
oat	əʊ	oᵘ	əʊ
mate	ɛɪ	eᶦ	eɪ
fair	ëə	ɛ	ɛə
bite	äɪ	əɪ	aɪ
out	æʊ	ʌʊ	aʊ
boy	ɔɪ	ɒɪ	ɒɪ

Keeping in mind what I said earlier about vowel length, the overall acoustic effects of NAE and SBE speech will generally be rather different (less for New York than Canada); [oᵛ] etc. represent diphthongs with short second elements, often nearly monophthongal in character, but not long monophthongs like Yorkshire or HE /oː/. Long vowels like CE /ɑː/ will be less apparently long in relation to shorts like /ɪ/ than would be the case with SBE generally, and /æ/ in particular may be rather long always. A few other features to note are: (a) the relatively closer *but* vowel (arguably an archaism, since this nucleus started out in ME as /u, and the lowering in SBE is post-17th-century); (b) the / / in NYC *foot*, which is unrounded (otherwise the same as [ʊ]) – a value typical for the northern and eastern U.S., but not normally reported in the literature; (c) the London-like pattern in NYC *bite, out* classes, with the front-gliding *bite* having a backer onset than the back-gliding *out*.

The New York dialect represented here has one 'extra' vowel phoneme, in common with many other U.S. varieties – a marginally contrastive segment rather like Scots '4a' (§5.7.1). This is a centralized half close front vowel [ï], distinct from /ɪ/, which appears as the stressed nucleus of *finish* (vs. /ɪ/ in *Finnish*), *just* (Adv) (vs. /ə/ in the adjective), and a few other forms. In the Americanist literature this vowel is usually represented as /ɨ/.

5.8.3 AUSTRALIA AND NEW ZEALAND

Although early geographers had claimed that human life at the Antipodes was impossible (since men living there would obviously be standing upside down), the first European visitors to the area, notably the Dutch explorer Abel Tasman in the 1640s, found thriving aboriginal populations, standing quite erect. The coastlines of Australia and New Zealand were extensively explored during the next century and a half, but it was not until near the end of the 18th century that the first English-speaking settlers arrived. The occasion was the establishment of a British penal colony near Botany Bay (what is now Sydney): the First Fleet, bearing about 1500 migrants, half convicts and half military personnel and officials, landed at Sydney Cove in January 1788.

By the time transportation was abolished in 1851, something like 160,000 convicts had been sent to Australia; up to the 1850s a majority of the population consisted of convicts, 'Emancipists' (freed convicts), 'Currency Lads and Lasses' (the children of convicts), and their descendants. In 1819, some 75% of the New South Wales population were convicts and their progeny, and later in the century one estimate gives these percentages for all of the country:

(5.50)

	% Convicts, etc.	% Free Immigrants
1828	87	13
1841	63	37
1851	59	41

So for something over sixty years, more than half the total settlement was of convict stock; and the majority of the convicts were working class, and from London and environs. This means that the major component of the emerging AusE was a southeastern English urban vernacular (and indeed early commentators remark on the similarities between AusE and Cockney – a point I will return to). The convicts and their descendants for a long time constituted a rather homogeneous and closed, or at least inward-looking, society: both because of their origins, and the natural solidarity that 'marginal' social position leads to, and because of the attitudes of both Government and free immigrants, who not unexpectedly were unenthusiastic about free social mixing.

The second component of the emerging dialect was the speech of the free immigrants: in addition then to a London-type vernacular there was a large input of standard SBE (RP and its ancestors), spoken by officials and the upper echelons of the military, and the wealthier and more upper- (or at least middle-) class free settlers; as well of course as other regional and class dialects, including in later periods American. There was also a large Irish element, though whether this left any significant traces is debatable (I am not very happy with most of the examples in Trudgill 1986 that purport to be HE). New Zealand, though, certainly had a large Scots input, which may have left relics in a tendency to maintain the /w̥/:/w/ opposition (*which*: *witch*), and the use of *will* as in *will I turn out the light*? as opposed to *shall/should I* ...?, which is otherwise restricted to Scotland.

The post-Sydney settlement was quite different from that in the U.S. Rather than a steady movement or series of migration waves in particular directions, pushing a receding frontier, there were scattered settlements, many based on a kind of 'plantation' system, with individuals (frequently immigrants from England) being given land grants, and having large numbers of convict labourers 'assigned' to them. This meant that from the outset internal migrations were multidirectional, and that both the convict and free populations were easily and unpredictably mobile. This internal mobility was increased in the 19th century by a series of gold rushes (in the 1850s to Victoria and New South Wales, in the 1860s to New Zealand, and in the 1890s to Western Australia). One result of this pattern is a lack of major, clearly defined regional distinctions in both AusE and NZE – though of course there is quite a bit of variation at the lexical level, very much like the U.S. (§4.8.2).

The colonization of New Zealand was largely Australian-based; linguistically it is an Australian colony in much the same way as Canada is a U.S. colony. In 1792 sealers first set up small enclaves on the South

Island, and there was a steady stream of missionaries, as usual where there are aboriginal populations ripe for conversion. But New Zealand did not become a separate colony until the Treaty of Waitangi with the Maoris in 1840.

Structurally (in terms of the number of phonemic contrasts, and the general deployment of phonemes in lexical classes), all Aus/NZ systems are virtually in one-to-one correspondence with SBE (London or RP), though the phonetic realizations are often markedly different – if closer to London than to RP. There are a few differences however in the apportionment of particular lexical items to phoneme classes, which we will look at below. Comparing the short vowel systems of standard 'General' Australian, standard New Zealand, London vernacular and RP, we find:

(5.51)

	Aus	NZ	Lon	RP
bit	ɪ̣	ï	ɪ	ɪ
bet	e	e~ë	e	ɛ
bat	æ̣~ɛ	ɛ	æ̣~ɛ	æ
foot	ʊ	ʊ	ʊ	ʊ
pot	ɒ	ɒ	ɒ	ɒ
but	ä	ä	ä	ʌ

(The symbols [ɪ̣], [æ̣] represent closer or raised variants: i.e. a somewhat [i]-like [ɪ] and a somewhat [ɛ]-like [æ].)

The vowels of the *bat*, *bet* classes are considerably higher than anywhere in the Northern Hemisphere: closer even than the most vernacular London. This feature is shared with South Africa, and may reflect an earlier southern English vernacular type. Raised /æ/, indicated by spellings in novels like *keb* for *cab*, was a 19th-century Cockney stereotype, and /ɛ/ for ME /a/ is widespread in southeastern traditional dialect, especially in Essex, Kent, and Surrey. The NZ nuclei are closer than the Australian, and *bet* tends to be markedly centralized, approaching [ɪ]: for outsiders, Aus/NZ *bat* is likely to be confused with their *bet*, and *bet* with their *bit*. The very central NZ *bit* vowel is probably the result of a chain shift of the short front vowels (see the discussion of the SA chain shift in §4.8.4). The very front and open *but* vowel is also London-like, and – historically – is quite advanced: given the history of ME /u/ (cf. §3.10, and §4.8.3 on U.S. *but*), it's likely that the closer the realization, the older the pronunciation type it represents.

297

The long vowels and diphthongs:

(5.52)

	Aus	NZ	Lon	RP
beet	ïi~əɪ	ïi	ïi	iː
boot	ʊɵ	ɵː	ɵː	uː
mate	æɪ~äɪ	æɪ~äɪ	äɪ	eɪ
oat	äʊ	äʊ	äʊ	əʊ
bite	ɑɪ~ɒɪ	ɑɪ	ɑɪ	aɪ
out	æʊ	æʊ	æʊ	aʊ
bought	ɔː	ɔː	oː	ɔː
fast	aː	aː	ɑː	ɑː
hurt	ɜː~ïː	œː~øː	ɜː	ɜː
fair	eə~eː	eə~ɪə	eə	ɛə
poor	ʊə~ɔː	ʊə~ɔː	ʊə~oː	ʊə
boy	ɔɪ	ɔɪ	ɔɪ	ɒɪ

The comparison makes it clear that – as we've seen from the discussion of North American English – we can't really characterize ETEs (or any other dialects for that matter) as wholly 'conservative' or 'innovating'. While Aus/NZ show innovatory qualities in *beet, boot, mate, oat, bite/out* and *hurt*, they have archaic /aː/ in *fast*, as against the later London/ RP /ɑː/ (§5.6.1). The following points are worth noting: (i) the 'crossover' of the first elements of the *bite/out* diphthongs (cf. §5.6.2 on Birmingham and London, §5.8.2 on New York, and §5.8.4 on South African); (ii) markedly diphthongal *beet, boot*, with centralized first elements; in some AusE varieties both elements of *boot* are unrounded, and instead of the [ʊɵ] above, we get [ïɯ], i.e. a half-close rather central starting point, moving to a close back unrounded vowel ([ɯ] = [u] without lip-rounding); (iii) lowered and centralized first morae in *mate, oat*: the former is of course responsible for the jocular name *Strine* for AusE: since /l/ is often deleted in the cluster /lj/ (as in *million, Australian*), this is a reasonable respelling. We might also mention (iv) the divergent developments in *hurt*: raising to [ïː] in AusE, and rounding in NZ (this is also the SA norm, and is widespread and increasing in non-RP southern English).

Another vowel feature is the unstressed nucleus in *city*, *happy*, etc.: Aus/NZE and London – along with all ETEs except some southern U.S. dialects – have the *beet* vowel here; RP, alone in the South, has that of *bit*.

Some lexical distributions in AusE are rather different from the usual SBE ones; one in particular appears to represent an earlier state of affairs. While ME /a/ before /f θ s/ is uniformly lengthened (e.g. /aː/ in *laugh*, *path*, *fast*), there is vacillation before nasal plus consonant: many Australians have the short *bat* vowel in *dance*, *plant*, *demand*, etc. This can even be a social and regional marker: South Australia has /aː/ in *dance*, etc., while Sydney has the *bat* nucleus: and the long vowel is considered 'posh' or 'affected' by some speakers. (The NZ distribution is much more like SBE, except for a short vowel in *-graph*.)

Australian accents are traditionally divided into three groups: Cultivated, General and Broad, in order of increasing distance from RP and increasing local uniqueness. The main distinguishers are the vowels in *beet*, *boot*, *mate*, *oat*, *out*, which in Broad are often described as 'slower' diphthongs than in the other varieties – i.e. with longer (and sometimes lower) first elements: thus [əːɪ] in *beet*, [əːʉ] in *boot*, etc. Cultivated AusE is phonetically more RP-like, e.g. often lacking the *bite/out* crossover, and having [ɪi] rather than [ïi] or [əɪ] in *beet*.

Among other phonetic features we might note that in both Aus/NZE /l/ tends to be dark in all positions (definitely not a London or SBE feature), though syllable-final /l/ is often vocalized to [o] as in London (cf. §5.6.2). Tapping of intervocalic /t/ is also very common, both within the word and across word boundaries (cf. §3.2.4).

Many of the diagnostic features of Aus/NZE – including the range of degrees of 'broadness' – stem from the rather complex way the original inputs have interacted. If we compare standard Aus/NZE with nonstandard London, we note that many originally (and still) vernacular features have been incorporated into the ET standards: the nonstandard inputs have contributed significantly to the formation of all ET social varieties. This is characteristic of ETE formation (if more perhaps of the southern than the northern varieties); in Australia and New Zealand (as well as in South Africa, but with special complications) we might envisage the growth of the new varieties something like (5.53). The broken lines represent continuing influence; in this case an external 'prestige focus' which maintains a kind of pressure toward a non-local norm on the upper reaches of the ET standard, and a vernacular 'influence from below' producing pressure in the opposite direction. The result is that the highest-class local standards are somewhat RP-like – if less so than speakers either feel that they are or ought to be; and this leads to a normative tradition, especially strong in the better schools, tending to stigmatize anything local,

(5.53)

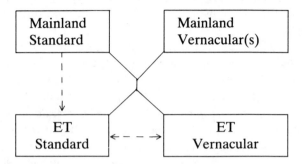

and holding up some kind of SBE norms as desirable (if in the end impossible) to imitate. (I will return to this in §5.8.4.)

There are few if any major grammatical features characterizing Aus/ NZE: the most clearcut diagnostics are lexical. In both countries the settlers came into contact with speakers of aboriginal languages, and this led to a certain amount of borrowing – if less than one might have expected. Some of these loans have passed into English generally (cf. §2.11): e.g. Australian *kangaroo*, *koala*, *wombat*, *budgerigar*, NZ *kiwi*, *moa*; but many are strictly or nearly strictly local, such as Aus *woomera* 'throwing stick', *yakka* 'work', *gunya* 'hut', NZ *pakeha* 'white man', *haka* 'war dance', *whare* 'small house, hut'.

Many of the other lexical differences involve changes in the sense or sense-range of particular (general English) words: e.g. *crook* 'ill/angry', *wog* 'gastrointestinal upset', *mob* 'flock, herd', *paddock* 'field', *creek* 'stream, small river' (but see below), *gully* 'valley' (NZ), *section* 'building plot' (NZ). There are also of course new formations like *outback*, *bach* (homophonous to *batch*) 'holiday cottage' (NZ), and numerous local slang terms that are now familiar abroad, but still stereotypically Antipodean, like *chunder* 'vomit', *Pom* 'Englishman', *sheila* 'girl'.

Some of the sense changes seem to be related to the largely urban background of the original settlers: the vocabulary for geographical features, for instance, has become restricted, so that terms like *brook*, *stream*, *rivulet* are not used, but the field is partitioned into *river* (relatively large) and *creek* (relatively small). Most authorities claim that the Aus/NZ sense of *creek* (as opposed to the usual British sense 'inlet') is a specifically Australasian innovation; but in fact 'stream'/'rivulet' is the normal (pretty much the only) U.S. interpretation as well. America is full of landlocked creeks, and I never knew that a creek was supposed to be an inlet until in the course of research for this book I read some material on Australian English where it isn't.

5.8.4 SOUTH AFRICA

The first European settlers in what is now South Africa were the Dutch. In 1652, under commission from the Dutch East India Company, Jan van Riebeeck set up a refreshment station and garden near Table Bay, the site of what is now Cape Town. It was designed to provide food, wine and postal services to ships on the Java-Holland run, but developed in time, against the wishes of the Company, into a colony. The English involvement dates from nearly a century and a half later; there was an established Dutch colony there when they arrived, and this has had significant implications for the development of South African English.

During the 18th century Britain had contemplated establishing a presence in southern Africa, but little had come of it; the Dutch East India Company had more or less complete control of the Cape sea route, and the Cape Colony was a trading monopoly run by agents of a foreign power. By the late 1770s, after the loss of America, the British were looking for new colonial sources of raw materials, and a way of stemming the tide of emigration to the United States; they also felt a need for a distant penal colony (Pitt in 1785 had suggested Algoa Bay in the Eastern Cape, but Sydney won), and a refreshment station for the merchant fleet.

An opportunity came in 1795, when it appeared necessary to counter French influence in the East, i.e. by closing off the Cape route. The British thereupon occupied the Cape, but did not set up a real colony; and in 1802 they returned it to Holland. But war with France erupted again, and the British recaptured the Cape in 1806, and remained until 1812. After the fall of Napoleon, Britain received the Cape as part of the spoils of the Congress of Vienna (1814), and from then till the establishment in 1910 of the Union of South Africa as a self-governing dominion there was a British governmental presence; South Africa retained at least some official ties with Britain until it left the Commonwealth in 1960 and became a republic.

During the early period there was relatively little permanent British settlement; the greater part of the Anglophone population increase was probably due to natural causes at work among resident officialdom and military personnel. At this point the British, except for residential enclaves like Cape Town, were essentially occupiers of a country whose European minority was mostly Dutch- (later Afrikaans-: see below) speaking, and whose indigenous majority was mainly Bantu-speaking (as it still is).

In 1819, Parliament, spurred on by a recession at home, continuous loss of emigrants to the U.S., and difficult frontier conditions in South Africa, authorized a settlement plan for the Eastern Cape. The purpose was, among other things, to establish a good-sized colony along the

Great Fish River as a buffer between the Xhosa and the English military – as well as a self-replenishing source of bodies for informal militias or 'commandos'. The settlement plan was based on assisted passage for emigrants, with land grants available at the end of a period of indentureship. In 1820 a group of between 4000 and 5000 settlers arrived in the Eastern Cape, and these were to form the nucleus of an emerging South African English community.

While the majority of the 1820 Settlers were probably from the Southeast of England, the urban – and in particular London – component was not dominant the way it was in Australia (§5.8.3); a large proportion of the immigrants were of rural rather than urban working-class origins, and there is evidence suggesting a fairly important component from the West Country.

In 1848 and onwards there was another wave of immigration, this time into Natal; these settlers were to a large extent of upper or middle class background, many of them retired officers and aristocrats down on their luck. Yet a third wave came later in the 19th century, with the discovery of diamonds and gold; this later influx, peaking in the last quarter of the century, brought many immigrants from London and other parts of the British Isles, as well as from the U.S. and Europe – but the effect of these later migrations on the development of SA English has been relatively slight: the outlines were fixed earlier.

The two basic formative elements of modern SAE were – oversimply – the largely vernacular Eastern Cape settlement of the 1820s, and the largely standard-speaking Natal settlement of the 1840s. The later immigrants eventually adopted the local range of ETEs that had been developed in the crucial half-century from 1820. The historical picture is, in outline, not dissimilar to the Australian one (though see below on language contact); and it bears some resemblance in social terms as well. There is still a strong normative tradition in South Africa, with its roots in the 19th-century vernacular/standard divide: even to the extent of a not uncommon lay use of the terms 'South African English' and 'Standard English' (= RP or SBE generally) as antonyms. One result of this can be seen in the relative valuation of accent types in the media: newsreaders, anchor-men and compères on the more prestigious channels tend to speak RP or quasi-RP, or what is called 'Conservative' SAE – an RP-focussed and minimally regional variety; while announcers on pop stations can be more local. Similarly with commercials: the more up-market ones are RP or Conservative, while those for down-market products have a more local flavour.

The developmental picture of SAE is complicated in a way not true of other ETEs in that there has been, from the beginning, extensive and intimate contact with another language: Afrikaans. (It's not entirely clear when Dutch 'became' Afrikaans, but it was well on its way during the 18th century; though the name Afrikaans did not come into full currency until late in the 19th century, we can assume that the most significant contacts, starting in the 1820s, were with it rather than Mainland Dutch.) There have also been contacts with indigenous languages (Bantu, Khoi-San), but these have left little beyond a scatter of lexical items.

In the 19th century, Afrikaans-speakers leaving the areas of British domination established the two 'Boer Republics' (Orange Free State and Transvaal); with the Union in 1910, these and the Cape and Natal came under a single government. From the beginning (despite attempts like Lord Charles Somerset's proclamation in 1822 of English as the only official language in the Cape), the country has been essentially bilingual: not in the sense that all individuals are, but that at least virtually all native-born English speakers have some knowledge of Afrikaans (if mainly as the result of doing it in school), and most Afrikaans speakers have some control of English. According to one recent survey, only 9.6% of first-language English speakers consider themselves fully bilingual, while 13.5% of Afrikaans speakers do; almost twice as many English speakers (22.4%) reported no competence in the other official language as Afrikaans speakers (12.9%).

Today both languages have official status; broadcasting, parliamentary debates and official forms are bilingual, and the level of exposure of English speakers to Afrikaans is relatively high. Because of a complex set of sociohistorical factors the degree of bilingualism and mutual exposure is still highest at the lower end of the socio-economic spectrum; this has an effect in that it is there that Afrikaans influence appears to be greatest.

As in AusE, the scholarly consensus is that there are three broad, general varieties: Conservative, Respectable, and Extreme, to use the terminology of Lanham (1978). These names do not of course refer to monolithic types: they are sections of a subtle continuum (as is indeed the case with the three Australian social types as well), and many of the differences, as is often the case, are reflected not in categorical features ('dialect X has sound [Y]'), but in patterns of variation ('dialect X has greater frequency of [Y] than dialect Z'): on this problem see the discussion in §5.5. But overall we can say that Conservative SAE is, like Cultivated AusE, relatively non-local and RP (or SBE) focussed; Respectable covers a range of standard but fully local varieties; and Extreme is generally nonstandard and to one degree or another stigmatized. Respectable SAE is probably the best reference accent for the country in general.

The short vowel system is very like that of NZE:

(5.54)

bit	ï
bet	e~ë
bat	æ~ɛ
foot	ʊ
pot	ɒ
but	ä~ɜ

The superficial similarities are however overridden by some complex allophonic variation, especially with respect to the *bit* vowel. For most Respectable speakers, the norm is a centralized [ï]; but in certain environments it has quite different realizations. Initially, after /h/, and next to velars and palato-alveolars it is fronter and occasionally closer, virtually identical to RP [ɪ]: e.g. [ɪ] in *it, hit, kit* vs. [ï] in *bit, sit, fit*. Thus (uniquely in English, as far as I know) *it*: *bit*, *hit*: *sit* are very obvious non-rhymes. Before /l/ in syllable codas (*fill, milk*) there is a very retracted [ÿ], so that to outsiders *fill/full*, *bill/bull* may sound like homophones (though the latter members of these pairs are distinguished by slight lip rounding). In this same context the *bet* and *bat* vowels are quite lowered and centralized.

The basic qualities of the three short front vowels probably derive from a very complex 19th-century chain shift (as the NZ seem to do from a later one): the principle can be seen if we represent the relative positions of RP *bit, bet, bat* (lower case below) and their SAE equivalents (in caps):

(5.55)

bit	BIT
BET	
bet	
BAT	
bat	

If RP represents an older state of affairs, then *bet, bat* have moved 'one up', and *bit* 'one back'. The internal chronology and mechanism of the shift are obscure, but it seems likely that what triggered it in the first place was the presence of SAE-type variants in the Eastern Cape input dialects. Raised *bet* and *bat* are well attested in the 19th century in the SE of England, and centralized *bit* is especially common in the West Country, though it occurs in Kent and other areas as well according to the SED.

The most likely scenario is this: the three innovative realizations, scattered as variables among the dialects in the Settler community, were accepted as 'basic'; from being variants they were 'recodified' into new, institutionalized norms, which became the basis for both standard and vernacular SAE. For instance: say one of the input dialects has [æ] for *bat*, and [ɛ] for *bet*, and borrows [ɛ] for *bat*. This could well trigger a raising of *bet* to [e], to 'prevent' merger of the two classes (on the assumption that a dialect may have a 'preferred spacing' of its vowels). The raising of *bet* would then trigger centralization of *bit*, since the new [e] quality is close enough to [ɪ] to exert a 'repelling force', if the distances are to be kept roughly as they were before. In fact, a little reflection will show that the introduction of any of the three new qualities into an RP-type system could be sufficient to trigger the sort of chain shift we have (what Susan Wright and I have called a 'stabilizing chain': Lass & Wright 1985, 1986).

The allophonic range of /ɪ̈/ is more extensive in Extreme SAE: here the fronter [ɪ] that appears initially, etc. in Respectable is replaced by a close front [i], so that e.g. *bit* and *hit* are even further apart, [bɪ̈t] vs. [hit], and the *hit* nucleus is qualitatively rather similar to the long *beet* vowel [iː].

The long vowels and diphthongs:

(5.56)

fast	ɑː
beet	iː
boot	ʉː
mate	eɪ~ɛɪ
oat	œʊ~œɤ
bite	aɪ~aː
out	ɑɤ
bought	oː
hurt	œː~ø̈ː
fair	eː
poor	ʊə
boy	ɔɪ

There is none of the London/Aus/NZ diphthongization in *beet, boot*; the *mate* vowel tends to be rather RP-like, and *boot* is central. The *oat* nucleus starts at a rounded, centralized half-open to half-close position, and in many upper middle class accents unrounds at the end. Note also the frequent monophthongization of *bite*, and the unrounded second mora in *out*.

The variety portrayed in (5.56) is what might be called Posher Respectable; it is distinctly upper-middle class, clearly local, but not at all tilted towards RP norms. Within the range of Respectable accents we also find less posh types, which would for instance have an opener and/or more retracted *mate* vowel [æɪ~ɜɪ], and a mild 'crossover' in *bite/out*: while the posh variety has a front onglide (if any) in *bite*, and a back one in *out*, many standard speakers will have [ɑɪ], [aʊ]. Virtually all non-Conservative speakers have a close London-like [oː] in *bought*, and monophthongal *fair*; monophthongization of *here* is also widespread, but seems to be commoner lower down the scale.

In the Extreme varieties more London-like (as well as Afrikaans-like: see below) features appear: [ɑɪ] in *bite* vs. [æʊ] ~ [ɛʊ] in *out*, [äʊ] ~ [ʌʊ] in *boat*, [äɪ] ~ [ʌɪ] in *mate*. Also (non-London) [ɒː] in *fast*.

As in the other ETEs, all varieties of SAE have the long *beet* vowel in the unstressed syllable of *happy*, *pity*, etc., often with full length and secondary stress, so that the contour of *pity* is like that of *pithead*, not *pitted* (i.e. -*y* constitutes a separate foot: cf. the discussion of *rabbi* vs. *rabbit* in §3.4).

Standard SAE is non-rhotic, though variable rhoticity does appear in some Extreme varieties. Linking /r/ (§3.2.2) is much rarer than in other non-rhotic dialects, and intrusive /r/ is virtually unknown. This appears to be tied in with a specifically SA development of a tendency common elsewhere in English: in many varieties, word-initial vowels (especially under primary stress) are preceded by a glottal stop; in SAE [ʔ] occurs before non-prominent vowels as well, and behaves like any other consonant in blocking linking. The following extracts from casual conversation on a radio show will illustrate this: glottal stops indicated; *r* = deleted /r/; r‿V = linking /r/; V̆ = a very low prominence or reduced vowel; V́ = very prominent vowel:

(5.57)

   i.   that is whe*r*e ʔĬ réally got hooked
   ii.   belíeve it o*r* not ... ʔI taught ʔÉnglish
  iii.   so that ʔĬ have no interest in ʔánything else
  iv.   fo*r* ʔănothe*r* one
   v.   the letters of ʔáll of ʔŏu*r* names
  vi.   ŏ*r* their ʔáttitude
 vii.   my bróther‿and I used to go ʔóver

This may relate to another local feature: the lack of distinct allomorphs of the definite article before consonants and vowels (in all varieties) and of the indefinite article in Extreme SAE. Thus [ðə ʔáðə] *the other* just like [ðə máðə] *the mother*, Extreme [əʔɛpət] *a(n) apple*.

In Conservative and Respectable varieties /r/ is usually a post-alveolar approximant as in most SBE; in Extreme it tends to be a tap or even a trill in some contexts – though these realizations are not unknown in the more standard forms. One consonantal variable that is particularly important as a social marker is aspiration of voiceless stops: Extreme SAE, like the English of first-language Afrikaans speakers, tends to lack aspiration; this may be a borrowing from Afrikaans.

Because of its long contact history (not only with Afrikaans but with indigenous languages, Portuguese, and various Indian languages) SAE has a lexicon extraordinarily rich in 'exotic' loans – i.e. forms unknown outside South Africa. A sample of items in common use will give some idea of the extent of this borrowing; the bulk are from Afrikaans, which I list first:

ag /äx/ 'oh'; *bakkie* /bäki:/ 'pickup truck'; *boep* /bʊp/ 'paunch'; *braai* /braɪ/ 'barbecue'; *brak* /bräk/ 'mongrel dog'; *broeks* /brʊks/ 'underpants'; *dassie* /dási:/ 'hyrax'; *doek* /dʊk/ 'scarf'; *hanepoot* /há:nəpʊət/ 'Muscadet grape/wine'; *kak* /käk/ 'shit'; *kappie* /kápi:/ 'sunbonnet, circumflex accent'; *kloof* /klʉːf ~ klʊəf/ 'ravine'; *mealies* /mí:li:z/ 'maize'; *naartjie* /ná:(r)tʃi:/ 'tangerine/clementine/satsuma'; *platteland* /plátəlänt/ 'rural areas'; *poep* /pʊp/ 'fart'; *sies* /sïs/ 'ugh!'; *skolly* /skóli:/ 'hoodlum'; *spanspek* /spá:nspek/ 'canteloupe'; *steen* /stɪən ~ sti:n/ 'Chenin blanc'; *stoep* /stʊp/ 'verandah'; *vetkoek* /fétkʊk/ 'unsweetened doughnut'; *voetsek ~ voetsak* /fútsək/ 'bugger off'; *voetstoots* /fútstòəts/ 'as it stands' (of property for sale); *vlei* /fleɪ/ 'pond, shallow lake'; *witblits* /vïtblïts/ 'home-distilled spirit' (lit. 'white lightning').

From Bantu languages (mainly Zulu and Xhosa) we have among others *amandla* 'power', *bundu* 'outback, wilderness', *fundi* 'expert', *lobola* 'bride-price', *muti* 'herbal medicine, magical potion' (often generalized to 'medicine', e.g. *cough muti*), *sangoma* 'witch-doctor', *songololo* 'millipede'. The contribution from Khoi languages is small, but includes two very common items: *dagga* /dáxä/ 'cannabis', and *gogga* /xóxä/ 'bug, creepie-crawlie'.

The transcriptions given above reflect the commonest pronunciations, in which Afrikaans phonemes are represented by what are apparently the closest English ones: thus /ʊ/ is usual for Afr short /u/, and the *but* vowel for Afr /ɐ/: though some speakers apparently have a distinct or partially distinct /ɐ/, which may overlap with some realizations of /ä/, for use specifically in loanwords. The pronunciation of many loans, how-

307

ever, also depends on other factors: e.g. the degree of competence the speaker has in Afrikaans, the other participants in a conversation, style, and so forth. This is especially clear with Afrikaans phonemes that have no very close equivalents in English, such as /œi/, e.g. in place-name elements like *Buite(n)*- 'outer'; there is a street in Cape Town called *Buitengracht Street*, and I have heard English speakers pronounce the first element /beɪtn̩-/ (perhaps the commonest) and /bœitn̩-/, and even /bjɵːtn̩-/; but the *-gracht* part is always /-xrᴁxt/: /x/ is one foreign segment that is virtually never 'Anglicized', and /x/ can be said to be a full member of the SAE consonant system in all varieties.

The more colloquial registers of SAE frequently incorporate Afrikaans expressions in their entirety, like *môre is nog 'n dag* 'tomorrow's another day', *alles sal regkom* 'everything will come out right', as well as loan-translations like *we'll make a plan* 'we'll organize something' (*ons sal 'n plan maak*). Many SAE lexical items in fact are calques, especially plant and animal names: *stinkwood* < *stinkhout*, *yellowwood* < *geelhout*, *baboon spider* (a large hairy wolf spider) < *bobbejaan spinnekop*; and Afrikaans animal names that are untranslated are usually pronounced (roughly) as in the original, which is often surprising to foreigners who know the names with English pronunciations: e.g. *gemsbok* /xémsbɒk/, *eland* /fəlänt/, *quagga* /kwáxä/.

There are also a number of (non-borrowed) items that seem to be peculiar to SAE: *bond* 'mortgage', *robot* 'traffic light', *takkies* (~ *tackies*) 'sneakers, tennis-shoes', *stand* 'building plot'.

Grammatically, SAE shows two features connected with the tense/aspect system and one connected with the modal verbs which are unique to SA, and appear to have a complex connection with Afrikaans. The first is an alternative progressive with *busy* + V-*ing*; this construction is an old one in English, and occurs in most varieties now as a marked progressive (*don't bother me, I'm busy working/reading/shaving*); in SAE however it can be used as an unmarked progressive (*what are you doing? I'm busy reading*); but more interestingly, it can be used with verbs that have no inherent sense of 'busy-ness' or activity: e.g. *I'm busy relaxing*. While the construction itself is English, the use as an unmarked progressive, especially with non-action verbs, seems to be influenced by a parallel construction in Afrikaans, which is used in precisely this way: Afr *ek is besig om te ontspan* = *I'm busy relaxing*.

The second time-related feature involves the range of temporal contexts in which the adverb *now* can be used, and one unique construction involving it. In non-SA English, *now* refers to the immediate present (*I'm doing it now*), or with perfect, to the immediate and present-relevant past (cf. §4.5.2), as in *I've (just) now done it*. If it's used with future reference, this can only be immediate: *now I'll put the spices into the pan* (in reference to a self-narrated exposition of cooking, for example). But in SAE, the range of both *now* and the modified *just now* have been extended into a much larger slice of future time, in a way that is quite opaque to speakers of other varieties.

So for instance, *I'll do it now* means 'I'll do it in the (reasonably near) future', not 'instantly'. So if one asks a South African to do something, and he says *I'll do it now*, and then returns to whatever he was doing before, he's not in fact being rude; *now* has a different sense. A more immediate future is specified by *just now*, which is more or less equivalent to *presently*, *shortly* (note that while there's a marginal future *now* in other dialects, there is definitely not a future *just now*). If even more immediate future reference is required, the reduplication *now-now* (with compound stress) is available. Thus future time is covered by *now* in the following way:

(5.58)

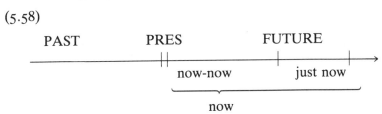

Reduplications like this are definitely not an English word-formation type, but they are productive in Afrikaans: *nou-nou* 'right now' (also with future sense, which is probably the source of *now-now*), *plek-plek* 'scattered, in places' (lit. 'place-place'), *tien-tien* 'in groups of ten' (lit. 'ten-ten'), etc. Afrikaans also has *net nou* as a marker of immediate future, and there seems little doubt that these constructions have influenced the English usage.

A final SAE peculiarity is the loss of obligative force in the deontic (cf. §4.5.3) reading of the modal verb *must*: it is generally equivalent to *should*, *shall* in other dialects: e.g. *what must I wear tonight?* = *what shall/should I wear tonight?*

CHAPTER 5: NOTES AND REFERENCES

Throughout this chapter I have deliberately stuck pretty much to structural and historical description of regional varieties of English, with very little discussion (mainly in §§5.5–6) of social variation and its implications. The reasons for this are laid out in §5.1: regional type is the input to social variation, and one has to draw the line somewhere. Readers of a politically 'committed' cast of mind will miss in this chapter any discussion of what might be called 'language politics' –

except for a few snide remarks in §5.7 on the British treatment of Celtic speakers. Issues of current concern like standard vs. nonstandard English in the schools, language as a means of social 'control', nonstandardness and disadvantage, language and ethnicity, racism/sexism/classism in language and language teaching, etc. have been deliberately avoided. Although my own general political stance and sympathies might be inferrable from self-indulgent remarks scattered here and there in the text, they are of no importance: this book is not intended to be 'engaged' in any direction, left or right. It is primarily about a language and its varieties and history as 'objects of contemplation', and about the application of techniques of linguistic description and analysis to these objects. The reader who is interested in the sociopolitical implications of varietal differences in English would do well to look at chs. 25–6, 32–3 in Trudgill (1984) for the U.K. and chs. 17–23 in Fergusson & Heath (1981) for the U.S. These and their bibliographies furnish a good start on current thinking on these matters.

5.1 The best overall introduction to dialectology is Chambers & Trudgill (1980); difficult and at times idiosyncratic, but sophisticated and well worth the trouble. For introductory treatment of the issues raised here, Hughes & Trudgill (1979: chs. 1–3). On the development of English dialectology, Wakelin (1972a: chs. 1–3). On 'Jewish English' see the interesting discussion in Gold (1981).

5.2 On boundaries and isoglosses, Chambers & Trudgill (chs. 7–8) give a somewhat untraditional and critical account; for more conventional views Wakelin as above, and Bloomfield (1933: ch. 19). On SW fricative voicing and its history, Fisiak (1984) and his references; this paper has a particularly nice set of maps showing isogloss recession.

5.3 For traditional dialect and boundaries in England, and the motivation and procedures of the SED, Wakelin (1972a) and the abbreviated but rich treatment in Wakelin (1984), with better maps. Wakelin was one of the original fieldworkers, and his (1972a) is a classic of this approach. The SED 'Basic Materials' (edited questionnaire responses by county) are available (see bibliography under Orton and various co-authors), and there is an index and introduction (Orton 1962). Some material is now in atlas format (Orton *et al.* 1978, Kolb *et al.* 1979); there are also a number of SED-based studies in Wakelin (1972b).

5.4 The regional divisions are traditional: see Wakelin (1972a: ch. 5, 1984). For the GVS in the North, Lass (1976: ch. 2). Material on *thou* and *be* from my own sampling of the SED. For some excellent work on the syntax of traditional dialects and an assessment of its importance Ihalainen (1985, 1986).

5.5 The literature on variation study and urban sociolinguistics is enormous; for a good account Chambers & Trudgill (chs. 9–11). There is an introductory treatment of phonological variation and its relation to change in Lass (1984b: §§12.4.5, 13.4). The tradition of 'variationist' dialect study stems from the work of William Labov and his followers (Labov 1963 is perhaps the earliest 'classic' paper, and see also Labov 1966). In Britain the tradition has been carried on, often with innovative methodology, in many important studies; for a monograph-length treatment Trudgill (1974). See also the papers in Trudgill (1978).

The role of variation in 'vernacular' communities has been studied in detail, especially the use of nonstandard forms as indices of 'solidarity': see L. Milroy (1980) on Belfast, and Cheshire (1982) on Reading.

5.6.1 Here and elsewhere in this book there may be a problem for readers without first-hand acquaintance with British English: exactly how does RP differ from other southern types? Actually the differences are becoming smaller, and younger RP speakers are shifting away from older norms. For some discussion see Gimson (1984); the best description of varieties of RP is Wells (1982: §§2.1–2, 3.1–2, ch. 4), which gives a lot of fine detail; a more pedagogical approach is taken in Gimson (1962). Among the diagnostics we can note final [ɪ] (not [i(:)]) in *city*, *happy*; and realization of foot-initial /iː uː/ before vowels as [ɪ ʊ:] rather than [iː uː]: *seer*[sɪ:ə], *doing* [dʊ:ɪŋ], and even across word boundaries as in *three o'clock* [θrì: ə klók]. The embedding of RP in the sociolinguistic continuum in Britain (and to some extent in Australia and South Africa) is enormously complex. The rather monolithic assumption of a 'unitary' RP (rather than in fact a complex dialect-cluster with its own internal structure) is a gross, if serviceable, oversimplification. The best overall treatment I know of the origins, development, social status and function of RP is Honey (1985), which has a rich bibliography as well.

5.6.2 The regional coverage is sketchy, and designed only to highlight some major features. General characterizations are based on my own experience with these areas, with help from Wells (1982: vol. II), Hughes & Trudgill, Trudgill (1978), Lodge (1984). For references for each area see Wells. Further: on West Yorkshire Petyt (1985); on Merseyside Knowles (1978); on Cockney Sivertsen (1960). There is a summary outline of modern regional variation in Wells (1984).

5.7.1 For Scotland today the best introduction is Romaine (1982a), with an excellent bibliography. On 'Scots' vs. 'English' and the uses of literary Scots, McClure (1974b, 1979), Aitken (1984b). For Scots phonology Abercrombie (1979), Aitken (1984a); on 'Aitken's Law' Aitken (1981), Lass (1974). Social variation in Scots is discussed in Romaine; see also Aitken (1984a, b). For a larger-scale sociolinguistic study, Macaulay (1977) on Glasgow; other good studies are Reid (1978), Romaine (1978).

The Linguistic Survey of Scotland, based at Edinburgh University, is in process of publishing an atlas (see Mather & Speitel 1975, 1977). Quotations: Douglas from Coldwell (1964), Boyd from Scott (1970), Fergusson from the 1851 edition, McDiarmid from Scott, Alexander Scott from McClure (1974b). Edinburgh discussion based on my own work. For Scots syntax see Brown & Millar (1980).

5.7.2 On English in Ireland generally, Barry (1981, 1982) and the papers in Harris *et al.* (1986). On the fortunes of Irish, Edwards (1984). A good recent overview of southern HE is Bliss (1984). Phonological description based on above sources, Wells (1982: §5.3), and my own observations.

For the North, Barry (1982) and Harris (1984a) for general coverage; for a detailed study of the evolution of northern HE phonology, Harris (1985) – one of the best studies of the history of a non-southern vernacular in existence. On aspect and Irish/English interaction in HE, Harris (1984b), and the rather different account in Kallen (1986). On HE stress, Ó Sé (1986). For Belfast, the best single overall study is Milroy & Milroy (1978); see also L. Milroy (1980), and the references to the work of the Milroys in the material by Harris cited above. HE examples in (5.31–34) from Harris (1984a, b).

5.7.3 For an overview of Welsh-English relations in Wales, and the changing fortunes of Welsh, Price (1984: ch. 8), Bellin (1984). On Welsh English, Thomas (1984), Wells (1982: §5.1), Hughes & Trudgill (1979: 51ff). For rural Welsh English, Parry (1972). The most detailed dialectological studies are in Parry (1977, 1979); for a phonological description of a South Welsh dialect, Connolly (1981). My exposition here is largely based on Thomas and Wells.

5.8.1 The ETE terminology at the beginning of this section (along with the term and abbreviation ET(E)) is nonstandard: I may have invented it. But it seems useful and accurate, and worth keeping. The overall division into 'British' and 'American' types is parallel to that of Trudgill & Hannah (1985), some of whose examples I have borrowed. For an interesting study of the interaction between BrE and AmE in the specific context of British pop-singers' pronunciation, see Trudgill (1983: ch. 8).

5.8.2 North American English is a vast field, and in keeping with the somewhat Anglocentric bias of this book, and limitations of space, I've barely scratched the surface. I'm grateful to Mari Blåfield for help with references and information about Canadian English; some of my material on CE is pinched from her very useful handouts for courses at the University of Helsinki.

For Mainland inputs into U.S. English, see Kurath (1928, 1964); figures on New England settlements from Cassidy (1957). On Canadian English, the best short survey is Bailey (1982), which has valuable references; for a richly detailed and accessible study, with a great deal of CE/USE comparison, McConnell (1979); other general works are Scargill (1974), Chambers (1975). On HE features in Newfoundland, Clarke (1986); on the Diphthong Rule Gregg (1973), Chambers (1973), and the discussion of similar alternations in other dialects (including New York City and the North of England) in Lass (1981). Figures for vowel durations in RP/USE from Jones (1950) and Peterson & Lehiste (1960) respectively.

For U.S. English generally, Mencken & McDavid (1963) is a classic: superbly documented, full of examples, quirky and idiosyncratic (McDavid in his revisions and notes is true to Mencken's style), and consistently delightful to read. For shorter general treatments, Marckwardt (1958) is useful, and for an older, very solid and scholarly treatment, Krapp (1925). On the American vocabulary, Mathews (1951).

Dialect study in the U.S has a long tradition, and there are some excellent SED-type studies (though with rather more sensitivity to social variation): see for instance Kurath & McDavid (1961), Kurath et al. (1939–43), and Allen (1973–6). The Americans have been particularly good on lexis: see Kurath (1949) and Atwood (1953) for particularly fine examples. For American dialectology in general, the papers collected in Allen & Underwood (1971) and Williamson & Burke (1971) give good coverage of regional dialects and dialectological method in the U.S. The vexed question of boundaries and the 'correct' regional divisions in the U.S. can perhaps best be approached by reading a convinced North/Midland/South believer like McDavid (1958), and comparing his account to one by a believer in General American: the most cogent arguments for GA I know of are in Wells (1982: §6.1). For a recent overall view of U.S. dialects, Cassidy (1982); and on social dialectology, including a good introduction and bibliography on Black and Hispanic English, Toon (1982). For the phonology of American English generally there is a clear and detailed overview of the major accent types, with some discussion of social variation, in Wells (ch. 6). Overall Wells is probably the best general account available, even if I disagree with him on a number of issues. The particular approach I take to the origins of U.S. (and other ET) Englishes, with its emphasis on the regional Mainland origins of ETE features, has been condemned by some writers; for a very different account, attempting to set the history of AmE in the framework of contact/pidgin/creole studies, Dillard (1985).

5.8.3 For general surveys of Australian and New Zealand English, see Turner (1972), Eagleson (1982), and the essays in Ramson (1966); very brief coverage as well in Trudgill & Hannah (1985: ch. 2). The literature on NZ is sparser than that on AusE, but there is good phonological discussion in Wells (1982: § 8.2); the centralization of the *bit* nucleus in NZ is well treated in Bauer (1979). Bauer (1986), which appeared as this book was going to press, is now the best treatment of NZ phonology. On general matters, especially vocabulary, Turner is the fullest easily accessible source on New Zealand (he is a native as well).

On AusE, aside from Turner and Eagleson, see Clyne (1976), Hammarström (1980); Mitchell & Delbridge (1965(a)) and Wells (§8.1) are useful on phonology. For sociolinguistic studies, see Mitchell & Delbridge (1965(b)) and Horvath (1985) – the latter one of the best sociolinguistic studies of a complex, multiethnic urban community I know of. Horvath's chs. 1–3 are also particularly good on the general methodological problems of ETE studies, and the vexed question of social class and social dialect in Australia. For phonology, the best recent description is Wells, and both Wells and Horvath have rich bibliographies. For Australian lexis see Ramson (1966), Turner, and the now standard *Macquarie dictionary* (Delbridge 1977).

The phonological description here largely follows Wells, with some alterations and reinterpretations based on Trudgill & Hannah and my own observations; lexical material based on Turner, Eagleson, and Trudgill & Hannah.

5.8.4 For a historical introduction and general description of SAE, see Lanham (1978, 1982); for a more detailed sociohistorical overview Lanham & Macdonald (1979). This book is controversial, and should be read along with Jeffery (1982), which is highly critical of some of their arguments and claims. On phonology see also Lanham (1967) and Wells (§8.3).

Current research being conducted by Susan Wright and myself has made us rather sceptical of some of Lanham's now classical assertions about the origin and nature of certain SAE phonological variables – particularly the analysis of the *bit* vowel, and the large-scale attribution of the more idiosyncratic features of SAE to Afrikaans contact. The descriptions here are based entirely on our own work with informants, not published sources, and the picture presented is quite different in a number of details from what is given in Lanham or Wells.

On the short front vowels and the chain shift see Lass & Wright (1985), which discusses the origin of the SAE system and the allophony of the *bit* vowel in detail; on the general problem of Afrikaans influence on SAE, and the methodological problems that arise in assessing contact influences in ETEs, see Lass & Wright (1986).

For South African lexis, the best source is Jean Branford's *Dictionary of South African English* (1980), which is a fund of useful information, and rich in illustrative quotations; the discussion of *busy* is based on Lass & Wright (1986); that of *now* and *just now* on unpublished work by Susan Wright.

6. ENGLISH AND GERMANIC REVISITED

6.1 Prologue: Innovativeness, Conservatism and Convergence

If a group of languages with a common ancestor now show great differences from one another, their evolutions must have been, to some extent, independent. The fact of common ancestry suggests that the degree of 'family resemblance' among the descendant languages will be connected with the speed and/or degree of diverging evolutionary change. That is, at any given time some family members will have diverged less from the ancestral condition than others, and will be defined as a group by having 'archaic' features; while others will show greater innovativeness, and be further from the original type.

So on the face of it, the members of a language family (or the dialects of a single language) will fall into 'conservative' and 'innovating' categories. But there's another dimension of classification and family resemblance that creates a different type of relation: abandonment of archaic features and innovation are not simply random radiations from a common core. Groups of languages can be defined by parallel abandonments of old features, or other innovations. Without a detailed historical perspective (including external history), it's often impossible to tell how a given set of family resemblances actually came about.

More concretely, a subgroup within a language family may show resemblances of two basic types:

(i) Common retention of archaic features;

(ii) Common innovation resulting in (a) abandonment of particular archaic features, or (b) common non-archaic ('novel') features.

But even this is oversimple: group (ii) resemblances can be due to at least three different historical patterns:

(iia) Innovations in the ancestor of the particular subgroup, carried down through all the members – as it were 'second-order' archaisms;

(iib) Innovations in one member diffused or transmitted by contact to the others;

(iic) Parallel independent development or convergence, without contact.

Complete family-wide resemblances are normally type (i) archaisms: an example is the presence in all Germanic languages of deictics or demonstratives that can be traced back to the IE root */to-/: Icelandic *þat*, E *that*, Sw *det*, G *das*: cf. L (*is*)-*t-ud* or the Greek neuter nom sg article *to*.

For type (ii) resemblances: the fact that all the Scandinavian languages have a postposed definite article (Sw *mann-en* 'the man') is a common inheritance from Proto-NGmc (iia); the fact that both Dutch (some varieties) and southwestern rural English dialects (§5.2) show signs of voicing of initial voiceless fricatives (e.g. /v-/ in *fish*, /z-/ in *sing*: cf. the Dutch spellings *vis*, *zingen*) is the result of diffusion from Continental Franconian dialects into English in early OE times (iib); and the fact that Afrikaans and English have both lost grammatical gender and infinitive marking, or that Afrikaans and Yiddish have lost the past/perfect distinction, are cases of convergent development (iic).

Of the three types, convergence is the hardest to understand. In evolutionary biology (the source of the term 'convergence') the motivation is generally pretty transparent, and we more or less understand the mechanisms involved. Thus both placental carnivores (cats, dogs) and marsupial carnivores (Tasmanian devil), while not in the same line of descent, have evolved nearly identical teeth: these can be seen as 'strategic' adaptations to the solution of specific ecological or survival problems, selected over time by the differential breeding success of those individuals with the right adaptations. But such neat 'Darwinian' explanations don't work for language evolution: structural change is not 'strategic' or 'adaptive'. A language with a postposed article is no better or worse for any conceivable purpose than one with a preposed article (or none at all). So when I come to speak of convergences in detail in later sections, I will not offer any explanations: they are simply a mystery.

But before we proceed, we must say something about innovativeness and conservatism in general. Those languages that have been isolated for a long time, out of contact with their parent languages or other related ones, are generally supposed to be more conservative. And indeed, there seems at first to be some evidence to support such a view: Icelandic and Faroese, the two geographically isolated 'insular' Scandinavian dialects, have a much richer and more archaic type of noun and verb morphology than the 'continental' dialects (Norwegian, Danish, Swedish). But if we look more closely at supposed correlations of this sort, we normally find that they are not in fact global, but restricted to particular aspects of the total structure – while others may be radically innovating. Thus the morphological conservatism of Icelandic and Faroese is 'balanced' by a great phonological innovativeness. And even within one area of structure, a language may be both innovating and conservative: e.g. Scots is phonologically innovating in having lost vowel length (§5.7.1), but conservative in retaining /x/ and being rhotic.

6.2 'Deviation from Type'

Still, in a wider perspective it often does make some sense to talk of overall conservatism or innovativeness – especially in terms of the retention of extremely ancient features. If we take Old English, for instance as a representative 'Old Germanic' dialect, we have a good point of departure for assessing relative degrees of 'Old Germanic-ness' in the living dialects – degrees of evolution away from an early common 'model'. It's certainly clear (cf. the examples of early texts in §2.2) that the Germanic languages were once a lot more similar than they are now; and there is a cluster of features whose possession characterizes (more or less) the historically archaic dialect types. These features may be of either PIE or Proto-Gmc date; and we can order the extant languages in terms of them. In addition, there are sets of later developments that are widely shared: we will look at some of them in the next section.

Some of the most important of these archaic features are:

(i) Grammatical gender. OE and the older Gmc dialects have three (m, f, n); modern languages may have two (neuter vs. non-neuter or 'common' as in standard Dutch and Swedish), three (as in German), or none (as in English). We will classify on a two-term grid: some gender distinction vs. none.

(ii) Rich noun morphology, with at least four cases (nom, gen, dat, acc) distinguished in the early dialects. The modern ones will be classified according to whether they have some case-marking (four as in Icelandic, three as in German, two as in Frisian) or none.

(iii) Rich verb morphology, with 1, 2, 3 persons distinct in the present, and plural distinct from singular. Also a distinction between indicative and subjunctive. We will classify under these three headings: (iiia) full distinction of person in pres sg vs. none (English with only one distinct form will count as not having any); (iiib) distinction between sg and pl; (iiic) distinction between indicative and subjunctive.

(iv) Strong vs. weak verb conjugations (§4.5.4).

(v) Strong vs. Weak adjective declension (§4.3.2) – or at least some inflected/uninflected distinction.

(vi) Verb-second rule. OE had a strong tendency (if not an absolute rule) that made the verb second in main clauses – regardless of what came before. Thus a preposed adverb brings the verb up with it to second position: OE *hē fōr* 'he went' vs. *þā fōr hē* 'then went he'. Not counting relics in English like *there goes John* or *never have I seen such a jerk*, we will classify by presence or absence of the basic rule.

(vii) Quantity. OE had a long/short vowel distinction, tied in with a contrast between heavy and light syllables (cf. §3.3). Any modern language that either has phonemic vowel length or makes use of the heavy/light distinction in its phonology will count as 'having quantity'.

(viii) Umlaut (§3.8). Alternations of the *mouse/mice* type played an important and productive role in OE and the other early dialects; we will be concerned here only with whether a language maintains a large number of these alternations, or has reduced them to marginal or virtually non-existent 'exceptions'.

We can now line up the modern Germanic dialects in terms of their possession (+) or lack (–) or these ten features:

(6.1)

	E	Fr	Du	Afr	G	Yi	Ic	Far	Nor	Da	Sw
(i) Gender	–	+	+	–	+	+	+	+	+	+	+
(ii) Case	–	+	–	–	+	–	+	+	–	–	–
(iiia) V-Person	–	+	+	–	+	+	+	+	–	–	–
(iiib) V-Number	–	+	+	–	+	+	+	+	–	–	–
(iiic) Ind/Subj	–	–	–	–	+	–	+	+	–	–	–
(iv) Strong/Weak V	+	+	+	–	+	–	+	+	+	+	+
(v) Strong/Weak A	–	+	+	+	+	+	+	+	+	+	+
(vi) V-2nd Rule	–	+	+	+	+	+	+	+	+	+	+
(vii) Quantity	+	+	+	+	+	–	+	+	+	+	+
(viii) Umlaut	+	–	–	–	+	+	+	+	+	+	+

We can extract from this a rather simple-minded but indicative ranking of overall innovativeness, in terms of typological distance from the archaic Germanic model. Counting each '–' as an innovation, we get a scale of distance like this:

(6.2)

> English, Afrikaans (7) > Yiddish, Norwegian, Danish, Swedish (4) > Dutch (3) > Frisian (2) > German, Icelandic, Faroese (∅)

This is of course somewhat misleading: Norwegian, Danish and Swedish are actually less innovating *qualitatively* than quantitatively, since three of their four losses cluster in the verb system. We will explore some of the more interesting and complex qualitative differences in later sections; but this rough quantitative measure does at least give an overall historical perspective on the family as a whole.

6.3 A Common Germanic Pattern: Erosion of Case Systems

One notable convergent pattern in virtually all of Germanic except insular Scandinavian is the loss of case-marking on the noun. This has occurred at different times and in somewhat different ways, but the end results are strikingly similar. The sharp +/– dichotomy in (6.1) has obscured some of the finer details: both Icelandic and German for instance have case-marking, but of quite different kinds: Icelandic distinguishes four cases, by and large, and generally keeps nominative and accusative separate, while German never distinguishes these two, but does mark dative plural for most nouns, genitive sg for most masculines and neuters, and dat sg for a vanishing minority of masculines. Still, German with its reduced system is more of an inflected language in this respect than English with only its problematical genitive (cf. §4.3.2), or Afrikaans with nothing at all.

The older Germanic pattern can be seen at its fullest in Gothic, which in a maximally differentiated declension marks all eight of the possible case/number forms: thus for the masculine *a*-stem (see §4.3.2) noun 'day', we have:

(6.3)

	Sg	Pl
nom	dag-s	dag-ōs
gen	dag-is	dag-ē
dat	dag-a	dag-am
acc	dag	dag-ans

(I will use this noun throughout as an example.) Gothic unfortunately did not survive in a full enough form for us to see how it might have developed; there were speakers of an EGmc dialect in the Crimea in the 16th century ('Crimean Gothic'), but all we have of their language is a word-list and a few expressions collected by a Flemish-speaking amateur.

So we'll concentrate here on the developments in languages that still survive: as examples Swedish, German, Dutch and English. The erosion of case-marking proceeded this way in Swedish:

(6.4)

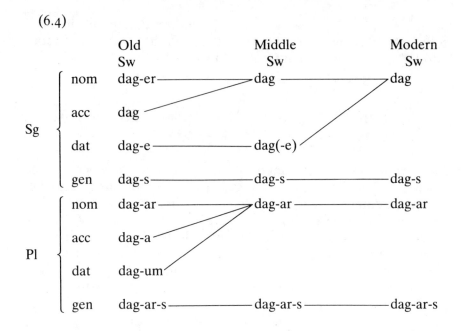

Characteristically (see English and German below), the genitive re-mains, and the nom/acc and dative distinctions erode; but the sg/pl distinction remains salient.

The German pattern is:

(6.5)

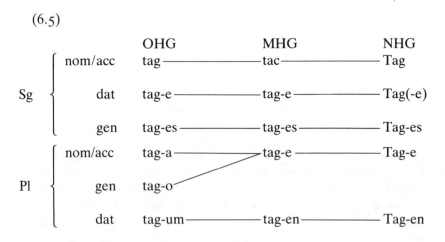

(The order in which the case-forms are presented is tailored to the needs of the diagrams: it has no theoretical significance.)

For Dutch, the pattern is:

(6.6)

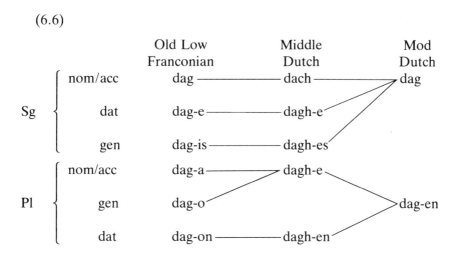

The Dutch pattern suggests – probably erroneously – that the dat pl is the 'source' of the modern plural: actually what happened is that nouns of this type tended to pass over into the *n*-stem declension, which marked plurality with a nasal (cf. §4.3.2). The distinct spellings for nom sg in Middle Dutch and Middle High German indicate a voiceless final consonant: *tac* [tak], *tage* [taːgə]: Modern German still has an alternation between /k/ and /g/, but doesn't bother to spell it anymore; Dutch in most varieties has a voiceless [x] in all forms nowadays.

The development in English is like this:

(6.7)

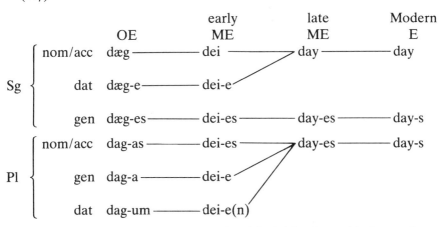

(I discount the difference between *days*/*day's*/*days'*, as this is purely a matter of spelling; the alternation between *æ* and *a* in the OE forms represents a kind of vowel-harmony: *æ* before front vowels or in monosyllables, *a* before back vowels; in ME the vowel of the singular was extended to the rest of the paradigm in nouns of this type.)

All these languages show a characteristic pattern: reduction of contrasts parallel to reduction in the number of unstressed vowel qualities in the transition from 'Old' to 'Middle' periods; a related tendency to retain as distinctive those endings that contain a consonant (since vowels – by and large – can be deleted more easily than consonants); and a tendency therefore to retain the genitive, at least for this declension, if any case-form at all is retained.

These brief sketches in fact can give us something of a working definition of terms that have been used undefined throughout this book: 'old', 'middle' and 'modern'. Typologically, the tendency is to use 'old' for those stages where there is a reasonably full range of unstressed inflectional vowel qualities (as in the Gothic, Old High German, Old English, and Old Low Franconian examples), 'middle' for those stages where unstressed vowels have fallen together in [ə] or something of the sort, usually spelled -*e*; and 'modern' or 'new' for those stages where the largest number of inflectional vowels have fallen away altogether. As a result, the old languages show full or relatively full noun paradigms, the middle and modern ones progressively reduced ones.

Usage, however, is not entirely consistent: in some cases the earliest attested form of a language is called 'old' even if it's a typical 'middle' variety: this is true for Old Frisian and Old Yiddish; in others, even where the structure is of an 'old' type (as in modern Icelandic), the terminology reflects simple time: anything from about the 17th century on is 'modern'. This produces confusions for the unwary, such as Old Frisian being roughly contemporary to Middle High German and Middle English. One other inconsistency arises in the case of Swedish, which is typically 'modern' in all respects except that it retains a number of inflectional vowel qualities, and hasn't reduced them to [ə]: thus it has plurals in -*ar* [ar], -*or* [ur], and -*er* [ər], as in *dag-ar* 'days', *flick-or* 'girls', *tänd-er* 'teeth'.

6.4 English, Yiddish, Afrikaans: A West Germanic Convergence Cluster

English, Yiddish and Afrikaans show some striking convergences in evolutionary pattern. At first sight, there are common 'ecological' factors that look as if they might be implicated: all three languages are geographical 'outposts' on the periphery of continental Germania (specifically, they have become outposts through emigration from the centre: English in the Northwest, Yiddish in the East, and Afrikaans in the Southwest).

In addition, they have all been in contact with other languages in a rather intimate way: English with French and Scandinavian as we've seen (ch. 2), Yiddish with Slavonic languages and English, and Afrikaans with English (§5.8.4).

But it would be hard to support a claim that geographical isolation or contact *per se* are 'causes' of the convergences. Isolation by itself means nothing; it can be implicated in conservativeness, not innovation. And even if Afrikaans and English were in contact in South Africa during the period when the innovations in Afrikaans were stabilized, (a) they began before extensive contact, and (b) the sociolinguistic situation makes it most unlikely that English could have a strong influence: as we've seen (ch. 2), even the longer and more intimate contacts between English and French and Scandinavian had negligible structural effects. And as we will see, the innovations in Yiddish took place considerably before any contact with English. In all cases the innovations in the three languages fail to match up temporally or geographically: all we can say is that their evolutions are often surprisingly parallel in detail and overall effect.

I simply note here that these three languages share a number of common developments, which are not as a group fully shared with the rest of Germanic – even West Germanic. And the developments are not common to all three languages – though each occurs in two out of the three. There is enough here to make this group of dialects fairly special within the larger picture. And – as we will see later – there is some evidence for other languages developing in a similar way, or for one of the innovations beginning to occur in a language in our group where it hasn't before.

The innovations in question are all of the same type: loss of older West Germanic structures or contrasts. We will look at each of them in some detail.

(i) *Loss of the Past/Perfect Distinction*

English (cf. §4.5.2) and the other West Germanic languages except Yiddish and Afrikaans, and North Germanic, all have a grammaticalized past/perfect distinction:

(6.8)

	Past	Perfect
E	I sang	I have sung
G	ich sang	ich habe ge-zung-en
Du	ik zang	ik heb ge-zong-en
Sw	jag sjung	jag har sjung-it

323

Afrikaans and Yiddish in contrast have only one past form, which is morphologically a perfect: Afr *ek het ge-sing*, Yi *ix hob ge-zung-n*. The old perfect has simple past meaning – or to put it more accurately, the past/perfect distinction is no longer grammaticalized, but any given form is ambiguous as to aspect.

Meaning can be derived from context in most cases: i.e. aspect is now a pragmatic rather than a grammatical category. So in Yiddish *ix hob ge-ges-n*, in Afrikaans *ek het ge-eët* both mean 'I ate'/'I have eaten'. But the context can disambiguate; thus in Yiddish

(6.9)

    a. ix bin nit hungerix, *ix hob gegesn*
       I am not hungry, I have eat-pp
       'I'm not hungry, *I've eaten*'

    b. *ix hob gegesn* lectn jor nur cvej mol a tog
       I have eat-pp last year only two times a day
       'Last year *I* only *ate* twice a day'

If it's necessary to specify perfect, this is done in both languages by adverbs: Yi *šojn* 'already', Afr *al* 'already', *klaar* 'completely': *ix hob šojn gegesn*, *ek het al/klaar geeët* are unambiguously 'I've eaten'.

I said above that Afrikaans had lost the past/perfect opposition, with all functions taken over by the old perfect: this is generally true, but there are a few old pasts left, which taken together with other evidence can shed some light on how oppositions like this typically get lost. A few verbs, which had very 'irregular' pasts, still retain them: the past of *ek is* 'I am' is *ek was* - not the expected **ek het gewees* (*wees* is the infinitive). (Though a hybrid *ek was gewees* is beginning to gain currency, and may eventually yield to *ek het gewees*.) Similarly, *dink* 'think' has the pasts *ek dog* and *ek het gedink* – with the old form now recessive and literary rather than colloquial. The verb *hê* 'have' shows a similar set-up, with *ek had* ~ *ek het gehad*; and the modal auxiliaries retain the old pasts (*sal/sou* 'shall/should', *kan/kon* 'can/could', *mag/mog* 'may/might'). These are now really not pasts, however, any more than *should, could, might* are in English (cf. §4.5.3). What we have in Afrikaans is a nearly completed restructuring of the system, with a set of fringe exceptions, one of which (*was*) seems on the way out.

In Yiddish, the change is complete: there are no pasts left. But if we look back historically, we can see a situation somewhat parallel to the current Afrikaans one. For instance, here is a piece of 16th-century Yiddish (all past forms italicized):

(6.10)

doû *bin* ix krank *gyvorn*, doû *iz* an alter iîd *gykimyn*
then *am* I sick *become*-pp, then *is* an old Jew *come*-pp

ci mir, in *hot* mix *gyfrêgt*, fin vanyn ix *vêr*
to me, and *has* me *asked*, from whence I *was*

doû *hob* ix *gyšproxyn*: 'fin Krôuky'. dôu *hot* er *gyšproxyn*
then *have* I *said*: from Kraków. then *has* he *said*

er *vêr* oyx fin Krôuky
he *was* also from Kraków.

A modern Yiddish version would be quite similar – except that *vêr* (= modern German *war*, E *was*) no longer exists: it's been replaced by a perfect-type construction with a form of *zajn* 'to be' as auxiliary, and the past participle of the verb, *geven* (= G *ge-wesen*). Thus *fin vanyn ix vêr* would be *fun vu ix bin geven*, *er vêr oyx* would be *er iz ojx geven*, etc. So we see the verb 'to be' – notoriously irregular in most IE languages – the last to retain its old forms: the scenario of loss in Yiddish is quite like that in Afrikaans.

Now English generally retains a grammaticalized past/perfect opposition; but some dialects – even standard ones – are beginning to lose it. In my own, for instance, both the following dialogues are acceptable (cf. §§1.2, 1.5):

(6.11)

    (i)   A.   Did you eat (yet)?
           B.   Yes, I ate (already).

    (ii) A.   Have you eaten (yet)?
           B.   Yes, I've eaten (already).

(Note that in Yiddish and Afrikaans, 'already' with the simple past can act as a marker of perfect.) In my dialect, the past-for-perfect is commonest (a) in casual speech, and (b) in *already/yet* contexts; but it seems not unlikely that it's going to spread. And if it does – even though formally the merger is to the simple past, with the perfect being lost, rather than the other way round – the effect on the aspect system will be the same as the Yiddish/Afrikaans developments. The same sort of thing is happening in many varieties of spoken German as well, with the more regular verbs appearing in speech only in the old perfect, and the simple pasts remaining only for the more irregular ones.

The loss of the perfect/past distinction in Afrikaans and Yiddish has drastically affected their structural 'Germanicness' ((6.1)): they have lost the strong/weak verb contrast. Obviously, since strong verbs form their pasts by internal vowel-change, and weak verbs by suffixation, loss of the past will obliterate the difference. We can see this by comparing the forms of a weak verb ('think') and a strong verb ('sing') in German, Yiddish, and Afrikaans:

(6.12)

		Inf	Past	Perfect
German:	WEAK:	denk-en	dach-*te*	habe ge-dach-*t*
	STRONG:	sing-en	sang	habe ge-sung-*en*
Yiddish:	WEAK:	denk-n		hob ge-dax-*t*
	STRONG:	zing-en		hob ge-zung-*n*
Afrikaans:	WEAK:	dink		het ge-dink
	STRONG:	sing		het ge-sing

In Yiddish, we can still tell which kind a verb was by the ending of the participle (-*n* for strong, -*t* for weak) – though this has no systematic significance; in Afrikaans, all the information is lost.

The change in Yiddish dates back to the 15th–16th centuries, and was complete by the 17th; in Afrikaans we see variation between past and perfect as early as the 1750s, and there is still some as late as the 1830s. We can assume completion by the late 19th century.

The loss of grammaticalized aspect is actually part of a recurrent or cyclical process in Germanic (as well as other branches of IE). Proto-IE had for instance a simple past (aorist) vs. perfect opposition, as in Greek *é-lipon* 'I left' vs. *lé-loipa* 'I have left'; this was lost in Proto-Gmc, leaving it with no aspectual distinctions, but a pure present vs. past tense system (or present vs. aorist, to keep the terminology consistent). In later Germanic times, a new perfect was created, using auxiliary 'have' or 'be' plus past participle (cf. §4.5.5); now this has been lost in Yiddish and Afrikaans. And it's not unlikely that say the Afrikaans *ek het al* + pp construction could be grammaticalized into a new perfect, while English lost the distinction. Thus we have the scenario;

(6.13)

Proto-IE   Proto-Gmc   Old Gmc   Yi, Afr

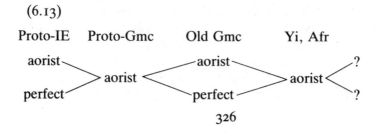

(ii) *Loss of the Infinitive Suffix*

The oldest Germanic languages uniformly marked the infinitive of the verb with a suffix /-an/; some relic of this has persisted in all of their descendants except English and Afrikaans. The origins and forms of the Germanic infinitive have been dealt with earlier (§4.5.5); to recapitulate briefly, the modern dialects show either a full /-Vn/ suffix (e.g. German -*en* /-ən/, Yiddish -*n* /-ən/), a reduced one with the nasal deleted (Swedish -*a* /-a/, Danish -*e* /-ə/, Dutch -*en* /-ə/: in Dutch the final nasal is generally not pronounced, though it surfaces in some styles), or none at all (English, Afrikaans).

Reduction of the ending in English began in the Northern dialects in OE times (perhaps under Scandinavian influence); Northumbrian texts beginning as early as the 7th–8th centuries show forms in -*a*, where the other dialects have -*an*. By ME times the infinitive form is -*en* in all dialects except in the North, where zero endings already occur; during the ME period loss of -*en* proceeds variably in the London Standard. It is still -*en* in the 14th century, but is gone by the 15th.

In Afrikaans we find the first textual evidence for loss of -*en* around 1750 (though it probably began at least half a century earlier); the current endingless state is reached around 1800.

(iii) *Loss of the 'Sentence-Brace'*

The sentence-brace (G *Satzklammer*) is an old West Germanic construction which involves the splitting, under certain conditions, of an auxiliary from a main verb. In simple intransitive clauses, the normal order for WGmc (and NGmc for that matter) is: Subject + Auxiliary + Infinitive/Participle:

(6.14)

	Modal + Infinitive	Perfect
G	ich kann schreiben	ich habe geschrieben
Afr	ek kan skryf	ek het geskryf
Yi	ix ken šrajbn	ix hob gešribn
E	I can write	I have written

But transitive clauses, or clauses containing adverbials (or pretty much anything except subjects, auxiliaries, and main verbs), have a different order in German and Afrikaans (and Dutch and Frisian): the subject and auxiliary come in the first two places as usual, but the infinitive or participle is extraposed to the end, coming after the object or adverb – a 'brace' enclosing the non-subject material. Thus:

(6.15)

German
- ich *kann* den Brief *schreiben*   'I can write the letter'
- ich *habe* den Brief *geschrieben* 'I've written the letter'
- ich *kann* jetzt *schreiben*   'I can write now'

Afrikaans
- ek *kan* die brief *skryf*
- ek *het* die brief *geskryf*
- ek *kann* nou *skryf*

The rule for brace-formation is roughly: (a) finite verb (aux) in position 2; (b) objects, adverbs, etc. in position 3; (c) nonfinite verbal material (i.e. the main verb) to the end.

English has lost the construction entirely (but see §5.7.2): *I can the letter write*, *I have the letter written* (the latter of course is fine if it's not a perfect, but means 'I've got the letter finished'). Yiddish at first appears to have lost it too: using the same examples as above:

(6.16)

    a. ix ken šrajbn   ix ken šrajbn dos brif
    b. ix hob gešribn   ix hob gešribn dos brif

But if we have an adverb, or if the object of the verb is a pronoun, we still have the brace:

(6.17)

    a. ix ken es šrajbn   'I can write it'
    b. ix hob es gešribn   'I wrote it'
    c. ix hob gestern gešribn 'I wrote yesterday'

The brace can also occur – optionally – in main clauses in conditional constructions:

(6.18)

    a. as got *zol vojnen* ojf der erd,
       if God *shall live* on earth
       volten di menšn baj im di fenster *ojsšlogn*
       would the men by him the windows *out-hit*
       'If God lived on earth, men would break his windows'

b. as me *ken* nit *bajsn*,
if one *can* not *bite*
zol men nit *ščirn* mit di cejn
shall one not grind with the teeth
'If you can't bite, don't growl'

(The initial position of the auxiliary (*zol, volten*) in the main clause is due to the fact that the subordinate ('if') clause comes first; according to the verb-second rule, the preposed subordinate clause takes up position 1, and attracts the finite verb to its immediate right.)

As in the past/perfect case, we can see distinct phases in the loss of a construction: Afrikaans and German have the original firmly established; Yiddish has lost it overall, but retains it obligatorily with adverbs and pronominal objects, and optionally in conditionals; English has lost it entirely. Clearly the current state of Yiddish represents a point 'between' the two, in terms of historical type, a process of diffusion from environment to environment caught in midstream.

(iv) *Loss of Split Word Order*

Since earliest West Germanic there has been a strong tendency toward a split word-order: verb-second in main clauses and verb-final in subordinate clauses. This tendency (strong in Old English, perhaps somewhat less so in the other dialects) became rigid in German and Dutch during the course of the 16th century. We can see the pattern in German and Afrikaans:

(6.19)

a. Relative Clause

Das Auto [das ich gekauft *habe*] ist neu
Die motor [wat ek gekoop *het*] is nuut
'The car [that I bought *have*] is new'

b. Complement Clause

Er dachte [daβ er krank *wäre*]
Hy het gedink [dat hy siek *was*]
'He thought [that he sick *was*]'

Compare this with Yiddish and English:

(6.20)

Dos kar [vos ix *hob* gekauft] iz naj
The car [that I *have* bought] is new

Er hot gedaxt [dos er *iz* geven krank]
He thought [that he *was* sick]

329

The loss of both the sentence-brace and the in principle very similar verb-final rule proceeded in the same way: by an increasingly common process of rightward movement of preverbal material. There is considerable evidence for this in OE; and even in modern German, which has quite rigid brace and verb-final constraints, extraposition is allowed under certain conditions: e.g. comparative phrases are normally moved to the right out of the brace ('exbraciated'):

(6.21)

> Expected:
> Wir *haben* [einen besseren Wein als diesen] *getrunken*
>
> We *have* [a better wine than this] *drunk*
> 'We've drunk a better wine than this'
>
> Actual:
> Wir *haben* [einen besseren Wein] *getrunken* als diesen

Verb-second subordinate clauses arose in English in a similar way: by extraposing preverbal material like objects. The type is:

(6.22)

> hē sægde þæt he [þone mann] seah
>
> hē sægde þæt he seah [þone mann]
>
> 'He said that he saw the man'

Both brace and verb-final subordinate clauses were variable in OE, and became steadily less frequent, virtually disappearing in the 14th century; Yiddish maintained both until the late 19th century.

(v) *Loss of Grammatical Gender*

Ancient Germanic retained the old IE three-gender system, as do modern German and Yiddish:

(6.23)

	m	f	n
OE	se mann	sēo fǣmne	þæt cild
G	der Mann	die Frau	das Kind
Yi	der man	die froj	dos kind

330

Dutch, like most Scandinavian dialects except Icelandic and Faroese, has reduced the system to a two-way contrast:

(6.24)

	Common	Neuter
Du	de man	het kind
Sw	mann-en	barn-et

Afrikaans and English both lost grammatical gender entirely: English by late ME times, Afrikaans beginning in the 18th century, but complete only in the 19th: thus *the man/women/child, die man/vrouw/kinder*. Traces of the original system, reorganized in terms of 'natural' gender, of course remain in the personal pronoun systems of both languages: the *man . . . he, the woman . . . she, the house . . . it*; *die man . . . hy, di vrouw . . . sy, die huis . . . dit*. (I've substituted *house* for *child* to make the concord with *it* more natural: though it's still normal to use *it* for a child of unknown sex, especially a very young one.)

(vi) *Loss of Person/Number Marking on the Verb*

The old Germanic languages (N, E, W) marked person and number throughout the present system of the verb, and to some extent in the past (cf. §4.5.5). German and Yiddish still retain relatively well-differentiated paradigms, whereas English has lost all but a distinct 3 sg, and Afrikaans has lost all marking:

(6.25)

		German	Yiddish
	1	ich schreib-e	ix šrajb
Sg	2	du schreib-st	du šrajb-st
	3	er schreib-t	er šrajb-t
	1	wir schreib-en	mir šrajb-n
Pl	2	ihr schreib-t	ir šrajb-t
	3	sie schreib-en	zej šrajb-n

English has *I, you, we they write* vs. *he writes*; Afrikaans *ek, jy, hy, ons, hulle skryf* (all persons and numbers). The loss in English began during the 15th century, and was pretty well completed by about 1600; in Afrikaans we get evidence for loss around 1750, and completion by the end of the 19th century.

In summary:

(6.26)

		E	Afr	Yi	G	Du
(i)	Loss of Past/Perfect	−	+	+	−	−
(ii)	Loss of Infinitive suffix	+	+	−	−	−
(iii)	Loss of sentence-brace	+	−	+	−	−
(iv)	Loss of split word order	+	−	+	−	−
(v)	Loss of gender	+	+	−	−	−
(vi)	Loss of verb marking	+	+	−	−	−

In terms of time-scale, the picture is:

(6.27)

	E	Afr	Yi
(i)	−	18th–19th	17th
(ii)	15th	19th	−
(iii)	14th	−	19th
(iv)	12th	−	19th
(v)	13th–15th	18th–19th	−
(vi)	15th–16th	18th–19th	−

If we look at the time-spans separating the same innovation in different languages, we find a minimum 'convergence distance' of about 200 years, and a maximum of about 700.

CHAPTER 6: NOTES AND REFERENCES

6.1 On the general problem of distinguishing convergence from inherited innovation, see the methodological discussion in Lass (1984c).

6.3 The material in this section is extracted from standard histories and historical grammars. For English, see the works cited in the relevant endnotes to ch. 4; for German, the most usable account in English is probably Russ (1978), and see also the shorter Chambers & Wilkie (1970). For Old Low Franconian and Middle Dutch, there is a good deal of material extractable from the notes in Markey (1976); the classic history of Dutch is only available in Dutch (van Loey 1970). For Swedish, there is a brief account in Bergman (1973: 52ff); for more details, a knowledge of Swedish will be necessary to cope with Wessén (1968).

6.5 The material on the history of Yiddish and Afrikaans is widely scattered, and not a good deal is available in English. Most of the datings for Yiddish changes are rough, based largely on the texts collected in Birnbaum (1965); for the history of Yiddish see Weinreich (1980), Birnbaum (1979). There is very little on Afrikaans in English; for short treatments see Combrink (1978), Scholtz (1970). For a general overview, Raidt (1980).

7. EPILOGUE: THE CONTENT OF A LANGUAGE HISTORY, OR WHAT DOES IT ALL MEAN ANYHOW?

This book has now come more or less full circle. I began with an attempt at defining English, and then went on to its emergence out of a (relatively) undifferentiated Proto-Germanic, and on through its development, an account of its present-day structure, geographical spread, and dialectology. And in chapter 6 back to a resetting of English in its Germanic context – in structural terms, but with a strong historical bias.

A similar account could be written for any of the Germanic dialects, even if the details are bound to be different. The external histories, for instance, would be quite similar in principle; the pattern of migration leading to new extraterritorial dialects that become culture-bearing or national languages, to take one Germanic *Leitmotiv*, has been repeated over and over. Yiddish in one sense is extraterritorial German on an extraterritorial Hebrew-cum-extraterritorial Old French/Old Italian base; Afrikaans is extraterritorial Dutch. Going back further, Icelandic and Faroese are extraterritorial Old Norwegian; and still further, English of course is extraterritorial North Sea Germanic. In terms of contributing elements or 'determinants' melded into emergent dialects, if ones with particular regional flavours, South African or American or Australian English bears the same relation to earlier Mainland English as Old English did to its continental ancestors – and as the emergent late medieval SEML standard did to the regional dialects of Middle English. Even the Mainland/Extraterritorial pattern is part of a more inclusive one.

In fact, as the Preacher says (Ecclesiastes 1: 9–10):

> The thing that hath been, it is that which shall be; and that which is done is that which shall be done: and there is no new thing under the sun. Is there any thing whereof it may be said, See, this is new? it hath been already of old time, which was before us.

One point therefore of the preceding chapter (and in a way of this whole book) is that, special as English is to its speakers, it's nothing special: at

333

least no more so than any other language. This is of course why a book about English must be a book about English linguistics, which in its own way is a branch of the general discipline of linguistics. All languages are equally deserving (or undeserving) of the patriotism and sentimental attachment their speakers feel for them; simply because, given the human condition, our language is perforce the vehicle of our culture, and everything we love most or hate most can only be expressed by means of it. And of course we learn our language more or less at the same time as we're being socialized and acquiring our personalities and cultural and individual identities, so that the two often seem inextricably connected, or even the same thing. But though a language is the vehicle of a culture, it's not the culture itself – any value-judgements that one makes about a language are value-judgements about its speakers and their culture; languages themselves are value-neutral.

As the history of category-loss and innovation we've been looking at here suggests, 'the language' in fact is a momentary phenomenon: 'the same language' can change enormously, in just about every way, over the course of its history. And when it does, it still remains the bearer of culture and identity in precisely the same way as it did before, and it mediates its necessary cultural and social tasks with unchanged and unchangeable efficiency and fitness.

This is an important point, given two complementary streams of romantic misconception about the nature of language change and its relation to language structure and use. The first of these is the scenario of 'decay': in the early 19th century for instance (unsurprisingly, given the importance of the Classical languages in education) there was a feeling among many linguists that loss of inflection and structural 'simplification' of the kind we looked at in chapter 6 represented a 'decadence'. That the 'expressive power' of the modern, simplified languages was somehow less than that of the earlier forms (German as compared to Old High German, any IE vernacular as compared to Latin, Greek or Sanskrit). Opposed to this was the 'progressivist' school, who held the view that simplification (in terms of increasing regularity, loss of morphology) was somehow 'progress', clearing away rubbish that impeded good communication.

The rather charming silliness of such a view can be seen in a characteristic passage from one of the great proponents of 'progress in language', Otto Jespersen. (I am impugning him here only as a thinker about language in general, not as either a historian or describer of English, where he ranks among the giants.) Thus (with a strong touch of 19th-century sexism to add spice), the following (Jespersen 1948 (originally 1905): 5):

334

The Italians have a pointed proverb: 'Le parole son femmine e i fatti son maschi.' [Words are feminine and facts are masculine.] If briefness, conciseness and terseness are characteristic of the style of men, while women as a rule are not such economizers of speech, English is more masculine than most languages. We see this in a great many ways. In grammar it has got rid of a great many superfluities found in earlier English as well as in most cognate languages, reducing endings, etc., to the shortest forms possible and often doing away with endings altogether. Where German has, for instance, *alle diejenigen wilden tiere*, *die dort leben*, so that the plural idea is expressed in each word separately (apart of course, from the adverb), English has *all the wild animals that live there*, where *all*, the article, the adjective, and the relative pronoun are alike incapable of receiving any mark of the plural number; the sense is expressed with the greatest clearness imaginable, and all the unstressed endings *-e* and *-en*, which make most German sentences so drawling, are avoided.

Jespersen is here comparing the non-comparable, or perhaps better, making a pseudo-comparison in the wrong terms. We might note first that he's writing in a foreign language (his own was Danish), and comparing this foreign language he chose to write in with another foreign language. His perspective is therefore one that strictly speaking doesn't count; it's not that of the native speaker, involved in the use of the language in his own community, but that of a non-involved aesthetic judge. A German's reaction to a 'stripped down' version like **all der wild tier, der dort leb*, for instance, would not be 'How economical!', but rather 'How like the "pidgin German" of a newly-arrived guest-worker', or 'How childish and ungrammatical', etc.

One could in fact turn Jespersen's argument around by pointing to the 'cumbersome' and 'unnecessary' use of *do*-support in English: where German forms all yes/no questions by simply shifting the finite verb to the left (*er singt* 'he sings', *singt er?*) English needs that 'extra' item in *does he sing?* instead of using the 'economical' **sings he?* And German has quasi-aspectual prefixes that could be said to be particularly efficient information-packaging devices: e.g. *stören* 'disarrange, disturb', *zerstören* 'destroy, lay in ruins', *sägen* 'to saw', *zer-sägen* 'saw up, cut to pieces', *trennen* 'separate', *zer-trennen* 'rip up', etc. It would be as pointless for an English speaker to 'miss' this kind of intensifying prefix in English as it would for a German speaker to 'regret' the need for concord in NPs and between subjects and verbs.

There is really no warrant for talking about qualitative differences between languages. A native speaker can (I would argue by definition) do anything he needs to with his language, and in general cannot import into it the 'desirable' traits of a foreign one. This means that nostalgia for the 'lost excellences' of one's own language is irrational, because they were excellent only for speakers who used them natively. It seems likely that there is essentially nothing you can say in one language that you can't (in some way) say in any other; which in fact follows pretty much from what I would take to be reasonable assumptions about the basic similarities of human brains across cultures, and the similar tasks that languages have to perform in human societies.

These reflections should make us at least cautious about claims that linguistic changes achieve anything of note for languages or their speakers; and, conversely, about accounts which talk of 'harm' done by changes, or about potential 'collapses' in linguistic systems 'avoided' by changes. (The plethora of scare-quotes here reflects my feelings about these notions.) It is frequently claimed for instance that the kind of morphological simplification discussed in chapter 6 and elsewhere (especially the loss of case-marking on nouns) 'caused' the stabilization of SVO order in English. I.e. the situation would occur where in certain contexts anyhow it was impossible to tell subjects from objects: hence the two grammatical functions were assigned invariable positions. But such a scenario implies one of two (impossible) kinds of 'linguistic action': either (a) speakers actually found themselves confusing subjects and objects, and took steps to remedy the situation; or (b) they foresaw that they might do so, if things went on the way they were, so they took the requisite steps in advance. Option (a) is as it were 'therapy', option (b) 'prophylaxis'. Under the therapeutic interpretation, speakers actually found themselves confusing subjects and objects, and took steps to remedy the situation; under the prophylactic, they foresaw that they would do so, if things went on the way they were, so they took the requisite steps in advance. The therapeutic option is incompatible with what we know of how languages function in speech communities (nobody has ever really demonstrated a clear case of a language whose native speakers had 'trouble' representing grammatical relations); the prophylactic option doesn't match up with what we know of speakers' knowledge of their languages and general talent for prophecy.

This may seem at first a rather negative conclusion to a book like this: in effect it's a confession that I don't understand the reasons why the things that interest me most, and figured so largely in the discussion, actually happen. As the author of an essentially 'instructive' work, maybe I shouldn't espouse such an attitude in public (whatever I feel about things in private); does it detract from (what I hope is) my scholarly 'authority'?

Frankly, I find this lack of understanding of the deeper motivations of linguistic change – if indeed there are any – exciting and hopeful, rather than a cause for pessimism or intellectual depression. Any subject where all the answers are in is bound to be boring; intellectual vitality depends in the long run on creative ignorance. I am therefore quite unapologetic about ending on an agnostic note: I don't understand why language changes, and I don't think anybody else does either; I'm not even sure if there is any reason in general for change – aside from a built-in lack of stability in all human cultural artifacts. But it's quite clear that modern English is no more better or worse than Old English than Haydn is better or worse than Bach; and it's equally clear that the evolution from one state to the other, and the enormously complex and intricate structural properties of the states, are fascinating, important, and well worth continued (maybe perpetual) study. I rest my case.

CHAPTER 7: NOTES AND REFERENCES

If the description of Yiddish in the second paragraph seems bizarre, see Weinreich (1980). The original vernacular of the Jews in Palestine was Hebrew, later succeeded by Aramaic; in the Diaspora, the nucleus of the later Yiddish-speaking community consisted of speakers of Loez ('Judaeo-Romance'), who learned German when they moved into the Rhineland, and later into other parts of Germany and further east. Iceland and the Faroes were 9th-century Norwegian colonies; Dutch was brought to South Africa in 1652 when van Riebeeck established his refreshment-station at the Cape for the Dutch East India Company. On English, of course, see chapter 2.

The rest of this epilogue is somewhat personal and idosyncratic, which at this late stage shouldn't surprise anyone. A technical account of this position (Lass 1980, especially ch. 4) opened up a large can of worms, many of which are still wriggling happily. There is no sense in which the 'meaningfulness' or 'meaning-lessness' of linguistic change, and the role of functional considerations as motivations for change, are settled issues, and my position is probably a minority one among historical linguists.

APPENDIX I
PHONETIC CLASSIFICATION AND
TRANSCRIPTION

The symbols used in this book are those of the IPA (International Phonetic Association): for detailed treatment see IPA (1949). Symbols are presented here with a conventional articulatory description (see glossary for unfamiliar terms), and rough 'key words' in familiar languages to indicate the general quality a symbol represents. If a specific dialect of English or some other language is intended in a key word, this will be specified; otherwise the symbols may be taken as roughly applicable to all dialects..

1 Vowels

Vowels are normally classified on a three-dimensional grid: Height (the position of the maximal constriction in the vocal tract on the vertical axis), Backness (position of maximal constriction on the horizontal axis), and Rounding (lip-attitude: rounded or unrounded). In terms of an idealized geometry of the vocal tract, the vowel-symbols used here can be represented as:

	front	central	back
close	i,y I,Y,ï	ɨ,ʉ ÿ,ʊ	ɯ,u
half-close	e,ø	ə	ɣ,o
half-open	ɛ,œ	3	ʌ,ɔ
open	æ a ä ɐ		ɑ,ɒ

Close vowels are also called high, open vowels low; half-close and half open vowels are grouped together as mid. In the chart above, if a pair of symbols is separated by a comma (e.g. x, y), the first is unrounded and the second rounded. For details see below:

338

The Individual Vowels

[i]   Close Front Unround. F v*i*te (short), G L*ie*d, SBE l*ea*d (long)

[y]   Close Front Round. F t*u* (short), G k*üh*ne, Afr v*uu*r (long)

[e]   Half-Close Front Unround. SAE, NZE, AusE b*e*t (short); G Th*ee* (long)

[ø]   Half-Close Front Round. F p*eu* (short), G sch*ö*n (long); Centralized version [ö:] in NZE, some SAE h*u*rt

[ɛ]   Half-Open Front Unround. E b*e*t (short), F m*aî*tre (long)

[œ]   Half-Open Front Round. F b*eu*rre, G G*ö*tter; centralized [œ̈:] in standard SAE h*u*rt

[æ]   Raised Open Front Unround. SBE *cat*, Finnish *käsi*

[a]   Open Front Unround. Scots c*a*t, F p*a*s (short), Dutch g*aa*n (long); centralized [ä] in vernacular London, AusE and some SAE b*u*t

[ɪ]   Centralized Front Half-Close Unround. SBE b*i*t, G l*i*tt; further centralized [ï] in SAE, NZE b*i*t

[ʏ]   Centralized Front Half-Close Round. G m*ü*ssen

[ɨ]   Close Central Unround. Polish zł*o*ty

[ʉ]   Close Central Round. Scots b*oo*t (short), SAE, NZE b*oo*t (long)

[ə]   'Schwa': General symbol for (mainly unstressed) vowels between half-open and half-close central. SBE moth*e*r, c*o*mmand

[ɜ]   Half-Open Central Unround. RP h*u*rt (long)

[ɐ]   Open Central Unround. SBE t*a*, some SAE b*a*kkie, E U.S. t*o*p

[u]   Close Back Round. F t*ou*t (short), RP b*oo*t, G g*u*t (long)

[ɯ]   Close Back Unround. Second element of some AusE *boot* [ïɯ]

[o]   Half-Close Back Round. Scots *oa*t, F h*au*t (short), G B*oo*t (long)

[ɣ]   Half-Close Back Unround. Second element in SAE *out* [ɑɣ]; centralized [ɣ̈] in New York f*oo*t, first element of b*oo*t [ɣ̈ʊ]

[ʊ]   Half-Close Centralized Back Round. SBE f*oo*t, G Schm*u*tz

[ɔ]   Half-Open Back Round. Scots p*o*t, F c*o*mme (short), SBE b*ou*ght (long)

[ʌ]   Half-Open Back Unround. Scots b*u*t; more central [ʌ̈] in much SBE

[ɑ]   Open Back Unround. Dutch d*a*t (short), SBE f*a*st (long)

[ɒ]   Open Back Round. SBE, SAE p*o*t (short), Extreme SAE f*a*st (long)

Diacritics: Centralized varieties of vowels marked with [¨]; long vowels [:]; nasalized vowels [˜]; particularly close variants, not warranting the symbol for the next closer vowel [.].

2 Consonants

Consonants are classified by glottal state (voiced: vocal folds are vibrating vs. voiceless: not vibrating); place of articulation (the point in the vocal tract where the maximal constriction occurs); manner (the type of stricture, i.e. the manner in which airflow is impeded); nasality (whether there is airflow through the nasal cavity); and laterality (whether airflow is down the centre of the vocal tract, or along one or both sides). The basic arrangement here will be by manner, subclassified by place and other features. All segments not particularly specified have central airflow, and are non-nasal.

(a) *Stops (Complete closure)*
[p]   Voiceless Labial. E *p*it
[b]   Voiced Labial. E *b*it
[t̪]   Voiceless Dental. E eigh*t*h, F *t*u
[d̪]   Voiced Dental. E wi*d*th (if not [t̪]), F *d*eux
[t]   Voiceless Alveolar. E *t*ip
[d]   Voiced Alveolar. E *d*ip
[c]   Voiceless Palatal. E *k*ey, Afrikaans -*tj*ie
[ɟ]   Voiced Palatal. E *g*eese
[k]   Voiceless Velar. E *c*ot
[g]   Voiced Velar. E *g*ot
[ʔ]   Glottal. Vernacular Scots bu*tt*er, most English foo*t*ball

(b) *Affricates (Complete closure shading off into friction at the same place)*
[tʃ]   Voiceless Palato-Alveolar. E *ch*ur*ch*
[dʒ]   Voiced Palato-Alveolar. E *j*u*dg*e

(c) *Fricatives (Incomplete closure, with turbulent airflow between the articulators)*
[Φ]   Voiceless Labial. Japanese *F*uji, E *ph*ew
[β]   Voiced Labial. Spanish sa*b*er
[f]   Voiceless Labiodental. E *f*ew
[v]   Voiced Labiodental. E *v*iew
[θ]   Voiceless Dental. E *th*igh
[ð]   Voiced Dental. E *th*y
[s]   Voiceless Alveolar. E *s*ip
[z]   Voiced Alveolar. E *z*ip
[ʃ]   Voiceless Palato-Alveolar. E *sh*ip, o*c*ean, na*t*ion
[ʒ]   Voiced Palato-Alveolar. E rou*g*e, vi*s*ion
[ç]   Voiceless Palatal. Std G i*ch*, some E *h*ue

340

[j]   Voiced Palatal. G *ja*
[x]   Voiceless Velar. G a*ch*, Scots lo*ch*
[ɣ]   Voiced Velar. Spanish a*g*o, N German sa*g*en
[χ]   Voiceless Uvular. Dutch, Afrikaans *g*oed
[ʁ]   Voiced Uvular. F *r*ouge, G *r*ot, older Northumberland *r*ed
[h]   Voiceless Glottal. E *h*ow, *wh*o
[ɦ]   Voiced glottal or breathy-voiced. E a*h*ead, SAE *h*ead

(d) *Nasals (Stops with opening into nasal cavity): all voiced*
[m]   Labial. E *m*oo
[n̪]   Dental. E te*n*th
[n]   Alveolar. E *n*ew
[ɲ]   Palatal. F vi*gn*e
[ŋ]   Velar. E si*ng*, si*n*k

(e) *Lateral*
[l̪]   Voiced Dental. E fi*l*th
[l]   Voiced Alveolar. E *l*ip
[l̥]   Voiceless Alveolar. E p*l*ay
[ɬ]   Voiceless Alveolar Fricative. Welsh *ll*an, Zulu Um*hl*anga

(f) *Central Approximants*
[j]   Voiced Palatal. E *y*ou
[w]   Voiced Labial-Velar. E *w*oo
[w̥]   Voiceless Labial-Velar. Scots, some U.S. English *wh*ich (where
                      distinct from *w*itch)
[ɹ]   Voiced Alveolar. E *r*eal

(g) *Taps and Trills*
[r]   Voiced Alveolar Trill. Italian *r*osso, Afrikaans *r*ooi
[ɾ]   Voiced Alveolar Tap. U.S. bu*tt*er, older RP ve*r*y, conservative
                      Scots *r*ed

The symbol [ʰ] indicates aspiration; [~] marks velarization, as in SBE syllable-final [ɫ]. In discussions of historical Indo-European and citations of Sanskrit, [ˌ] under a consonant means that it's syllabic; otherwise [˳] = voicelessness, and [ˌ] syllabicity.

APPENDIX II
OTHER SYMBOLS

[ ]   Encloses phonetic transcriptions. In syntax, marks off a subordinate clause or other constituent under discussion

/ /   Encloses phonemic transcription

>   'Becomes', 'Develops into'

<   'Derives from'

[$_x$Y]   Item Y belongs to category x

*   In historical discussion, a reconstructed category; in non-historical discussion, an ungrammatical or unacceptable structure or sequence

S   Relatively prominent category (with respect to stress)

W   Relatively non-prominent category (with respect to stress)

σ   Syllable

 σ́   Stressed Syllable

V́   Stressed Vowel (primary stress)

V̀   Stressed Vowel (secondary stress)

Ø   Zero, null

~   Varies with

{ }   Encloses a set

GLOSSARY

This glossary contains virtually all technical linguistic terms used in this book. Those defined fully in the text are given minimal entries – sometimes only section references, if this seems to be adequate. Others are treated more fully, with references to the text, and occasional suggestions for further reading. In some cases new technical terms or synonyms are introduced in an entry; these are in SMALL CAPS. Items in **boldface** refer to an entry elsewhere in the glossary. For fuller definitions, Crystal (1985c) is very useful, as are most of the introductory texts cited in the notes to chs. 1, 3, 4, 5 – especially Lyons (1968). In general, ordinary commercial dictionaries are likely to be unhelpful or misleading for technical definitions; specialist dictionaries like Crystal or textbooks in the field are likely to be both more accurate and more in keeping with current professional usage.

ablative The **case** typically expressing movement-from, or any expression (e.g. a prepositional phrase) with that function.

ablaut A set of **Indo-European** vowel **alternations**, showing up as differences in vowel quality and/or length: e.g. the **root** vowels in L *regō* 'I rule' vs. *rēxī* 'I have ruled'. In **Germanic**, the vowel **grades** of the **strong verb**. [§4.5.5]

accent (a) The **phonetic** and **phonological** features of a particular **dialect**; (b) prominence (e.g. **stress**) assigned to a particular **syllable**. [§§3.4–5]

accessibility hierarchy [§4.6.3]

accusative The **case** typically marking the **direct object** of a verb.

acronym A 'word' formed by reading a set of initials as if they constituted a real spelling: e.g. UNESCO /juːnéskəʊ/.

active see **voice** (a)

adposition An item typically marking local relations between some other expression and a noun or NP, its **object** (e.g. *to* [*New York*]). Those preceding are PREPOSITIONS, those following POSTPOSITIONS. [§4.2]

adversative A construction indicating opposition or antithesis, e.g. *X, whereas Y*.

affix A grammatical item, normally incapable of standing alone, attached to a full word or **stem** (its BASE); those preceding the bases are PREFIXES, those following SUFFIXES, those inside INFIXES. [§4.2]

affricate A consonant consisting of a **stop** closure released into a **fricative** at the same **place of articulation**: e.g. [tʃ dʒ] in *chew, Jew*. [Appendix I, §2(b)]

agent A **semantic role** indicating the deliberate or intentional performer of an action, as distinct in principle from the **grammatical role** of **subject**. [§4.7.1]

agglutinating [§4.2]

agreement see **concord**

Aitken's Law The **rule** controlling the length of vowels in Scots. [§5.7.1]

allegro rule A **rule** governing modifications in rapid or connected speech. [§§3.1, 3.7]

allophone A **realization** of a **phoneme**. [§3.1]

alternation A situation where some linguistic unit has different **realizations** under different (normally **rule**-governed) conditions: e.g. **allophones** of a **phoneme** alternate in particular environments ([tʰ] in *top*, [t] in *stop* both realizing /t/). Or phonemes may alternate in grammatical environments, e.g. the stressed vowels of *divíne, divínity*, etc.

alveolar Articulated at the ALVEOLAR RIDGE, the bony projection of the **palate** behind the upper incisors: e.g. [t d n].

analytic Of the expression of a category by means of separate words rather than in SYNTHETIC form via **affixes**: e.g. analytic *more beautiful* vs. synthetic *ugli-er*.

anaphoric Of a pronoun or other item referring back to some preceding one, its ANTECEDENT: e.g. *he* in *Sam left and then he came back*.

Anglo-Frisian [§1.4]

animate Denoting a living being, e.g. *man, dog*.

antecedent see **anaphoric**

antepenult Third from last **syllable** in a word.

aorist A verb form unspecified for **aspect**: e.g. the English **past** (*he went*) vs. the **perfect** (*he has gone*).

approximant A **segment** produced with the articulators neither making a full closure, nor producing a channel narrow enough to cause friction: e.g. [j w]. Normally of consonants, but on this definition applies to vowels as well. [Appendix I, §2]

articulator Any structure either moving to effect a **stricture** in the vocal tract (ACTIVE articulator), or serving as a target of such a movement (PASSIVE articulator). E.g. respectively the tongue tip and upper incisors in [θ ð].

aspect A time-related category distinct from **tense**, indicating such properties of an action or state as completeness, duration, habitualness, etc. [§4.5.2]

aspiration A period of **voiceless** airflow between the release of a consonantal closure and the onset of **voice** on a following vowel. [§§3.2.1, 3.2.3]

assimilation Any process by which some **segment** becomes more like or identical to another. [§3.7]

attributive Of an adjective in pre-noun position, e.g. *red socks*; as opposed to PREDICATE adjective, one following its **head**, typically after a **copula**, as in *Max is hyperactive*.

auxiliary A verb typically appearing in a two-verb or longer sequence, where the central meaning is carried by the **(nonfinite) main verb**, and **tense, number** etc. by the auxiliary. [§§4.5.1, 4.5.4–5]

back-formation Creation of a new 'simple' word by (erroneous) analysis of an apparently complex one: e.g. *burgle* < *burglar* interpreted as *burgle* + *er*; or extracting a not-yet-existing simple form from a complex one, e.g. *edit* < the earlier *editor*.

back vowel One whose maximal **stricture** is toward the rear of the oral cavity, opposite the **velum, uvula** or **pharynx**: e.g. [u o ɑ]. [Appendix I, §1]

bahuvrīhi A compound of the type *redskin, barefoot*. [§4.8.2]

Baltic [§1.3]

base see **affix**

basic word-order The characteristic and statistically dominant 'neutral' order of sentence elements in a language. [§4.2]

beneficiary A **semantic role** encoding 'person/thing for whom/which something is done'. [§4.7.1]

blend A word formed by deleting material in two words set back to back: e.g. *motel* < *mo*(tor ho)*tel*. Also PORTMANTEAU WORD. [§4.8.6]

borrowing Perhaps better TRANSFER; taking items from one language into another. Borrowed items are LOANS. [ch. 2, *passim*]

boundary (a) A linguistically significant interface between items, with (normally) no physical existence in itself, but which triggers linguistic processes of one kind or another. E.g. word- and **morpheme**-boundaries [see discussion in §5.7.1]; (b) a division between dialect areas. [§5.2]

breathy voice A state of the **glottis** in which the **vocal folds** vibrate for part of their length, but there is a chink open at the back of the larynx through which **voiceless** non-vibrating air passes simultaneously with **voiced** air, giving a 'breathy' or 'sighing' effect. E /h/ between vowels (e.g. *ahead*) is usually breathy voiced, as opposed to the voiceless **allophone** in *head*; *bh, dh, gh* in transliterations from Indian languages (*bhaji, ghee, Gandhi*) usually represent consonants of this kind.

Brythonic [§§1.3, 2.3]

case (a) An abstract category involving the relations (both grammatical and **semantic**) contracted by NPs with verbs and with each other, or

345

their roles within **clauses** and **phrases**; (b) the explicit marking of such relations and roles with **affixes** or other formal devices. So in sense (a) *Mary* in *Mary loves John* is grammatically '**nominative**' – being **subject** of a verb; but formally (in sense (b)) it is not distinct from 'accusative' *Mary* in *John loves Mary* (**direct object**). Whereas in Latin, the same noun in these two case-roles would be marked differently, i.e. *Mari-a Iohann-em amat* 'Mary loves John' vs. *Mari-am Iohann-es amat* 'John loves Mary'. Here case-relations in sense (a) are also marked in sense (b).

calque Or LOAN-TRANSLATION. A form of partial **borrowing** where a complex item is literally translated, piece-by-piece: e.g. E *skyscraper* > G *Wolkenkratzer*, F *gratte-ciel*.

Celtic [§§1.3, 2.3]

central vowel One formed with the maximal **stricture** opposite the juncture of the **palate** and **velum**, e.g. unstressed [ə] in *mother*, stressed [ɜː] in SBE *bird*. [Appendix I, §1]

centralized Of a vowel rather advanced from **back** or retracted from **front**, but not fully **central**: e.g. [ɪ ʊ]. [Appendix I, §1]

chain shift A set of related sound changes, with an internal relation of mutual implication: e.g. where a **low** vowel raises and 'pushes' the vowel above it into raising (a PUSH CHAIN), or a **high** vowel diphthongizes and 'drags' the vowel below it into its own former position (DRAG CHAIN). [See discussion and diagrams in §§3.10, 5.4, 5.8.4]

citation-form The maximally careful pronunciation of a word in isolation. [§§3.1, 3.7]

clause (a) A grammatical unit consisting at least of a **subject** and verb (in this sense a simple **sentence** – consisting only of a **main clause** – is itself a clause); (b) a subject + verb sequence within a **complex** or **compound** sentence; (c) a unit of roughly this type within a complex sentence serving in the role of a noun or adjective or adverb. [§§4.6.1–2]

clear see **dark**

clefting [§4.7.2]

clipping [§4.8.6]

clitic A grammatical item, essentially an independent word rather than an **affix**, attached to and forming a phonological unit with another form (its HOST): e.g. *-n't* in English 'contracted' negatives, where the full word *not* is reduced and rhythmically attached to an **auxiliary** verb. [§3.4]

close vowel One with maximal **stricture** between the tongue and upper part of the vocal tract. Also HIGH: e.g. [i y u]. [Appendix I, §1]

cluster A sequence of **segments** (either vowels or consonants) normally forming (part of) a basic **syllable** constituent (**onset, peak, coda**): e.g. /aɪ/, /ts/ in *bites* /baɪts/.

coda The constituent of a **syllable** following the **peak**: e.g. /t/ in *cat*, /ts/ in *cats*. [§3.3]

cognate Having the same ancestor. English and German are cognate languages, descending from **Proto-Germanic**; E *tooth*, G *Zahn*, F *dent*, Welsh *dant*, Lith *dantìs* are cognate words, descending from the same IE **root**.

comitative The **case** relation or **semantic role** involving accompaniment: e.g. (*I came*) *with my friends*.

comparative (a) Involving the **reconstruction** of earlier linguistic forms by comparing and projecting from attested ones: e.g. comparison of L *pater*, E *father*, OIr *athir* allows reconstruction of initial */p-/ in the IE **root** 'father': see discussion in §§1.3, 1.6; (b) a form of an adverb or adjective: see **comparison**.

comparison The specification of 'degree of' a property attributed by an adjective or adverb. Typically involving the degrees POSITIVE (*big*), COMPARATIVE (*bigger*), SUPERLATIVE (*biggest*).

complement (a) A **clause** or clause-like structure serving a noun-like function in relation to a verb or other noun or NP: [§§4.6.1–2]; (b) a noun or NP following a **copula** (often called a PREDICATE NOMINAL), e.g. *John is* [*a cannibal*].

complementary distribution The occurrence of two or more items in mutually exclusive environments: e.g. in SBE **clear** [l] occurs only syllable-initially and **dark** [ɫ] only syllable-finally.

complementizer A form introducing or otherwise marking a **subordinate clause**; in traditional grammars often a SUBORDINATING CONJUNCTION. [§§4.6.2–3]

complex (a) Of a word containing more than one formative element, e.g. a **compound** like *blackbird* or an **inflected** form like *walk-s*; (b) of a **sentence** containing at least one **subordinate clause**.

compound (a) A form consisting of two or more independent words collapsed under a single **stress**-contour (*bláckbird*): [§4.8.2]; (b) of a **phrase** or **sentence** containing two or more elements of equal status and identical or similar grammatical structure, e.g. *boys and girls*, *Adam delved and Eve span*. Note (unfortunately) that the usual terminology allows a compound noun like *blackbird* to be described as 'complex'; but not a compound phrase or sentence.

compound stress rule (CSR) The **rule** assigning initial stress to **compounds** in English and related languages. [§§3.4, 3.6]

concord Also AGREEMENT. The imposition of a particular form by some other element in a **sentence** or **phrase**, specifically the triggering of formal modification by some property of the controlling element: e.g.

347

English verbs agree with their **subjects** in **person** and **number**, French adjectives agree with their **head** nouns in **gender** and number. [§4.1]

conditional Of any item or sequence expressing a condition: e.g. *if I were king* (*I'd have a decent salary*).

conjugation (a) The set of forms of a verb; (b) a class of verbs whose conjugation is generally the same, e.g. Latin 'first conjugation' verbs with **infinitive** in *-āre*, pres I sg in *-ō*, 2 sg *-as*, etc.

conjunction A form that relates two like or equal constituents (e.g. the COORDINATING conjunctions *and*, *but*, *or*).

contrastive Capable of signalling a difference in meaning. E.g. the **phonemes** /p/ and /t/ in English are shown to be contrastive by the fact that the substitution of one for the other effects a distinction in meaning (*pat* ≠ *tat*, etc.).

conversion see **zero-derivation**

copula A 'linking' verb whose **subject** and **complement** are of the same status, e.g. a verb expressing notions of identity or equality; characteristically the verb *to be*.

coreferent Of NPs or similar expressions that refer to the same entity: e.g. JOHN *came in and then* HE *sat down*, I *admire* MYSELF.

creole A **pidgin** that has acquired native speakers, and is losing typical pidgin features and acquiring those of a full language.

dark Of consonants with a secondary or additional articulation toward the rear of the oral cavity, most often used of **velarized** /l/; as opposed to CLEAR, i.e. either with no additional articulation, or **palatalized**.

dative A **case** expressing the general notion 'motion toward'.

deadjectival Of a process or **affix** forming some other part of speech from an adjective. [§4.8.5]

declarative A **sentence** type used for assertions or statements, e.g. *the world is flat*.

declension (a) The set of forms (**case**, **number**, etc.) of a noun, pronoun or adjective; (b) a class of nouns, etc. declined the same way, e.g. the Latin 'fourth declension' with nom sg in *-us*, gen sg in *-ūs*.

deictic see **deixis**

deixis The linguistic reflection of the orientation of discourse participants and their surroundings in time and space, normally with reference to the speaker. (Adj. DEICTIC.) [§4.4]

demonstrative A **deictic** pronoun or adjective, e.g. *this, that*.

denominal Of a process or **affix** forming some other part of speech from a noun. [§4.8.5]

dental Of a consonant produced with the fore part of the tongue making a **stricture** with the upper incisors: e.g. [θ ð].

deontic A **modality** expressing obligation or command. [§4.5.4]

derivation Word-formation by **affix** or other processes, excluding forma-

tion of **compounds**. The set of such processes in a language is its
DERIVATIONAL MORPHOLOGY, and a word formed by such a process is
DERIVED. [§4.8, *passim*]

determiner An article, **demonstrative**, etc. introducing and defining the
overall character of a **noun phrase**. [§§4.3.1–2, 4.3.4]

deverbal Of a process or **affix** forming some other part of speech from a
verb. [§4.8.5]

dialect A regionally, temporally or socially defined variety of a
language, i.e. any member of the set of varieties generally going under
a particular language name. [§§1.1–2, ch. 5]

diphthong A syllable **peak** with two detectably different vowel qualities:
e.g. [ɔɪ] in *boy*.

direct object see **object**

distal A parameter of **deixis** reflecting location/motion away from the
speaker.

distribution The set of constraints on the occurrence of some linguistic
item: e.g. the occurrence of *him*, *her* only in non-**subject** positions, the
limitation of /h/ to syllable-initial position.

do-**support** The use of an 'empty' form of *do* as a carrier of **tense** and
number in English questions and negations lacking an overt **auxiliary**
verb (e.g. DO *you know*?). [§4.5.4]

drag chain see **chain shift**

Dravidian A language family mainly of southern India, including Tamil,
Malayalam, Kannada.

dual see **number**

dvandva A compound of the type *Alsace-Lorraine*. [§4.8.2]

Early Modern English The conventional term for the language roughly
1500–1700.

East Germanic The branch of the **Germanic** family containing Gothic.
[§§1.1–2]

ejective A consonant produced not with lung air, but with an airstream
produced by the closed **glottis** moved rapidly upwards like a piston,
with an audible 'pop' on release.

entailment A logical relation between **sentences**, where the truth of one
implies the truth of certain others. [§4.7.1]

epistemic Of a **modality** expressing a speaker's mental state with respect
to his assessment of the possibility, probability etc. of a state of affairs.
[§4.5.4]

extraposition The 'movement' of a constituent to a position outside the
boundaries of a **clause**, as a way of expressing a relationship between
two sentences with the same constituent in different positions (e.g. *a
man* [*that I used to know*] *was there* vs. *a man was there* [*that I used to
know*]. [§4.6.2]

extraterritorial Of a **dialect** that results from the movement of speakers from an original homeland to some other place outside national boundaries. [§5.8]

finite Of a verb form marked for **tense, person, number** (or at least tense). [§4.5.1]

focus The speaker's psychological 'centre of interest' in an **utterance**; where this does not coincide with the grammatical subject various focussing rules can shift NPs to unaccustomed or 'marked' positions, e.g. moving a non-subject to the head of a sentence in *John, I really hate him*. [§4.7]

foot A rhythmic unit consisting of a **stressed syllable** plus any material to its right not including another stress: *would, wouldn't, wouldn't he* are all single feet. [§3.4]

fricative A consonant produced with a narrow aperture between two **articulators**, so the airstream passing between is turbulent and displays audible friction: e.g. [f v s z]. [Appendix I, §1]

fronting Movement of any articulation forward in the mouth.

front vowel One whose maximal **stricture** is opposite the **palate**: e.g. [i y e]. [Appendix I, §1]

future A **tense** or tense-like category referring primarily to future time. [§4.5.2]

geminate A long or 'double' **segment**, interpreted as a sequence of two identical short ones: e.g. Sw *natt* 'night' [nat:] alternatively [natt].

gender Any organization of nouns (and/or pronouns) into a classificatory system, where the classes control **concord**. Gender systems may be arbitrary (e.g. the neuter vs. non-neuter system of Dutch) or completely or partly based on 'real-world' properties like sex, animacy, humanness, shape, etc. [§§4.1–3]

genitive A **case** normally encoding notions like 'possession' or 'origin'. [§§4.3.1–3]

Germanic A family within **Indo-European**, containing English in one of its branches. [§§1.3.4, ch. 6]

gerund A noun derived from a verb, e.g. *walking* (*is healthy*); in English distinct (functionally) from the PRESENT PARTICIPLE in *-ing*. [§§4.5.1, 4.5.5]

glottal stop A **stop** consonant formed by a complete closure of the **vocal folds**.

glottis The space between the **vocal folds**, acting as a valve between the oral cavity and trachea, controlling airflow to and from the lungs.

Goidelic [§§1.3, 2.3]

government In traditional terminology, the determination of particular **case** forms of nouns or pronouns by their 'governing' verbs or prepositions: e.g. some Latin verbs govern **accusative** (*libr-um legō* 'I read the book'), others the **ablative** (*libr-ō utor* 'I use the book'). [§4.2]

grade The vowel associated with a particular **tense** form of a **strong verb**: e.g. the /ɪ/ in *sing* vs. the /ʌ/ in *sung*. [§4.5.5]

grammaticalized Encoded obligatorily in the grammatical structure of a language; e.g. since every (full) **sentence** in English must have at least one verb marked for **tense**, tense is a grammaticalized category.

grammatical role The syntactic function of a noun, pronoun or NP with respect to the verb of a **clause**: e.g. **subject, direct object**. [§§4.7.1–2]

Great Vowel Shift (GVS) A massive transformation of the English long vowel system, starting in the 15th century. [§3.10]

Grimm's Law A systemic shift of the **Proto-Indo-European stops**, one of the defining features of **Germanic**. [§1.3]

habitual An **aspect** encoding the notion 'action typically or habitually performed'. [§4.5.2]

half-close vowel A vowel lower in **height** than **close**, but higher than **half-open**: e.g. [e o]. [Appendix I, §1]

half-open vowel One higher than **open**, lower than **half-close**: e.g. [ɛ ɔ]. [Appendix I, §1]

head (a) An obligatory and characteristic constituent of a **phrase**; (b) that which is modified by an adjective or adjectival **clause**; (c) the element in a **compound** that determines its part of speech, is marked for **number**, etc. (e.g. *-man* in *milkman*). [§4.3.1 on heads in general, §4.3.6 on heads of relative clauses]

heavy syllable One whose **rhyme** contains a long vowel or **diphthong**, or a short vowel plus two or more consonants. [§§3.3.4–6]

height The degree of **stricture** of a vowel. [Appendix I, §1]

High German The group of dialects originating in the interior uplands of Germany, characterized by the High German Consonant Shift. [§1.4]

high vowel see **close vowel**

homophones Two or more words different in meaning but phonologically identical: e.g. *but/butt, right/write/rite/wright*.

hortatory A **modality** expressing 'exhortation'. [§4.5.3]

hypercorrection The creation of anomalous forms through attempts at imitating prestige forms, or avoiding stigmatized ones, without real understanding of the issues involved. E.g. avoidance of *it's me* and *me and him went* leading to **he brought it to my wife and I*.

hypotaxis **Subordination** explicitly marked by a **complementizer** or in some other way. [§4.6.2]

imperative (a) A **mood** expressing commands or orders; (b) a **sentence**-type characteristically so used. [§4.5.3]

imperfect A combined **tense/aspect** form indicating **progressive** aspect in the past (e.g. F *je disais* 'I was saying').

inchoative An **aspect** expressing the idea of 'coming into being' or 'becoming'; e.g. *become, grow* are inherently inchoative verbs. [§4.5.2]

independent clause see **main clause**

indicative A **mood** expressing assertion. [§4.5.3]

indirect object see **object**

Indo-European (IE) The language family containing most of the languages of modern Europe and northern India. [§1.3]

infinitive A **nonfinite** verb form that functions like a noun; in English, either the bare **stem** of the verb (*I can* SWIM*)* or a form preceded by *to* (*I like* TO SWIM). [§§4.5.1, 4.5.5]

infix see **affix**

inflected Carrying an **affix** or other marker of grammatical category of function; e.g. *walk-ed, took* are marked in different ways for **tense**. See **inflectional**.

inflecting [§4.2]

inflectional Of that portion of a language's **morphology** that is not used in **word-formation**, but for the marking of grammatical categories like **case, number, gender, tense**. [§4.2]

Ingvaeonic [§1.4]

instrumental A **case** or expression encoding the notion 'instrument' or 'means by which something is done': e.g. (*I hit him*) *with a hammer*.

interrogative A **mood** expressing questioning; a **sentence** type characteristically used for asking questions. [§4.5.3]

intransitive Of a verb that does not take an **object**. As opposed to **transitive**.

isochrony The rhythmic spacing of **phonological** elements at roughly equal time-intervals; usually **stresses** (in STRESS-TIMED languages) or **syllables** (in SYLLABLE-TIMED languages). [§3.4]

isogloss A line on a dialect map separating regional features or defining a **boundary**. [§5.2]

koiné A **standard**(ized) language with components from various **dialects** spoken in a multidialectal community, used as a *lingua franca* throughout the community, and not identical with any regional dialect; e.g. literary Greek of the early Christian Era, the Old English 'poetic dialect'.

labial Of consonants with the lips as primary articulators: (a) labials proper or BILABIALS with both lips involved ([p b m]); (b) LABIODEN-TALS where the upper incisors articulate with the lower lip ([f v]).

labiodental see **labial**

lateral A consonant in whose articulation the airstream passes out along one or both sides of the tongue, rather than down the centre of the vocal tract: e.g. [ɬ]. [Appendix I, §2(e)]

length The (relative) duration of a consonant or vowel; a language 'has length' if some subset of its vowels and/or consonants is consistently – all things being equal – relatively longer than another. [§3.2.3]

lexicalization The encoding of a concept in a single word; the process by which this comes about. E.g. most dialects of English don't lexicalize the concept 'bovine animal of either sex'; but some do, having *beast* in this sense.

lexis Vocabulary, especially as a level of linguistic description, distinct from **phonology**, **syntax**, etc.

liquid A **sonorant** consonant, typically not **nasal**; in standard terminology mainly '*r*-sounds' (**taps**, **trills** and others) and **laterals**; in some frameworks (as in this book) including what other writers call 'semivowels' or 'glides', e.g. [j w].

loan(word) see **borrowing**

locative A **case** or other expression encoding 'location-in-which'; e.g. the prepositions *in, on, at* are locative.

Low German The northern dialect group within West Germanic that has not undergone certain changes typical of **High German**. Crudely, the dialects in which 'water' has a medial /t/ rather than /s/: E, Du *water* vs. G *Wasser*. The term is sometimes restricted to dialects of German proper; in a larger historical context it can be extended to Dutch and even English.

low vowel see **open vowel**

main clause Also INDEPENDENT. One capable of 'standing alone', i.e. typically containing a **finite verb**, not introduced by any marker of **subordination**. [§4.6.1]

main stress rule (MSR) The **rule** assigning **stress** to regularly accented English words. [§§3.4–6]

main verb The one carrying 'primary' meaning in a construction with an **auxiliary**. [§§4.5.1, 4.5.4]

margins The 'outside' constituents of a **syllable**, i.e. **onset** and **coda**.

merger The falling together of two or more linguistic categories: e.g. the collapse of OE dat sg *him* and acc sg *hine* in *him*, or of ME /e:/ in *beet* and /ɛ:/ in *beat* in Modern /i:/.

Middle English The traditional name for the language roughly 1100–1400.

mid vowel A category conflating **half-open** and **half-close** vowels: e.g. [e ɛ o ɔ]. [Appendix I, §1]

minimal pair A pair of words differing in only one **phoneme**; thus a test for **contrastive** status (e.g. *tip: dip*).

modal (a) Of or pertaining to **modality**; (b) a class of **auxiliary** verbs (*can, may, must, shall, will*) with certain peculiarities of both form and function. [§§4.5.3–5]

modality The category expressing speakers' attitudes toward the content of an **utterance**, e.g. in terms of certainty, desire to impose obligations on others, etc. [§4.5.3]

modification A relation between an item like an adjective, adverb or **clause** acting as one and some other item, in which a property is attributed to the **head** of the construction.

monophthong A steady-state vowel, long or short; the change of a **diphthong** to a monophthong is MONOPHTHONGIZATION.

mood The grammatical category encoding **modality**, e.g. **indicative**, **subjunctive**, **imperative**. [§4.5.3]

mora A unit of **quantity** or WEIGHT, e.g. one element of a **diphthong** or long vowel or consonant **cluster**. [§3.2]

morph A piece of linguistic material at the **phonetic** or **phonological** level, unanalyzable into any smaller items without loss of meaning, but not necessarily realizing a single **morpheme**. E.g. *-s* in *walk-s, -ed* /t/ in *walk-ed, walk-*.

morpheme The grammatical equivalent of a **phoneme**: a minimal piece of grammatical material, which may or may not correspond to a single **morph**. E.g. the morpheme (= 'category') {past} is represented in both *walk-ed* and *drove, fit* (past of *fit*), but only in *walked* does it correspond to a morph. But for purposes of grammatical analysis it is often useful to represent (say) all pasts of verbs as fundamentally the same, sequences of {stem} + {past}, so that *walked* = {walk} + {past}, *drove* = {drive} + {past}.

morphology (a) The subdiscipline of linguistics concerned with word-structure (i.e. the deployment of **morphemes** in words); (b) the means at a language's disposal for **inflection** and **derivation**, and its rules for word-structure and formation. [§§4.1, 4.8]

morphophonology Also MORPHOPHONEMICS. (a) The linguistic subdiscipline concerned with **alternations** of **phonemes** in morphological contexts; (b) the set of such alternations in a language. E.g. the consonant alternations in *divide* ~ *divisive* ~ *division* are part of English morphophonology. [§§3.1, 4.8.4]

nasal (a) Of a segment produced with lowered velum, allowing air to pass through the nasal cavity and cause it to resonate: e.g. nasal(ized) vowels like [ã], nasal consonants like [m n]; (b) as a noun, a nasal consonant.

nominative The **case** typically marking the **grammatical role** of **subject**.

nonfinite Of a verb form not marked for **tense**, etc. (see **finite**); e.g. **gerund**, **participle**, **infinitive**. [§§4.5.1, 4.5.5]

nonrestrictive see **restrictive**

non-rhotic see **rhotic**

North Germanic The branch of **Germanic** containing the Scandinavian languages. [§§1.3–4]

Northwest Germanic The ancestor of both **North** and **West Germanic**. [§1.4]

noun phrase (NP) A **phrase** whose **head** is a noun or pronoun, and which has the typical distribution and function of a noun. [§4.3.1]

nuclear stress rule (NSR) The **rule** in English governing the assignment of **stress** to a **phrase** (e.g. *black bírd*). [§3.4]

nucleus An alternative term for **peak**; most often used in identifying the members of the vowel system of a language, since it covers both simple vowels and diphthongs.

number A grammatical category (roughly) involving the 'counting' of objects, frequently deployed in **concord** systems, as well as being a primary or inherent feature of nouns and pronouns. The two basic terms of number systems are SINGULAR (one and one only) vs. PLURAL (more than one); some languages also have a DUAL (two and two only, as in OE or Classical Greek), and some a TRIAL (three . . .). [§§4.3.1–3].

object (a) A **noun phrase** in a non-**subject** function, normally one standing after any verb except a **copula**. The single object of a **transitive** verb (as in *I saw John*) is a DIRECT OBJECT; one appearing in two-object constructions (*him* in *I gave him the book*) is an INDIRECT OBJECT; (b) a noun phrase following a preposition and serving as its 'goal': e.g. *the table* in *on the table, under the table*, etc.; also called OBLIQUE OBJECT.

oblique Of any non-**nominative** form of a noun or pronoun.

obstruent A consonant of the class consisting of **stops, fricatives** and **affricates**, grouped together because of their tendency toward similar behaviour, and certain **phonetic** attributes (e.g. a tendency to be **voiceless**).

offglide The second **mora** of a **diphthong**; a short transitional segment. E.g. [-ɪ] in [aɪ], [ə] before [ɬ] as in some dialects' realization of *feel* as [fiːəɬ].

onomatopoeia The 'imitation' in linguistic form of nonlinguistic sounds; e.g. *mew, burp, thump, ding-dong*.

onset The **syllable** constituent preceding the **rhyme**: e.g. /sk/ in *scat*. [§3.3]; the first element of a diphthong.

open syllable One with an empty **coda**: e.g. *eye* /aɪ/.

open vowel One with a low tongue position, or a minimal degree of **stricture**. Also LOW vowel. E.g. [æ ɑ]. [Appendix I, §1]

optative A **modality** or **mood** expressing wishing. [§4.5.3]

orthographic Referring to spelling.

palatal Pertaining to the (hard) PALATE, the bony roof of the mouth extending from behind the **alveolar** ridge to the **velum**. **Close front** vowels and [j] are palatal.

palatalize (a) To impose a palatal colour (i.e. an [i]-resonance) on a

355

non-palatal segment: e.g. /l/ in English tends to be palatalized before /j/ as in *million*; (b) to shift the articulation of a consonant from non-palatal (usually **alveolar** or **velar**) to palatal or **palato-alveolar**: e.g. changes like [t] > [tʃ], [k] > [tʃ].

palate see **palatal**

palato-alveolar Of a consonant articulated toward the rear of the **alveolar ridge**, with the body of the tongue normally raised toward the palate: e.g. [ʃ ʒ].

paradigm The set of forms belonging to a particular word-class or member of a word-class: e.g. the paradigm of the E noun encompasses its **singular**, **plural** and **genitive**; the paradigm of *man* is *man/men/man's/men's*.

parataxis The linking of **clauses** in a loose way, 'side-by-side', with no overt marker of their relationship. [§4.6.2]

participle A **nonfinite** verb form, functioning in English either as an adjective or along with an **auxiliary** in marking **aspect**. English has a PRESENT PARTICIPLE (*a writing man*, *he's writing*) and a PAST PARTICIPLE (*a written document*, *he has written*). [§§4.5.1, 4.5.5]

partitive A **case** category expressing the notions 'part of a whole' or 'portion': e.g. constructions with *some* (*of*).

passive see **voice** (a)

past A **tense** locating the content of an utterance as prior to the moment of speaking, and having secondary functions such as indicating 'non-reality' or 'psychological distance'. [§§4.1, 4.5.2]

past participle see **participle**

patient A **semantic role** involving the property of being the animate or sentient 'recipient' of the action of a verb. [§4.7.1]

peak The constituent of a syllable rhyme that bears SYLLABICITY, or the maximal output of acoustic energy; normally a vowel, but also a SYLLABIC CONSONANT as in *sh!*, *mm*. [§3.3]

penult The next-to-last **syllable** of a word.

perfect An **aspect** or aspect-like category encoding the notions 'completion', 'present relevance', 'anteriority'. [§4.5.2]

person A **deictic** category specifying the relation of the speaker (1 person) to addressee(s) (2 person) and other participants or objects in the field of discourse (3 person). Person may also be a secondary category of the verb, e.g. verbs may show **concord** with their subjects (*I walk* vs. *he walk-s*). [§§4.4–5]

pharyngeal Pertaining to the PHARYNX, the muscular tube forming the rear wall of the vocal tract between the larynx and the entry to the nasal cavity; a pharyngeal articulation involves movement of the root of the tongue toward the rear pharyngeal wall, or constriction of the tube itself.

phoneme A **phonological** unit serving a **contrastive** function; a minimal **segment**-sized unit capable of distinguishing meaning. [§3.1]

phonetic Pertaining to the physical realization of a **phonological** category or unit; or to the physical and perceptual aspects of the sound-structure of a language or of language in general. [§3.1]

phonological Pertaining to the structure, organization and overall behaviour of the sound-system of a language or of language in general; the phonology of a language is the inventory of **phonemes** and the **rules** for their deployment, among other things. In this latter, wider sense, 'the phonology of English' would include phonetics as well. [§§3.1–4]

phonotactics The **rules** for the **distribution** and grouping of **phonemes** in a language. [§§3.1, 3.2–3 *passim*]

phrase A construction type defined by a characteristic and obligatory element or **head**, and that typically has the same overall **distribution** as its head. [§4.3.1]

pidgin A special-purpose language with much reduced and simplified structure, that is not anyone's native language, and normally arises through the requirements of a contact situation, in which speakers of different languages have to communicate for limited purposes like trade.

place of articulation The location in the vocal tract where a **stricture** is formed (e.g. teeth, lips, etc.).

pluperfect past perfect (e.g. *I had gone*).

postposition see **adposition**

pragmatic Having to do with features of meaning embedded in or derived from the speech situation, including speaker's knowledge of conventions, the extralinguistic context, etc. E.g. the decision as to whether *can you pass the salt?* is a question about your ability at salt-passing (which is what it looks like grammatically) or a request to pass the salt is a pragmatic one. Generally, discourse or context-bound aspects of meaning, as opposed – roughly – to **semantic**.

predicate adjective see **attributive**

predication A **semantic** or logical structure in which some action or property is attributed to one or more entities; grammatically, most characteristically a **clause** with at least one NP.

prefix see **affix**

preposition see **adposition**

present A **tense** locating the content of an **utterance** as coterminous with the moment of speech; or in an extended sense expressing 'timeless truth'. [§4.5.2]

present participle see **participle**

preterite-present verb [§4.5.5]

principal parts A set of forms (particularly of a verb) which contain all the information necessary for constructing the rest of the forms in the **paradigm**. [§4.5.5]

progressive An **aspect** encoding the notion 'action currently in progress'. [§4.5.2]

proposition A logical or **semantic** construct, roughly equivalent to the 'basic content' of a **sentence**, devoid of **modality**, **tense**, etc. E.g. any sentence referring to John's falling (*John fell, John's falling, did John fall? John might not have fallen* ...) 'contains' the proposition 'John fall'. See further §4.5.3 and the entry in Crystal.

prosodic Pertaining to **stress** or rhythm or aspects of pitch (e.g. intonation).

Proto-Germanic [§§1.3–4]

Proto-Indo-European [§1.3]

proximal A parameter of **deixis** reflecting motion/location in the speaker's vicinity. See also **distal**. [§4.4]

pseudo-cleft [§4.7.2]

push chain see **chain shift**

qualifier An item further **modifying** an adjective or adverb, e.g. *very, quite, rather*, etc.

quantifier An item expressing general (not numerical) quantity: e.g. *some, any, all, each*.

quantity see **weight**

realization The concrete form taken by an abstract linguistic category: e.g. the **allophones** [p pʰ] are realizations of the **phoneme** /p/; the syntactic structure *be* + V-*ing* realizes **progressive.**

Received Pronunciation (RP) The **phonetic** and **phonological** attributes of a particular non-regional **dialect** of **standard** Southern British English; a class rather than local variety, what used to be (and sometimes still is) called 'Oxford' or 'BBC' English. [§§1.2, ch. 5, *passim*]

reconstruction Any process for recovering unattested or lost historical material; see discussion and examples in §1.6.

reduced vowel A short and/or **centralized** 'version' of another vowel; any 'neutral' (**central, mid**) vowel in an unstressed position: e.g. the unstressed vowels in *refér, cháracter*.

reduplication The complete or partial copying of a linguistic unit for **inflection** or **derivation**: e.g. L *canō* 'I sing', perf 1 sg *ce-cinī*, SAE *now-now* 'in the very near future, immediately'.

reflex The descendant of an older historical category.

reflexive Pertaining to the general function of self-reference; e.g. the special form of pronouns in object position **coreferent** to the subject of a clause (*myself* in *I'm shaving myself*); of the semantic property of a verb in which the subject normally implies itself as object (in *I'm shaving*, under normal conditions, the assumption is that I'm shaving myself).

register A stylistic, occupational or other context-determined or context-appropriate variety of a language: e.g. 'formal speech', 'clergyman's style', 'casual speech'. *Could you direct me to the bog, your Highness?* shows incongruities arising from mixing of registers. See Crystal at *register* (2) and his references.

relative clause One acting as an adjectival modifier of a noun or NP (its head). [§§4.6.1, 4.6.3]

relative pronoun One inside a **relative clause**, **coreferent** to some outside NP, and serving as a marker of the construction.

relativization strategy A particular formal way of constructing relative clauses (e.g. with a pronoun as in *the man* [WHO *was there*] vs. 'zero' as in *the man* [*I saw*]).

relic area A geographical area showing an archaic feature that was once more widespread, but now remains only in 'islands' of conservatism. [§5.2]

restrictive/nonrestrictive [§4.6.3]

retroflex Of an articulation produced with the tongue-tip curled back so that its underside contacts the rear of the **alveolar ridge** or the front of the **palate**.

rhotacism The change of some consonant (usually [s z]) to [r]. [§§1.3–4]

rhotic Of a dialect pronouncing historical /r/ in all positions, as opposed to a NON-RHOTIC one where /r/ occurs only before vowels. [§3.2.3]

rhyme The syllable constituent consisting of the **peak** and **coda**: e.g. /-æts/ in *cats*. [§3.3]

Romance The subfamily of languages descending ultimately from the spoken Latin of the late Empire: e.g. French, Spanish, Italian. [§1.3]

root (a) In a language with a particular kind of structure, the minimal string of segments carrying a particular sense – not a 'word', but a base for word-building. Thus L *dom-* 'house' as in *dom-u-s* (nom sg), *dom-u-m* (acc sg), etc. See also **stem**. (b) In (slightly loose) historical usage, the source of a word or group of words in a later language. Thus the Greek root *kard-* appears in E *card(iac)*, *card(iovascular)*, *(peri)cardium*; and the IE root */kr̥d- ~ kord- ~ kerd-/ appears in Gr *kard-*, L *cord-* and its derivatives in English (*cord(ial)*, *(re)cord*) – as well as in E *heart* and its cognates in Germanic (Du *hart*, G *Herz*, etc.).

rounding Protrusion and/or 'pouting' of the lips, as in the vowels of *boot, bought* in most British dialects.

rule In technical usage, a statement of a (perceived) regularity in a language: e.g. 'English verbs take -*s* in pres 3 sg', '/h/ appears only initially in the foot', etc. A 'rule of grammar' in this sense is not a prescription like 'don't end a sentence with a preposition', but a (statement of) a generalization from data, or a statement intended not only to generalize over a corpus of data, but to predict the properties of any not-yet-observed piece of a language. The status of a rule (whether it's a linguist's artifact or something 'inside the head' of a speaker) is dependent on beliefs associated with a linguist's general theory of language. This is a contentious issue at the moment. See Crystal's useful discussion and references.

runes The system used for writing Germanic languages before the introduction of the Latin alphabet by missionaries in the West, and a modified Graeco-Latin one for Gothic. [§1.3]

scope The domain over which a linguistic element operates: e.g. in *I do not want to do it*, the scope of *not* is [*want to do it*]; in *I don't think he'll arrive until tomorrow*, the scope of the negative doesn't include *think*; the paraphrase is *I think he won't arrive until tomorrow*.

segment A cover term for any vowel or consonant, at any level of description: e.g. *cat* is a sequence of three segments /kæt/, [kʰæt].

semantic Pertaining to 'inherent' or 'intralinguistic' meaning, i.e. divorced (as far as possible) from context. E.g. semantically *It's cold in here* is an assertion about the temperature; in **pragmatic** terms (given a particular discourse situation, the rules for normal interactions in English, etc.) it may be a request to turn on the heat or close the window.

semantic role The **semantic** contribution of an item (usually an NP) to the meaning of a sentence. [§4.7.1]

sentence A complex and controversial concept. The sense in which I use it in this book can perhaps be indicated by Crystal's definition (1985c, at *sentence*): 'The largest structural unit in terms of which the grammar of a language is organized'. This has its problems, but can serve as a beginning. Without going into the issue of 'completeness' (is *yes*, as an answer to *are you there?*, grammatically a sentence?) we can say at least that in general any main clause is a sentence. But the term is to be interpreted in a special way: a sentence is the 'abstract' or 'ideal' grammatical structure which is realized in some particular **utterance**. E.g. If I say *I am pregnant* five times, and write it twice, each of the seven 'performances' is of the same sentence, though the places, situations, even the physical media (speech vs. writing) are different. A coarse analogy to the sentence/utterance distinction might be that between a musical score and a performance: any performance of Mozart's Symphony No. 40 is an 'utterance' with respect to 'Mozart's 40th Itself'. Crystal's discussion and references are useful.

sentential Referring to a sentence, or any relation between parts of a sentence; having sentence-like properties.

shadow pronoun An 'extra' pronoun inside a **relative clause**, e.g. *his* in *the man [that I knew his daughter]*. [§§4.6.3–4]

sibilant A consonant (usually a **fricative**, but also an **affricate**) marked by high-frequency friction noise or 'hissing': e.g. [s z].

simple past A **past tense** form consisting of a verb alone (e.g. *went*, *walked*) with no **auxiliary**.

Slavonic [§1.3]

sonorant A consonant with a relatively high acoustic energy output, typically **voiced** (as opposed to an **obstruent**); especially a **nasal** or **liquid**. Also RESONANT.

split The development of a single category at any level into two or more distinctive categories: e.g. ME /u/ splits into modern /ʊ/ (*put*) and /ʌ/ (*putt*); Proto-Germanic splits into the various modern descendant languages, etc.

split infinitive An infinitive prefixed by *to*, with material between *to* and the verb itself: e.g. *to boldly go*.

standard A **dialect** with particular prestige and a certain degree of uniformity and official status, used as a community's medium for public discourse, education, etc. [§1.2]

stem In a language of a certain structural type, a **root** (sense (a)) plus a STEM-FORMATIVE: the unit made of the two is the base to which endings are attached. Thus L *domus* 'house' (nom sg) consists of root *dom-*, stem-formative *-u-*, and nom sg ending *-s*: i.e. it has the structure:

$$[_{\text{word}} [_{\text{stem}} [_{\text{root}} dom] \text{ -}u\text{- }] \text{ -}s]$$

In languages without a clear root/stem distinction, the term 'stem' is generally preferred: e.g. in *hous-es* the ending is attached to the noun stem. [§4.3.2]

stranding Leaving a preposition at the end of a **relative clause**, without a contiguous **object**: e.g. *the man [that I gave it* TO]. [§§2.6, 4.6.3]

stress A particular kind of **accent**, not normally associated primarily with pitch, but more characteristically with intensity ('loudness') and duration. Sometimes referred to as 'expiratory stress/accent' as against 'pitch-accent'. [§3.4]

stress-timing see **isochrony**

stricture The general term for a closure of any degree between two articulators: **stops**, **fricatives** and **approximants** represent three decreasing degrees of stricture.

strong adjective In Germanic languages of a more archaic type, the form of the adjective used with no preceding **inflected determiner**, and carrying maximal information (marking for **case**, **number**, **gender**, etc.). E.g. G *gut-es Bier* 'good beer', where the *-es* carries the information that the following noun is neuter, and not dative, and singular. Whereas in *das gut-e Bier* 'the good beer' (nom sg), the WEAK ADJECTIVE, the *-e* tells us little except that the adjective is preceded by a determiner; it's *das* that carries gender and number. [§§1.3, 4.3.4]

strong verb A Germanic verb-type that forms its **past tense** and **past participle** by means of vowel change within the **stem** rather than by a suffix. E.g. the type *drive/drove/driven* as opposed to *walk/walk-ed*, which are WEAK VERBS. Some verbs with internal vowel change however are counted as weak: *buy/bought, think/thought, leave/left* – since the past forms are easily segmented into stem + suffix: *bough-t, lef-t*, etc. [§§1.3, 4.5.5]

subject A **grammatical role** characterized among other things by a tendency to appear in the position of **focus**, and more importantly as a controller of **concord** on the verb. The notion is however extremely complex, and it's not clear whether all languages have such a category, and what its defining criteria ought to be. See Comrie (1981: ch. 5) for an illuminating discussion.

subjunctive A **mood** form of a verb (a) encoding **modalities** like **optative**, contrary-to-fact, doubt; (b) in Latin and German and some other languages, tending to mark certain kinds of **subordinate clauses**. [§§4.5.3, 4.5.5]

subordinate clause One that (a) performs the function of some other part of speech (e.g. a noun or adjective), and (b) is in some way not 'independent' or able to stand alone. As opposed to **main clause**. [§§4.6.1–4]

subordination A 'downgrading' of the status of one element with respect to another; e.g. modifiers are subordinate to their **heads**, subordinate clauses to main clauses.

suffix see **affix**

superlative see **comparison**

supine A **participle** (particularly in Latin) expressing a passive sense: e.g. *captus* '(having been) captured'.

suppletion 'Irregular' or unmotivated (i.e. not **rule**-governed) **alternation** within a **paradigm**: e.g. *went* as the past of *go*, *worse* as the comparative of *bad* (vs. 'regular' *walk/walked, red/redder*).

syllable A structured string of **segments**, the primary organizational unit in **phonology**; the domain of **phonotactics**, **stress**-assignment, etc. [§3.3]

syllable-timing see **isochrony**

syntax The level of linguistic organization involved with the distribution of higher-level units like words, **phrases** and **clauses** and the internal structure of the latter two; the study of this level; the set of **rules** controlling it in a given language.

tag-question One ending with a sequence designed to express the speaker's expectation of a particular answer: e.g. *he did, didn't he?/he didn't, did he?*

tap A consonant produced by a rapid BALLISTIC movement of an **articulator**, i.e. 'throwing' it against another; in effect a very short stop. E.g. [ɾ] in U.S. English *bitter, bidder* for medial /t d/.

tatpuruṣa A compound of the type *onion-skin, milk-bottle*. [§4.8.2]

tense A deictic category involving the relation of the content of an **utterance** to the moment of speaking. [§4.5.2]

traditional dialect The older type of rural dialect, insulated from influences of the **standard** and modern urban dialects. [§§5.2–4]

transformational grammar A type of syntactic theory characterized, among other things, by deriving occurring sentence-types from abstract 'underlying forms', often by means of formal operations called TRANSFORMATIONS, which 'move', delete and otherwise alter constituents. See Crystal at *transformation(al)*, and his references.

transitive Of a verb whose action is 'carried over' from **subject** to **direct object**; any verb that characteristically takes a direct object, or a **clause** containing such a construction.

trill A consonant produced by allowing an articulator to be vibrated by an airstream passing over it, producing a sequence of very short taps: e.g. [r] as in Italian *rosso*. Sometimes called a ROLL.

truth-conditions The circumstances under which a **sentence** is a true description of the state of 'the world'. [§4.7.1]

Turkic A family including a number of languages of the Near East, e.g. Turkish, Azerbaidjani, Uzbek.

umlaut A type of **assimilation** in which a vowel changes in response to some element (normally another vowel) in a following syllable. [§3.8]

utterance A particular use of a **sentence** at a given time and place.

uvula The small non-muscular appendage at the back of the **velum**; the back of the tongue can articulate with it to form UVULAR sounds, like the **fricative** [ʁ] (as in F *rouge*).

uvular see **uvula**

variable A set of alternative **realizations** of a linguistic category, each of which has a particular social value. [§5.5]

velar(ized) see **velum**

velum Also SOFT PALATE, a muscular flap at the rear of the oral cavity, behind the hard **palate**. It acts as a valve controlling the opening between the oral and nasal cavities; when it's lowered, air can pass through the nose, producing **nasal** consonants and vowels. It can also be an articulator: the back of the tongue can form a stricture with it, giving VELAR consonants like [k g x]. A constriction between the back of the tongue and velum, along with another articulation, imposes [u]- or [o]-colouring, giving a VELARIZED segment, like many varieties of E **dark** /l/, [ɫ]. 363

vernacular (a) A non-classical spoken language in a culture that has a different classical language for at least some purposes: e.g. Old and Middle English as opposed to Latin; (b) a non-**standard** variety of a language characteristic of the lower socio-economic classes in a community.

Verner's Law [§1.3]

vocal folds Sometimes (inaccurately) VOCAL CORDS. Two bands of muscle stretching from front to back of the larynx, capable of cutting off and otherwise controlling airflow to and from the lungs; the source of **voice** (a).

vocative The **case** expressing direct address.

voice (a) A category of the verb, involving primarily an opposition of ACTIVE (subject 'acting on' the verb) and PASSIVE (subject 'acted on'); not relevant to the English active/passive contrast, which is better treated as a matter of **focus** [§4.7.1]; (b) the vibration of the **vocal folds**. Segments with vibration during articulation (e.g. vowels, [b d g m n r l j w]) are VOICED; those without such vibration are VOICELESS (e.g. [p t k f s]).

voiced, voiceless see **voice** (b).

weak adjective see **strong adjective**

weak verb see **strong verb**

weakening Also LENITION. Any process in which (a) the degree of **stricture** of a consonant decreases (e.g. **stop** > **fricative** > **approximant**); (b) a **voiceless** segment becomes **voiced**; (c) a consonant articulated in the oral cavity loses its oral articulation and becomes **glottal**, e.g. [s] > [h], [t] > [ʔ]. [§1.6; Lass 1984b: ch. 8]

weight Also QUANTITY. A property of syllables related to the structural complexity of their **rhymes**; **heavy** and **light** syllables are the poles of the weight scale. [§§3.3–4]

word-formation Any process producing new words, e.g. the formation of **compounds**, **derivational** affixation, etc. [§4.8]

zero-derivation Also CONVERSION. A type of **word-formation** in which a word belonging to one grammatical category is used as a member of another with no formal change. [§4.8.1]

zero syllable A construct devised to account for the rhythmic behaviour of monosyllabic words in stress-timed languages, and some properties of **clitics**. See **isochrony**, and §§3.3–4.

REFERENCES

Abercrombie, D. (1964). Syllable quantity and enclitics in English. In Abercrombie *et al.* (1964).

—————— (1979). The accents of Standard English in Scotland. In Aitken & McArthur (1979).

——————, Fry, D.B., MacCarthy, P.A.D., Scott, N.C., Trim, J.L.M. (1964). *In honour of Daniel Jones. Papers contributed on the occasion of his eightieth birthday, 12 September 1961.* London: Longmans.

Aitken, A.J. (1981). The Scottish vowel-length rule. In M. Benskin & M.L. Samuels, *So many people longages and tonges: Philological essays in Scots and mediaeval English presented to Angus McIntosh.* Edinburgh: Middle English Dialect Project.

—————— (1984a). Scottish accents and dialects. In Trudgill (1984).

—————— (1984b). Scots and English in Scotland. In Trudgill (1984).

—————— & McArthur, T. (1979). *Languages of Scotland. The Association for Scottish Literary Studies, Occasional Paper No. 4.* Edinburgh: Chambers.

Allen, H.B. (1973–6). *The linguistic atlas of the Upper Midwest.* 3 vols. Minneapolis: University of Minnesota Press.

—————— & Underwood, G.N. (1971). *Readings in American dialectology.* New York: Appleton-Century Crofts.

Antonsen, E.H. (1975). *A concise grammar of the older runic inscriptions.* Tübingen: Niemeyer.

Atkinson, M., Kilby, D., Roca, I. (1982). *Foundations of general linguistics.* London: Allen & Unwin.

Atwood, E.B. (1953). *A survey of verb forms in the Eastern United States.* Ann Arbor: University of Michigan Press.

Bailey, R.W. & Görlach, M. (1982). *English as a world language.* Ann Arbor: University of Michigan Press.

Bailey, R.W. (1982). The English language in Canada. In Bailey & Görlach (1982).

Baldi, P. (1983). *An introduction to the Indo-European languages.* Carbondale & Edwardsville: Southern Illinois University Press.

Barry, M.V. (1981). *Aspects of English dialects in Ireland.* Belfast: Institute of Irish Studies, The Queen's University of Belfast.

—————— (1982). The English language in Ireland. In Bailey & Görlach (1982).

Bauer, L. (1979). The second Great Vowel Shift? *Journal of the International Phonetic Association* 9.57–66.

—————— (1986). Notes on New Zealand English phonetics and phonology. *English World-Wide* 7.225–58.

Baugh, A.C. (1957). *A history of the English language.* 2nd ed. New York: Appleton Century Crofts. Revision with T. Cable (1978).

Bellin, W. (1984). Welsh and English in Wales. In Trudgill (1984).

————— (1986). Notes on New Zealand English phonetics and phonology. *English World-Wide* 7. 225–58.

Bennett, W.H. (1955). The southern English development of Germanic initial *[f s þ]. *Language* 31.367–71. Repr. Lass (1969).

Bergman, G. (1973). *A short history of the Swedish language*. Lund: The Swedish Institute for Cultural Relations with Foreign Countries.

Berndt, R. (1965). The linguistic situation in England from the Norman Conquest to the loss of Normandy 1066–1204. *Philologica Pragensia* 8.145–63. Repr. Lass (1969).

Birnbaum, S. (1965). Specimens of Yiddish from eight centuries. In U. Weinreich (1965), *The field of Yiddish*, 2. The Hague: Mouton.

————— (1979). *Yiddish. A survey and a grammar*. Manchester: Manchester University Press.

Blake, N. & Jones, C. (1984). *English historical linguistics: studies in development*. Sheffield: Centre for English Cultural Tradition and Language, University of Sheffield.

Bliss, A.J. (1984). English in the South of Ireland. In Trudgill (1984).

Bloomfield, L. (1933). *Language*. New York: Henry Holt.

————— (1944). Secondary and tertiary responses to language. *Language* 20.45–55.

Bourcier, G. (1981). *An introduction to the history of the English language*. English adaptation by C. Clark. Cheltenham: Stanley Thornes.

Branford, J. (1980). *A dictionary of South African English*. Cape Town: Oxford University Press.

Bronstein, A.J. (1960). *The pronunciation of American English. An introduction to phonetics*. New York: Appleton-Century-Crofts.

Brown, C. (1932). *English lyrics of the XIIIth century*. Oxford: Clarendon Press.

Brown, E.K. & Millar, M. (1980). Auxiliary verbs in Edinburgh speech. *Transactions of the Philological Society* 81–133.

————— & Miller, J.E. (1980). *Syntax: a linguistic introduction to sentence structure*. London: Hutchinson.

Brown, G. (1977). *Listening to spoken English*. London: Longmans.

————— & Yule, G. (1983). *Discourse analysis*. Cambridge: Cambridge University Press.

Bynon, T. (1977). *Historical linguistics*. Cambridge: Cambridge University Press.

Campbell, A. (1959). *Old English grammar*. Oxford: Oxford University Press.

Cassidy, F.G. (1957). Language on the American frontier. In Wyman, W.D. & Kroeber, C.B. (1957), *The frontier in perspective*. Repr. in Kerr, E.M. & Aderman, R.M. (1971), *Aspects of American English* (2nd ed.). New York: Harcourt Brace Jovanovich.

————— (1982). Geographical variation of English in the United States. In Bailey & Görlach (1982).

Cawley, A.C. (1958). *The Wakefield pageants in the Townely Cycle*. Manchester: Manchester University Press.

Chambers, J.K. (1973). Canadian raising. *Canadian Journal of Linguistics* 18.2.113–35.

————— (1975). *Canadian English*. Agincourt, Ont.: Methuen.

————— & Trudgill, P. (1980). *Dialectology*. Cambridge: Cambridge University Press.

Chambers, W.W. & Wilkie, J.R. (1970). *A short history of the German language*. London: Methuen.

Cheshire, J. (1982). *Variation in an English dialect. A socio-linguistic study*. Cambridge: Cambridge University Press.

Chomsky, N. & Halle, M. (1968). *The sound pattern of English*. New York: Harper.

Clarke, S. (1986). Sociolinguistic patterning in a New World dialect of Hiberno-English: the speech of St John's, Newfoundland. In Harris *et al.* (1986).

Clyne, M.G. (1976). *Australia talks*. Canberra: Australian National University Press.

Coldwell, D.F.C. (1964). *Selections from Gavin Douglas*. Oxford: Clarendon Press.

Comrie, B. (1976). *Aspect*. Cambridge: Cambridge University Press.

———— (1981). *Linguistic universals and language typology*. Oxford: Blackwell.

———— (1985). *Tense*. Cambridge: Cambridge University Press.

Connolly, J.H. (1981). On the segmental phonology of a South Welsh accent of English. *Journal of the International Phonetic Association* 11.51–6.

Craigie, W.A. (1946). *The critique of pure English from Caxton to Smollett*. S.P.E. Tract No. LXV. Oxford: Clarendon Press.

Crawford, S.J. (1922). *The Old English version of the Heptateuch, Ælfric's treatise on the Old and New Testament and his Preface to Genesis*. EETS OS 160.

Crotch, W.J.B. (1982). *The prologues and epilogues of William Caxton*. EETS OS 176.

Crystal, D. (1985a). To use or not to use. *English Today* 1.27.

———— (1985b). How many millions? The statistics of English today. *English Today* 2.7–9.

———— (1985c). *A dictionary of linguistics and phonetics*. 2nd ed. Oxford: Blackwell.

Davenport, M., Hansen, E., Nielsen, H.F. (1983). *Current topics in English historical linguistics*. Odense: Odense University Press.

De Camp. D. (1958). The genesis of the Old English dialects: a new hypothesis. *Language* 34.232–44. Repr. Lass (1969).

Delbridge, A. (1977). *The Macquarie dictionary*. St Leonards, NSW: Macquarie Library Pty Ltd.

Dickens, B. & Wilson, R.M. (1956). *Early Middle English texts*. 3rd ed. London: Bowes & Bowes.

Dillard, J.L. (1985). *Toward a social history of American English*. Berlin: Mouton.

Dobson, E.J. (1955). Early Modern Standard English. *Transactions of the Philological Society* 25–54. Repr. Lass (1969).

———— (1968). *English pronunciation 1500–1700*. 2nd ed. 2 vols. Oxford: Clarendon Press.

Douglas-Cowie, E. (1978). Linguistic code-switching in a Northern Irish village: social interaction and social ambition. In Trudgill (1978).

Duncan, P. (1972). Forms of the feminine pronoun in modern English dialects. In Wakelin (1972b).

Dykema, K. (1961). Where our grammar came from. *College English* 22.455–65.

Eagleson, R.D. (1982). English in Australia and New Zealand. In Bailey & Görlach (1982).

Eaton, R., Fischer, O., Koopman, W., van der Leek, F. (1985). *Papers from the 4th International Conference on English Historical Linguistics, Amsterdam, 10–13 April, 1985*. Amsterdam: John Benjamins.

Edwards, J. (1984). Irish and English in Ireland. In Trudgill (1984).

Ekwall, E. (1930). How long did the Scandinavian language survive in England? In *A grammatical miscellany offered to Otto Jespersen*. Copenhagen: Levin & Munksgaard. Repr. Ekwall, E., (1963), *Selected papers*. Lund: Gleerup.

———— (1956). *Historische neuenglische Laut- und Formenlehre*. Berlin: De Gruyter.

Ellegård, A. (1953). *The auxiliary do: the establishment and regulation of its use in English*. Stockholm: Almqvist & Wiksell.

Elliott, R.W.V. (1959). *Runes. An introduction*. Manchester: Manchester University Press.

Ferguson, C.A. & Heath, S.B. (1981). *Language in the U.S.A.* Cambridge: Cambridge University Press.

Fergusson, R. (1851). *The works of Robert Fergusson, edited, with life of the author and an essay on his genius and writings, by A.B.G.* London, Edinburgh & Dublin: A. Fullarton.

Fisher, J.H. (1977). Chancery and the emergence of standard written English in the fifteenth century. *Speculum* 52.870–99.

Fisiak, J. (1968). *A short grammar of Middle English. Part One: Graphemics, Phonemics and Morphemics*. Warsaw: PWN/London: Oxford University Press.

———— (1983). *A bibliography of writings for the history of the English language*. Poznań: Adam Mickiewicz University.

———— (1984). The voicing of initial fricatives in Middle English. *Studia Anglica Posnaniensia* 17.3–16.

Francis, W.N. (1958). *The structure of American English*. New York: Ronald Press.

Fudge, E.C. (1983). *English word stress*. London: Allen & Unwin.

Giegerich, H. (1985). *Metrical phonology and phonological structure: German and English*. Cambridge: Cambridge University Press.

Gimson, A.C. (1962). *An introduction to the pronunciation of English*. London: Arnold.

———— (1984). The RP accent. In Trudgill (1984).

Gold, D.L. (1981). The speech and writing of Jews. In Ferguson & Heath (1981).

Goosens, L. (1984). The interplay of syntax and semantics in the development of the English modals. In Blake & Jones (1984).

Gordon, E.V. (1957). *An introduction to Old Norse*. 2nd ed. Oxford: Clarendon Press.

Görlach, M. (1974). *Einführung in die englische Sprachgeschichte*. Heidelberg: Quelle & Meyer.

———— (1986). Middle English – a creole? In Kastovsky & Szwedek (1986).

Greenberg, J. (1966). Some universals of grammar with particular reference to the order of meaningful elements. In Greenberg, J. (1966), *Universals of language*. 2nd ed. Cambridge, Mass.: MIT Press.

Gregg, R.J. (1973). The dipththongs əi and ai in Scottish, Scotch-Irish and Canadian English. *Canadian Journal of Linguistics* 18.2.136–45.

Grzegorek, M. (1984). *Thematization in English and Polish*. Poznań: Adam Mickiewicz University.

Halliday, M.A.K. (1976). *Language as social semiotic*. London: Arnold.

Hammarström, G. (1980). *Australian English: its origin and status*. Hamburg: Buske.

Harris, J. (1984a). English in the North of Ireland. In Trudgill (1984).

————— (1984b). Syntactic variation and dialect divergence. *Journal of Linguistics* 20.303–28.

————— (1985). Phonological variation and change. Studies in Hiberno-English. Cambridge: Cambridge University Press.

—————, Little, D., Singleton, D. (1986). *Perspectives on the English language in Ireland. Proceedings of the first Symposium on Hiberno-English*. Dublin: Trinity College Dublin, Centre for Language and Communication Studies.

Harris, M. (1986). English *ought* (*to*). In Kastovsky & Szwedek (1986).

Hart, J. (1569). *An orthographie, conteyning the due order and reason, howe to write or paint thimage of mannes voice, most like to the life or nature*. Facsimile ed. Menston: The Scolar Press.

Haugen, E. (1966). Dialect, language, nation. *American Anthropologist* 68.922–35. Repr. Pride, J.B. & Holmes, J. (1972), *Sociolinguistics: selected readings*. Harmondsworth: Penguin.

Hepher, S. (1954). The phonology of the dialect of Scotswood, Newcastle-on-Tyne. Unpublished B.A. Thesis. Leeds: University of Leeds.

Hoad, T.F. (1984). English etymology: some problematic areas in the vocabulary of the Middle English period. *Transactions of the Philological Society* 27–57.

Hockett, C.F. (1958). *A course in modern linguistics*. New York: Macmillan.

Holmberg, B. (1964). *On the concept of standard English and the history of modern English pronunciation*. Lund: Gleerup.

Honey, J. (1985). Acrolect and hyperlect: the redefinition of English RP. *English Studies* 66.241–57.

Horn, W. & Lehnert, M. (1954). *Laut und Leben*. 2 vols. Berlin: Deutsche Verlag der Wissenschaften.

Householder, F. (1966). Phonological theory: a brief comment. *Journal of Linguistics* 2.99–100.

Huddleston, R.D. (1980). Criteria for auxiliaries and modals. In Greenbaum, S., Leech, G., & Svartvik, J. (1980), *Studies in English linguistics for Randolph Quirk*. London: Longmans.

————— (1984). *Introduction to the grammar of English*. Cambridge: Cambridge University Press.

Hudson, R. (1980). *Sociolinguistics*. Cambridge: Cambridge University Press.

Hughes, A. & Trudgill, P. (1979). *English accents and dialects. An introduction to social and regional varieties of British English*. London: Arnold.

Ihalainen, O. (1985). Synchronic variation and linguistic change: evidence from British English dialects. In Eaton *et al.* (1985).

————— (1986). An inquiry into the nature of mixed grammars: two cases of grammatical variation in dialectal British English. In Kastovsky & Szwedek (1986).

IPA (1949). *The principles of the International Phonetic Association*. London: University College.

Itkonen, E. (1981). Review of Lass (1980). *Language* 57.688–97.

Jackson, K.H. (1953). *Language and history in early Britain*. Edinburgh: Edinburgh University Press.

Jacobsson, U. (1962). *Phonological dialect constituents in the vocabulary of standard English*. Lund: Gleerup.

Jeffery, C. (1982). Review of Lanham & Macdonald (1979). *Folia Linguistica Historica* 3.251–63.

Jespersen, O. (1909–49). *A modern English grammar on historical principles*. 7 vols. Copenhagen: Munksgaard.

———— (1948). *Growth and structure of the English language*. 9th ed. Oxford: Blackwell.

Johnson, S. (1785). *A dictionary of the English language: in which the words are deduced from their originals, and illustrated in their different significations by examples from the best writers*. 2 vols. London: J.F. & C. Rivingon et al.

Jones, C. (1972). *An introduction to Middle English*. New York: Holt, Rinehart & Winston.

Jones, D. (1950). *The phoneme: its nature and use*. Cambridge: Heffer.

Jordan, R. (1968). *Handbuch der mittelenglischen Grammatik. I Teil: Lautlehre*. Rev. Ch. Mathes. Heidelberg: Winter.

Kallen, J.L. (1986). The co-occurrence of *do* and *be* in Hiberno-English. In Harris *et al.* (1986).

Karsten, T.E. (1928). *Die Germanen*. Berlin: De Gruyter.

Kastovsky, D. & Szwedek, A. (1986). *Linguistics across historical and geographical boundaries in honour of Jacek Fisiak. Vol I: Linguistic theory and historical linguistics*. Berlin: De Gruyter.

Keenan, E. & Comrie, B. (1977). Noun phrase accessibility and universal grammar. *Linguistic Inquiry* 8.63–99.

Knowles, G.O. (1978). The nature of phonological variables in Scouse. In Trudgill (1978).

Kolb, E., Glauser, B., Elmer, W., Stamm, R. (1979). *Atlas of English sounds*. Berne: Francke.

Krahe, H. (1963). *Germanische Sprachwissenschaft*, I. Berlin: De Gruyter.

Krapp, G.P. (1925). *The English language in America*. 2 vols. New York: Century.

Kurath, H. (1928). The origin of the dialectal differences in spoken American English. *Modern Philology* 25.385–95. Repr. Williamson & Burke (1971).

———— (1949). *A word geography of the eastern United States*. Ann Arbor: University of Michigan Press.

———— (1956). The loss of long consonants and the rise of voiced fricatives in Middle English. *Language* 32.434–45. Repr. Lass (1969).

———— (1964). British sources of selected features of American pronunciation: problems and methods. In Abercrombie *et al.* (1964). Repr. Allen & Underwood (1971).

————, Hanley, M.L., Bloch, B., Lowman, G.S. Jr, Hansen, M.L. (1939–43). *Linguistic atlas of New England*. 3 vols. Providence: Brown University Press.

————, & McDavid, R.I. Jr (1961). *The pronunciation of English in the Atlantic states*. Ann Arbor: University of Michigan Press.

Labov, W. (1963). The social motivation of a sound change. *Word* 19.273–309.

———— (1966). *The social stratification of English in New York City*. Washington: Centre for Applied Linguistics.

Ladefoged, P. (1975). *A course in phonetics*. New York: Harcourt Brace Jovanovich.

Lanham, L.W. (1967). *The pronunciation of South African English*. Cape Town: Balkema.

———— (1978). South African English. In Lanham & Prinsloo (1978).

———— (1982). English in South Africa. In Bailey & Görlach (1982).

———— & Macdonald, C.A. (1979). *The standard in South African English and its social history*. Heidelberg: Julius Groos Verlag.

———— & Prinsloo, K.P. (1978). *Language and communication studies in South Africa*. Cape Town: Oxford University Press.

Lass, R. (1969). *Approaches to English historical linguistics*. New York: Holt, Rinehart & Winston.

———— (1974). Linguistic orthogenesis? Scots vowel quantity and the English length conspiracy. In Anderson, J.M. & Jones, C. (1974), *Historical linguistics II*. Amsterdam: North-Holland.

———— (1976). *English phonology and phonological theory: synchronic and diachronic studies*. Cambridge: Cambridge University Press.

———— (1980). *On explaining language change*. Cambridge: Cambridge University Press.

———— (1981). Undigested history and synchronic 'structure'. In Goyvaerts, D. (1981), *Phonology in the 1980s*. Ghent: E. Story-Scientia.

———— (1984a). Language and time: a historian's view. University of Cape Town Inaugural Lecture. Cape Town: UCT.

———— (1984b). *Phonology: an introduction to basic concepts*. Cambridge: Cambridge University Press.

———— (1984c). Vowel system universals and typology: prologue to theory. *Phonology Yearbook* 1.75–112.

———— (1984d). Quantity, resolution and syllable geometry. *Folia Linguistica Historica* 4.151–80.

———— (1984e). Survival, convergence, innovation: a problem in diachronic theory. *Stellenbosch Papers in Linguistics* 12.17–36.

———— & Anderson, J.M. (1975). *Old English phonology*. Cambridge: Cambridge University Press.

———— & Higgs, J.A.W. (1984). Phonetics and language history: American /r/ as a candidate for an archaism. In Higgs, J.A.W. & Thelwall, R. (1984), *Topics in linguistic phonetics in honour of E.T. Uldall*. Occasional Papers in Language and Language Learning No. 9. Coleraine: The New University of Ulster.

———— & Wright, S. (1985). The South African chain shift: order out of chaos? In Eaton *et al.* (1985).

———— & Wright, S. (1986). Endogeny vs. contact: 'Afrikaans influence' on South African English. *English World-Wide* 7. 201–24.

Legge, M.D. (1941). Anglo-Norman and the historian. *History* 26.163–75.

Lehmann, W.P. (1952). *Proto-Indo-European phonology*. Austin: University of Texas Press.

———— (1967). *A reader in nineteenth-century historical Indo-European linguistics*. Bloomington: Indiana University Press.

Leith, D. (1983). *A social history of English*. London: Routledge & Kegan Paul.

Levinson, S.C. (1983). *Pragmatics*. Cambridge: Cambridge University Press.

Lockwood, W.B. (1966). *Indo-European philology*. London: Hutchinson.

Lodge, K.R. (1984). *Studies in the phonology of colloquial English*. London: Croom Helm.

Lorenz, K. (1975). *Vergleichende Verhaltensforschung: Grundlagen der Ethologie*. Vienna: Springer-Verlag.

Luick, K. (1968). *Historische Grammatik der englischen Sprache*. 2 vols, reprint. Oxford: Blackwell.

Lyons, J. (1968). *Introduction to theoretical linguistics*. Cambridge: Cambridge University Press.

———— (1977). *Semantics*. 2 vols. Cambridge: Cambridge University Press.

Macaulay, R.K.S. (1977). *Language, social class and education: a Glasgow study*. Edinburgh: Edinburgh University Press.

Marchand, H. (1969). *The categories and types of present-day English word-formation. A synchronic-diachronic approach*. München: C.H. Beck.

Marckwardt, A.H. (1958). *American English*. New York: Oxford University Press.

Markey, T.L. (1976). *A North Sea Germanic reader*. München: Wilhelm Fink Verlag.

Mather, J.Y. & Speitel, H.H. (1975). *The Linguistic Atlas of Scotland. Scots Section, vol. 1*. London: Croom Helm.

———— (1977). *The Linguistic Atlas of Scotland. Scots Section, vol. 2*. London: Croom Helm.

Mathews, M.M. (1951). *A dictionary of Americanisms on historical principles*. Chicago: University of Chicago Press.

Matthews, P.H. (1974). *Morphology*. Cambridge: Cambridge University Press.

———— (1981). *Syntax*. Cambridge: Cambridge University Press.

McClure, D. (1974a). *The Scots language in education*. Association for Scottish literary studies, Occasional Papers No. 3. Aberdeen: Waverley Press.

———— (1974(b)). Modern Scots prose writing. In McClure (1974(a)).

———— (1979). Scots: its range of uses. In Aitken & McArthur (1979).

McCoard, R.W. (1978). *The English perfect: tense-choice and pragmatic inferences*. Amsterdam: North-Holland.

McConnel, R.E. (1979). *Our own voice. Canadian English and how it is studied*. Toronto: Gage Educational Publishing Ltd.

McDavid, R.I. (1958). The dialects of American English. In Francis (1958).

Mencken, H.L. & McDavid, R.I. (1963). *The American language: an inquiry into the development of English in the United States by H.L. Mencken. Revised and abridged by R.I. McDavid and D.W. Mawrer*. New York: Knopf.

Miller, J.E. & Brown, E.K. (1982). Aspects of Scottish English syntax. *English World-Wide* 3.3–17.

Milroy, J. (1980). Lexical alternation and the history of English: evidence from an urban vernacular. In Traugott *et al.* (1980).

———— (1983). On the sociolinguistic history of /h/-dropping in English. In Davenport *et al.* (1983).

———— & Milroy, L. (1978). Belfast: change and variation in an urban vernacular. In Trudgill (1978).

———— (1985). *Authority in language.* London: Routledge & Kegan Paul.

Milroy, L. (1980). *Language and social networks.* Oxford: Blackwell.

Minkova, D. (1982). The environment for open syllable lengthening in Middle English. *Folia Linguistica Historica* 3.29–58.

Mitchell, A.G. & Delbridge, A. (1965a). *The pronunciation of English in Australia.* Sydney: Angus & Robertson.

———— (1965b). *The speech of Australian adolescents.* Sydney: Angus & Robertson.

Moore, S. (1964). *Historical outlines of English sounds and inflections.* Rev. A.H. Marckwardt. Ann Arbor: Wahr.

Morsbach, L. (1888). *Über den Ursprung der neuenglischen Schriftsprache.* Heilbronn: Henninger.

Mossé, F. (1950). *A handbook of Middle English.* Baltimore: Johns Hopkins Press.

Murison, D. (1979). The historical background. In Aitken & McArthur (1979).

Ó Sé, D. (1986). Word-stress in Hiberno-English. In Harris *et al.* (1986).

Orton, H. (1962). *Survey of English dialects. A, Introduction.* Leeds: Arnold.

———— & Barry, M.V. (1969). *Survey of English dialects. B, Basic Material: the West Midland Counties.* Leeds: Arnold.

———— & Halliday, W. (1962). *Survey of English Dialects. B, Basic Material: The Northern Counties and the Isle of Man.* Leeds: Arnold.

———— & Tilling P.M. (1969). *Survey of English Dialects. B, Basic Material: the East Midland Counties and East Anglia.* Leeds: Arnold.

———— & Wakelin, M. (1967). *Survey of English Dialects. B, Basic Material: the Southern Counties.* Leeds: Arnold.

———— & Wright, N. (1974). *A word geography of England.* London: Seminar Press.

————, Sanderson, S., Widdowson, J. (1978). *The linguistic atlas of England.* London: Croom Helm.

Palmer, F.R. (1974). *The English verb.* London: Longmans.

Parry, D. (1972). Anglo-Welsh dialects in South-East Wales. In Wakelin (1972b).

———— (1977). *The survey of Anglo-Welsh dialects. Vol. 1, the South-East.* Swansea: University of Wales Press.

———— (1979). *The survey of Anglo-Welsh dialects. Vol. 2, the South-West.* Swansea: University of Wales Press.

Peterson, G.E. & Lehiste, I. (1960). Duration of syllable nuclei in English. *Journal of the Acoustical Society of America* 32.693–703. Repr. Lehiste, I. (1967), *Readings in acoustic phonetics.* Cambridge, Mass.: MIT Press.

Petyt, K.M. (1985). *Dialect and accent in industrial West Yorkshire.* Amsterdam: Benjamins.

Plank, F. (1984). The modals story retold. *Studies in Language* 8.305–64.

Poussa, P. (1982). The evolution of early Standard English. *Studia Anglica Posnaniensia* 14.69–85.

Price, G. (1984). *The languages of Britain.* London: Arnold.

Prokosch, E. (1938). *A comparative Germanic grammar*. Baltimore: Linguistic Society of America.

Quirk, R., Greenbaum, S., Leech, G., Svartvik, J. (1972). *A grammar of contemporary English*. Harlow: Longmans.

———— & Greenbaum, S. (1972). *A university grammar of English*. Harlow: Longmans.

———— & Wrenn, C.L. (1957). *An Old English grammar*. 2nd ed. London: Methuen.

Radford, A. (1981). *Transformational syntax*. Cambridge: Cambridge University Press.

Raidt, E.H. (1980). *Afrikaans en sy europese verlede. Van Tacitus tot van Wyk Louw*. 2nd. ed. Goodwood: NASOU.

Ramson, W.S. (1966). *Australian English: An historical study of the vocabulary 1788–1898*. Canberra: Australian National University Press.

———— (1970). *English transported. Essays on Australasian English*. Canberra: Australian National University Press.

Reid, E. (1978). Social and stylistic variation in the speech of children: some evidence from Edinburgh. In Trudgill (1978).

Robertson, S. & Cassidy, F.G. (1954). *The development of modern English*. 2nd ed. Englewood Cliffs: Prentice-Hall.

Robinson, F.N. (1957). *The works of Geoffrey Chaucer*. Boston: Houghton Mifflin.

———— (1973). Syntactical glosses in Latin manuscripts of Anglo-Saxon provenance. *Speculum* 48.443–75.

Romaine, S. (1978). Postvocalic /r/ in Scottish English: sound change in progress? In Trudgill (1978).

———— (1980). The relative clause marker in Scots English: diffusion, complexity, and style as dimensions of syntactic change. *Language in Society* 9.221–47.

———— (1982). The English language in Scotland. In Bailey & Görlach (1982).

———— (1984). Towards a typology of relative clause formation strategies in Germanic. In Fisiak, J. (1984), *Historical syntax*. Berlin: Mouton.

Russ, C.J.V. (1978). *Historical German phonology and morphology*. Oxford: Oxford University Press.

Samuels, M.L. (1963). Some applications of Middle English dialectology. *English Studies* 44.81–94. Repr. Lass (1969).

———— (1972). *Linguistic evolution*. Cambridge: Cambridge University Press.

Sapir, E. (1921). *Language*. New York: Harcourt Brace.

Scargill, M.H. (1974). *Modern Canadian English usage*. Toronto: McClelland & Stewart.

Schlauch, M. (1959). *The English language in modern times (since 1400)*. Warsaw: PWN/London: Oxford University Press.

Scholtz, J. du P. (1970). Internal history of Afrikaans. In Potgieter, D.J. (1970), *Standard Encyclopaedia of Southern Africa*. Cape Town: NASOU.

Scott, T. (1970). *The Penguin book of Scottish verse*. Harmondsworth: Penguin.

Sherley-Price, L. (1955). *Bede: a history of the English church and people*. Harmondsworth: Penguin.

Sivertsen, E. (1960). *Cockney phonology*. Oslo: Oslo University Press.

Sommerstein, A. (1977). *Modern phonology*. London: Arnold.

Stenton, D.M. (1952). *English society in the earlier Middle Ages, 1066–1307.* Harmondsworth: Penguin.

Stenton, F.M. (1955). *Anglo-Saxon England.* Oxford: Oxford University Press.

Stockwell, R.P. (1961). The Middle English 'long close' and 'long open' mid vowels. *University of Texas Studies in Literature and Language* 2.4.529–38.

————— (1985). Assessment of alternative explanations of the Middle English phenomenon of high vowel lowering when lengthened in the open syllable. In Eaton *et al.* (1985).

Strang, B.M.H. (1968). *Modern English structure.* 2nd ed. London: Arnold.

————— (1970). *A history of English.* London: Methuen.

Strevens, P. (1985). Standards and the standard language. *English Today* 2.5–8.

Sweet, H. (1885). *The oldest English texts.* Early English Text Society OS 83.

————— (1891/98). *New English grammar.* 2 vols. Oxford: Clarendon Press.

————— (1957). *Anglo-Saxon primer.* 9th ed., rev. N. Davis. Oxford: Clarendon Press.

————— (1967). *Sweet's Anglo-Saxon reader in prose and verse.* Rev. D. Whitelock. Oxford: Clarendon Press.

Szemerényi, O.L.J. (1985). Recent developments in Indo-European linguistics. *Transactions of the Philological Society* 1–71.

Thomas, A.R. (1984). Welsh English. In Trudgill (1984).

Thomson, R.L. (1984). The history of the Celtic languages in the British Isles. In Trudgill (1984).

Tolkien, J.R.R. (1934). Chaucer as a philologist. *Transactions of the Philological Society* 1–70.

Toon, T.E. (1982). Variation in contemporary American English. In Bailey & Görlach (1982).

————— (1983). *The politics of early Old English sound change.* New York: Academic Press.

Trager, G.L. & Smith, H.L. (1951). *An outline of English structure.* Studies in English Occasional Papers, 3. Norman, Oklahoma: Battenburg Press.

Traugott, E.C. (1972). *A history of English syntax.* New York: Holt, Rinehart & Winston.

—————, LaBrum, R., Shepherd, S. (1980). *Papers from the 4th International Conference on Historical Linguistics.* Amsterdam: Benjamins.

Trudgill, P. (1974). *The social differentiation of English in Norwich.* Cambridge: Cambridge University Press.

————— (1978). *Sociolinguistic patterns in British English.* London: Arnold.

————— (1982). On the limits of passive 'competence': sociolinguistics and the polylectal grammar controversy. In Crystal, D. (1982), *Linguistic controversies.* London: Arnold.

————— (1983). *On dialect.* Oxford: Blackwell.

————— (1984). *Language in the British Isles.* Cambridge: Cambridge University Press.

————— (1986). The role of Irish English in the formation of colonial Englishes. In Harris *et al.* (1986).

————— & Hannah, J. (1985). *International English. A guide to varieties of standard English.* 2nd ed. London: Arnold.

Turner, G.W. (1972). *The English language in Australia and New Zealand.* London: Longmans.

van Coetsem, F. & Kufner, H. (1972). *Toward a grammar of Proto-Germanic*. Tübingen: Niemeyer.

van Loey, A. (1970). *Schönfelds historische grammatica van het Nederlands: klankleer, vormleer, woordvorming*. 8th ed. Zutphen: Thieme & Cie.

Verner, K. (1875). Eine Ausnahme der ersten Lautverschiebung. *Zeitschrift für vergleichende Sprachforschung auf dem Gebiete der Indogermanischen Sprachen* 23.97–130. Translation in Lehmann (1967).

Viereck, W. (1985). *Focus on England and Wales*. Amsterdam: Benjamins.

Visser, F. (1963–9). *An historical syntax of the English language*. 4 vols. Leiden: E.J. Brill.

Wakelin, M. (1972a). *English dialects. An introduction*. London: Athlone Press.

————— (1972b). *Patterns in the folk speech of the British Isles*. London: Athlone Press.

————— (1984). Rural dialects in England. In Trudgill (1984).

Warner, A. (1982). *Complementation in Middle English and the methodology of historical syntax*. London: Croom Helm.

Weinreich, M. (1980). *History of the Yiddish language*. Chicago: University of Chicago Press.

Weinreich, U., Labov, W., Herzog, M. (1968). Empirical foundations for a theory of language change. In Lehmann, W.P. & Malkiel, Y. (1968), *Directions for historical linguistics. A symposium*. Austin: University of Texas Press.

Wells, J.C. (1982). *Accents of English*. 3 vols. Cambridge: Cambridge University Press.

————— (1984). English accents in England. In Trudgill (1984).

Wessén, E. (1968). *Svensk språkhistoria. I. Ljudlära och ordböjningslära*. 18th ed. Stockholm: Almqvist & Wiksell.

Whitelock, D. (1952). *The beginnings of English society*. Harmondsworth: Penguin.

Williamson, J.V. & Burke, V.M. (1971). *A various language: perspectives on American dialects*. New York: Holt, Rhinehart & Winston.

Wolfe, P.M. (1972). *Linguistic change and the Great Vowel Shift in English*. Berkeley & Los Angeles: University of California Press.

Wright, J. (1905). *The English dialect grammar*. Oxford: Frowde.

————— & Wright, E.M. (1925). *Old English grammar*. 3rd ed. Oxford: Clarendon Press.

————— (1928). *An elementary Middle English grammar*. 2nd ed. Oxford: Clarendon Press.

Wyld, H.C. (1927). *A short history of English*. 3rd ed. London: John Murray.

————— (1936). *A history of modern colloquial English*. 3rd ed. Oxford: Blackwell.

INDEX

INDEX

This index is roughly complementary to the glossary and table of contents; most of the section-headings are explicit enough to be used for accessing topics, and technical and theoretical notions discussed in detail are referenced in the glossary. For regional dialects or larger areas (e.g. Canada, Scotland) see *dialects, regional*; for smaller locations (cities, counties) see under specific names. For loans from specific languages, see under *loans*. The index is not exhaustive; I have used my judgement about what is worth putting in. Alphabetization: phonetic symbols for categories discussed (e.g. '/æ/', '/a/, ME') are listed at the beginning of each alphabetical section; long vowels follow short. Non-roman symbols as follows: æ after ad, ð after d, ʒ after g, ŋ after n, þ, θ after t.